(*continued on back*)

ACQUAINTANCE RAPE

Acquaintance Rape
The Hidden Crime

Edited by
Andrea Parrot
Laurie Bechhofer

A WILEY-INTERSCIENCE PUBLICATION

JOHN WILEY & SONS, INC.

New York • Chichester • Brisbane • Toronto • Singapore

Library of Congress Cataloging-in-Publication Data

Acquaintance rape : the hidden crime / edited by Andrea Parrot and
    Laurie Bechhofer.
       p.   cm.—(Wiley series on personality processes)
    "A Wiley-Interscience publication."
    Includes bibliographical references.
    ISBN 0-471-51023-8
    1. Acquaintance rape. I. Parrot, Andrea. II. Bechhofer, Laurie.
  III. Series.
  HV6558.A27   1991
  362.88′3—dc20   90-38127

Printed in the United States of America

91 92 10 9 8 7 6 5 4 3 2

To the hidden victims of acquaintance rape

Series Preface

This series of books is addressed to behavioral scientists interested in the nature of human personality. Its scope should prove pertinent to personality theorists and researchers as well as to clinicians concerned with applying an understanding of personality processes to the amelioration of emotional difficulties in living. To this end, the series provides a scholarly integration of theoretical formulations, empirical data, and practical recommendations.

Six major aspects of studying and learning about human personality can be designated: personality theory, personality structure and dynamics, personality development, personality assessment, personality change, and personality adjustment. In exploring these aspects of personality, the books in the series discuss a number of distinct but related subject areas: the nature and implications of various theories of personality; personality characteristics that account for consistencies and variations in human behavior; the emergence of personality processes in children and adolescents; the use of interviewing and testing procedures to evaluate individual differences in personality; efforts to modify personality styles through psychotherapy, counseling, behavior therapy, and other methods of influence; and patterns of abnormal personality functioning that impair individual competence.

IRVING B. WEINER

University of South Florida
Tampa, Florida

Preface

Approximately one in four women in the United States will be victims of rape or attempted rape by the time they are in their mid-twenties, and over three quarters of those assaults will occur between people who know each other. Because the problem of acquaintance rape is so widespread, it has been receiving increasing attention. A wealth of scholarly research conducted over the past 10 years has examined the incidence and prevalence of acquaintance rape, the contributing factors, the profile of assailants and victims, and the effects on the victims. Those empirical findings have been presented at professional conferences and published in scholarly journals, but by and large have not been readily available to practitioners who work outside of academia.

Acquaintance Rape: The Hidden Crime is an attempt to bridge the gap. The book is relevant not only for those in academia, but also for professionals working in applied areas such as treatment, prevention, law enforcement, and public policy. Four other books dealing specifically with acquaintance rape have gained widespread attention. *I Never Called It Rape: The MS. Report on Recognizing, Fighting, and Surviving Date and Acquaintance Rape,* by Robin Warshaw (1988), and *Coping with Date Rape and Acquaintance Rape,* by Andrea Parrot (1988), were written for the lay audience. *Real Rape: How the Legal System Victimizes Women Who Say No,* by Susan Estrich (1987), and *The Ultimate Violation,* by Judith Rowland (1985), focus on the legal issues related to acquaintance rape. The topic has often been presented in articles or as a chapter or section in books on sexual coercion, sexual exploitation, and sexual assault, but to date it has not been the primary focus of a book intended for professionals in the field.

We felt strongly that the content of the chapters should include not only a review of the empirical findings related to acquaintance rape, but also practical suggestions for educators and clinicians. Therefore, we have attempted to utilize a research-based, service-oriented approach.

There have been substantial developments in the field of sexual assault, but many fundamental questions remain unanswered. We hope that researchers will continue to receive support in their efforts to understand the antecedents, dynamics, and consequences of acquaintance rape. All too often, faculty are encouraged to study those areas that are more theoretical than applied. Acquaintance rape is too prevalent and its effects are too far-reaching to be neglected on the research front.

We have titled the book *Acquaintance Rape: The Hidden Crime* because forced sex between people who know each other is often not viewed as a legitimate crime by its victims and assailants or by society at large. The victims of these assaults usually do not consider their assaults to be rape; they rarely come forward and identify themselves as victims to authorities, families, or friends. Furthermore, acquaintance rapists are rarely convicted, and cases are generally not viewed as "real" rape by the legal system. Thus, the crime remains deeply hidden in our culture.

It is our hope that much of the information in this book will no longer be needed in the near future. Perhaps as people become more sensitive to and aware of acquaintance rape as a serious and pervasive crime, such a formal justification will not be necessary. Once we establish it as a crime, efforts can be channeled to treatment, prosecution, and, most importantly, prevention.

We hope that this book will serve as a conceptual and practical tool to help individuals from all areas of the field to view themselves as part of a larger effort working toward the common goal of reducing the incidence of acquaintance rape. Acquaintance rape is a problem that impacts on all of us.

ANDREA PARROT
LAURIE BECHHOFER

Ithaca, New York
St. Paul, Minnesota
January 1991

Acknowledgments

Many individuals have contributed greatly toward the production of this book. First, we would like to thank the contributors for their tireless research efforts and interest in this important problem. Also, we would like to express our appreciation to those who have contributed their valuable insights to the content of the volume: Dr. Steve Allen, Robin Bechhofer, Debby Bors, Jim Isaak, Reverend Kurt Katzmar, Tom McCormick, J.D., Colleen Nolan, Dennis Raverty, Dr. Barry Roessler, and Carla Waterman. A special thanks goes to the secretarial help that kept us afloat: Mary Jo Stewart, Melissa Doak, Penny Neno, and Laurie Michelman. Finally, we thank our families for their continuous support.

About the Contributors

Antonia Abbey, PhD, is an assistant professor in the Department of Community Medicine at Wayne State University. She received her doctoral degree in social psychology from Northwestern University in 1982 and completed a postdoctoral fellowship at the Institute for Social Research at the University of Michigan. Dr. Abbey's first research project on gender differences in sexual intent was reported in her Master's thesis, and she has maintained this research interest since then. In her doctoral dissertation, she examined how rape victims' attributions of responsibility for the attack influenced their adjustment. She has also conducted research on how people cope with health crises, with an emphasis on gender differences. One of her current studies examines how couples cope with infertility and whether women's and men's responses to infertility differ.

Py Bateman, MS, has been working in the field of sexual assault prevention for 20 years. She founded "Alternatives to Fear" in Seattle in 1971. Her current focus in working with acquaintance rape prevention is to incorporate theater into her programs. She has taught sociology and women's studies at Western Washington University and the University of Washington. She served as the editor of the *Journal of Sexual Assault and Coercion* from 1986 to 1987.

Laurie Bechhofer, BA, is a sexuality educator with Planned Parenthood of Minnesota, where she speaks to schools, community groups, detention centers, churches, and youth groups about sexuality issues, with a special focus on acquaintance rape prevention. She received her degree in psychology from Cornell University. Under the supervision of Dr. Sandra Bem and Dr. Andrea Parrot, she pursued a personal research interest in the nature of miscommunication as an antecedent of date rape. Her study, "Divergent Perceptions of Men and Women and the Risk of Date Rape," earned the T. A. Ryan award for the most outstanding psychology honors thesis in 1989. Ms. Bechhofer has also conducted a review of the scholarly literature and compiled a bibliography of more than 200 scholarly research articles related to the issue of acquaintance rape.

Carol Bohmer, PhD, is a member of the Sociology Department at Cornell University. She trained as a lawyer in her native New Zealand before obtaining a degree in criminology at Cambridge University, England, and a PhD in sociology at the University of Pennsylvania. She has taught at several law schools and medical schools in the United States and Canada. Her major focus of research has been on the relationship between law and social change. She has published articles on the subjects of sex offenders, rape law, comparative family law, and the use of psychiatry in the legal system.

Barry R. Burkhart, PhD, ABPP, is a diplomate in clinical psychology and a professor of psychology at Auburn University, Alabama, and is one of the nation's authorities in the areas of sexual violence and victimization. He and his students have conducted pioneering research on the epidemiology of sexual aggression, particularly "hidden" victimization, with both offenders and victims. Additionally, his research programs include the development and evaluation of conceptual models describing psychological dynamics of offenders and effects of and coping with victimization in both adult and child populations.

In his clinical practice, Dr. Burkhart is involved in the treatment of both victims and offenders. Through his clinical work and research, he has helped develop effective individual treatment and community-based, prevention-focused intervention programs for victims and offenders. As Chair of the Auburn University Rape Awareness Committee, Dr. Burkhart produced *It Still Hurts,* a videotape on acquaintance rape, which is in widespread use in prevention programming on college campuses. In recognition of his scientific and professional expertise, Dr. Burkhart has been asked to present numerous lectures and workshops on sexual violence and to serve as a consultant to universities and other agencies in the development of sexual assault prevention and treatment programs.

Martha R. Burt, PhD, is director of the social services research program at the Urban Institute. She received her doctoral degree in sociology in 1972 from the University of Wisconsin—Madison. She has been involved in research on rape since 1976, when she conducted her study on rape myths and other attitudes that help maintain rape myths. Her other rape research includes a study of the characteristics and goals of rape crisis centers 10 years after the first center opened in 1972, and a study of long-term recovery from rape, the role of counseling in recovery, and personal growth as an outcome of women's efforts to recover from a rape. Dr. Burt worked as a rape hotline counselor for two years in 1973-1974, helped organize rape centers in Minnesota from 1974-1978, and served on the board of the Washington, DC, Rape Crisis Center from 1983-1989. She has directed numerous policy-oriented research studies in the areas of services for pregnant and parenting teens, the chronically mentally ill, the low-income elderly, disabled adults, and the homeless.

Karen S. Calhoun, PhD, is a professor of psychology and director of clinical training at the University of Georgia. She was 1989-1990 President of the Southeastern Psychological Association. She has published a number of articles on the psychological adjustment of rape victims over time and is coauthor of a book on treatment of rape victims. Her area of current interest is personality of date rapists and their interpersonal interaction styles.

Karol E. Dean, BS, is a graduate student in personality at the University of California, Los Angeles. Her primary research interests are in the areas of violence against women and sexual aggression.

Christine A. Gidycz, PhD, is an assistant professor of psychology at Ohio University in Athens, Ohio, teaching graduate and undergraduate courses. She obtained her doctorate from Kent State University in 1988 and did her internship at Harvard Medical School (The Cambridge Hospital). Her field of specialization is in clinical psychology and her area of concentration has been in the treatment of children, adolescents, and families. She has been actively involved in the supervision of clinical psychology graduate students' practice experiences. Dr. Gidycz began conducting research in the area of sexual victimization while she was a graduate student at Kent State University. She worked with Dr. Mary Koss on her national study of sexual victimization and aggression on college campuses. At Ohio University, she has continued to investigate the impact of acquaintance rape and the process of recovery for acquaintance rape victims.

Theresa Gilmore, MA, received her degree in psychology from California State University. She has been actively pursuing research on women's issues for six years.

Georgina S. Hammock, PhD, is an assistant professor of psychology at Clarkson University in Potsdam, New York. She received her doctoral degree in 1986 at the University of Georgia, under the direction of Dr. Deborah Richardson. Her dissertation dealt with situational and individual predictors of human physical aggression. Her current research interests include conflict resolution, provocation in relation to aggressive behavior, and perceptions of violent behavior. She has been actively pursuing a research program that focuses on the effects of the victim/perpetrator relationship and the consumption of alcohol on perceptions of responsibility for rape.

Patricia A. Harney, MA, is currently pursuing doctoral studies in clinical psychology at the University of Kansas. She graduated with distinction in 1987 from Cornell University, where she received a BS in human development. Ms. Harney has extensive clinical experience with the chronically mentally ill and has particular clinical interest in working with survivors of sexual abuse. Her research experiences have been varied, including such topics as the identification of children at risk from families with abusive parents and the effects of individual difference variables on health status. She plans to continue her research in the area of rape and sexual abuse.

John A. Humphrey, PhD, is a professor of sociology at the University of North Carolina at Greensboro. He received his doctoral degree from the University of New Hampshire. Dr. Humphrey has conducted research on criminal homicide, suicide, and drug and alcohol use. He is coauthor of three books in the field of deviant behavior.

Bonnie L. Katz, PhD, is in clinical practice in Columbus, Ohio. She has been active in research and clinical work in the area of rape recovery for over 10 years. She received her doctorate in clinical psychology from Boston University in 1987. Her dissertation compared the relative psychological effects on women of rape by strangers versus rape by nonstrangers, and she was awarded the Society for the Psychological Study of Social Issues Dissertation Prize in 1988. This research was done in collaboration with Dr. Martha R. Burt at the Urban Institute in Washington, DC. Dr. Katz continues to do research on rape recovery.

Mary P. Koss, PhD, is a professor of psychiatry (with a joint appointment in the Department of Psychology) at the University of Arizona College of Medicine. She is associate editor of *Psychology of Women Quarterly* and *Violence and Victims* and is a member of the editorial boards of the *Journal of Consulting and Clinical Psychology* and *Journal of Interpersonal Violence*. For over 10 years she has conducted research on hidden rape, that is, sexual aggression and victimization among the general population. One project, a national study of more than 6,000 college students, was the subject of the book, *I Never Called it Rape: The MS. Report on Recognizing, Fighting, and Surviving Date and Acquaintance Rape*. She recently completed a study of the impact of crime victimization on health and medical utilization among working women. Under contract from the National Institute of Mental Health, she prepared a mental health research agenda in the area of violence against women. In addition to many papers published in the scientific literature, Dr. Koss is the coauthor of the book, *The Rape Victim: Clinical and Community Approaches to Treatment*. In 1986 Dr. Koss was recipient of a distinguished publication award from the Association of Women in Psychology.

Neil M. Malamuth, PhD, is a professor and Chair of the Communications Studies Program, and a professor of psychology at the University of California, Los Angeles. He received his doctoral degree in personality and social psychology from UCLA. His primary research interests include the causes and prevention of violence against women, particularly rape, and mass media effects.

Catalina A. Mandoki, PhD, is a clinical psychologist, with expertise in the area of sexual victimization, and is presently employed as a psychologist at Searcy State Hospital in Mobile, Alabama. She received her PhD from Auburn University in 1989. While on internship, she participated in research and treatment at the Crime Victim's Research and Treatment Center of the Medical University of South Carolina in Charleston. Her research has focused on effects of victimization in adult victims of child sexual abuse, acquaintance rape, and repeated sexual victimization.

Charlene L. Muehlenhard, PhD, holds a joint appointment as an assistant professor of psychology and women's studies at the University of Kansas. She received her doctorate in psychology in 1981 from the University of Wisconsin—Madison, after a clinical internship at the University of Mississippi Medical Center/VA Consortium. She began her career as an assistant professor of psychology at Texas A&M University and moved to the University of Kansas in 1988. Her research program initially focused on social skills training; her interest in changing gender roles led her to study women's dating initiation and the possible consequences of its misinterpretation by men. She has pursued research on date rape and sexual coercion for several years. Her special interest is the relationship between sexual coercion and traditional gender roles.

Chris S. O'Sullivan, PhD, specializes in the study of campus gang-rape and is developing a questionnaire on group sexual assault on campus. After earning a master's degree in linguistics, she held a research position at Stanford University and then briefly ran a women's center on Martha's Vineyard. Returning to graduate study, she first worked in chimpanzee sign language research at the University of Oklahoma and later completed her doctorate in cognitive psychology. As a postdoctoral fellow at Michigan State University, her attendance at a gang-rape trial, in support of the complaining witness, initiated her continuing interest in the study of the crime and its prevention. She formerly taught social psychology at the University of Kentucky.

Andrea Parrot, PhD, a nationally recognized expert in the field of acquaintance rape prevention, is an assistant professor in the Department of Human Service Studies at Cornell University. In addition, she is a clinical assistant professor of psychiatry at the SUNY Health Sciences Center, Syracuse, New York, where she teaches a medical school course on sexuality. Dr. Parrot travels extensively, conducting programs on acquaintance rape prevention. She has been a consultant to numerous colleges, universities, educational media producers, federal and state agencies, and crime prevention programs. She received her doctorate at Cornell University in 1981, and now teaches a course on human sexuality to up to 1000 students per year at Cornell. She has developed improvisational-theater video tapes on acquaintance rape prevention, one for college audiences, called "STOP DATE RAPE!," and another for high school audiences, called "I Know You Said 'No' But I Thought You Meant 'Yes.'" Her *Acquaintance Rape and Sexual Assault Prevention Manual* is viewed as a leading work in the field and has been recommended by MS. magazine. She is the author of *Coping with Date Rape and Acquaintance Rape* and other writings directed toward heightening awareness of sexual assault and developing prevention strategies.

C. Dale Posey, PhD, is the director of case management services and director of psychology training at 45th Street Mental Health Center in West Palm Beach, Florida, and is in the private practice of forensic clinical psychology in Boynton Beach, Florida. He received his doctoral degree from Auburn University. His research has included studies of the personality characteristics of criminals, the detection of faking on psychological tests, and the diagnosis of affective disorders in psychiatric patients. He is on the editorial board of *Criminal Justice and Behavior* and recently edited a special issue on the psychological classification of offenders. His current research projects are related to characteristics of successful psychotherapy supervisors, psychiatric hospital admission criteria, and prediction of suicidality in psychiatric patients. Dr. Posey's clinical work has involved diagnosis and psychotherapy of adjudicated offenders, psychiatric hospital patients, and schoolchildren with academic and emotional problems.

Karen R. Rapaport, PhD, consults on diagnostic and treatment issues with the Palm Beach County school system and a number of psychiatric hospitals and is currently in independent practice in Boynton Beach and Boca Raton, Florida. Her specialty areas include eating disorders, adult children of dysfunctional families, and women's issues. She also provides clinical supervision related to psychodiagnostics and psychotherapy. She received her doctorate from Auburn University. Her professional experience has included treatment of sexually abused children and rape victims, diagnostic and therapeutic work with offenders, and administrative and supervisory positions with a group of adolescent treatment facilities. In her research, she has investigated the characterological features of sexually coercive college students and their differential responsiveness to pornography.

Deborah R. Richardson, PhD, is a social psychologist affiliated with the Department of Sociology and Social Psychology at Florida Atlantic University in Boca Raton, Florida. She also serves as the director of the Computer-Administered Panel Study at the University of North Carolina. Since 1974, Dr. Richardson has been doing research on human physical aggression, particularly the factors that influence males' violence toward females. Her dissertation, "The Effect of Alcohol and Verbal Provocation on Male Violence Toward Female Targets," was completed at Kent State University under the direction of Stuart P. Taylor. Her current research focuses on factors that lead to aggressive interactions in the context of interpersonal conflict, and the role of empathy in regulating aggressive interactions.

Patricia D. Rozée, PhD, is an assistant professor of psychology and women's studies at California State University, Long Beach. She received her doctorate in social psychology from the University of California, Davis, in 1984, and went on to complete a two-year fellowship in applied social psychology at Peabody College of Vanderbilt University. Dr. Rozée's research and teaching specialization is in the psychology of women, especially violence against women. Her research program explores the institutionalization of values supportive of violence against women across cultures. She is currently investigating the relationship of cultural factors in the psychological response of female Cambodian refugees to wartime physical and sexual abuse. She is also studying corporate work environments that create safety problems for women employees, increase their fear of rape, and contribute to safety-related barriers to career advancement.

Diana E. H. Russell, PhD, is a professor of sociology at Mills College, where she has taught since 1969. She is the author of *The Politics of Rape, Rape in Marriage, Sexual Exploitation: Rape, Child Sexual Abuse and Workplace Harassment, The Secret Trauma: Incest in the Lives of Girls and Women,* and *Lives of Courage: Women for a New South Africa.* She was awarded the 1986 C. Wright Mills Award for *The Secret Trauma.* She has contributed to and coedited *Crimes Against Women: The Proceedings of the International Tribunal, Against Sadomasochism: A Radical Feminist Analysis,* and *Exposing Nuclear Phallacies.* Dr. Russell received her PhD from Harvard University in 1970. Her prior education had been at the University of Cape Town, South Africa and the London School of Economics and Political Science, where she received a postgraduate diploma with distinction.

Jennifer L. Schrag, BS, is an undergraduate in psychology and women's studies at the University of Kansas. She received her degree in cellular biology from the University of Michigan. She is currently working toward completion of an honors thesis based on research, with Charlene Muehlenhard, in the area of sexual coercion. Ms. Schrag has worked extensively with battered women and is active in the hospice movement.

Cindy Struckman-Johnson, PhD, is an applied social psychologist and an associate professor at the University of South Dakota, where she teaches courses in social psychology and sex roles. She received her doctoral degree in psychology from the University of Kentucky at Lexington in 1978. Professor Struckman-Johnson's research topics include sex-role issues such as coercive sexuality, contraceptive motivation, and changing standards of masculinity and femininity. She regularly designs and conducts applied survey research in traffic safety and academic image. As faculty advisor for Psi Chi, the honor society for psychology majors, she assists the group in developing its annual research project.

Ruth M. Townsley, MS, is a doctoral student in clinical psychology at the University of Georgia and is currently completing her clinical internship at Western Psychiatric Institute and Clinic, University of Pittsburgh Medical School. Her interest in attributions began with an undergraduate thesis project on students' attributions for performance. The topic of her master's thesis was offender alcohol use and attributions for rape. She has authored and coauthored papers on attributions and expectancies for rape, adjustment following childhood sexual abuse, predictors of abuse, and attributions made by spouses in the context of marital discord. She has participated in workshops on the treatment of victims of sexual abuse and has contributed to book chapters on the treatment of rape victims.

Robin Warshaw is an award-winning journalist who writes on social issues and other subjects for national magazines and newspapers. She is the author of *I Never Called It Rape: The Ms. Report on Recognizing, Fighting, and Surviving Date and Acquaintance Rape,* a book based on the findings of scholarly research conducted by Dr. Mary P. Koss and on Warshaw's own reporting.

Jacquelyn W. White, PhD, is an associate professor of psychology at the University of North Carolina at Greensboro. Her doctoral degree in social/personality psychology was received from Kent State University. She has published extensively on gender, aggression, and social influence.

Contents

Introduction

Until recently, acquaintance rape was not viewed as a real phenomenon. In the past decade, however, more and more scholars have acknowledged the existence of date and acquaintance rape and females as the primary victims. Since most of the research on acquaintance rape has examined female victims and male assailants, that approach is the focus of the majority of the chapters in this book. The recent research of social scientists who have begun to study male victims is discussed to a limited extent. We do acknowledge the existence of male victims and we recognize their special difficulties in being viewed as legitimate.

The book is organized into nine parts: Defining the Problem, Attitudes About Acquaintance Rape, Factors Contributing to Acquaintance Rape, Types of Acquaintance Rape, Victims, Assailants, Effects of Acquaintance Rape, Societal Response, and Avoidance and Prevention. Each part contains chapters written from the unique perspectives of researchers in the field.

DEFINING THE PROBLEM

In the opening section, the editors of the book, Laurie Bechhofer and Andrea Parrot, set the stage by providing an overview and theoretical framework. The first chapter, "What Is Acquaintance Rape?", explores the hidden nature of the crime, the changes in public perceptions, and some of the hypotheses posited to explain the presence of the crime in American culture.

Martha Burt's chapter presents an analysis of how rape myths contribute to acquaintance and date rape. The chapter focuses on the reason for the existence of rape myths. Dr. Burt develops her analysis from three central questions: Why do patriarchal societies maintain prejudicial, stereotyped, and false beliefs about rape, rape victims, and rape myths? What are the rape myths and how do they work to deny that a specific incident is a "real" rape? What is the larger context in which rape myths are found?

ATTITUDES ABOUT ACQUAINTANCE RAPE

This section explores the common and often alarming attitudes among various groups in American society toward acquaintance/date rape.

Acquaintance rape has become prevalent partly because these attitudes are so pervasive.

Jacquelyn White and John Humphrey focus on young people's attitudes about acquaintance/date rape. Their chapter deals with how adolescents and young adults perceive male–female sexual relationships in a dating context, the true range of attitudes and beliefs about forced sexual relations, and how research on young people's attitudes toward acquaintance/date rape fits with rape theories.

Karen Calhoun and Ruth Townsley address the attribution of responsibility for acquaintance/date rape. They begin by discussing different types of attributions that relate to acquaintance rape. They then explore how these attributions affect the perceptions of responsibility of victims and assailants for acquaintance rape. Finally, they present the legal and social implications for the treatment of assailants and victims and for the prevention of acquaintance rape.

FACTORS CONTRIBUTING TO ACQUAINTANCE RAPE

This section focuses on several factors that contribute to acquaintance/date rape—alcohol, sex-role socialization, media messages, and communication problems between men and women.

In the chapter that deals with the contributions of sex role socialization to acquaintance rape, Robin Warshaw and Andrea Parrot explore the contribution of the media, peer group pressures, and social milieu that allow young people to believe that acquaintance rape is acceptable. In addition, the authors analyze an acquaintance rape and discuss the socialization messages that contribute to it.

Deborah Richardson and Georgina Hammock identify the role of alcohol in acquaintance rape situations. Their chapter responds to these questions: What evidence exists to suggest that the victim and/or perpetrator are drinking alcohol when acquaintance rape occurs? Is alcohol the *cause* of acquaintance rape? How does drunkenness of the victim and/or perpetrator affect judgment of culpability for acquaintance rape?

"Misperceptions as an Antecedent of Acquaintance Rape: A Consequence of Ambiguity in Communication Between Women and Men," the chapter written by Antonia Abbey, probes the role of the media in perpetuating misperceptions of sexual intent, and the differences between male and female perceptions of friendliness as implying sexual intent. Dr. Abbey also addresses these questions: What types of men are likely to perceive friendliness as sexual interest? What verbal or nonverbal cues might contribute to these misperceptions?

TYPES OF ACQUAINTANCE RAPE

Nonviolent coercive sex, marital rape, and gang rape are addressed in this section. These forms of rape are included in this book because all of them occur between people who know each other and all are treated similarly under the law. Charlene Muehlenhard and Jennifer Schrag examine rape that is achieved through nonviolent sexual coercion and ways in which women are coerced into engaging in sex. In addition, they explore the relationship between traditional gender roles and the advantages and disadvantages of broadening our conceptualization of sexual coercion.

Marital rape is presented by Diana Russell. This chapter is excerpted from her landmark book *Rape in Marriage* (published in 1982, revised in 1990), based on a study of marital rape in San Francisco. Both the historical and contemporary aspects of the criminalization of wife rape are included in this review.

Chris O'Sullivan's presentation of the topic of gang rape on college campuses includes her studies of the differences in the prevalence of gang rape among college men and noncollege men of the same age. She endeavors to determine whether particular groups of college students are most likely to organize and commit group sexual assaults and what characteristics of these groups make them participate in gang rapes. Finally, she investigates why acquaintance gang rapes are so difficult to prosecute.

VICTIMS

When we think of rape victims we think first of women; however, men can also be victims of forced sex. This section examines the factors that increase the likelihood that someone will become a victim of sexual assault and profiles male and female victims.

Patricia Harney and Charlene Muehlenhard identify factors associated with victimization. Without blaming the victims, these authors examine the cultural, situational, and personal variables that heighten the risk of sexual victimization for women. (Men are not discussed as potential victims in this chapter.)

Catalina Mandoki and Barry Burkhart present information on the antecedents and consequences when women are rape victims. They discuss women's social roles as victims and sexual beings, how cultural influences impact on the lives of women, and the factors that increase a woman's vulnerability to acquaintance rape. Finally, they propose behavioral strategies for women to avoid rape.

Cindy Struckman-Johnson, in her discussion of male victims of acquaintance rape, reports on the prevalence of male sexual assault in America and explores the question of why so little is known about this phenomenon. Dr.

Struckman-Johnson considers how men can be sexually assaulted by both male and female acquaintances. She examines the short- and long-term psychological impact of rape on male victims. Finally, she discusses what can be done about sexual assault of males, in terms of research, education, and prevention.

ASSAILANTS

What factors contribute to men becoming assailants? Which men are likely to become acquaintance rapists, and why are they likely to do so?

Karen Rapaport and Dale Posey present an analysis of those college men who are most likely to become sexually coercive. The personality characteristics that distinguish self-reported sexually coercive and noncoercive college males are described, and the self-reported rapists' responses to depictions of rape are compared to those of nonrapists. The authors also explore the attitudes toward women and sexual behavior that predominate among self-reported sexually coercive males.

Neil Malamuth and Karol Dean discuss why some men are attracted to sexual aggression—how the construct of sexual aggression fits with psychodynamic, sociobiological, and feminist theoretical perspectives. They examine how research on attraction to sexual aggression might help to explain why some men are sexually aggressive and some men are not. Finally, they address the question: Which other areas of research might benefit from the introduction of an attraction concept?

EFFECTS OF ACQUAINTANCE RAPE

What are the psychological effects of acquaintance/date rape on female victims? The differences between the coping mechanisms of stranger rape victims and acquaintance rape victims are identified in this section.

Bonnie Katz writes about the psychological effects of prerape familiarity on recovery from rape. She compares the differences in recovery of several groups of rape victims, based on their degree of familiarity with the rapist. She also considers why prerape familiarity can lead to differences in the rape experience and the process of recovery. Finally, she discusses the areas of personality and social functioning that are likely to be affected by rape and those that are likely to be involved in recovery.

Christine Gidycz and Mary Koss explore the effects of acquaintance rape on female victims by examining the prevalence of acquaintance rape and comparing the recovery processes in women who have been raped by strangers and victims of acquaintance rape. The authors also evaluate the central assumptions of cognitive theories that have been used to explain a rape victim's reaction to trauma.

SOCIETAL RESPONSE

In this section the responses of the medical community, legal community, and psychological community to rape are examined. Suggestions are made regarding how each of these three groups can help rape victims and how they can improve their understanding and protocol for dealing with acquaintance/date rapes.

Barry Burkhart presents a conceptual and practical analysis of treatment for acquaintance rape victims. He addresses how the social context of acquaintance rape defines and controls this phenomenon and how it is experienced by victims and offenders. In addition, Dr. Burkhart considers why denial is such an impediment to treatment of acquaintance rape victims. Finally, he proposes a 10-step protocol for counseling acquaintance rape victims.

The chapter on the medical community's response to acquaintance rape, written by Andrea Parrot, focuses on the rape trauma syndrome and the medical and psychological needs of the victim following a rape. Suggestions are made for medical practitioners regarding evidence collection immediately following a rape, as well as long-term and follow-up care necessary for victims of acquaintance rape.

In the chapter on acquaintance rape and the law, Carol Bohmer reviews why the spousal rape exemption has been part of the law historically and why it still exists today. Dr. Bohmer also examines how rape laws have changed, why those reforms were instigated by the legal system, and the legal similarities between how acquaintance rape and marital rape are viewed.

AVOIDANCE AND PREVENTION

This section offers prevention strategies from the personal as well as the institutional perspective. The institutional suggestions are most appropriate for colleges and universities, because acquaintance rapes are particularly common in such environments, but they are also valid for other institutions such as boarding schools and high schools.

Patricia Rozée, Py Bateman, and Theresa Gilmore write about acquaintance rape avoidance on three levels. First, they discuss how to handle an acquaintance rape in progress. Second, they present suggestions on how we can structure our everyday lives to avoid being in an acquaintance rape situation. Finally, they describe the types of social changes that need to come about, to reduce the incidence of acquaintance rape.

Andrea Parrot presents the chapter on how institutions can help to prevent acquaintance rape. She discusses educational changes an institution can make to improve its approach to acquaintance rape. She strongly encourages prevention programs for students, faculty, and staff and suggests that personnel on campus who are likely to deal with acquaintance rape victims should be educated about how to best respond to the needs of the victims and assailants.

The final chapter of the book, also written by Dr. Parrot, recommends policies and procedures that colleges should employ to deal most effectively with acquaintance rape on their campuses. Specific recommendations are made: to college judicial boards, for revision of their approach to cases presented to them, and to campus administrators regarding funding, research, alcohol policies, and training needs.

Because this book is written by scholars in the United States, its perspectives are specific to this culture. In addition, because very little research has been done on any groups other than caucasian college students, much of the information presented is specific to that group and may not be generalizable to other age and/or racial or ethnic groups.

The contributors to this book represent many different disciplines; the perspectives presented are therefore broad in scope. It is our hope that, by making this information available, acquaintance rape will be viewed more seriously so that victims will receive better treatment, assailants will be held more accountable for their actions, and ultimately the crime will be better prevented.

PART 1

Defining the Problem

CHAPTER 1

What Is Acquaintance Rape?

LAURIE BECHHOFER and ANDREA PARROT, PhD

He kissed her. When he started to unbutton her blouse, she asked him to stop. He continued to unbutton her blouse. She begged him to stop. She told him "No!" emphatically. He continued anyway. He pulled up her skirt and pulled down her panties. While holding both of her arms down with one of his hands, he unzipped his fly and took out his erect penis and penetrated her.

Would you consider the above incident to be rape? Now consider the following situation:

Mary and John had been dating for two weeks. Both John and Mary had slept with people in the past but they hadn't had sexual intercourse with each other. On their fourth date, after John took Mary out for a lobster dinner and then to a wild party to meet some of his friends, the couple went to John's apartment. Mary was wearing a sexy, provocative dress. She had spent a lot of time getting ready, because she wanted to look her best for a special evening. After they got to his apartment, they shared a bottle of wine, listened to music, talked, laughed, and kissed. Mary told John what a wonderful time she was having with him. John suggested that they move to his bedroom where they could get more comfortable. She nodded in agreement. In the bedroom, they started dancing erotically and kissing passionately. John caressed Mary's breasts, and Mary moaned. When he started to unbutton her blouse, Mary asked him to stop. He kissed her gently and continued to undress her. She begged him to stop. She told him "No!" emphatically and said that she was not ready for sex with him. He continued anyway, telling her that he knew she wanted it. He told her to relax and that she was really going to like it. John assured Mary that he loved her and that he had been thinking about this moment ever since they first met. He pulled up her skirt and pulled down her panties. While holding both of her arms with one of his hands, he unzipped his fly, took out his erect penis, and penetrated her.

Would you consider this incident to be rape? Why or why not? What are the elements that must be present for an incident to be rape?

The woman was raped in both scenarios. She told the man "No," and he proceeded to penetrate her while holding her down. She was forced to have sexual intercourse against her will and without her consent. Many people would characterize the first scenario as rape but not the second, even though both contain the same key elements. How can we account for this inconsistency?

Mary and John were involved in a typical date rape, an act that many people fail to view as a criminal sexual assault. Why is date rape not taken seriously? First, it is difficult, if not impossible, to reconcile the concept of rape with our preconceptions about dating and courtship. Dating brings to mind images of happiness, enjoyment, friendship, sexual exploration, cooperation, and sharing. Rape evokes images of force, power, hurt, violation, pain, guilt, and scars. The very term "date rape" is an oxymoron.

Date and acquaintance rape occur in a social context where consensual sex is a possibility; in stranger rape, sex is generally out of context. It is hard to imagine that a woman who was attacked, raped, and beaten while walking down the street at night *wanted* to have sex with her assailant (although some people do believe this myth). However, if a man and woman kiss and slow dance together in the privacy of the man's apartment (as Mary and John did in the second scenario), consensual sex would certainly be one possible outcome for the evening; most people would not expect the date to end in rape.

Finally, date rape diverges from the *common perception* of rape, or the *stereotype rape,* which is the mental image of rape that many people ascribe to: a crazed stranger jumps out of the bushes and drags a victim into an alley at night. The perpetrator uses a weapon such as a knife or a gun to obtain compliance. The victim is severely battered and bruised because she fought back. After the rape, she rushes to a hospital emergency room in a state of hysteria and immediately reports the crime to the police.

In fact, very few rapes fit the above description. The vast majority are perpetrated by someone known to the victim (Kanin, 1957; Koss, Gidycz, & Wisniewski, 1987; Parrot, 1985; Russell, 1982). Most assailants do not appear to be psychopaths. The majority of rapes take place in the residence of the victim or perpetrator (Parrot & Link, 1983). Assailants are more likely to use verbal or psychological coercion to overpower their victims than guns or knives (Rapaport & Burkhart, 1984). Consequently, victims often exhibit few external cuts or bruises. Contrary to the stereotype, victims may appear calm and collected after they have been raped; researchers have identified this controlled reaction as one possible response in the *disorientation phase* of the rape trauma syndrome experienced by many rape and sexual assault victims (Burgess & Holmstrom, 1974).

Although acquaintance rape is much more common than stranger rape, it is largely a *hidden crime* that is critically unacknowledged. At the deepest level, a victim of acquaintance rape does not usually label her* experience as

---

* The female pronoun will be used to refer to the victim and the male pronoun will be used to refer to the assailant because the majority of sexual assault victims are female and assailants are male.

such. "Most women forced to have sex by men they know see themselves as victims but not as *legitimate crime* victims [emphasis added]" (Estrich, 1987, p. 12). And those who admit to themselves that they have been raped rarely tell anyone about the incident out of fear that they will not be believed or that they will be blamed for inviting the rape. It is estimated that less than one percent of acquaintance rape victims report the crime to the police (Burkhart, 1983). Finally, in the rare case that the victim presses criminal charges, a conviction is unusual since acquaintance rape victims usually lack bruises or other external marks that are judged as indicators of the use of force (Estrich, 1987; Rowland, 1985). All of these factors contribute to the invisibility of acquaintance rape. The blind spot that obscures society's ability to recognize acquaintance rape as a crime is far-reaching: the victim must label the crime as rape and come forward to report the assault, and a court must convict the assailant in order to confirm that rape did indeed occur.

The bottom line is that acquaintance rape is viewed by most people as something other than "real rape." A victim who knows her assailant seems to be automatically considered at least partially to blame for the incident. Consider the case of *State of Florida v. Lord,* in which a woman was raped at knife point by someone she knew. In the October 4, 1989, verdict, the assailant was found not guilty because the woman was wearing lace "short shorts" and no underwear. The verdict was particularly shocking because the assailant was armed.

Often, acquaintance rape is viewed as a charge a woman frivolously brings against her partner if she wants revenge or if she feels guilty about having consented to sex. In fact, however, the number of acquaintance rapes falsely reported to the police is negligible (New York City Police Department, 1972). When very few legitimate rapists are punished, a woman stands to gain little more than negative attention by falsely pressing charges.

The motivations for stranger and date rape often differ. In stranger rape, the assailant usually premeditates the rape. He plans to rape for the purposes of degradation and humiliation of the victim. Sex is secondary to domination. This is not generally the case in date rape. A man who rapes on dates usually premeditates sex, not rape. He plans the evening with the intent of sex, but if the date does not progress as planned and his date does not comply, he becomes angry and takes what he feels is his right—sex. Afterward, the victim and assailant usually view the incident differently; the victim feels raped, while the assailant believes that he has done nothing wrong. He may even ask the woman out on another date.

Acquaintance rape is still largely hidden from public perception. It is reported far less frequently than stranger rape despite the fact that it is much more common. Rape statistics derived from the Federal Bureau of Investigation and rape crisis centers do not begin to reflect the magnitude of the problem since they are based only on reported cases. While the public is finally acknowledging the *existence* of rape and sexual assault between acquaintances, it is still reluctant to view such behavior as criminally and morally reprehensible. Our goal in writing this chapter is to call attention to the problem of acquaintance rape by defining the phenomenon, discussing it in its historical context, and recognizing it for what it is: a punishable crime.

DEFINING THE PARAMETERS OF ACQUAINTANCE RAPE

Acquaintance rape is treated with ambivalence by society and the legal system partly because it is difficult to identify situations that clearly constitute acquaintance rape. Therefore, a working definition of the terms is in order. We define *acquaintance rape* as nonconsensual sex between adults* who know each other. The word *acquaintance* is sometimes used to describe a person who is known but not a close friend ("He is a casual acquaintance"). The word can also be used to describe any person who is known to the victim—anyone who is not a stranger. This broader definition is the one used in this book. The acquaintance relationship can be any one of a variety of acquaintanceships including platonic, dating, marital, professional, academic, or familial. *Date rape* is a narrower term referring to nonconsensual sex between people who are dating or on a date. Although the two terms "acquaintance rape" and "date rape" are often used interchangeably (particularly in the lay press), they do not have the same meaning. Date rape is one form of acquaintance rape.

Nonconsent is much more difficult to define than acquaintance. The ambiguity surrounding consent can be illustrated by examining a nonsexual situation.

Suppose that Liz wanted to borrow her friend Sarah's car. What would Liz have to do to obtain permission or consent? She could ask Sarah directly whether she could borrow the car and Sarah could either grant or deny permission. Alternatively, Liz could assume that since Sarah allowed her to use the car on three previous occasions, it would be acceptable if she uses it this time without her permission. Or if Liz heard that Sarah lent out her car all the time, she might assume that it would be acceptable to simply borrow it without asking. And what if Sarah was sleeping when Liz needed to use the car? Liz might think that it would be acceptable to borrow the car since Sarah wouldn't be needing it.

There are some similarities between the dynamics of this scenario and those of acquaintance rape situations. First, there is often an assumption that a person has consented to sex if he or she has had sex with the same person on a previous occasion. Also, consent is assumed if a woman is known to have

---

* We are excluding instances of child sexual abuse from our discussion of acquaintance rape, primarily because the antecedents and dynamics differ substantially from those of adult sexual assault.

had sex with many other people and has a "loose reputation." Finally, a person is often considered to be "fair game" if she or he is asleep or drunk. In each of the above circumstances, consent is falsely assumed based on a person's past or current behavior. In addition, if a person does not explicitly say "no" to sex, it is assumed that he or she is implicitly saying "yes."

None of the above criteria should be used in determining consent. For a person to give consent in a sexual situation, legally and morally, she or he must say "yes" *and* not say "no." Consent must be obtained on every separate occasion and cannot be assumed from previous interactions. According to this definition, most people do not give true consent in their sexual interactions. However, a situation is rape only if the person not consenting *does not want to have sex.* To reduce ambiguity regarding whether a person has consented, one must use the above criteria. To violate or ignore these conditions is to enter the gray zone and take the risk of committing rape.

In real-life situations, the stranger/acquaintance and consent/nonconsent distinctions are often obscured. Figure 1.1 provides a visual depiction of how the two dimensions (stranger/acquaintance and consent/nonconsent) intersect to create a quadrant with indistinct boundaries. Acquaintance rape is in a unique position: It is rape and yet it borders lovemaking (consensual sex between acquaintances). Moreover, the border between lovemaking and acquaintance rape is not always clear. If it were, there would be no ambiguity regarding whether rape occurred. But, the very fact that acquaintance rape and lovemaking often have similar antecedents and dynamics contributes to the blurring of the line and the mislabeling of many forced sex incidents.

Both males and females can be either assailants or victims of acquaintance rape. Although it is statistically unusual for males to be victims and females to be assailants, it does occur. Men report being forced into sexual encounters by other men (sometimes gangs) as well as by females. Because these types of sexual assaults are rarely reported to the police, many believe that they do not

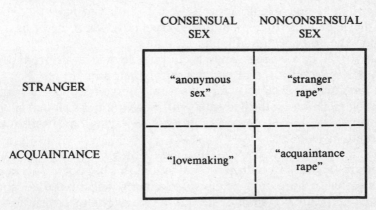

Figure 1.1.   Stranger/acquaintance and consent/nonconsent interactions.

occur. The Federal Bureau of Investigation (FBI, 1982) estimated that 10% of all sexual assault victims are male, although male victims rarely report the crime unless they are physically injured.

Some people believe that it is inappropriate to consider marital rape as a type of acquaintance rape. There are compelling reasons, however, to do so. At the simplest level, marital rape is rape between adults who know each other; hence it fits into our definition of acquaintance rape. But beyond that, marital relationships usually contain the elements of trust and intimacy which are present in many nonmarital dating relationships. Therefore, it would seem somewhat arbitrary and inappropriate to include date rape in our discussion while excluding marital rape. The law has viewed rape between cohabitating couples and spouses similarly, in that marital exclusion statutes in some states have been extended to nonmarried couples who are living together (Finkelhor & Yllo, 1987).

WHY DISTINGUISH ON THE BASIS OF DEGREE OF ACQUAINTANCE?

To characterize all incidents of forced sex as either acquaintance rape or stranger rape is not always meaningful or even possible. Some cases do not clearly fit into either category; a case in which the victim met the assailant 10 minutes prior to the assault is an example. Nevertheless, researchers, educators, and health practitioners have found it helpful to distinguish between acquaintance and stranger rape because the antecedents, dynamics of the assault, and psychological consequences for victims often differ.

Furthermore, some researchers have hypothesized that the degree of trust and emotional intimacy may matter more than the type of relationship per se (e.g., acquaintance, friend, intimate) in determining the victim's path to recovery (Katz, 1987). Emotional intimacy is not synonymous with physical intimacy. A person can have an intimate bond with his or her parent, for example, that is not sexual. Conversely, a person can have a "one-night stand" that is not emotionally intimate, especially when she or he doesn't even know the other person's first name.

While we will be focusing on how acquaintance rape *differs* from stranger rape, it is important to point out several of their similarities. First, both involve the same physical act—forced sexual intercourse. Second, both are devastating violations of the body and will. The victim is stripped of dignity and personal control. The recovery process following rape and sexual assault usually takes years.

Although acquaintance rape victims are coming forth to get help and to work toward recovery from their victimization, this has not always been the case. Historically, acquaintance rapes were rarely if ever reported, and victims suffered in isolation because they didn't know where to turn for help— or even that they were eligible for help.

CHANGES IN THE PUBLIC PERCEPTION OF ACQUAINTANCE RAPE

While people have only recently begun to hear about acquaintance rape, the phenomenon is not new. Forced sex between acquaintances has probably occurred as long as people have been involved in relationships with each other. A reference to acquaintance rape can be found in the Old Testament (2 Samuel 13: 1–15):

Absalom son of David had a beautiful sister whose name was Tamar; Amnon son of David fell in love with her. Amnon was so obsessed with his sister Tamar that it made him ill, for she was a virgin and it seemed to Amnon impossible to do anything to her. But Amnon had a friend called Jonadab son of Shimeah, David's brother, and Jonadab was a very shrewd man. "Son of the king," he said, "tell me why, morning after morning, you look so worn? Will you not tell me?" Amnon answered, "I am in love with Tamar, my brother Absalom's sister." Then Jonadab said, "Lie down on your bed, pretend to be ill and when your father comes to visit you, say, 'Let my sister Tamar come and give me something to eat; let her prepare the food before my eyes for me to see; only at her hands will I eat.'" So Amnon lay down and pretended to be ill. The king came to visit him and Amnon said to the king, "Let my sister Tamar come and make a cake or two; I will eat at her hands." David then sent word to Tamar at the palace, "Go to your brother Amnon's house and prepare some food for him." Tamar went to the house of her brother Amnon who was lying there in bed. She took dough and kneaded it, and she made cakes there before his eyes and baked the cakes. Then she took the pan and dished them up in front of him, but he refused to eat. "Let everyone leave me," he said; so they all withdrew. Then Amnon said to Tamar, "Bring the food to the inner room so that I can eat at your hands." So Tamar took the cakes she had made and brought them to her brother Amnon in the inner room. And as she was offering the food to him he caught hold of her and said, "Come lie with me, my sister." But she answered, "No, my brother! Do not violate me. This is not a thing men do in Israel. Do not commit such an outrage. Wherever should I go, bearing my shame?" . . . But he would not listen to her; he overpowered her and, raping her, lay with her.

Then Amnon was seized with extreme hatred for her; the hatred he now felt for her was greater than his earlier love. "Get up and go," he said. "No, my brother," she said, "to send me away would be a greater wrong than the other you have done me." But he would not listen to her. . . . "Get rid of this woman for me," he said, "throw her out and bolt the door after her." . . .

Tamar took dust and put it on her head, tore the long-sleeved gown she was wearing, laid her hand on her head, and went away uttering cries as she went. Her brother Absalom said to her . . . "Be quiet now, my sister; he is your brother; do not take this so much to heart."

(The Jerusalem Bible, 1968, pp. 341–342.)

The dynamics of acquaintance rape have not changed significantly over the past 2,000 years. Amnon forced Tamar to have sex despite her wishes. He got her into his bed through manipulation and then rejected her after the rape. Tamar was emotionally distraught by the rape, yet others simply trivialized her feelings.

Despite its long history, rape between acquaintances wasn't reported in the scholarly literature until the 1950s. Sociologist Eugene Kanin (1957) of Purdue University documented the existence of sexual aggression within courtship relationships. Of the women he sampled 30% had been victims of rape or attempted rape while on a date. These cases, however, were probably reported to authorities less often than cases are today. Since no term was in use to describe the event, many victims did not know what to call it or where to report it. In addition, the law governing rape in the 1950s made it all but impossible to prove because an eye witness to the crime was usually required for a conviction.

It wasn't until the early 1980s that rape between acquaintances was given a name. In September of 1982, Karen Barett wrote an article in *Ms.* magazine based on the research findings of Dr. Mary Koss, and she referred to this "new and unusual" form of sexual aggression as "date rape." Giving sexual aggression between acquaintances a name was a crucial first step in addressing the problem.

Changes in the Law

In addition to changes in our language, modifications in the laws are reflecting society's changing attitudes toward rape. For example, only fairly recently has rape been viewed as a crime against the rape victim; it used to be considered as a crime against another man's property (Brownmiller, 1975). In addition, the laws have been changed to allow males who have been forced to have sex to be considered rape victims. Unfortunately, many state statutes still reflect the antiquated view that rape can happen only to a woman and can be perpetrated only by a man. In the past 15 years, wife rape has come to be considered a punishable offense in the eyes of the law. Most state laws no longer stipulate that a man commits rape only when he has "sexual intercourse with a female, *not his wife,* by force and against her will." As of January 1990, 43 out of 50 states have changed their laws to provide legal protection to married women who are sexually victimized by their husbands (Russell, 1990, p. 23). The laws are beginning to reflect the reality that rape can happen to any person under a variety of circumstances.

The definition of rape varies from state to state, but generally for an incident to be considered rape or sexual assault, three conditions must be present: The sexual act must be against the victim's will and without the victim's consent; some degree of force or threat of force must be applied; and penile/vaginal penetration must occur.

State laws differ in their classification of rape situations. Some states have gender neutral laws: Either males or females can be victims or assailants.

Others have restrictions that effectively fail to recognize that both men and women can be assailants or victims; in such states, only men can be assailants and only women can be victims. Several states have completely eliminated the term rape and defined any forced sexual act (e.g., vaginal, anal, or oral intercourse) as sexual assault. But in a majority of states, only penile/vaginal intercourse is considered rape and other forced sex crimes are included in the sodomy or sexual abuse statutes.

When the law is interpreted in its broadest form, rape occurs any time a person is forced to have sex (usually vaginal intercourse) against his or her will and without his or her consent. But other factors—such as a victim's inability to consent because of physical or mental incapacitation, or a victim's capitulation to sex out of fear for his or her personal safety or life—would render a situation rape in most jurisdictions.

A legal distinction is made between "simple" and "aggravated" rape (Estrich, 1987); the latter is rape that occurs in conjunction with some other crime, such as kidnapping, physical assault, or breaking and entering. Simple rape occurs without any other crime being committed in conjunction with it. Most cases of acquaintance rape are simple, and for that reason are extremely difficult to prosecute and convict (Estrich, 1987; Rowland, 1985); this pattern has not changed much over the past few decades.

Acquaintance Rape Perception Since 1955

The time line in Table 1.1 illustrates changes in our perceptions and awareness of the crime of acquaintance rape since 1955. As noted earlier, researchers did not begin to identify the phenomenon of date rape until 1957; even then, they did not have a term to characterize sexual aggression between acquaintances. Surprisingly little significant research was conducted on the issue over the next two decades. In the early 1980s, several landmark studies indicated that many people considered forced sex to be acceptable (Goodchilds, Zellman, Johnson, & Giarrusso, 1988) and desirable (Malamuth, 1981) under certain circumstances. At the same time, researchers were learning that acquaintance rape and sexual assault were prevalent on college campuses. The issue then began to be addressed by the popular media. By the late 1980s, movies and television shows focusing almost exclusively on acquaintance rape were released. Finally, research findings that had accumulated during the 1980s were disseminated to the general public. The time line illustrates how the researchers, the legal system, and the popular media simultaneously addressed the problem of acquaintance and date rape, thereby promoting a greater understanding of the issue. None of these avenues alone would have been sufficient to raise public consciousness.

Much of the reform and promotion of public awareness regarding acquaintance rape and other forms of violence against women must be credited to the emergence of the Women's Movement. As a result of the movement, within academia, fields of inquiry specifically related to women were finally legitimated. In addition, the Women's Movement helped to bring about changes in

TABLE 1.1   Landmark Events in Acquaintance/Date Rape History Since 1955

1957	First documentation (by Kanin) in the scholarly literature of sexual aggression between dating couples.
1975	Rape laws changing to allow for easier prosecution.
1976	*Against Our Will,* Susan Brownmiller's historical treatise on rape, published.
1978	*Rideout* case in Oregon; first husband still effectively living with his wife to be tried for marital rape.
1979	Landmark two-part study by Giarrusso, Goodchilds, Johnson, and Zellman revealed significant percentage of teenagers believed forced sex on dates was sometimes acceptable (Giarrusso et al., 1979; Goodchilds et al., 1979; *see also* Goodchilds, et al., (1988).
1979	Irresponsible portrayal of date rape on the soap opera "General Hospital," in which Luke raped Laura, and she left her husband to marry him.
1981	Study by Neil Malamuth, in which 35% of college men indicated some likelihood that they would rape if they could be assured of getting away with it.
1982	First use of the term "date rape" in widely circulating publication (*Ms.* magazine article based on Koss's research).
1984	First syndicated talk show (Donahue) on date rape.
1985	Cathleen Crowell Webb admitted to falsely accusing Gary Dotson of rape, after he spent eight years in prison for the alleged crime, thereby reinforcing the myth that women frequently charge rape falsely.
1985	Nationwide survey of rape by Dr. Mary Koss, including more than 6,100 college students and 30 college campuses, documented that one in four college women have experienced rape or attempted rape.
1986	National television commercial condemning date rape (from a male perspective) produced by the Santa Monica rape treatment center.
1986	Syracuse University football player earned national recognition for pleading guilty to sexual misconduct, after being charged with rape and sexual assault. Syracuse University found him innocent of any wrongdoing.
1987	ABC aired After-School Special on acquaintance rape, "Between Friends," aimed at teenagers.
1987	Harvard Law School Professor Susan Estrich's *Real Rape* was published, a book about how acquaintance rape is treated by the legal system.
1987	Soap opera "All My Children" ran segment on date rape in which rapist was convicted and sent to prison.
1988	Robin Warshaw's book, *I Never Called It Rape,* based on Koss's nationwide survey of college campuses, published; first book on acquaintance rape written for general audience.
1988	Film, "The Accused," about acquaintance gang rape, released. Jody Foster won Academy Award for role as rape victim.
1989	Made-for-television documentary, "Against Her Will," focusing on date rape on college campuses, narrated by Kelly McGillis on Lifetime Cable Network.
1989	Jury in *State of Florida v. Lloyd* acquitted defendant on rape charges because victim was wearing lace "short shorts" and no underwear.
1989	Made-for-television, prime-time movie, "When He's Not a Stranger," portraying date rape on a college campus.
1989	Since 1955, over 200 scholarly papers and articles written on acquaintance/date rape, over 175 of which were written during the past decade.

the way that women viewed themselves physically and sexually. Increasingly, women came to feel that it was acceptable to take control of their bodies, their sexual selves, and their lives. Women actively spoke out against sexual violence and other forms of male control over women. As a result of the Women's Movement, however, some women may have developed a false sense of security in their dating interactions. They naively believe that all men have been converted to a "feminist" way of thinking and that they respect women's wishes in sexual situations. Unfortunately, this is not the case. As recently as 1981, 35% of college men indicated some likelihood that they would rape if they could be assured of not getting caught (Malamuth, 1981). In another recent study, one in 12 college men admitted to committing acts that met the legal definition of rape (Koss, 1988). While the Women's Movement did not bring about an end to rape and sexual assault, "It did identify sexual violence as a key element maintaining the subordination of women, provided women with new ways of understanding their situation, and expanded the resources that women had for fighting back" (D'Emilio & Freedman, 1988, p. 315).

Changes in Research Methodology

With the evaluation of laws and common perception has come the improvement of research methodology for acquaintance rape. The biased research that was conducted prior to the 1980s colored the way that we view rape.

Social scientists have often relied on prison inmates as subjects, when studying the characteristics of assailants. This population was chosen for several reasons: (a) the guilt of the inmates was nearly certain; (b) the population was easy to access and to question; and (c) the prisoners were sometimes offered incentives if they volunteered to be research subjects. Assailants undergoing psychological treatment were also a readily accessible population for study. By focusing on such populations, however, researchers learned a great deal about those who were caught and convicted of sexual assault, and very little about the majority who were not. The emerging picture of a "typical rapist" or a "typical rape circumstance" was misleading. Violent stranger rapes and/or serial rapes appeared to be the norm.

Not until the early 1980s were social scientists able to tap into the population of "hidden" rape victims and assailants. Koss and Oros (1982) developed the Sexual Experiences Survey, a behavioral self-report instrument with questions about a range of coercive sexual experiences. The survey identified the population of unacknowledged victims and assailants—those women who had been rape victims (according to the legal definition) and men who had been assailants, but had not labeled their experiences as such. The survey also allowed researchers to determine the incidence and prevalence of acts of sexual aggression other than forced sexual intercourse.

Koss's (1988) nationwide survey of more than 6,100 college students revealed several startling facts about rape. First, rape and sexual assault were much more common than previously imagined. One in four college women reported being victims of rape or attempted rape. Second, a majority of those rapes happened between people who knew each other and/or were dating. Finally, the perpetrators of the rapes were, for the most part, not psychologically deviant men. In summary, the profile of rape derived from the Sexual Experiences Survey looked nothing like those derived from studies of incarcerated assailants and self-acknowledged rape victims who had reported to crisis centers. Since Koss first conducted her survey in the early 1980s, other researchers who examined the incidence and prevalence of acquaintance rape and sexual assault in college (Aizenman & Kelley, 1988; Berger, Searles, Salem, & Pierce, 1986; Muehlenhard & Linton, 1987; Parrot, 1985) and noncollege (Russell, 1982; Sorenson, Stein, Siegel, Golding, & Burnam, 1987) populations corroborated her findings.

Most of the acquaintance rape researchers have utilized college students as subjects. For several reasons, this has been a useful population to study. First, college students are easily accessible and often willing to participate in difficult research. Second, they are most at risk for sexual aggression by acquaintances. They are at the most active dating stage of their life and frequency of dating is one of the best predictors of involvement in sexual assault (Koss, 1985; Mahoney, Shively, & Traw, 1986). The more one dates, the greater the likelihood of sexual victimization. Of the people aged 18 to 24 (the highest-risk group for acquaintance rape) in the United States, 26% attend college (Koss et al., 1987), so by focusing on college students, researchers have reached a substantial proportion of the at-risk population. Finally, research on college campuses is likely to yield information about acquaintance rape because college environments often are conducive to sexual assault. Fraternities, sororities, sports teams, and similar organizations found on most college campuses have been implicated in numerous cases of acquaintance rape (Bausell & Maloy, 1990; Ehrhart & Sandler, 1985).

It is now important for researchers to move beyond college populations. Other groups of individuals, such as adolescents and recently divorced women, are particularly vulnerable to acquaintance rape. Adolescents are at high risk because they often have low self-esteem and they lack maturity and experience in dealing with difficult dating interactions. Furthermore, adolescents frequently believe they are invincible: "It can't happen to me." Recently divorced women are likely to be high-risk for several reasons. They too may suffer from low self-esteem, particularly if they were rejected by their husbands. They may feel inexperienced in dating, especially in the new AIDS-conscious decade of the 1990s, when the unwritten rules of dating are nothing like those of previous decades. Finally, as women grow older, the pool of eligible men shrinks and their chances of dating a sexually assaultive man increase. One point is important to remember: Just because individuals possess characteristics that have been found to increase the likelihood of victimization does not mean that they *will* be victimized; nor does it mean that they *will not* be victimized because they lack those characteristics.

FACTORS CONTRIBUTING TO ACQUAINTANCE RAPE

Over the past decade, researchers have investigated the incidence and prevalence of acquaintance rape, the profiles of assailants and victims, and the
psychological impact on victims. (Much of this research is reviewed in Chapters 11 through 17 of this book.) To date, however, there has been relatively
little research exploring the antecedents of acquaintance rape. Focus has been
on the "what" and "how" and has avoided the "why." Part of the reason for
this is political. There is a concern that by pointing to the things that women
do that increase their risk for victimization, blame will be placed on them for
what happened. Rape, however, is never the victim's fault. It is possible to
examine risk factors for acquaintance rape without blaming the victim. And
by identifying those factors which put people at greater risk for victimization,
researchers can provide concrete risk-reduction strategies that are empower-
ing to potential victims. Following is a brief discussion of some of the theories
posited to explain the prevalence of acquaintance rape in our culture.

When the common perception of rape was that it was committed by
perverted, crazy men, "nice" women didn't feel threatened because they
doubted that they would interact with such men. But now we know that
"nice" men do rape, and that they rape "nice" women. The crime is far too
common to be blamed on a small minority of psychopaths. We must therefore reevaluate our theories regarding the factors contributing to rape, and
acquaintance rape in particular.

Feminist theorists have suggested that the pathology lies not in a few
deviant men but rather in our contemporary American culture. Our culture
condones and even encourages acquaintance rape. For example, parents
frequently socialize their male children to set their goals and go after them
regardless of whom they hurt. This behavior is visible on the peewee football
field, where boys are told to "act like a man" when they are knocked down:
"Don't cry; get out and win the game, and put the opponent out of commission." Little girls, on the other hand, are socialized to make things better in
relationships, to not "make waves," and to do things for males.

We also teach boys and girls to "play games" in sexual relationships rather
than to be assertive and ask for what they really want. Boys are taught to be
aggressive and girls are taught to be passive. Boys are taught to never take
"no" for an answer because girls do not really know what they want sexually,
and even if girls do say "no," it is because they are trying to protect their
reputation. The somewhat twisted logic goes like this: He thinks that if he
pushes her further than she wants to go, she will be thankful in the end,
because she will have gotten what she wants (which is sex), and he will have
gotten what he wants (which is sex), and he will have done her a favor by
sexually satisfying her and giving them both what they needed. This type of
thinking completely denies the woman any choice of rational thought, or any
opportunity to be believed if and when she says "no" to sex.

Women are taught that they should not openly ask for or concede to sex because they might be viewed as sexually "loose" and "easy." They are expected to be reticent about sex. Given the double standard, it is not surprising that 39% of college women report that they have said "no" to sex when they meant "yes" (Muehlenhard & Hollabaugh, 1988). It is to a woman's disadvantage to ask for what she wants sexually (if she does want sex) because she risks being viewed negatively by her partner and anyone else who might hear about the incident. As a consequence, many women learn that the best way to get what they want, sexually or otherwise, is to be unclear rather than assertive. Such behavior can easily contribute to misperceptions in a dating situation and ultimately lead to nonconsensual sex. (For an in-depth discussion of the role of sex-role socialization, refer to Chapter 5.)

Beyond this type of socialization, the media, especially television and movies, portray acquaintance rape as acceptable behavior. There have been numerous irresponsible depictions of nonconsensual sexual relations on television shows (e.g., "General Hospital," "Moonlighting"), movies (e.g., "Gone with the Wind"), and MTV videos. In these portrayals, the woman was clearly forced to do something sexual that she did not want to do, and the man was either rewarded or not punished for his actions. Young people who watch these shows or movies receive the harmful message that women want to be sexually coerced and men who engage in coercive behaviors are desirable.

The socialization messages that young people hear about acquaintance rape begin early in their lives and impact as early as the preteen years. Kikuchi (1988) studied 1,700 sixth through ninth graders in Rhode Island and asked them when, if ever, forced sex was acceptable. More than half of the young people responded that it was acceptable for a man to force sex on a woman if she was wearing seductive clothing or if the couple had been dating for more than six months, and almost one-third said it was acceptable if he spent a lot of money on her. When asked what constituted "a lot of money," the teenagers said ten dollars. Goodchilds and colleagues (1988) asked similar questions of high school students and found that more than a quarter of the females and half of the males believed that forced sex was acceptable if "she led him on," if she "first said 'yes' and then changed her mind," or if "he was so excited he couldn't stop."

These norms for appropriate male and female behavior, as well as the belief that forced sex is sometimes acceptable, set the stage for conflicts in sexual situations. In addition, males and females enter the heterosexual dating interaction with a readiness to interpret important cues differently. Males frequently misjudge a woman's friendly intent as an indication of sexual interest (Abbey, 1982). And if a male perceives strong sexual interest on the part of the woman, he may feel "led on," which is considered justification for forcing sex by many young people. Males are much more likely to view bargaining behaviors such as verbal persuasion or physical seduction as acceptable after a woman has said "no" to sex (Bechhofer & Bem, 1989). If a woman says "no" several times and her partner fails to take her refusal seriously, she may eventually believe that her protests or verbal refusals are ineffectual and may see no alternative but to acquiesce to sex.

Parties with heavy alcohol and drug use, loud music, heavy peer pressure, and a general attitude of sexism create an atmosphere where those scripts and rape conducive beliefs can easily surface and lead to acquaintance rape. Alcohol, in particular, reduces people's inhibitions against using coercion and/or force, dulls people's ability to recognize uncomfortable situations early on, and is inappropriately used by assailants as an excuse for assaultive behavior ("It wasn't my fault; I was drunk"). The degree of intoxication of a man is the single most important factor in determining whether acquaintance rape will occur (Polonko, Parcell, & Teachman, 1986). Approximately 75% of men and at least 55% of women involved in acquaintance rapes had been drinking or taking drugs just before the act (Koss, 1988).

CONCLUSION

To reduce the incidence of acquaintance rape, the problem must be simultaneously attacked at several levels. We need educators in the schools, colleges, and communities to talk about those behaviors and situations that put individuals at greater risk for being victims or assailants. (See Chapter 22.) Moreover, we need to radically alter the way that the younger generation is socialized, so that little boys and girls are no longer cast into molds that set them up to be assailants and victims respectively. No doubt this will be a very difficult process. People will be forced to question and challenge some of the most basic assumptions concerning what it means to be male and female in our culture. But both steps are necessary to bring about substantial change.

Acquaintance rape is too prevalent and too insidious a crime for us to ignore any longer. We must work to bring it out from under the "cloak of silence or tacit acceptance" (The Boston Women's Health Book Collective, 1988, p. 100). Forced sex between people who know each other is *real* rape with *real* consequences for its victims. It is essential that people from all disciplines and backgrounds work together to bring about improvements in the laws, in public attitudes, in the media, in the power inequity between the sexes and in the socialization of our young people. Only then can we hope to bring about a reduction in the incidence of acquaintance rape in our society.

REFERENCES

Abbey, A. (1982). Sex differences in attributions for friendly behavior: Do males misperceive females' friendliness? *Journal of Personality and Social Psychology, 42*, 830–838.

Aizenman, M., & Kelley, G. (1988). The incidence of violence and acquaintance rape in dating relationships among college men and women. *Journal of College Student Development, 29,* 305–311.

Barett, K. (1982, September). Date rape: A campus epidemic. *Ms. Magazine,* pp. 40, 50–51, 130.

Bausell, C., & Maloy, C. E. (1990, January). *The links among drugs, alcohol, and campus crime: A research report.* Paper presented at the Fourth National Conference on Campus Violence, Towson, MD.

Bechhofer, L., & Bem, S. L. (1989). *Divergent perceptions of men and women and the risk of date rape.* Unpublished manuscript, Cornell University, Ithaca, NY.

Berger, R. J., Searles, P., Salem, R. G., & Pierce, B. (1986). Sexual assault in a college community. *Sociological Focus, 19,* 1–26.

The Boston Women's Health Book Collective (1988). *The new our bodies, ourselves.* New York: Simon & Schuster.

Brownmiller, S. (1975). *Against our will: Men, women, and rape.* New York: Simon & Schuster.

Burgess, A. W., & Holmstrom, L. L. (1974). Rape trauma syndrome. *American Journal of Psychiatry, 131,* 981–86.

Burkhart, B. (1983, December). *Acquaintance rape statistics and prevention.* Paper presented at the Rape Prevention on College Campuses Conference, Louisville, KY.

D'Emilio, J., & Freedman, E. B. (1988). *Intimate matters: A history of sexuality in America.* New York: Harper & Row.

Ehrhart, J. K., & Sandler, B. R. (1985). *Campus gang rape: Party games?* Washington, DC: Association of American Colleges.

Estrich, S. (1987). *Real rape: How the legal system victimizes women who say no.* Cambridge, MA: Harvard University Press.

FBI (Federal Bureau of Investigation). (1982). *Uniform crime reports.* Washington DC: U. S. Department of Justice.

Finkelhor, D., & Yllo, K. (1987). *License to rape: Sexual abuse of wives.* New York: Free Press.

Giarrusso, R., Johnson, P. B., Goodchilds, J. D., & Zellman, G. (1979, April). *Adolescent cues and signals: Sex and assault.* Paper presented at the meeting of the Western Psychological Association, San Diego.

Goodchilds, J. D., Zellman, G., Johnson, P. B., & Giarusso, R. (1979, April). *Adolescent perceptions of responsibility for dating outcomes.* Paper presented at the meeting of the Eastern Psychological Association, Philadelphia, PA.

Goodchilds, J. D., Zellman, G., Johnson, P. B., & Giarrusso, R. (1988). Adolescents and their perceptions of sexual interaction outcomes. In A. W. Burgess (Ed.), *Sexual assault,* (*Vol. II,* pp. 245–270). New York: Garland. (Original work published in 1979.)

The Jerusalem Bible: Reader's Edition. (1968). New York: Doubleday.

Kanin, E. J. (1957). Male aggression in dating–courtship relations. *American Journal of Sociology, 63,* 197–204.

Katz, B. L. (1987). *Prerape victim–rapist familiarity and recovery from rape: Psychological consequences.* Unpublished doctoral dissertation, Boston University.

Kikuchi, J. J. (1988, April). *What do adolescents know and think about sexual abuse?* Paper presented at the National Symposium on Child Victimization, Anaheim, CA.

Koss, M. P. (1985). The hidden rape victim: Personality, attitudinal, and situational characteristics. *Psychology of Women Quarterly, 9,* 193–212.

Koss, M. P. (1988). Hidden rape: Incidence, prevalence, and descriptive characteristics of sexual aggression and victimization in a national sample of college students. In A. W. Burgess (Ed.), *Sexual assault, Vol. II* (pp. 1–25). New York: Garland.

Koss, M. P., Gidycz, C. A., & Wisniewski, N. (1987). The scope of rape: Incidence and prevalence of sexual aggression and victimization in a national sample of higher education students. *Journal of Consulting and Clinical Psychology, 55,* 162–170.

Koss, M. P., & Oros, C. J. (1982). Sexual experiences survey: A research instrument investigating sexual aggression and victimization. *Journal of Consulting and Clinical Psychology, 50,* 455–457.

Mahoney, E. R., Shively, M. D., & Traw, M. (1986). Sexual coercion & assault: Male socialization and female risk. *Sexual Coercion & Assault, 1,* 2–8.

Malamuth, N. M. (1981). Rape proclivity among males. *Journal of Social Issues, 37,* 138–157.

Muehlenhard, C. L., & Hollabaugh, L. C. (1988). Do women sometimes say no when they mean yes? The prevalence and correlates of women's token resistance to sex. *Journal of Personality and Social Psychology, 54,* 872–879.

Muehlenhard, C. L., & Linton, M. A. (1987). Date rape and sexual aggression in dating situations: Incidence and risk factors. *Journal of Counseling Psychology, 34,* 186–196.

New York City Police Department (1972). *Special rape analysis squad report.* NY: Author.

Parrot, A. (1985, November). *Comparison of acquaintance rape patterns among college students in a large co-ed university and a small women's college.* Paper presented at the annual meeting of the Society for the Scientific Study of Sex, San Diego, CA.

Parrot, A., & Link, R. (1983, April). *Acquaintance rape in a college population.* Paper presented at the eastern regional meeting of the Society for the Scientific Study of Sex, Philadelphia, PA.

Polonko, K., Parcell, S., & Teachman, J. (1986, November). *A methodological note on sexual aggression.* Paper presented at the annual meeting of the Society for the Scientific Study of Sex, St. Louis, MO.

Rapaport, K., & Burkhart, B. R. (1984). Personality and attitudinal characteristics of sexually coercive college males. *Journal of Abnormal Psychology, 93,* 216–221.

Rowland, J. (1985). *The ultimate violation.* New York: Doubleday.

Russell, D. E. H. (1982). The prevalence and incidence of rape and attempted rape of females. *Victimology, 7,* 81–93.

Russell, D. E. H. (1990). *Rape in marriage* (2nd ed.). New York: Macmillan.

Sorenson, S. B., Stein, J. A., Siegel, J. M., Golding, J. M., & Burnam, M. A. (1987). The prevalence of adult sexual assault: The Los Angeles epidemiologic catchment area project. *American Journal of Epidemiology, 126,* 1154–1164.

Warshaw, R. (1988). *I never called it rape: The Ms. report on recognizing, fighting, and surviving date and acquaintance rape.* New York: Harper & Row.

CHAPTER 2

*Rape Myths and Acquaintance Rape**

MARTHA R. BURT, PhD

Rape myths are prejudicial, stereotyped, or false beliefs about rape, rape victims, or rapists. Rape myths have the effect of denying that many instances involving coercive sex are actually rapes. To understand how a rape myth works, one must understand the legal definition of rape and then ask why, when faced with a sexual assault that fits this legal definition, many people are still not willing to call this assault a rape.

As used in this book, rape is defined as: penetration, however slight, of any bodily orifice, obtained against the victim's will by using force, or threat of force, of any part of the assailant's body or any object used by the assailant in the course of the assault. (See Chapter 1 for definitions of acquaintance rape and date rape.)

This definition does not require resistance on the part of the victim. Its critical elements are that the sexual acts have occurred against the victim's will, by the assailant's use of force or the threat of force.

In a world without rape myths, the general public would understand that every act of coerced sex involving penetration is a rape. Unfortunately, the common perception does not match the legal definition, because rape myths influence the common perception. What is a rape to the general public? Much depends on how people answer this question and what specific acts their definitions include.

The rape definitions held by individuals in this culture may be broad and inclusive or narrow and restrictive. People whose definitions are at the

---

* Portions of this chapter first appeared in Burt (1983a) and Burt (1988).
Author's note: I came to victim studies first through active work on a rape crisis telephone line, public speeches, and community organization work to develop integrated services for sexual assault victims. Slightly later, and while still pursuing those activities, I began to study rape using my professional training as a social psychologist. Although the need to understand victims' reactions to sexual assault was great, my field experience led me to the position that another need was even greater: to understand how society was structured to create opportunities that sexually victimize women, excuse assailants, and blame victims. The results were a focus on understanding rape myths and research to learn what they are and how they work.

M.R.B.

inclusive extreme believe that all coerced sex is rape, whether the coercion used is physical, psychological, or economic. Those whose definitions lie at the restrictive extreme believe that there is no such thing as rape—no matter what occurred, these people will find a way, using rape myths, to conclude that no rape happened.

Most people's definition of rape falls somewhere between these two extremes, including some acts of coerced sex but also excluding many on the basis of belief in rape myths. People have in their heads an idea of a "real" rape. Usually their idea is a good deal narrower than the legal definition given above and excludes many types of rape that happen more frequently than the classic "real" rape. When they hear of a specific incident in which a woman says she was raped, they look at the incident, compare it to their idea of a "real" rape, and, all too often, decide that the woman was not "really" raped.

The classic "real" rape, for many people, is a rape by a stranger who uses a weapon—an assault done at night, outside (in a dark alley), with a lot of violence, resistance by the victim, and hence severe wounds and signs of struggle. In fact, except for "at night," every element of this "classic" rape scenario is absent for a majority of rape victims in this country. More than half of all rapes are committed by someone known to the victim; most do not involve a weapon, or injury beyond minor bruises or scratches; most occur indoors, in either the victim's or the assailant's home (Ageton, 1983; Amir, 1971; Burgess & Holmstrom, 1979; Koss, 1985; Macdonald, 1979; Russell, 1984; Warshaw, 1988).

Note how thoroughly the classic rape scenario excludes acquaintance and date rape from the category of "real" rape. A rape by a date or an acquaintance is not a rape by a stranger. Further, it is relatively rare for date or acquaintance rapes to involve a weapon or serious injury to the victim, and they are most likely to take place indoors. In addition, the victim often has engaged in some type of voluntary interaction with the assailant, which may be as slight as giving the time of day to a neighbor's brother-in-law or as extensive as being married to the assailant. The problem in determining whether a "real" rape occurred then becomes perceiving that voluntary interaction ended and coercion began.

Rape myths are the mechanism that people use to justify dismissing an incident of sexual assault from the category of "real" rape. Accepting or believing rape myths leads to a more restrictive definition of rape and is thus rape-supportive, because such beliefs deny the reality of many actual rapes. Rejecting these assaults as not being "real" rapes makes rape prosecution harder, the victim's recovery more difficult, and the assailant's actions safer. Rejecting or disbelieving rape myths has the opposite effect. It leads to including more concrete instances within the definition of what is a real rape (Burt & Albin, 1981).

There are, of course, important consequences for the victims of "unreal" rape—people blame them, belittle them, treat them badly, do not take their situation seriously, and do not offer needed support (Burt & Estep, 1981a). Since rapes by acquaintances are very likely to be considered "unreal" rapes, their victims may have a particularly hard time with certain aspects of recovery (Katz, 1986; Russell, 1984; Warshaw, 1988).

ANALYSIS OF RAPE MYTHS

Rape myths are part of the general culture. People learn them in the same way they acquire other attitudes and beliefs—from their families, their friends, newspapers, movies, books, dirty jokes, and, lately, rock videos. I group rape myths into four main classifications of myths focused on the victim/woman (other myths, discussed below, focus on the assailant/man): nothing happened; no harm was done; she wanted or liked it; and she asked for or deserved it.

Nothing Happened

The first group of myths remove an incident from the category of a "real" rape by denying that any incident, either sex or rape, occurred at all. A number of myths promote the idea that women falsely accuse men of rape. For years, judges in rape trials cautioned juries to be wary of women's claims of rape by reading them the warning of Lord Hale, a British judge during the 18th century: "A rape accusation is easily made, and, once made, is difficult to defend against, even if the accused person is innocent." Juries were instructed to weigh the woman's claim with special care. Many people believe that women lie, "crying rape" to cover up an out-of-wedlock pregnancy or to get back at men who have jilted them or refused their advances. Yet according to police records, false reports are no more likely for rape than they are for other serious crimes (Lear, 1972). Many myths in this group have the effect of negating a claim of rape against someone known to the victim—an acquaintance, neighbor, family member, coworker, ex-husband, or ex-lover—especially if the prerape relationship involved conflict.

Also in this category of "nothing happened" are myths that women's rape claims are sheer fantasy or wishful thinking. The elderly spinster calling the police to find the "rapist under the bed" is a common theme of dirty jokes, implying that the woman is sex-starved and making up her accusations to convince herself that she is desirable. And, women's "rape" fantasies usually involve very handsome and attractive men who find them so irresistible that masculine self-control is momentarily overwhelmed, and the men sweep them off their feet. These fantasies do not resemble real rapes: they lack the degradation, the ignoring of one's personhood, the threat of death, the fear of physical injury, and the forced necessity to have intimate contact with someone against one's will.

No Harm Was Done

The second group of myths remove an incident from the category of a "real" rape by denying that any harm was done. Sexual intercourse is admitted, but its coerced and harmful nature is denied. Beliefs that rape is "just sex" belong in this group. Remarks such as "If you're not a virgin, what difference does it make?" and "Relax and enjoy it" reflect this belief, implying that the rape is no different from other acts of sex the victim has experienced. They deny the violent, life-threatening nature of rape. Acquaintance rape involves the humiliation of realizing that the assailant does not care what the victim wants and that part of the payoff for the assailant is his ability to control the victim, ignore her wishes, and force her to do anything he says. Although it often involves less outright fear of death than stranger rape, acquaintance rape still involves force and fear of bodily injury.

Other rape myths in this category of "no harm done" are based on the assumption that a woman's value lies in her sexual exclusiveness. If she is not a virgin, or she is not the exclusive sexual property of her lawful husband, there is no more harm that can be done. Indeed, until very recently rape statutes in this country, as in England, were based on property rights incorporating this assumption. The person harmed by a rape was presumed to be the man who owned the woman—either her father, who had lost the marriage value of a virgin daughter, or her husband, who had lost the ability to enjoy her as exclusive sexual property. As of 1990, seven states still do not include marital rape as a prosecutable offense and an additional 26 states allowed prosecutions only under restricted circumstances. Laws allowing prosecution of marital rape are very recent; they have resulted from political pressure from women's groups. The earlier laws were based on the husband's property right to use his wife sexually and her presumed forfeiture of a right to refuse.

Many "no harm done" myths refer to women of societally devalued status or women who are stereotyped as sexually available. The most extreme implication of these myths is that once a woman has "said yes" and had sex with one man, she is never again in a position where she can legitimately say "no." So, if a woman can be shown to have had sex with someone other than her husband, she is no longer worthy of the law's protection—she is fair game, or an "open territory victim" as Clark and Lewis (1977) phrased it. Prostitutes are a special case of the open territory victim, so devalued that many people believe that prostitutes cannot be raped (Silbert, 1988).

This is the type of myth that traps many minority women, whose experiences of sexual violation are not taken seriously because they are stereotyped as sleeping with many men and therefore already devalued. Any group of women stereotyped as being sexually active outside of marriage, such as divorcées or prostitutes, or any women who frequent places associated with being sexually available, such as bars, run the risk of being dismissed as unworthy of the law's protection or of sympathetic concern when they press a charge of rape.

Even if a woman is raped by a complete stranger under circumstances fitting the "classic" rape and in which her normal sexual behavior is completely irrelevant, once it becomes known that she belongs to a stereotyped group the general public is less likely to believe that she was the victim of a "real" rape. If her rape occurred in connection with dating, frequenting a bar, or other circumstances connected in the public mind with impropriety or promiscuity, her report of a rape will be received with even greater skepticism.

The myth that "only bad girls get raped" works to cast suspicion on any woman who has been raped. The reasoning goes, "If she was raped, she must have done something to bring it on, she must be a 'bad girl.'" Common defense attorney tactics follow directly from this premise; in their efforts to obtain a not-guilty verdict, defense attorneys will try to convince juries that victims are sexually promiscuous. Too often, this defense tactic works, even in states with laws rewritten specifically to exclude this type of testimony as prejudicial to the victim (Berger, 1977; Borgida, 1981; New York Task Force on Women in the Courts, 1986–87; Wood, 1973).

She Wanted It

The third group of myths remove an incident from the category of a "real" rape by maintaining that the woman wanted it, invited it, or liked it. The issue of consent lies at the crux of this type of myth. In one sense, these myths simply pose the question: Did she want to or did she have to? Did her observed behavior stem from personal motivation, in which case it was consensual sex, or from environmental coercion by an assailant, in which case it was rape?

Complications arise in answering this seemingly simple question because the culture's many myths concerning women and sex are distilled to a belief that "women never mean no." At some level, women are always presumed always to "want it," no matter what they say. Think of the meaning of some common phrases: "Your lips say 'no, no, no' but your eyes say 'yes, yes, yes,'" or "Come on, baby, you know you really want it." As a result of these assumptions about women and sex, the practical requirements of proof of environmental coercion ("real" rape) are often extreme, precisely because the situations activate rape myths and sexual stereotypes.

To differentiate a rape from "just sex," one must be convinced that the victim did not consent to the sexual acts performed. To people who have experience with victims and with rape trials, it is quite clear that in the public mind a victim's reputation or identity enters this judgment; women with certain reputations or identities (e.g., divorcées, minority women, women out alone at night) are stereotypically assumed to consent more readily, to more men, in more situations. Having assumed a generalized propensity to consent and attached it to whole classes of women, this line of reasoning then particularizes this argument to this woman (victim) in this situation (alleged rape) and infers consent to this man (alleged assailant). Therefore, following this line of reasoning, this situation is not a rape.

One can also see why women who are raped by acquaintances or dates have a very hard time getting their listeners to credit their claim that what happened was actually a rape. The closer the prerape situation is to a context in which sex is a possibility (e.g., a party, a date, consensual necking or petting), the more difficult it is to convince the world that a rape occurred. The difficulties are further compounded by some people's perception that any interaction between a man and a woman is potentially sexual, and therefore anything that occurs should be considered to be sex, not rape.

Even judges share this myth. A recently censured New York judge opined, about a brutal and lengthy rape incident "I think it started without consent, but maybe they ended up enjoying themselves" (New York Commission on Judicial Conduct, 1984). The big issue around consent is, "What do women want?" If one believes, as many people do, that women never mean "no," that women tease, that women do not want to take responsibility for their own sexual desires, that they lead a man on but then they want to be able to say that they resisted at the end, one is more likely to conclude that the women consented—that she really wanted it, despite her denials.

Among this group of myths is the idea that any healthy woman can resist a rapist if she really wants to, particularly if the rapist is someone she knows. The corollary is that if she got raped, she must not have resisted enough and therefore she wanted it or consented to it. Frighteningly, some people also still believe that women like to be treated violently and that force is sexually stimulating to women. This line of reasoning ultimately comes down to: "There's no such thing as rape."

She Deserved It

The fourth group of myths remove an incident from the category of "real" rape by claiming that the woman deserved it or did something to bring it on. These myths admit that there was sex and that the sex was forced, but they hold the woman responsible—therefore the act was not a rape. If she was flirting; if she was attractively dressed; if she was, in the man's perception, a tease; if she went out with a man, necked with him, and invited him to her apartment for coffee; even if she only said "hello" to him at the office—it was her fault. She "got into the game" of sexuality, this reasoning goes, and once in the game, society loads her with the full responsibility for whatever happens. The myths do not differentiate between her "asking for" companionship, friendship, and a date and her "asking for" rape.

There are also some underlying ideological assumptions that women are sly, manipulative, devious, underhanded; that women are teases; that they like to make men jump through hoops. And if they lose control and the situation goes too far (they get raped), then getting raped is simply what they deserve and their own fault for trying to control and manipulate men.

Women are also blamed or seen as deserving the rape if they put themselves in risky circumstances, even when they have no choice but to do so. If a woman hitchhikes, or is out late at night, even if she works late-night shifts, a rape is still her fault. There is no parallel for this in other crimes. If someone walking in a bad neighborhood is robbed, or if someone does not lock an apartment door and is burglarized, no one denies that the *crime* happened, even when it is clear that the victim used poor judgment. The robber or burglar is perceived as intending to commit a crime and actually carrying it out; the victim simply made it a little easier. Not so with rape, where the rape myths operate to blame the victim even when the facts show that a majority of rapists plan their rapes in advance, thus showing an intent to commit a crime independent of the behavior of any potential victim (Amir, 1971; Groth, 1979; Macdonald, 1979).

Myths Regarding Men

All of the myths discussed so far focus on women—as does most of the cultural ideology. To have everyone judging the victim is a good smokescreen; the attacker usually gets away with hardly a glance. However, there are complementary myths about male sexuality and about rapists which also serve to reduce perceptions of the assailant's culpability. One is that only crazy men rape. Therefore, faced with a sane accused assailant, the average person finds it hard to imagine that he is a rapist. In fact, rapists are no more "insane" than the average man (Groth, 1979), and significant numbers of normal college men admit that they have raped (Koss, Leonard, Oros, & Beezley, 1985) or would rape if they could get away with it (Malamuth, 1981).

Second, the myths promote the idea that men cannot control their sexuality. The idea that wearing revealing clothing is provocation to rape implies that rape results from a spontaneous, unplanned response to a sexually attractive woman. This myth once again presumes that rape is simply forceful sex ("assault with a friendly weapon," as the joke has it) and that only sexually attractive women will be the targets of this male response ("Who would want to rape *her*?", said of a very unattractive woman). To be somewhat facetious, this myth implies that if a scantily clad woman walks down the street and a man sees her, he will go out of control, the situation can end only in rape, and the man is not responsible for it because he saw her knees and they drove him over the edge. Put this way, it should be obvious that this myth excuses men's assaultive behavior and helps remove such incidents from the category of "real" rapes.

A corollary of this myth is that men's sexuality is not active but is simply a response to stimuli supplied by women. Variations on this theme occur every day in dating situations, even when no rape results. When a boy or man argues that the girl or woman got him all excited and now is obliged to "finish what she (!) started" and have intercourse, this myth is brought into play. The often implied alternative to her "cooperation" is that he might go ahead and take what he considers she owes him (i.e., rape her) because she is responsible for getting him so excited. The underlying assumption is that men are not to be held responsible for their own excitement and what they do with it. Further and equally important, women *are* to be held responsible, not only for keeping themselves chaste but also for controlling men's sexuality.

THE CONTEXT OF RAPE MYTHS

Rape myths do not exist in a vacuum, however powerful they are in themselves. One of the things my research has documented (Burt, 1980; Burt & Albin, 1981) is the surrounding set of attitudes that support the myths. This research showed strong positive associations between acceptance of rape myths and higher levels of sex role stereotyping, adversarial sexual beliefs, sexual conservatism, and acceptance of interpersonal violence.

People's sense of themselves as male and female is tied into whether they believe rape myths or see males and females as relating to each other as adversaries. Contemplating this set of attitudes can be quite discouraging for the prospects of making serious changes in the cultural ideology of rape, because these attitudes represent an aspect of people's core identity and cannot readily be changed through public education programs that deal with facts. Anyone who has ever tried knows how hard it is to change core identities of what maleness means, what femaleness means, and what the underlying assumptions I have just described mean for sexual violence.

Check (1984) has further generalized my work by expanding my adversarial sexual beliefs scale beyond the sexual into the concept of general hostility toward women—an attitude that is also very strongly associated with rape myth acceptance and sex role stereotyping. Further, the culture reinforces these feelings by representing women as sly, manipulative, vindictive, and untrustworthy. If one has hostile feelings toward women, the culture will provide ample support for the "truth" of these feelings. Those who have hostile feelings will not therefore have to confront them as feelings, but will be able to sustain a (false) belief that women "really are" untrustworthy. However, if a woman feels hostile toward men, she will experience a lot of baiting and rejection. The culture does *not* support women's hostility toward men, however justified. Rather, women who express these feelings are called "manhaters," "ball breakers," and similar epithets.

Researchers have measured some important consequences of beliefs in rape myths and their supporting attitudes. The more one believes rape myths, the narrower is one's definition of a "real" rape, the less likely is one to convict someone of a rape, and the lighter the sentence is one to recommend in a mock jury situation (Borgida, 1981; Burt & Albin, 1981). There is an association between believing rape myths and admitting that one has had intercourse with a woman by force (Koss et al., 1985). High myth acceptors are also more likely to say that they would rape if they thought they could get away with it (Malamuth, 1981). Finally, high myth acceptors are more aroused by violent pornography (Malamuth & Donnerstein, 1984).

All of these beliefs and attitudes form an interlocking web of victim blame. The culture reinforces the behavior, and the behavior reinforms the culture and becomes the reality. A continuing cycle of beliefs denies real victim status to women and makes it very hard to be a woman who has been raped.

Another thing that the myths do is to clearly define a "free rape." A rapist can easily figure out how to carry out a rape so that the odds are very high that the woman will not report it or, if she does, will not be believed. Pick someone up in a bar; date the woman a few times; have sex at an office party; pick her up hitchhiking—do anything that will leave her defined as a bad girl or as having asked for it.

Other cultural elements such as dirty jokes and movies reinforce rape myths. With dirty jokes, the questions to ask are: Who is the target of aggression, who is "it" in the jokes, and who is the audience for the jokes? Who squirms, who is put down? Another question is: What image of male and female sexuality is portrayed by dirty jokes? By and large, women are the targets of aggression in dirty jokes, both as characters in the jokes and as the audience to whom they are told. Dirty jokes generally portray women as sexually insatiable (and therefore too demanding of the male), always ready to go, never saying no, and seductive. Women's bodies and genitals are portrayed as foul and their bodily fluids as harmful. They are depicted as unfaithful, untrustworthy, and untruthful, as whores who have no real affection for their faithful men. Jokes about rape incorporate all of the myths described above but concentrate mostly on the idea that women like rape, or really cooperate, and therefore there is no such thing as rape.

Movies likewise reinforce rape myths. Pornographic films do this outright, by portraying rape incidents in which the woman ultimately responds with enjoyment, and by frequent and repeated association of sex and violence. But movies for the general public are culpable in their own way, from the famous scene in "Gone with the Wind" to more modern versions such as "Swept Away" and "Blume in Love."

Teenagers and young women are the most likely victims of rape, and most will be raped by people they know. These victims are very likely to believe an extensive array of rape myths that lead them to accept responsibility for their own rapes in dating, party, and acquaintance situations (Goodchilds, Zellman, Johnson, & Giarusso, 1988). Films aimed at the teenage audience reinforce these myths and teach young women that sex is likely to be violent and violence is frequently the price one pays for being sexual. Slasher films, now very popular with teenagers, implicitly reinforce violence against women. The victims are almost invariably young, attractive women alone (with no male protector); these films associate emotional climax and release with stalking and ultimately committing violence on women, repeatedly (sometimes as many as ten times in a single movie). Finally, rock videos commonly portray strong associations between sex and violence. Adolescents who spend a lot of time watching rock videos are highly likely to believe rape myths and to hold other beliefs that foster women's sexual victimization (Deiter & Heeter, 1989). The next generation is being taught to acquiesce to its own victimization.

THE FUNCTION OF RAPE MYTHS

The analysis that has guided my research was developed by women in the antirape movement in the early 1970s. The evolution of this analysis and explanations of the causes and consequences of sexual assault occurred hand-in-hand. The analysis assisted attempts to understand sexual assault; the daily experience of trying to help sexual assault victims provided both a great push for theory to guide counseling practice and data for theory development. This analysis, developed by feminists, offers a radical critique of women's victimization through sexual assault and other sex- and sex-role-related phenomena such as battering, incest, prostitution, and pornography. Feminist analysis approaches women's sexual victimization in a way that shifts the focus away from victim reactions and immediate contributing factors, both of which often fail to address the question of why victimization occurs in the first place. Feminists started to ask who benefits from women's sexual victimization and focused their attention on the structural conditions that promote certain forms of victimization as mechanisms for maintaining the current distribution of power between the sexes. That distribution of power is embodied in patriarchy.

Most present societies, including our own, are patriarchies. Patriarchy is a system designed to maintain societal power, control, and privilege in male hands. Many writers have examined the mechanisms used to maintain male advantage, including economic and familial structures, and child-rearing and socialization practices (see Chafetz, 1984; Eagly, 1987; and Epstein, 1988 for the social science perspective; and Benjamin, 1988; and Westkott, 1986 for the psychoanalytic perspective). Far less analysis illuminates the support provided for patriarchy by culture and ideology and, ultimately, by overt physical and sexual violence; that which exists has been produced by feminists (Benjamin, 1988; Brownmiller, 1975; Burt, 1980, 1983a, b; 1988; Burt & Albin, 1981; Burt & Estep, 1981a, b; Clark and Lewis; 1977; Deiter & Heeter, 1989; Dinnerstein, 1976; Farley, 1978; Griffin, 1981; Holliday, 1978; MacKinnon, 1982; Miller, 1976; Rowbotham, 1973; Webster, 1978; Westkott, 1986).

To retain themselves in control, groups in power may use many means, including overt violence and coercion, training or socialization, and cultural beliefs about what is "right," "good," "true," and "natural." The part of patriarchal ideology relevant to this chapter is our culture's set of beliefs about what is right, good, true, and natural about men, women, and their relationship to each other. Rape myths are part of this ideology.

Ideologies are most easily seen when they are not our own. Under those circumstances it is also easy to see that the ideology supports one group's interests and suppresses those of other groups. This may be why the word *ideology* has a slightly pejorative connotation in the United States. It is relatively easy to see that beliefs about the cultural inferiority and mental incapacities of colonized or enslaved peoples, which were prevalent among western powers during periods of empire building, were both false and supportive of the exploitive interests of the colonizers. Believing a people to be childlike, lazy, and incapable of looking out for its own best interests is a strong justification for taking it over, whether as a colony or by making slaves of its members. It is less easy to see or to admit that one's own beliefs are not necessary or natural. The purposes of an ideology, if it is functioning well, are to make a particular world view appear natural and normal, to make alternative belief structures impossible, and to make rebellion against the powerful group supported by the ideology unlikely.

The ideology that supports a patriarchal power structure contains several important elements. First is the belief that men are "better" than women—smarter, more active, more capable, stronger, and so forth (Vogel, Broverman, Broverman, Clarkson, & Rosenkrantz, 1972; Broverman, Broverman, Clarkson, Rosenkrantz, & Vogel, 1970; Chafetz, 1984; Eagly, 1987; Epstein, 1988). Second, patriarchy's ideology appropriates certain behaviors to the male role as its exclusive prerogative. For our purposes, physical violence and sexuality are the two most important behaviors so appropriated (Benjamin, 1988; Brownmiller, 1975; MacKinnon, 1982). Patriarchy's ideology of sex roles encourages average expressions of violence and sexual behavior for males and tolerates extreme expressions. It also encourages suitably passive, complementary behavior for females. Conversely, inappropriate cross-sex behavior is punished, and the strongest condemnations are reserved for women who "unnaturally" indulge in behavior that forms the core of male privilege—violence and sexuality (New York Task Force on Women in the Courts, 1986–87; Schneider, Jordan, & Arguedas, 1978). Finally, patriarchy's ideology contains beliefs that deny, excuse, exonerate, or justify extreme forms of male behavior that epitomize men's power position vis-à-vis women, such as rape, wife-beating, and incest, or that blame the victims of these acts for their own victimization.

Ideology usually operates to make the powerless (the potential victims of violence) at least as likely to acquiesce in it as the powerful (Fanon, 1966). Thus the powerless may believe in their own inferiority; rape victims often express a sense of self-blame for their rapes (Katz & Burt, 1988). In essence, ideology works to reduce the need for much overt violence to maintain power, because the powerless, believing the ideology, will not act in their own behalf. Rape victims often will not report a rape because they are humiliated and they fear they will not be believed.

Research has begun to document instances of how a justifying ideology accomplishes this end of stifling the powerless. Rape myths justify and excuse rape (Burt, 1980, 1983a, 1988; Burt & Albin, 1981; Schwendinger & Schwendinger, 1974; Weis & Borges, 1973) and deny victims appropriate support (Burt & Estep, 1981a; Warshaw, 1988), while an ideological commitment to the sanctity of the home withholds protection for women and children against violence in the family (Calvert, 1974; Finkelhor, 1979; Gil, 1973; Greenblat, 1985; Steinmetz & Straus, 1974; Walker, 1979).

CONCLUSION

Rape myths allow rapists to rape with near-impunity. They teach women to blame themselves for their own victimization. They transform rape by acquaintances, friends, and intimates into no rape at all. They support the use of violence, coupled with sexuality, as a mechanism for keeping women powerless. At base, every woman lives with the fear of rape and modifies her behavior in large and small ways to reduce the likelihood of becoming a rape victim (Burt & Estep, 1981b; Burt & Katz, 1985; Riger & Gordon, 1988). The myths make clear to her that avoiding rape is her responsibility and that she will find little sympathy for her situation should she be so careless as to allow herself to be raped. They make especially clear the disbelief and blame she will encounter should she be so foolish as to be raped by someone she knows. Rape myths keep her quiet and keep her controlled. Rape and the threat of male violence are one of patriarchy's mechanisms for maintaining male control.

REFERENCES

Ageton, S. S. (1983). *Sexual assault among adolescents.* Lexington, MA: Lexington Books.

Amir, M. (1971). *Patterns in forcible rape.* Chicago, IL: University of Chicago Press.

Benjamin, J. (1988). *The bonds of love: Psychoanalysis, feminism and the problem of domination.* New York: Pantheon Books.

Berger, V. (1977). Man's trial, woman's tribulation: Rape cases in the courtroom. *Columbia Law Review, 77,* 1–103.

Borgida, E. (1981). Legal reform and rape laws: Social psychological and constitutional considerations. In L. Bickman (Ed.), *Applied social psychology annual* (Vol. 2). Beverly Hills, CA: Sage.

Broverman, I. K., Vogel, S. R., Broverman, D. M., Clarkson, F. E., & Rosenkrantz, P. S. (1972). Sex-role stereotypes: A current appraisal. *Journal of Social Issues, 28,* 59–72.

Broverman, I. K., Broverman, D. M., Clarkson, F. E., Rosenkrantz, P. S., & Vogel, S. R. (1970). Sex-role stereotypes and clinical judgments of mental health. *Journal of Consulting Psychology, 34,* 1–7.

Brownmiller, S. (1975). *Against our will: Men, women, and rape.* New York: Simon & Schuster.

Burgess, A. W., & Holmstrom, L. L. (1979). *Rape: Crisis and recovery.* Bowie, MD: Brady.

Burt, M. R. (1980). Cultural myths and supports for rape. *Journal of Personality and Social Psychology, 38,* 217–230.

Burt, M. R. (1983a). Justifying personal violence: A comparison of rapists and the general public. *Victimology: An International Journal, 8,* 131–150.

Burt, M. R. (1983b). A conceptual framework for victimological research. *Victimology: An International Journal, 8,* 261–268.

Burt, M. R. (1988). Cultural myth, violence against women, and the law. *Drew Gateway, 58,* 25–37.

Burt, M. R., & Albin, R. S. (1981). Rape myths, rape definitions, and probability of conviction. *Journal of Applied Social Psychology, 11,* 212–230.

Burt, M. R., & Estep, R. E. (1981a). Who is a victim: Definitional problems in sexual victimization. *Victimology: An International Journal, 6,* 15–28.

Burt, M. R., & Estep, R. E. (1981b). Apprehension and fear: Learning a sense of sexual vulnerability. *Sex Roles, 7,* 511–522.

Burt, M. R., & Katz, B. L. (1985). Rape, robbery, and burglary: Responses to actual and feared criminal victimization, with special focus on women and the elderly. *Victimology: An International Journal, 10,* 325–358.

Calvert, R. (1974). Criminal and civil liability in husband-wife assaults. In S. Steinmetz & M. Straus (Eds.), *Violence in the family* (pp. 88–90). New York: Dodd, Mead.

Chafetz, J. S. (1984). *Sex and advantage: A comparative macro-structural theory of sex stratification.* Totowa, NJ: Rowman & Allanheld.

Check, J. V. P. (1984). *The hostility toward women scale.* Unpublished doctoral dissertation, University of Manitoba.

Clark, L. M. G. & Lewis, D. J. (1977). *Rape: The price of coercive sexuality.* Toronto: The Women's Press.

Deiter, P., & Heeter, C. (1989, March). *"Shooting her with video, drugs, bullets and promises. . .": MTV videos and adolescent viewers' beliefs about sex, violence and sexual violence.* Paper presented at the annual meeting of the Association for Women in Psychology, Newport, RI.

Dinnerstein, D. (1976). *The mermaid and the minotaur: Sexual arrangements and human malaise.* New York: Harper & Row.

Eagly, A. (1987). *Sex differences in social behavior: A social role interpretation.* Hillsdale, NJ: Erlbaum.

Epstein, C. F. (1988). *Deceptive distinctions: Theory and research on sex, gender and the social order.* New Haven, CT: Yale University Press.

Fanon, F. (1966). *The wretched of the earth.* New York: Grove Press/Evergreen.

Farley, J. (1978). *Sexual shakedown: The sexual harassment of women on the job.* New York: McGraw-Hill.

Finkelhor, D. (1979). *Sexually victimized children.* New York: Free Press.

Gil, D. G. (1973). *Violence against children* (2nd ed.). Cambridge, MA: Harvard University Press.

Goodchilds, J. D., Zellman, G. L., Johnson, P. B., & Giarruso, R. (1988). Adolescents and their perceptions of sexual interactions. In A. W. Burgess (Ed.), *Rape and sexual assault* (Vol. II, pp. 245–270). New York: Garland.

Greenblat, C. S. (1985). Don't hit your wife . . . unless . . .: Preliminary findings on normative support for the use of force by husbands. *Victimology: An International Journal, 10,* 221–241.

Griffin, S. (1981). *Pornography and silence.* New York: Harper & Row.

Groth, A. N. (1979). *Men who rape: The psychology of the offender.* New York: Plenum.

Holliday, L. (1978). *The violent sex: Male psychobiology and the evolution of consciousness.* Guerneville, CA: Bluestocking Books.

Katz, B. L. (1986, August). *Effects of familiarity with the rapist on post-rape recovery.* Paper presented at the annual meeting of the American Psychological Association, Washington, DC.

Katz, B. L., & Burt, M. R. (1988). Self-blame in recovery from rape: Help or hindrance? In A. W. Burgess (Ed.), *Rape and sexual assault (Vol. II,* pp. 191–212). New York: Garland.

Koss, M. P. (1985). The hidden rape victim: Personality, attitudinal, and situational characteristics. *Psychology of Women Quarterly, 9,* 193–212.

Koss, M. P., Leonard, K. E., Oros, C. J., & Beezley, D. A. (1985). Nonstranger sexual aggression: A discriminant analysis of the psychological characteristics of undetected offenders. *Sex Roles, 12,* 981–992.

Lear, M. W. (1972). Q: If you rape a woman and steal her TV, what can they get you for in New York? A: Stealing her TV. *New York Times Magazine,* January 30, 1972, 10–11.

Macdonald, J. M. (1979). *Rape: Offenders and their victims.* Springfield, IL: Thomas.

MacKinnon, C. (1982). Feminism, marxism, method and the state: An agenda for theory. *Signs, Journal of Women in Culture and Society, 7,* 515–544.

Malamuth, N. M. (1981). Rape proclivity among males. *Journal of Social Issues, 37,* 138–157.

Malamuth, N. M., & Donnerstein, E. (Eds.). (1984). *Pornography and sexual aggression.* New York: Academic Press.

Miller, J. B. (1976). *Toward a new psychology of women.* Boston: Beacon Press.

New York Commission on Judicial Conduct. (1984). Matter of Fromer. *1985 Annual Report, 135,* October 25, 1984.

New York Task Force on Women in the Courts. (1986–87). Report of the New York Task Force on Women in the Courts. *Fordham Urban Law Journal, 15,* 1–198.

Riger, S., & Gordon, M. T. (1988). The impact of crime on urban women. In A. W. Burgess (Ed.), *Rape and sexual assault* (Vol. II, pp. 293–316). New York: Garland.

Rowbotham, S. (1973). *Woman's consciousness, man's world.* Hammondsworth, England: Penguin.

Russell, D. E. H. (1984). *Sexual exploitation.* Beverly Hills, CA: Sage.

Schneider, E. M., Jordan, S. B., & Arguedas, C. C. (1978). Representation of women who defend themselves in response to physical or sexual assault. *Heresies, 6,* 100.

Schwendinger, J., & Schwendinger, H. (1974). Rape myths: In legal, theoretical, and everyday practice. *Crime and Social Issues, 1,* 18–26.

Silbert, M. (1988). Compounding factors in the rape of street prostitutes. In A. W. Burgess (Ed.), *Rape and sexual assault* (Vol. II, pp. 75–90). New York: Garland.

Steinmetz, S. K., & Straus, M. A. (Eds.). (1974). *Violence in the family.* New York: Dodd, Mead.

Walker, L. (1979). *Battered women.* New York: Harper & Row.

Warshaw, R. (1988) *I never called it rape: The Ms. report on recognizing, fighting, and surviving date and acquaintance rape.* New York: Harper & Row.

Webster, P. (1978). Politics of rape in primitive society. *Heresies, 6,* 16.

Weis, K., & Borges, S. (1973). Victimology and rape: The case of the legitimate victim. *Issues in Criminology, 8,* 71–115.

Westkott, M. (1986). *The feminist legacy of Karen Horney.* New Haven, CT: Yale University Press.

Wood, P. L. (1973). The victim in a forcible rape case: A feminist view. *American Criminal Law Review, 11,* 335–354.

PART 2

Attitudes About Acquaintance Rape

CHAPTER 3

Young People's Attitudes Toward Acquaintance Rape

JACQUELYN W. WHITE, PhD and JOHN A. HUMPHREY, PhD

There was a part of me back then that thought that is the way "it" was done. Guys pounced on you, you struggled, then forgot about the whole thing . . . I never told anyone I was raped. I would not have thought that was what it was. It was unwilling sex. I just didn't want to and he did. Today, at 29, I know it was rape.

(STATEMENT FROM A RAPE VICTIM;
WARSHAW, *1988, pp. 119–120)*

I know you must like this because a lot of women like this kind of thing. . . . [later] Can I call you tomorrow? Can I see you next week-end? . . . [after several weeks of trying to see his victim again, and she avoiding him] Oh, I guess you didn't get enough.

(AN ACQUAINTANCE RAPIST'S STATEMENT;
WARSHAW, *1988, pp. 16–17)*

An apparent paradox exists among American young people with regard to rape. On the one hand, rape is consensually viewed as an abhorrent form of interpersonal violence. On the other hand, many young people do not believe that forced sex between acquaintances and intimates is particularly wrong or problematic and they do not think that there is such a thing as rape between acquaintances and intimates.

The purpose of this chapter is to explore the social context of this contradiction. We do this by addressing the conflicting attitudes, beliefs, and norms about male–female roles and sexual relationships that legitimate sexual violence in a dating situation and result in reluctance to label its expression criminal. The chapter examines the content of these attitudes, where they come from, and how they are perpetuated.

The study of attitudes provides insight into the contemporary social norms governing sexual behavior in dating situations. Attitudes about male–female relationships, and about sexual interactions specifically, give young people a frame of reference for understanding their own and others' behaviors, allow them to choose behaviors that will be acceptable to others, and serve as a basis for justifying their actions ("It's okay; everyone does it").

The establishment of meaningful relationships with members of the opposite sex occurs during adolescence, usually in the dating context (Conger & Petersen, 1984; Rice, 1984). Yet, little attention has been given to issues related to adolescent sexual socialization. Goodchilds, Zellman, Johnson, and Giarusso (1988) defined adolescent sexual socialization as

the sets of attitudes and expectations about the sexually intimate relationship which evolve and coalesce as the individual becomes sexually mature and sexually active

(p. 245)

Since forced sexual encounters most often occur among acquaintances, typically in a dating situation (Ageton, 1983; Koss, 1985), an understanding of adolescents' sexually assaultive experiences and their attitudes about these experiences are crucial to rape prevention.

A SOCIOCULTURAL OVERVIEW

Sociocultural considerations are central to explanations of rape-supportive attitudes and sexual assault. American culture influences the ongoing sex-role socialization of the young, attitudes toward rape, and sexually aggressive behavior (Weis & Borges, 1973). Furthermore, rape reflects the power differential between women and men. Rose (1979) noted:

From the feminist perspective, rape is a direct result of our culture's differential sex role socialization and stratification . . . the association of dominance with the male sex role and submission with the female sex role is viewed as a significant factor in the persistence of rape as a serious social problem.

(p. 78)

Brownmiller (1975), in her landmark book *Against Our Will: Men, Women, and Rape,* described society as not only tolerating but ideologically encouraging sexual hostility toward women. Other investigations confirmed Brownmiller's assertion that rape is a manifestation of a social ideology of male domination over women (Burt, 1980; Costin & Schwarz, 1987; Feild, 1978; Sanday, 1981; Schwarz & Brand, 1983). The traditional view of women as powerless sex objects, who must exchange sexual favors for male protection and financial and emotional support, inevitably leads to an adversarial relationship between the sexes, characterized by confused sexual expectations and aggression (Weis & Borges, 1973).

The sociocultural environment influences socialization both within the family and within the adolescent subculture. Fagot, Loeber, and Reid (1988) suggested that there are three essential familial determinants of male-to-female aggression: (a) parents who are unable to control their demanding children, for example, children who use coercion to get what they want; (b) female members of the family who become targets for male aggression; and (c) attitudes that devalue women (male dominance is supported and aggression toward women is legitimated).

Parents have been found to socialize daughters to resist sexual advances and sons to initiate sexual activity (Ross, 1977), although fathers' strong disapproval of their sons' sexual activities has been found important in reducing sexual aggression (Kanin, 1985). Adolescent peer groups foster similar expectations for male and female sexual behavior. LaPlante, McCormick, and Brannigan (1980, p. 339) suggested that adolescents learn "sexual scripts." These scripts provide "norms which prescribe that the man should be the initiator of sexual activity while the woman is the 'limit setter.'"

Berger, Searles, Salem, and Pierce (1986, p. 20) argued that the pervasiveness of male sexual aggression is viewed by young women as "an inevitable part of the dating game." Forced sexual activity between acquaintances has become culturally normative behavior (Ageton, 1983). Berger et al. (1986) found that undergraduate women tend to downplay the seriousness of most unwanted sexual contact as harmless, commonplace in bars or at parties, and something that "should" therefore be endured. Such rationalizations provide a basis for tolerance of sexually exploitive behavior. Furthermore, young women are socialized to accept responsibility for controlling sexual interaction on a date and to assume blame for their own sexual victimization. Young men, however, are socialized to view female attempts to resist their sexual advances as a part of the "game" that must be disregarded. Young men commonly believe that when a young woman says "no" she actually means "yes" or that if a young woman consents to any sexual activity, she is willing to have sexual intercourse (Brodyaga, Gates, Singer, Tucker, & White, 1975; Dull & Giacopassi, 1987; Kanin, 1969). Misperception of sexual cues becomes the norm in the male–female interactions (Burkhart & Stanton, 1988). Culturally sanctioned sexual scripts are continuously played out in the dating situation. As a consequence, sexual assault perpetrated by an acquaintance is rarely reported to the police. Only rape committed by a stranger is viewed as real rape (Check & Malamuth, 1983; Estrich, 1987; Johnson & Jackson, 1988; Klemmack & Klemmack, 1976; Tetreault & Barnett, 1987; Williams, 1984). Thus, sexual scripts promote a conspiracy of silence among the victim, perpetrator, and larger society. Acquaintance rape is implicitly fostered.

THE STRUCTURE OF STUDENTS' BELIEFS ABOUT DATE RAPE

The general consensus among American students from junior high school through college is that forced sexual intercourse on a date rarely constitutes rape. A large-scale survey of Los Angeles teenagers, a group that might be expected to hold egalitarian sex-role values, revealed some startling results.

Though these teenagers understood the difference between consensual and nonconsensual sex, they were frequently reluctant to apply the label "rape" to the examples of forced sexual relations described in the survey (Goodchilds et al., 1988). Two factors affected the likelihood that nonconsensual sex would be labeled rape: the amount of force used and the type of relationship. The greater the force used by the man to obtain intercourse, the more likely the act was labeled rape, but the label rape was used less frequently if the couple had been dating for a while than if they had just met. Goodchilds and her colleagues (1988) concluded that:

> in fact they [adolescents] were pretty unsure about whether rape occurred between dating partners . . . . Adolescents appear reluctant to label nonconsensual sex within a dating relationship as rape, even when the guy slugs the girl.
>
> *(p. 268)*

Surveys by Goodchilds and her colleagues (1988) and others (Fischer, 1986a, b, 1987; Muehlenhard, Friedman, & Thomas, 1985) identified other factors that affect whether forced sex will be justified or labeled rape: the woman's type of dress, location of the date, use of drugs and/or alcohol, the woman's and man's reputations, how much money the man spends, the man's level of sexual arousal, and the level of previous sexual intimacy, that is, the amount of petting and whether intercourse had previously occurred. However, there were marked gender differences in the meaning imparted to the various circumstances surrounding forced sex. In general, there was a consistent tendency for the girls to view certain circumstances and behaviors in a less sexualized way. These gender differences help us to understand the various ways in which young women and young men may misinterpret what is going on during a date.

To elaborate, adolescent girls were more likely to mention personality and sensitivity as desirable attributes in a date, whereas boys were more likely to mention physical appearance. Girls were less likely than boys to see clothing of any type (low-cut top, shorts, tight jeans, see-through clothes) worn by either sex as a signal for the female's interest in sexual activity. Girls were less likely than boys to see any particular location or activity as a signal for sex, but both girls and boys judged "going to the guy's house alone when there is nobody home" as most indicative of the female's willingness for sex. Girls were less likely than boys to feel that a female who accepts a date with a guy with a bad reputation has agreed to sex but were more likely than boys to feel that a male has a right to expect sex from his date if she has a "tarnished" reputation.

Further gender differences were observed in perceptions of circumstances that might signal that the girl has forfeited her right to say no to sexual intercourse. Significantly more girls (44%) than boys (24%) indicated there are *no* circumstances under which it is "OK for a guy to hold a girl down and force her to have sexual intercourse." This means that 56% of the girls and 76% of the boys believed forced sex is acceptable under at least some circumstances. The largest differences between girls and boys were for the situations in which "he spends a lot of money on her" (61% of the males and 88% of the females said forced sex was not acceptable) and "she's led him on" (46% of the males and 73% of the females: not acceptable); the smallest difference was for "she gets him sexually excited" (49% of the males and 58% of the females: not acceptable). Goodchilds and her colleagues (1988) concluded that otherwise innocent female behaviors may be construed by a male to have sexual meaning.

Findings consistent with Goodchilds et al. (1988) have been reported for a younger group of adolescents. A survey of 1,700 11-to-14-year-olds conducted by the Rhode Island Rape Crisis Center (1988) found that 51% of the boys and 41% of the girls believed that a man has a right to force a woman to kiss him if he had "spent a lot of money" on her; 31% of the boys and 32% of the girls said it is not improper for a man to rape a woman who had past sexual experiences; 87% of the boys and 79% of the girls said rape is OK if a man and woman are married; and 65% of the boys and 47% of all of these seventh-to-ninth graders said it is OK for a man to rape a woman he has been dating for more than six months.

Other studies have confirmed that sex role stereotyping, acceptance of rape myths, and adversarial sex beliefs are related to college students' judgments that acquaintance rape is within the realm of normative acts (Check & Malamuth, 1983; Jenkins & Dambrot, 1987). However, undergraduate women and men typically perceive sexual aggression differently (Barnett & Feild, 1977). Studies suggest a consistent tendency for college women to judge rape more seriously than do college men (Costin, 1985; Costin & Schwarz, 1987; L'Armand & Pepitone, 1982) and to blame the victim less (Jenkins & Dambrot, 1987; Thornton, Robbins, & Johnson, 1981). For example, Tieger (1981), in a study of junior college students, found that male students were more likely than female students to: (a) perceive that rape victims failed to adequately resist the assault; (b) consider the offense less serious, more normative behavior; and (c) view the victim as seductive and taking pleasure in being raped.

Differences Among Men

It is important to recognize that although college men apparently are more tolerant of forced sexual relations than are college women, not all men adhere to sexist attitudes toward female sexual victimization and not all young men are sexually assaultive. Numerous studies have identified groups of men who vary in their beliefs about rape (Briere & Malamuth, 1983; Koss, Leonard, Beezley, & Oros, 1985; Lisak & Roth, 1988; Rapaport & Burkhart, 1984). College men who are willing to admit on anonymous surveys that they have sexually aggressed against a woman are the ones most likely to accept rape myths, show reluctance to view forced sexual relations on a date as rape, perceive the victim as desiring sexual relations, and consider rape more justifiable under various circumstances, for example, when the couple goes to the man's apartment, the woman initiates the date, or the man pays all the expenses (Burt, 1980; Jenkins & Dambrot, 1987; Koss, 1985; Muehlenhard et al., 1985; Muehlenhard & Linton, 1987).

Malamuth's (1981) integration of the findings of several studies on the proclivity of men to rape showed that about 35% of male college students reported some willingness to rape if they were assured of not getting caught. The higher the reported likelihood of committing rape, the greater the acceptance of rape myths. And the greater the reported likelihood of raping, the more likely that individuals would aggress against women in a psychological experiment (Malamuth, 1986).

Tieger (1981) found that men who expressed a willingness to commit rape tended to view rape as less violent, underplayed the harm to the victim, and blamed the female for her victimization. According to Rapaport and Burkhart (1984), men who viewed women as manipulative and untrustworthy and who considered male–female relations as adversarial were more apt to engage in sexual coercion. These authors characterized aggressive men as immature, irresponsible, and lacking in social conscience. Integration into a rape-supportive culture and marked character defects appear to produce coercive sexual behavior.

Koss and Dinero (1988) provided more refined analyses of sexual aggression toward acquaintances by looking at three types of sexually aggressive men: (a) sexually assaultive—they used physical force or its threat to obtain oral, anal, or vaginal intercourse; (b) sexually abusive—they used threat of force to obtain sex contact not involving intercourse; (c) sexually coercive—they used verbal coercion to obtain sexual intercourse. Sexually nonaggressive men—those who engaged in only consensual sexual relations—were also included in the analyses. Findings were consistent with an earlier study (Koss et al., 1985) which showed that the

> more sexually aggressive a man has been, the more likely he was to attribute adversarial qualities to interpersonal relationships, to accept sex-role stereotypes, to believe myths about rape, to feel that rape prevention is a woman's responsibility, and to view as normal an intermingling of aggression and sexuality.
>
> *(p. 989)*

Verbally coercive men differed from physically coercive men. Men who used physical force viewed women as more sexually free than did those who used verbal force. These results agreed with Brownmiller's (1975) assertion that sex-role stereotyping was causally related to rape attitudes. Males who believed rape was normal and acceptable and who judged the victim as seductive and therefore blameworthy were less inhibited from engaging in forced sexual relations.

Differences Among Women

Acceptance of traditional gender role attitudes and belief in rape-supportive myths have not been found to increase young women's vulnerability to sexual assault. And endorsement of a feminist ideology does not itself decrease the likelihood of sexual victimization (Korman & Leslie, 1982). The failure of attitudes to predict sexual victimization has been found for both adolescent and undergraduate women (Ageton, 1983; Koss, 1985; Koss & Dinero, 1989).

Furthermore, attitudes toward gender roles and sexual aggression have not been found to differentiate among levels of victimization. Koss (1985) analyzed women who experienced one of four levels of sexual assault: no victimization, verbal coercion into sexual intercourse, unwanted physical contact or attempted intercourse, and forcible rape. She found that attitudes alone did not adequately differentiate victimized from nonvictimized women, nor did they differentiate among levels of victimization. Koss and Dinero (1989) concluded:

> Although much has been written about the ways that rape is maintained at a societal level by culturally transmitted beliefs and attitudes . . . [there is] no justification for continuing to focus on gender role behavior or rape supportive attitudes as risk factors by which some women are rendered uniquely vulnerable to victimization.
>
> *(p. 249)*

STRATEGIES FOR ATTITUDE CHANGE

Research on attitudes toward rape reveals a fundamental contradiction that for too long has been disregarded: rape is regarded as an abhorrent crime, yet there is a denial of the reality of this crime between acquaintances. A climate of inertia mitigates efforts to change attitudes that support this contradiction. Various beliefs about women, violence, and rape have been consistently identified as risk factors predicting sexually assaultive behavior in men. Therefore, it is imperative to identify strategies for changing these attitudes; the assumption is that a change in attitudes will contribute to behavioral change. The consequences of acquaintance rape for young people and for society at large are too grave to ignore. Social beliefs and norms create a rape-tolerant atmosphere. Many young men continue to believe forced sex is acceptable in certain situations; young women reluctantly accept forced sex as part of the dating game; victims do not report the offense, blame themselves, and suffer long-term consequences alone. When an acquaintance rape is reported, family and friends and medical, mental health, and law enforcement personnel may not believe the victim, and/or discount the seriousness of the attack; prosecution of the perpetrator becomes unlikely (Hall, Howard, Boezio, & Boezio, 1986). As recognition of this problem has grown, various suggestions to promote attitude change have been offered.

It is useful to consider change strategies at three levels: public, institutional, and individual. At each level the goal is to teach people to label all instances of forced sexual contact as criminal and to label forced sexual intercouse as rape. Part of this entails young people's adopting egalitarian attitudes toward women and men, communicating honestly about sexual activities, and rejecting rape myths.

Public Level

Public education about rape is an important facet of strategies for attitude change, because values about women, men, sex, and violence are communicated to young people through parents, schools, churches, the media, and other social institutions. Several studies have shown that misconceptions about rape can be changed using straightforward information-giving strategies (Check & Malamuth, 1984; Donnerstein & Berkowitz, 1981; Malamuth & Check, 1984).

Institutional Responses

Institutional intolerance of sexism and violence must be communicated and demonstrated through policy statements; integration of rape awareness elements into the curriculum; programs and workshops for faculty, staff, and students; and swift and effective services for dealing with victims and perpetrators (Sandberg, Jackson, & Petretic-Jackson, 1987). Fischer (1986a), who demonstrated the effectiveness of a human sexuality course in changing college students' attitudes toward forcible date rape, recommended using a feminist-oriented textbook, teaching facts about sexuality, educating students about rape laws, and avoiding a confrontational style.

Individual Level

Recommendations have been directed toward women, to assist them in avoiding victimization, and toward men, to prevent them from becoming sexual assaulters. Beneke (1982) in *Men on Rape,* stated that "rape is a man's problem, and collectively, men can solve it." He and other rape awareness advocates (see Warshaw, 1988) have argued persuasively for the development of men's support groups. In these groups, men let each other know that forced sex is unacceptable and that it is not unmanly to have a woman say "no" and to take "no" for an answer.

Other suggestions for effecting attitude change focus on assertiveness and communication training (Parrot, 1988), values clarification, and empathy training (Deitz, Blackwell, Daley, & Bentley, 1982).

The emphasis on empathy training holds particular promise. Deitz and her colleagues (1982) argued that an empathetic person can assume the perspective of the victim and, in a jury decision-making context, be more certain about the defendant's guilt, give harsher sentences to the rapist, and hold the victim less responsible. The central role of empathy in changing men's attitudes was underscored in a study by Quackenbush (1989), who found that masculine sex-typed men reacted to various rape vignettes and attitude measures in a rape-supportive manner. He argued that these men "lacked the social skills of femininity, which encompass such expressive competencies as concern for, and ability to empathize with other persons" (p. 336). Quackenbush went on to argue that these men, because of their social skills deficits, rely on social myths in negotiating social interactions; sexually aggressive behavior is one consequence.

Quackenbush's (1989) observations about femininity as having a mitigating effect on sexually aggressive proclivities and on rape-supportive attitudes underscored the role of feelings. Femininity reflects the expressive, other-oriented side of oneself (Spence, Helmreich, & Stapp, 1975). Rape awareness programs should direct attention to people's *feelings* about rape, not just their beliefs.

Attitudes have a belief component and a feeling component. These do not always correspond, making it difficult to say whether an attitude is positive or negative. For example, people may believe in a woman's right to abortion but feel that abortion is an abhorrent act. Is their attitude toward abortion positive or negative? Conversely, one may believe that capital punishment is an ineffective deterrent to crime but feel that certain criminals should die.

Regarding attitudes toward rape, it is not always clear that one's attitudes are positive, just because one endorses stereotypic cultural beliefs about rape. The research on attitudes toward rape has told us more about young people's beliefs than about their feelings. However, case studies make it clear that female victims of forced sex do not feel good about what happened to them, though they may believe it is something they must tolerate as part of the dating game. College women indeed have negative emotional reactions to realistic descriptions of a rape (Bond & Mosher, 1986). Thus, for women the connection between beliefs and feelings about forced sex is complex. Women should be encouraged to trust their feelings; if they are not interested in sex, they should say no rather than acquiesce because they think it is expected. For male perpetrators, we believe the connection between their beliefs and feelings is probably straightforward. These men believe the cultural myths and feel okay about their sexually aggressive behavior. They do not have negative feelings. Herein may lie an important key to successful rape prevention education programs: men need to learn abhorrent *feelings* toward rape. It may not be enough to change stereotypic beliefs. Men should feel as repulsed by the idea of forcing a woman into sex as by the idea of sexually abusing a child.

CONCLUSIONS

Our examination of the literature on young people's attitudes toward rape made three points clear. First, acquaintance rape is viewed differently and less seriously than stranger rape. It is less often judged "real" rape, which results in a contradiction: The crime for which young women are most vulnerable, and the one "normal" young men are likely to perpetrate, is the one least likely to be labeled criminal. Second, various cultural norms, and sexual scripts in particular, mitigate efforts to label forced sex as real rape under a variety of circumstances: how long the couple has dated, prior level of sexual intimacy, who initiates the date, who pays, where the couple goes, how the woman dresses, use of alcohol or drugs, the man's and woman's reputations, and the man's level of sexual arousal. Third, various rape-supportive beliefs and adversarial attitudes toward women predict sexually aggressive behavior in men, and competencies such as empathy, emotional expressiveness, and femininity reduce the likelihood of sexually aggressive behavior.

We conclude that the cultural conception of *consent* lies at the core of understanding this problem (See Berger et al., 1986; Burt & Albin, 1981, for further discussions of consent.) Cultural support for the notion that the presence of certain circumstances means a woman has forfeited her right to refuse sexual intercourse leads to the conclusion that she consented and a crime did not occur. Acceptance of this premise legitimates a man's entitlement to sex under these circumstances. The logic is that a woman's earlier actions (accepting the date, going to isolated locations, choosing certain clothing, engaging in any action that sexually arouses the man, and so on) negate the legitimacy of any subsequent refusal to have further sexual interaction. Her resistance, seen as either token or inappropriate, must be overcome (Lakoff & Johnson, 1987). Forced sex is justified and ceases to be labeled a crime, either by young people or by the law (MacKinnon, 1983). "If the man believed that the woman's resistance was not genuine—and he has probably been socialized to believe this—it becomes difficult to define the act legally as a crime" (Berger et al., 1986, p. 5). Furthermore, as the review of the literature strongly indicated, young women and men frequently perceive the same dating circumstances differently. Misunderstanding and conflict result, and the woman has difficulty communicating her unwillingness (Lewin, 1985). Thus, current cultural norms dictate that the woman who wants to resist must go "beyond what is normally expected of women who want intercourse but wish to maintain a 'moral' appearance" (Weis & Borges, 1973, p. 92).

All of this points to the necessity of changing attitudes and beliefs about acquaintance rape. Young people must learn to define all instances of forced sexual contact as criminal. Furthermore, young men need to feel good about themselves even when their sexual desires go unfulfilled. They need to learn that having a woman say "no" to sex is okay and that part of their male integrity is the ability to respect the woman's decision.

A rape-supportive culture and concomitant social organization are socially constructed realities and, as such, are subject to change (Berger & Luckmann, 1966). To the extent that attitudes, beliefs, and social norms conducive to sexual assault are scientifically scrutinized and publicly confronted, relations between the sexes can be markedly altered. Forced sexual activity between acquaintances will become socially unacceptable.

REFERENCES

Ageton, S. S. (1983). *Sexual assault among adolescents.* Lexington, MA: Heath.

Barnett, N., & Feild, H. (1977). Sex differences in university students' attitudes toward rape. *Journal of College Student Personnel, 2,* 93–96.

Beneke, T. (1982). *Men on rape.* New York: St. Martin's.

Berger, R. J., Searles, P., Salem, R. G., & Pierce, B. A. (1986). Sexual assault in a college community, *Sociological Focus, 19,* 1–26.

Berger, P. L., & Luckmann, T. (1966). *The social construction of reality.* Garden City, NY: Doubleday.

Bond, S. B., & Mosher, D. L. (1986). Guided imagery of rape: Fantasy, reality and the willing victim myth. *Journal of Sex Research, 22,* 162–183.

Briere, J., & Malamuth, N. M. (1983). Self-reported likelihood of sexual aggression: Attitudinal vs. sexual explanations. *Journal of Research in Personality, 17,* 315–323.

Brodyaga, L., Gates, M., Singer, S., Tucker, M., & White, R. (1975). *Rape and its victims: A report for citizens, health facilities, and criminal justice agencies.* Washington, D.C.: U.S. Government Printing Office, J 1. 8/3: R18.

Brownmiller, S. (1975). *Against our will: Men, women, and rape.* New York: Simon & Schuster.

Burkhart, B. R., & Stanton, A. L. (1988). Sexual aggression in acquaintance relationships. In G. W. Russell (Ed.), *Violence in intimate relationships,* 43–45. New York: PMA Publishing Corp.

Burt, M. (1980). Cultural myths and supports for rape. *Journal of Personality and Social Psychology, 38,* 217–230.

Burt, M. R., & Albin, R. S. (1981). Rape myths, rape definitions, and probability of conviction. *Journal of Applied Social Psychology, 11,* 212–230.

Check, J. V. P., & Malamuth, N. M. (1983). Sex role stereotyping and reactions to depictions of stranger versus acquaintance rape. *Journal of Personality and Social Psychology, 45,* 344–356.

Check, J. V. P., & Malamuth, N. M. (1984). Can there be positive effects of participation in pornography experiments? *Journal of Sex Research, 20,* 14–31.

Conger, J. J., & Petersen, A. D. (1984). *Adolescence and youth: Psychological development in a changing world (3rd ed.).* New York: Harper & Row.

Costin, F. (1985). Beliefs about rape and women's social roles. *Archives of Sexual Behavior, 14,* 319–325.

Costin, F., & Schwarz, N. (1987). Beliefs about rape and women's roles: A four-nation study. *Journal of Interpersonal Violence, 2,* 46–56.

Deitz, S. R., Blackwell, K. T., Daley, P. C., & Bentley, B. J. (1982). Measurement of empathy toward rape victims and rapists. *Journal of Personality and Social Psychology, 43,* 372–384.

Dull, R. T., & Giacopassi, D. J. (1987). Demographic correlates of sexual and dating attitudes. *Criminal Justice and Behavior, 14,* 175–193.

Donnerstein, E., & Berkowitz, L. (1981). Victim reactions in aggressive erotic films as a factor in violence against women. *Journal of Personality and Social Psychology, 41,* 710–724.

Estrich, S. (1987). *Real rape: How the legal system victimizes women who say no.* Cambridge, MA: Harvard University Press.

Fagot, B. I., Loeber, R., & Reid, J. B. (1988). Developmental determinants of male-to-female aggression. In G. W. Russell (Ed.), *Violence in intimate relationships,* 91-105. New York: PMA Publishing Corp.

Feild, H. S. (1978). Attitudes toward rape: A comparative analysis of police, rapists, crisis counselors, and citizens. *Journal of Personality and Social Psychology, 36,* 156–179.

Fischer, G. J. (1986a). College student attitudes toward forcible date rape: Change after taking a human sexuality course. *Journal of Sex Education and Therapy, 12,* 42–46.

Fischer, G. J. (1986b). College student attitudes toward forcible date rape: I. Cognitive predictors. *Archives of Sexual Behavior, 15,* 457–466.

Fischer, G. J. (1987). Hispanic and majority student attitudes toward forcible date rape as a function of differences in attitudes toward women. *Sex Roles, 17,* 93–101.

Goodchilds, J., Zellman, G., Johnson, P., & Giarusso, R. (1988). Adolescents and their perceptions of sexual interactions. In A. W. Burgess (Ed.), *Rape and sexual assault, Vol. II,* 245–270. New York: Garland.

Hall, E. R., Howard, J. A., Boezio, S. H., & Boezio, L. (1986). Tolerance of rape: A sexist or antisocial attitude? *Psychology of Women Quarterly, 10,* 101–118.

Jenkins, M. J., & Dambrot, F. H. (1987). The attribution of date rape: Observer's attitudes and sexual experiences and the dating situation. *Journal of Applied Social Psychology, 17,* 875–895.

Johnson, J. D., & Jackson, L. A. (1988). Assessing the effects of factors that might underlie the differential perception of acquaintance and stranger rape. *Sex Roles, 19,* 37–44.

Kanin, E. J. (1969). Selected dyadic aspects of males' sex aggression. *Journal of Sex Research, 5,* 12–28.

Kanin, E. J. (1985). Date rapists: Differential sexual socialization and relative deprivation. *Archives of Sexual Behavior, 14,* 219–231.

Klemmack, S. H., & Klemmack, D. L. (1976). The social definition of rape. In M. Walker & S. Brodsky (Eds.), *Sexual Assault,* 135–147. Lexington, MA: Lexington Books.

Korman, S. K., & Leslie, G. R. (1982). The relationship of feminist ideology and date expense sharing to perception of sexual aggression in dating. *Journal of Sex Research, 18,* 114–129.

Koss, M. P. (1985). The hidden rape victim: Personality, attitudinal, and situational characteristics. *Psychology of Women Quarterly, 9,* 193–212.

Koss, M. P., Leonard, K. E., Beezley, D. A., & Oros, C. J. (1985). Nonstranger sexual aggression: A discriminant analysis of the psychological characteristics of undetected offenders. *Sex koles, 12,* 981–992.

Koss, M. P., & Dinero, T. E. (1988). Predictors of sexual aggression among a national sample of male college students. In R. A. Pretkney & V. L. Quinsey (Eds.), *Human sexual aggression: Current perspectives,* pp. 113–146. *Annals of the New York Academy of Sciences, 528.*

Koss, M. P., & Dinero, T. E. (1989) Discriminant analysis of risk factors for sexual victimization among a national sample of college women. *Journal of Consulting and Clinical Psychology, 57,* 242–250.

L'Armand, K., & Pepitone, A. (1982). Judgments of victim-rapist relationship and victim sexual history. *Personality and Social Psychology Bulletin, 8,* 134–139.

Lakoff, G., & Johnson, M. (1987). The metaphorical logic of rape. *Metaphor and Symbolic Activity, 2,* 73–79.

LaPlante, M. N., McCormick, N., & Brannigan, G. G. (1980). Living the sexual script: College students' views of influence in sexual encounters. *Journal of Sex Research, 16,* 338–355.

Lewin, M. (1985). Unwanted intercourse: The difficulty of saying no. *Psychology of Women Quarterly, 9,* 184–192.

Lisak, D., & Roth, S. (1988). Motivational factors in nonincarcerated sexually aggressive men. *Journal of Personality and Social Psychology, 55,* 795–802.

MacKinnon, C. A. (1983). Feminism, Marxism, method and the state: Toward feminist jurisprudence. *Signs: A Journal of Women in Culture, 8,* 635–658.

Malamuth, N. M. (1981). Rape proclivity among males. *Journal of Social Issues, 37,* 138–157.

Malamuth, N. M. (1986). Predictors of naturalistic sexual aggression. *Journal of Personality and Social Psychology, 50,* 953–962.

Malamuth, N. M., & Check, J. V. P. (1984). Debriefing effectiveness following exposure to pornographic rape depictions. *Journal of Sex Research, 20,* 1–13.

Muehlenhard, C. L., Friedman, D. E., & Thomas, C. M. (1985). Is date rape justifiable? The effects of dating activity, who initiated, who paid, and men's attitudes toward women. *Psychology of Women Quarterly, 9,* 297–310.

Muehlenhard, C. L., & Linton, M. A. (1987). Date rape and sexual aggression in dating situations: Incidence and risk factors. *Journal of Counseling Psychology, 34,* 186–196.

Parrot, A. (1988). *Acquaintance rape and sexual assault prevention training manual.* Ithaca, NY: Cornell University.

Quackenbush, R. L. (1989). A comparison of androgynous, masculine sex-typed, and undifferentiated males in dimensions of attitudes toward rape. *Journal of Research in Personality, 23,* 318–342.

Rapaport, K., & Burkhart, B. R. (1984). Personality and attitudinal characteristics of sexually coercive college males. *Journal of Abnormal Psychology, 93,* 216–221.

Rhode Island Rape Crisis Center (1988). *The question of rape.* Providence, RI: Author.

Rice, F. P. (1984). *The adolescent: Development, relations, and culture.* Boston: Allyn & Bacon.

Rose, S. (1979). *The youth values project.* Washington, DC: The Population Institute.

Ross, V. M. (1977). Rape as a social problem: A byproduct of the feminist movement. *Social Problems, 25,* 75–89.

Sanday, P. R. (1981). The socio-cultural context of rape: A cross-cultural study. *Journal of Social Issues, 37,* 5–27.

Sandberg, G., Jackson, T. L., & Petretic-Jackson, P. (1987). College students' attitudes regarding sexual coercion and aggression: Developing educational and preventive strategies. *Journal of College Student Personnel, 28,* 302–311.

Schwarz, N., & Brand, J. F. (1983). Effects of salience of rape on sex role attitudes, trust, and self-esteem in non-raped women. *European Journal of Social Psychology, 13,* 71–76.

Spence, J. T., Helmreich, R. L., & Stapp, J. (1975). Ratings of self and peers on sex role attributes and their relation to self-esteem and conceptions of masculinity and femininity. *Journal of Personality and Social Psychology, 32,* 29–39.

Tetreault, P. A., & Barnett, M. A. (1987). Reactions to stranger and acquaintance rape. *Psychology of Women Quarterly, 11,* 353–358.

Thornton, B., Robbins, M. A., & Johnson, J. A. (1981). Social perception of the rape victim's culpability: The influence of respondent's personal-environmental causal attribution tendencies. *Human Relations, 34,* 225–237.

Tieger, T. (1981). Self-rated likelihood of raping and the social perception of rape. *Journal of Research in Personality, 15,* 147–158.

Warshaw, R. (1988). *I never called it rape: The Ms. report on recognizing, fighting, and surviving date and acquaintance rape.* New York: Harper & Row.

Weis, K., & Borges, S. (1973). Victimology and rape: The case of the legitimate victim. *Issues in Criminology, 8,* 71–115.

Williams, L. S. (1984). The classic rape: When do victims report? *Social Problems, 31,* 459–467.

CHAPTER 4

Attributions of Responsibility for Acquaintance Rape

KAREN S. CALHOUN, PhD and RUTH M. TOWNSLEY

One of the most controversial issues related to rape is: Who is blamed for rape—the victim or the assailant? Indeed, the question of who is blamed for a rape is of central importance in the definition of rape itself. Legally, rape occurs when an assailant forces a victim to engage in vaginal, anal, or oral sexual intercourse against her will. (This definition varies by state.) Therefore, if a man is *not* blamed—in other words, is *not* seen as forcing a woman into having sexual intercourse against her will—the situation would not be defined as a rape.

The low arrest and conviction rate of assailants and the lack of support given to rape victims by lay people and professionals with whom they come in contact strongly suggest that *not* blaming the assailant and actually blaming the victim for a rape may be the rule rather than the exception. For those of us who work with victims and offenders, this situation is upsetting and confusing in light of the devastating effects of rape on victims. Many would suggest that this situation is urgently in need of change for the sake of victims and the prevention of rape. Yet, it is unlikely that changes will occur without a clear understanding of current attitudes and of why such views are maintained. Questions as to when and why assailants are not found blameworthy and when and why victims are held responsible for rape are of crucial importance in bringing about change and are the focus of this chapter.

These questions can be examined from a psychological, sociological, historical, or legal perspective. As psychologists, we examine these questions from a psychological point of view, that is, we examine factors "within" individuals that are related to tendencies to place blame on a victim or an assailant. This perspective is not unrelated to the sociological, historical, and legal perspectives and does not encompass all of the potential factors related to the current pattern of blaming victims and not blaming offenders. However, the psychological perspective offers a number of explanations for the current situation and is an important component for consideration.

Our goal in writing this chapter is to offer the reader an objective, thorough presentation of the theoretical and research work that suggests explanations for why victims might be blamed for rape and offenders might be relieved of the blame. As is often the case in research, the findings in this area do not always offer a coherent picture that is easily interpreted and acted upon. If we were to suggest that a clear understanding of this issue has been achieved, this suggestion would be misleading; our goals are to stimulate thought regarding the various issues discussed in the chapter and to raise the reader's awareness of the types of factors that are important to consider when one is faced with decisions about blameworthiness or with the implications of such decisions made by others.

Our discussion begins with an examination of (a) the definition of blameworthiness and of other related concepts and (b) how these definitions impact one's views of offenders and victims. Several psychological/theoretical explanations for why individuals might attribute blameworthiness to victims rather than offenders are examined. Finally, we review the research findings related to various factors that might impact on whether victims or offenders get blamed for a rape.

THE NATURE OF ATTRIBUTIONS

From a psychological perspective, blameworthiness can be viewed as a subset of attributions. Attributions are the explanations people offer to explain why events happen (Heider, 1958). For example, a person trying to understand why a rape occurred might attribute the event to factors such as the male's lack of empathy for the woman or the woman's walking alone at night. The study of attributions is one of the largest areas in social psychology and one of its applications is derived from the assumption that people's attributions affect their behavior. In the case of rape, it is assumed that if one attributes a rape to a woman's behavior, then one is less likely to be supportive of her attempts to have her rapist convicted than if one attributes the rape to the man.

An aspect of attributions that is particularly important in rape situations is the distinction among attributions of cause, responsibility, and blame (Bradbury & Fincham, 1990). *Attributions of cause* are merely explanations given for the occurrence of an event. Thus, causes of a rape might include any factor that increased the likelihood of the rape's occurring. Attributions of cause could include the clothing that a woman wore, which attracted her rapist's attention; her agreeing to go on a date with him, or the man's having previously been told "no" by women who eventually agreed to have sex with him.

Attributions of responsibility are concerned with an individual's accountability or answerability for some event (Bradbury & Fincham, 1990). For example, responsibility might be attributed to a rapist because he is accountable for his own behavior. Attributions of cause can be made to an individual without an attribution of responsibility or accountability. For example, a woman's seductive behavior might be seen as contributing to the likelihood of a man's raping her. Although she is responsible for her own seductive behavior, it does not follow that her seductive behavior is responsible for the man's behavior. Furthermore, cause and responsibility can be distinguished from blameworthiness.

Attributions of blame are concerned with an individual's liability for censure or condemnation (Bradbury & Fincham, 1990). For example, blame might be attributed to a rapist because his behavior was worthy of condemnation. The study of attributions assumes that attributions of blame, responsibility, and cause are related hierarchically. For blame to be attributed to someone, both responsibility and cause also must be attributed; for responsibility to be attributed to someone, cause must be attributed as well. Thus, an individual can be perceived as a contributing cause of a rape but not as responsible, or can be seen as a cause and as responsible, but not as worthy of blame.

According to general principles regarding blame and responsibility attributions (Bradbury & Fincham, 1980), one's responsibility and blame attributions for rape victims and offenders will be a function of one's *perceptions* of the following:

1. The degree of the rapist's intention to force a woman to engage in sexual activity (against her will) (Heider, 1958);
2. The amount of negative, selfish motivation involved in raping her;
3. The presence of free choice to do otherwise;
4. The degree of foresight regarding the consequences of forcing her to have sex;
5. The appreciation of wrongfulness of forcing a woman to have sex; and
6. The capacity to have done otherwise (the ability to not rape her under the circumstances).

Thus, for example, if one perceives that an offender selfishly intended to harm his victim, more blame will be attributed to the offender than if one perceives that the offender did not intend to harm the victim and did not foresee the consequences of his behavior.

It is important to recognize that, by definition, attributions involve individuals' *perceptions* of events (Heider, 1958) and thus are not statements of absolute truth which can be proven. Individuals' attributions of causes, responsibility, and blameworthiness will vary according to subjective factors. These factors include ethical and moral values, differences in the information available, and past experiences. The six factors above, which affect the types of blame and responsibility attributions made, are a function of individual, subjective factors. For example, one's perception of a rapist's capacity to have done otherwise will be a function of one's beliefs about whether a man has control over his sexual behavior. Although it seems somewhat ridiculous to many, there are those who believe that men do not have control over their sexual behavior in situations where a sexual partner is potentially available. Attempts to change attributions must address these subjective perceptions, which determine the types of attributions made.

The distinction among causal, responsibility, and blame attributions seems to be crucial in situations where victims might be held responsible for their rape, particularly if it was an acquaintance rape. Lack of recognition of the distinction among the three types of attributions leads one to make logical errors regarding rape. For example, without recognizing this distinction, one might believe that if a woman's behavior contributed to the likelihood of a rape, she must be to blame for the rape. Such a conclusion is illogical because although a woman's behavior might increase her risk of being raped (an attribution of cause) this does not make her to blame for a man's behavior (an attribution of blame). Alternatively, it would be illogical to state that because a woman cannot be blamed for rape (an attribution of blame), she plays no causal role in rape and therefore is helpless in preventing rape (an attribution of cause). Finally, it is illogical to state that because a woman might have prevented being raped (an attribution of cause) she was to blame for the rape (an attribution of blame).

These distinctions are particularly important in cases of acquaintance rape. Compared to stranger rape, acquaintance rape by definition involves a woman's behavior to a much greater extent; therefore, a greater proportion of the cause of the rape is likely to be attributed to the woman. Indeed, if the woman had not known the man, let him into her apartment, or gone on a date with him, the rape would probably have been less likely to occur. Again, this does not mean that the woman is to blame or is responsible for the man raping her.

This distinction is important to bear in mind when determining the guilt of an offender or when preventing rape. Among the psychological concepts of attributions, blame attributions seem to relate most strongly to the legal concept of guilt. Yet, it is not difficult to see how law enforcement officials and juries could easily operate under the assumption that an attribution of cause is equivalent to guilt and therefore could absolve an offender of guilt if his victim contributed in any way to the rape. Secondly, the belief that a woman's behavior contributes nothing to the rape leaves women helplessly at the mercy of would-be rapists. Recognition of the distinction among cause, responsibility, and blame allows women to take protective action and to avoid perceptions of helplessness that put them at risk for victimization and psychological distress.

Although a lack of distinction among the various types of attributions may partly account for the pattern of "blaming" victims for rape, there are many situations in which people attribute "true" responsibility to victims. Psychologists have made several hypotheses as to why individuals make such attributions. Rather than suggesting that individuals who make victim-blaming attributions do so merely out of malice and ignorance, these hypotheses suggest that such attributions serve an adaptive function for the individual and are maintained by the fact that they serve this function. Therefore, it is necessary to understand the function that victim-blaming attributions might serve, in order to maximize the likelihood of effecting a change in this pattern.

The belief in one's ability to predict and control one's environment is related to the maintenance of physical and emotional well-being. Lack of this belief has been shown to increase risk for physical and psychological distress. Therefore, it has been hypothesized that individuals are motivated to *maintain* the belief that they can predict and control their environment (Heider, 1958). Furthermore, it is hypothesized that attributions about all types of situations, not just rape, serve to maintain this belief (Heider, 1958). An important aspect of this belief is the idea that events are predictable and operate according to rules. It is additionally important to maintain the belief that these "rules" according to which the world functions are fair and just.

Studies have supported this hypothesis. For example, in 1965 Melvin Lerner found that subjects behaved as if they believed that "people deserve what happens to them." His subjects were told whether hypothetical workers did or did not get paid for their work. Afterward, the subjects were asked to make judgments as to whether the workers deserved to get paid. Interestingly, workers who got paid were viewed as more deserving of payment than those who did not get paid, even though there were no differences in the work performed by the two groups. Lerner explained this finding by suggesting that people feel more comfortable if they can believe that others get what they deserve. When he examined this type of belief in the domain of victimization, he found a similar pattern: victims seemed to be blamed for their own misfortune and often were rejected by subjects in the study despite serious suffering (Lerner & Simmons, 1966).

Lerner and Simmons (1966) suggested that the operating "force" behind these attributions of blame is the belief that bad things do not happen to good people. They called this the "just world hypothesis." According to this principle, people are strongly motivated to maintain the belief that the world operates according to just principles, "for the sake of maintaining their own sanity" (p. 203), even if it means that one must reject a suffering victim. In their study, women subjects were given to believe that they were watching another person receive moderately painful shocks. In one condition, the women had some control over the shocks received by the other person; in a second condition, they had no control over the shocks. When the women had no control over the shocks, they tended to blame the person for the shocks being received, presumably because they were motivated to maintain the belief that people deserve what they get.

This study might parallel the behavior of would-be supporters of rape victims (emergency room personnel, law enforcement officials, juries).

Given that they have no control over the victim's suffering, they might be motivated to maintain their own sense of well-being by blaming the victim for her own misfortune. By doing so, they maintain a belief that the world operates according to just principles.

In a related study, Walster (1966) found additional evidence for the idea that victim-blaming attributions serve a self-protective function for the person making the attributions. Men and women heard accounts of car accidents and made attributions of responsibility to the victim or to another cause. The more severe the consequences of the car accident, the more responsibility was assigned to the victim. Walster suggested that such attributions are reassuring to people and allow them to perceive that the world is predictable and controllable. Without making such attributions, people would have greater fear that such an event might happen to them.

Shaver (1970) extended the notion that victim-blaming attributions are self-protective by suggesting that they also serve a "defensive function." Shaver found that the types of attributions made by people (that is, either victim-blaming or non-victim-blaming) vary according to how vulnerable the persons making the attribution might feel, as potential victims. If the persons had a high likelihood of being victims themselves, they made fewer victim-blaming attributions than if they had a low likelihood of becoming victims. Balancing the self-protective function of maintaining a belief in a just world would seem to be influenced by the need to protect oneself from being blamed for future victimization.

FACTORS INFLUENCING ATTRIBUTIONS

Several factors have been found to influence attributions of responsibility for acquaintance rape and the division of that responsibility between the victim and assailant. These factors include: the sex of the person assigning responsibility, the person's attitude toward women in general, the characteristics of the victim (for example, physical attractiveness), and the victim's resistance to the assault. These factors have not been studied systematically but some patterns have begun to emerge.

Sex Differences

The sex of the person making the attribution has received considerable attention in the literature. The vast majority of studies have found that men hold female victims more responsible than do female subjects (Calhoun, Selby, Cann, & Keller, 1978; Cann, Calhoun, & Selby, 1979; Kanekar & Vaz, 1983; Muehlenhard, 1988). Therefore, in the absence of other information about subjects, we can predict that men will make more victim-blaming attributions than women will.

However, other variables are important as well. The one that has been studied most is general attitudes toward women and women's role; their scale of measurement placed traditional attitudes at one pole and conservative attitudes at the other. Studies that have included this measure have typically found it to be a more important predictor of victim-blaming attributions than sex of subject alone. Because men tended to have more traditional, less egalitarian attitudes toward women, they appeared to be more victim-blaming in studies that did not control for general attitudes toward women and sex roles. In other words, attitudes toward women's roles appeared to influence attributions more than sex per se. Shotland and Goodstein (1983), for example, found when they examined subjects equated on their attitudes toward women, that women subjects actually blamed victims more than did men.

Other studies that have included measures of sex role attitudes generally supported the overriding importance of this measure in perceptions of blame, with more traditional subjects blaming victims more. For example, Coller and Resick (1987) found that women with more traditional gender-role attitudes blamed victims more in a date rape situation than did those with more egalitarian attitudes, and saw the victim as "leading him on." Muehlenhard (1985) and Muehlenhard, Friedman, and Thomas (1988) found that men and women with traditional attitudes saw forced sex as more justifiable than did subjects without such views. In addition, traditional men rated rape as more justifiable than did any of the other groups, including traditional women.

Those with traditional role attitudes were more likely to blame women for their own victimization in a variety of situations, not just rape. Howard (1984) compared attributions blaming male versus female victims of various kinds of assaults (including rape). Whereas gender of victim made no difference to egalitarian subjects, those with traditional gender-role attitudes attributed more blame to female than to male victims.

The only study not consistent with these findings on gender-role effects dealt with a stranger rape situation, not acquaintance rape (Krulewitz & Payne, 1978). Traditional and nontraditional subjects did not differ in their attributions of blame to the victim or assailant, but nontraditional men and women attributed more blame to society. Thus, some blame was shifted to a broader, less personal cause, consistent with the feminist view of rape. Because subjects will probably blame a victim less when she is attacked by a total stranger, a different pattern of attributions might be expected. Surprisingly few studies, however, have compared perceptions in acquaintance and stranger assaults, and they have not included measures of gender-role attitudes.

Differences in responsibility attributed to victims of stranger and acquaintance rapes were found by Tetreault and Barnett (1987), and these attributions varied by subject sex. Women attributed greater responsibility to victims of acquaintance rape, but men viewed victims of stranger rape as more responsible. The authors suggested that men's attributions were influenced by greater devaluation of the stranger rape victim. Devaluation of victims is a major problem generally, but it is not clear why men and women would differ. Perhaps this is a self-protective mechanism: women who blame the victim can think it was something *she* did, and therefore feel less vulnerable. Possibly men viewed the stranger victim as less warm and likable, and thus more deserving of her fate. Because these findings were based on a relatively small sample and have not been replicated, more research is needed to fully understand perceptions of victims. Research should examine the effect of varying degrees of acquaintanceship, rather than assuming that all relationships between victim and assailant will be viewed similarly. The level of acquaintance between victim and assailant has traditionally been important for the outcome of criminal court cases, although it should not play a major role. In some cases, even a nodding acquaintance with the assailant was enough to cast doubt on a victim's nonconsent.

Other Contributing Factors

A variety of other factors related to victim characteristics and behavior, offender characteristics, observer characteristics, and situational variables might be expected to influence attributions of responsibility. None of these has been examined very thoroughly. Offender characteristics have been almost totally neglected, while victim characteristics have received constant attention. This is interesting in light of society's general attitude that women are primarily responsible for preventing rape and for how they are perceived and treated when they are raped. This research focus on the victim seems to imply that the assailant's behavior, character, or history of sexual aggression influences attributions less than victim characteristics do.

Situational variables and circumstances of rapes have received little formal attention, although most studies use sets of written or taped vignettes describing rape scenes. Little effort has been made to standardize these across studies, and the result is confusion. Systematic study is needed of such variables as degree of acquaintance and prior intimacy. Progress is being made along these lines in certain areas. For example, Muehlenhard et al. (1985) determined that date rape is considered more justifiable by college students when the man pays for the date, when the date is initiated by the woman, and when they go to his apartment or a movie rather than to a religious event. Shotland and Goodstein (1983) examined both the level of force used by the offender and the timing of the victim's protest. Victims received greater blame when low levels of force were used and when clear resistance was not demonstrated at the first indication of sexual intent on the part of the male. These results were supported by Amick (1985), who found that early initiation of protest was the most critical factor in preventing date rape and avoiding blame. Potential victims who protested only after having consented to kissing and petting were blamed more than those who made their nonconsent clear as soon as any sex play was initiated. This perception did not change even when victims added strong physical resistance to their verbal protests.

The effects of successful resistance have been studied only in the stranger rape literature and it is clear that victims are blamed more when the rape is completed rather than merely attempted (Krulewitz & Nash, 1979). Apparently, victims gain respectability in the eyes of others when they "fight for their honor" even at the risk of their lives. Resistance is an important variable because it is a primary determinant of whether an assault is perceived as rape. Juries' decisions on guilt are based in large part on the level of resistance a victim displays. The self-blame often shown by victims tends to center on questions of resistance ("Should I have fought harder?" "Is there something else I could have done?").

Other victim variables that have been studied include race, physical attractiveness, self-blame, and sexual history. Race has not been identified in the victim descriptions used in most studies. Only Johnson and Byrne (1989) specifically compared reactions to black and white victims and defendants. No differences were found on ratings of responsibility, seriousness of the crime, or appropriate sanctions for the defendant.

Physical attractiveness of the victim has been included only in the literature on rapes by strangers, and results have been mixed. Seligman, Brickman, and Koulack (1977) found that less attractive victims were blamed more by both men and women than those higher in attractiveness. However, Calhoun et al. (1978) found that both sexes blamed the more attractive victims slightly more. Whereas social science research has generally held physical attractiveness to be an advantage for both sexes, it may put women at greater risk for becoming targets of rape and for being blamed for their own victimization.

A victim's sexual history often is used against her in court if it can be construed to reflect on her respectability. She is a witness (usually the only witness) to the crime, and the primary defense strategy is usually to attack her credibility. Juries are thought to be more lenient toward the accused assailant when they regard the victim as less respectable, either because they fail to identify with the victim or feel she deserves her fate. However, research has not entirely supported the notion that more respectable victims will always be held less blameworthy. Jones and Aronson (1973) found that both sexes faulted "respectable" (married or virgin) victims more than "less respectable" (divorced). This was not supported by Kahn et al. (1977), however, who found that attributions of blame were not related to respectability of victim or defendant or identification with either. Factors other than respectability may have played a role in these studies. Cann et al. (1979) examined more directly the effects of testimony about a victim's prior sexual experiences. Victims who refused to testify were seen as more responsible for the assault. However, if a judge blocked the victim's testimony, she was seen as less responsible than a sexually inexperienced victim.

Some level of self-blame is commonly seen in rape victims as they struggle to make sense of the experience and why it happened to them. Those who work with victims may be concerned that expressions of self-blame may cause others to hold a victim more responsible or to be more negative toward her. Research findings are mixed. Coates, Wortman, and Abbey (1979) found that victims who blamed themselves were not held more responsible than those who didn't. However, the self-blaming victim was rated as more emotionally disturbed. Thornton et al. (1988) examined effects of victim self-blame from the perspective of crisis counselors and lay observers. Both groups attributed less responsibility to a victim who verbalized chance attributions than to one who expressed self-blame. Overall, counselors attributed less blame to victims than did lay observers, but they considered self-blaming victims to be more emotionally disturbed, just as in the Coates et al. (1979) study.

Similarity to victims, identification with victims, and empathy for victims are related concepts that have been studied. Fulero and Delara (1976) looked at victim–observer similarity and found that observers attributed less responsibility to a similar victim than a dissimilar one. However, Kahn et al. (1977) found identification with either the victim or the offender to be unrelated to attributions. Perhaps identification and similarity are less closely related than they would appear.

Identification with a victim should be enhanced by observers' own experience with victimization. However, previous victimization did not influence blame attributions in a study by Jenkins and Dambrot (1987). A history of victimization on the part of the observer does enhance empathy for a victim (Barnett, Tetreault, & Masbad, 1987). But whether this empathy affects blame attributions has not been assessed.

Greater empathy toward victims is generally shown by women than men, perhaps as a result of women having experienced more victimization and feeling more vulnerable to it. A general tendency to empathize with others, in the absence of a history of victimization, does not appear to influence blame attributions (Coller & Resick, 1987).

Tendencies related to empathy and lack of it should be studied more carefully as they relate to rape attributions. They may influence the way accused assailants are treated by juries as well as the support given to victims. A good example is punitive tendencies. In a study of empathy and punitiveness not related specifically to rape, Sulzer and Burglass (1968) found that more empathetic and less punitive subjects held others less responsible for negative outcomes. Punitiveness appeared to be a more important determinant than empathy. General punitiveness has not been examined in the rape literature.

It is worth remembering that research outcomes can be affected by how blame is defined. Most studies discussed here used the term blame without further definition. Subjects were left to define blame in their own idiosyncratic ways. Some studies used other wording, such as "How much was the victim/offender at fault?" or "How justifiable was the behavior?" This presents problems for interpretation, since these terms are not interchangeable.

Blaming victims does not exonerate their assailants. Consistently, assailants are held more responsible than victims, even though victims may be assigned some share of the blame. It is easy to lose sight of this fact when so much of the research seems to reveal a fascination with victim blame. However, all the studies that have included a measure of blame to the assailant have found the greatest share of fault assigned to him, whether the subjects were male or female. This area of research represents an attempt to sort out the balance of blame/responsibility assigned to victim and assailant, and how person/situation variables affect that balance. The study of attributions for responsibility and blame appears to hold promise for a greater understanding of why rape victims are often blamed and why rapists are often absolved, at least in part, of responsibility.

IMPLICATIONS

The implications of attributing blame and responsibility to victims include a lack of medical, social, psychological, and legal support for victims as well as a lack of punishment and control over offenders. These theoretical explanations for why people might attribute responsibility and blame to victims of rape do not justify victim-blaming attributions; they merely suggest the reasons for such attributions. Only by understanding the factors that serve to maintain this pattern of attributions can we hope to change it. Perhaps the task of modifying people's patterns of attributions involves not only changing their conceptions of rape but also impacting on their general beliefs about the control that people have over others and over their environment. These explanations suggest that those who blame victims will not easily change their beliefs, for doing so would have deleterious effects on their sense of control and their feeling that the world operates according to predictable and just principles. The lack of these very factors (a sense of control and predictability) has been found to be strongly related to symptoms of depression, anxiety, and the onset of physical symptoms.

Perhaps the most deleterious effect of victim-blaming attributions is that they allow assailants and would-be assailants to justify their behavior, at least in part. Rape prevention efforts need to target rape-justifying attitudes much more directly. Men must accept responsibility for their behavior and its consequences. Women must be taught that rape is not justifiable behavior and that prevention is not entirely up to them. Victim-blaming is a rape-supportive attitude that interferes with the mobilization of personal and societal resources to prevent rape, punish rapists, and help victims. Changing such attitudes is essential and must start early because rapists tend to become sexually active at a younger age and have more partners than nonrapists (Koss, 1985). Continued research efforts should be aimed at exploring how attributions of responsibility affect behavior and at developing effective behavior change methods.

REFERENCES

Amick, A. E. (1985). *Perceptions of victim nonconsent to sexual aggression in dating situations: The effect of onset and type of protest.* Unpublished doctoral dissertation, University of Georgia.

Barnett, M. A., Tetreault, P. A., & Masbad, I. (1987). Empathy with a rape victim: The role of similarity of experience. *Violence and Victims, 2,* 255–262.

Bradbury, T. N., & Fincham, F. D. (1990). Attributions in marriage: Review and critique. *Psychological Bulletin, 107,* 3–33.

Calhoun, L. G., Selby, J. W., Cann, A., & Keller, G. T. (1978). The effect of victim physical attractiveness and sex of respondent on social reactions to victims of rape. *British Journal of Social and Clinical Psychology, 17,* 191–192.

Cann, A., Calhoun, L. G., & Selby, I. W. (1979). Attributing responsibility to the victim of rape: Influence of information regarding past sexual experience. *Human Relations, 32,* 57–67.

Coates, D., Wortman, C. B., & Abbey, A. (1979). Reactions to victims. In I. H. Frieze, D. Bar-Tal, & J. S. Carroll (Eds.), *New approaches to social problems* (pp. 21–52). San Francisco: Jossey-Bass.

Coller, S. A., & Resick, P. A. (1987). Women's attributions of responsibility for date rape: The influence of empathy and sex-role stereotyping. *Violence and Victims, 2,* 115–125.

Fulero, S. M., & Delara, C. (1976). Rape victims and attributed responsibility: A defensive attribution approach. *Victimology, 1,* 551–563.

Heider, F. (1958). *The psychology of interpersonal relations.* New York: Wiley.

Howard, J. A. (1984). Societal influences on attribution: Blaming some victims more than others. *Journal of Personality and Social Psychology, 47,* 494–505.

Jenkins, M. J., & Dambrot, F. H. (1987). The attribution of date rape: Observer's attitudes and sexual experiences and the dating situation. *Journal of Applied Social Psychology, 17,* 875–895.

Johnson, J. D., & Byrne, A. (1989). *Perceptual correlates in acquaintance and stranger rape scenarios.* Paper presented at the annual meeting of The Southeastern Psychological Association, Washington, DC.

Jones, C., & Aronson, E. (1973). Attribution of fault to a rape victim as a function of respectability of the victim. *Journal of Personality and Social Psychology, 26,* 415–419.

Kahn, A., Gilbert, D. A., Latta, R. M., Deutsch, C., Hagen, R., Hill, M., McGaughey, T., Ryen, A. H., & Wilson, D. W. (1977). Attribution of fault to a rape victim as a function of respectability of the victim. A failure to replicate or extend. *Representative Research in Social Psychology, 8,* 98–107.

Kanekar, S., & Vaz, L. (1983). Determinants of perceived likelihood of rape and victim's fault. *Journal of Social Psychology, 120,* 147–148.

Koss, M. P. (1985). *Hidden rape: Survey of psychopathological consequences.* Unpublished final report #R01MH31618 to National Institute of Mental Health.

Krulewitz, J. E., & Nash, J. E. (1979). Effects of victim resistance, assault outcome, and sex of observer on attributions about rape. *Journal of Personality, 47,* 558–574.

Krulewitz, J. E., & Payne, E. J. (1978). Attributions about rape: Effects of rapist force, observer sex and sex role attitudes. *Journal of Applied Social Psychology, 8,* 291–305.

Lerner, M. J. (1965). Evaluation of performance as a function of performer's reward and attractiveness. *Journal of Personality and Social Psychology, 1,* 355–360.

Lerner, M. J., & Simmons, C. H. (1966). Observer's reaction to the "innocent victim": Compassion or rejection? *Journal of Personality and Social Psychology, 4,* 203–210.

Muehlenhard, C. L. (1988). Misinterpreted dating behaviors and the risk of date rape. *Journal of Social and Clinical Psychology, 6,* 20–37.

Muehlenhard, C. L., Friedman, D. E., & Thomas, C. M. (1985). Is date rape justifiable? The effects of dating activity, who initiated, who paid, and men's attitudes toward women. *Psychology of Women Quarterly, 9,* 297–310.

Seligman, C., Brickman, J., & Koulack, D. (1977). Rape and physical attractiveness: Assigning responsibility to victims. *Journal of Personality, 45,* 555–564.

Shaver, K. G. (1970). Defensive attribution: Effects of severity and relevance on the responsibility assigned for an accident. *Journal of Personality and Social Psychology, 14,* 101–113.

Shotland, R. L., & Goodstein, L. (1983). Just because she doesn't want to doesn't mean it's rape: An experimentally based causal model of perception of rape in a dating situation. *Social Psychology Quarterly, 46,* 220–232.

Sulzer, J. L., & Burglass, R. K. (1968). Responsibility attribution, empathy and punitiveness. *Journal of Personality, 36,* 272–282.

Tetreault, P. A., & Barnett, M. A. (1987). Reactions to stranger and acquaintance rape. *Psychology of Women Quarterly, 11,* 353–358.

Thornton, B., Ryckman, R. M., Kirchner, G., Jacobs, J., Kaczor, L., & Kuehnel, R. H. (1988). Reaction to self-attributed victim responsibility: A comparative analysis of rape crisis counselors and lay observers. *Journal of Applied Social Psychology, 18,* 409–422.

Walster, E. (1966). Assignment of responsibility for an accident. *Journal of Personality and Social Psychology, 3,* 73–79.

PART 3

Factors Contributing to Acquaintance Rape

CHAPTER 5

The Contribution of Sex-Role Socialization to Acquaintance Rape

ROBIN WARSHAW and ANDREA PARROT, PhD

From the moment children are born in the United States, their sex becomes an important factor in their social growth. In hospital nurseries, infants who are otherwise indistinguishable from each other are placed in cribs marked with pink or blue name tags so visitors will know which ones are girls and which are boys. What sex they are makes no difference to the newborns; their cribs are color-coded because the adults in their world consider that information significant.

As these babies become toddlers and then preschoolers, they are deluged with direct and indirect messages about how they are to behave based solely on their sex. These messages come from parents and relatives, other adults, siblings, and friends and from cultural media such as movies, television, books, and song lyrics. Even the most egalitarian parents cannot fully insulate their daughters or sons from being affected by many of the gender-linked roles society expects them to adopt.

For example, girls learn, early on, that they should be "sugar and spice and everything nice" while boys learn that they should be "snips and snails and puppy dogs' tails." The girls' labels sound sweet and passive. The boys' labels sound daring and active.

From such social imprints, many girls proceed along a "niceness" track. They learn that they are supposed to be friendly and to yield to others' needs and wants even if it means sacrificing their own. They may develop a sense of physical and intellectual helplessness in areas deemed unsuitable for females, such as physical achievement and mechanical ability. As girls grow into young womanhood, they often are discouraged from becoming self-reliant and independent. They learn to defer to men, to rely on men to provide them with social status, protection, and, ultimately, a secure future. Many of our society's rape-supportive attitudes and myths about rape are rooted in beliefs about appropriate behavior for women.

For example, if a woman is too friendly, men are likely to perceive her behavior as seduction (Abbey, 1982). If a woman gets drunk and goes back to a man's apartment after a party or a date, many people would say she deserves to be raped, because "nice" girls are not supposed to do those things and in a "just world" she is getting what she deserves. However, if a man gets drunk and forces himself sexually on a woman, his behavior is likely to be excused, because "he couldn't help himself."

Many boys are steered onto an "aggression" track that guides them toward a self-centered view of their place in society. They learn to set aside the needs of others, to use physical responses to beat an opponent when faced with conflict, and to equate showing empathy with being weak and "girlish." This training often leads to beliefs in sexual entitlement and social superiority over women. The result is a string of myths that boys and men are expected to live up to.

Given these divergent social development patterns, some of the travelers on the "niceness" track and some of those on the "aggression" track are on a collision course with each other. They may collide as preteens or teenagers in junior high and high schools or at after-school jobs; as young single adults in college or the workplace; or as marriage partners, dates, or friends in later years.

Whenever it happens, aggressive or assaultive behavior between people who know each other is not an isolated or even an unusual event in society at large. Koss (1988) reported that fewer than half of the undergraduate women she surveyed had *never had* an unwanted sexual aggression committed against them. Makepeace (1981) reported in his study of dating college-age students, that 14% had been pushed by a date or did the pushing, 13% were slapped by a date or did the slapping, and 4% were involved in punching incidents on dates.

Historically, sexual assault is not a new problem. Kirkpatrick and Kanin (1957) reported that more than half of the college women they studied had been sexually "offended" within the past year. Kanin (1967) also found that 25% of male college students reported having been sexually aggressive since the beginning of college. In 1980, Malamuth and Check reported that 17% of the males they sampled indicated some likelihood that they would rape a female, but 69% reported some likelihood that they would rape a female if they could be assured of not being punished.

The continuum of aggression escalates to produce victims and perpetra-tors in acquaintance rapes and date rapes. As pointed out by Weis and Borges (1973), dating brings together two people who may have firmly socialized roles regarding sex and social behavior—including expectations for the outcome of the date—that may be in opposition with each other. Such roles and expectations, coupled with the ambiguity of a dating relationship and the privacy in which it generally takes place, mean that dating can easily lead to rape. Koss (1988), in a survey of college women, learned that 84% of the rape victims knew the men who attacked them; 57% of the assaults happened on dates. Russell (1984) studied a random sample of women in San Francisco and found that 88% of the rape victims knew their attackers.

THE BATTLE OF THE SEXES

For many men and women, "the battle of the sexes" may be just that. From their socialization in childhood and adolescence, they developed different goals related to sexuality—goals that set them up as adversaries. Both groups learned that women, to maintain their own "worth," are supposed to control men's sexuality and that men are supposed to singlemindedly go after sexual intercourse with a female, regardless of how they do it. Both groups were influenced by traditional stereotypic sexual scripts: men should use any strategy to get women to have sexual intercourse and women should passively acquiesce or use any strategy to try to avoid sexual intercourse (LaPlante, McCormick, & Brannigan, 1980). Even if these patterns are known to be dysfunctional or dangerous by the actors, it is often easier and more comfortable for them to repeat familiar patterns than to counteract them (Burnstein, 1975).

Many men have stereotypic sexual scripts that are tempered by other moral and ethical influences, but a significant number do not. Kanin (1984) called these men, who are products of a hypermasculine, hypererotic peer group culture, "sexually predatory."

By the reasoning of this socialization, if intercourse happens, the woman has "let" the man do something to her. He has won and she has lost. No wonder that in his 1984 study of self-disclosed date rapists, Kanin found that two-thirds of the subjects felt the fault for the incident rested with the woman.

Koss (1988) and others, have found that opportunity is the best predictor of who will be raped but that a strong belief in macho attitudes is an important indicator of who will rape. Because the male sex role formed by socialization attitudes pushes boys toward goals of power, success, and aggression (Gross, 1978), it is not surprising that college males show a stronger belief in rape-supportive and sexist attitudes than do their female counterparts (Barnett & Feild, 1977).

Rape myth acceptance is associated with kissing a woman without her consent on a first date, in long-term dating, and within marriage (Margolin, Miller, & Moran, 1989). Disregarding a woman's feelings is usually the first step toward rape. Margolin et al. (1989) believed that the process of rape-supportive attitudes which leads to expressions of male sexual dominance usually occurs on an unconscious level. Unwanted intercourse usually results from four societal norms: male supremacy, male initiative, the expectation that women should not be sexually experienced, and the "stroking norm" for women (Lewin, 1985). The stroking norm results from the notion that women should put their man's needs before their own.

Men's social training tells them that they must initiate sexual activity and that women who say "no" don't really mean it. In fact, Muehlenhard and Hollabaugh (1988), in a study of 610 undergraduate women, discovered that 39% had engaged in "token resistance" (saying "no" when they did not mean it) at least once. These women believed that token resistance was common, that male/female relationships were adversarial, that it was acceptable for men to use physical force in male/female relationships, and that women enjoy it when men use force. These beliefs all relate to traditional sexual scripts in which women should exhibit an insincere display of resistance and men should be sexually aggressive and overcome the women's token resistance (Muehlenhard & Hollabaugh, 1988). When those factors combine with the commonly held belief that sex is a biological need for males but not for females (Peplau, Rubin, & Hill, 1977), some men develop feelings of entitlement to force sex (Rapaport & Burkhart, 1984).

Many men have been socialized to be deaf to women's objections to unwanted sexual aggression, even when women physically resist. Koss (1988) reported that 70% of the college women she surveyed (most raped by men they knew) physically fought with their attackers, but only 12% of the men who committed rape (nearly all against women they knew) said their victims had physically struggled.

Mahoney, Shively, and Traw (1986) believed that traditional male learning provides attitudes, beliefs, and motivations that make sexual assault possible. In addition, personal characteristics—such as lack of social conscience, irresponsibility, and attitudinal acceptance of sexual aggression—and/or situational characteristics—such as heavy alcohol consumption at a party, or peer pressure—lessen learned inhibitions against sexual assault (Mahoney et al., 1986).

Studies with children show that boys and girls expect different outcomes for aggressive behavior, and these expectations may color what happens in an acquaintance rape. Perry, Perry, and Weiss (1989) reported that girls expect to feel guilty and upset after being aggressive but boys believe aggression increases their self-esteem. The boys they studied said that aggression against a girl would win less disapproval from their male peers than aggression against a boy. Mahoney et al. (1986) found that the basis for sexual assault is rooted in normal aspects of traditional male learning, and the most important factors related to whether a woman will be sexually assaulted are the number of men a woman has had sexual intercourse with and the degree of her attraction to macho males.

In any battle, the outcome usually depends on which side has better fighting skills. Many women learn, through direct social messages as well as media images, that they are unable to physically protect themselves in the event of a rape attack. Young girls generally do not have opportunities (as boys do on the football field, for example) to learn that they can withstand a physical thrashing and still survive. Indeed, for years, many police departments have advocated that women simply give up in rape situations. The fear created by that often misguided advice is frequently enough to debilitate a woman from taking action that might prevent her from being raped. Running away, yelling, and kicking the man have all been shown to be among the most effective rape-thwarting strategies (Bart & O'Brien, 1985).

When faced with acquaintance rape, many women are disabled further by socially ingrained beliefs: A friend wouldn't hurt you; rapists are crazy strangers, not people you know; and so on. Sexual abuse is more common among people who believe rape myths, who don't believe that sexual assault is a problem, and who hold traditional views of women's role in American society (Peterson & Franzese, 1987). Women mistakenly believe that since the threat is coming from a man they know, they can reason or argue him out of it. Instead, talking or quarreling have been shown to more likely end in rape, with either strangers or acquaintances (Levine-MacCombie & Koss, 1986). Some women who would be willing to physically strike a stranger who is attacking them often hesitate to hurt someone they know.

The actual battle between the sexes may be encouraged by movies, television scripts, books, and magazines that depict women as really liking it when men are physically rough with them. That theme was clearly portrayed in "Gone with the Wind," when Rhett Butler and Scarlett O'Hara fought and he forcibly carried her upstairs against her will. The next morning, Scarlett was humming and smiling, presumably because she enjoyed being forced to have sex. Thousands of film and TV scripts have repeated that message since the landmark movie's release in 1939, and pornographic magazines and books have reiterated it in more explicit terms. On "General Hospital," for example, Luke raped Laura and she subsequently married him.

Men get these messages from childhood on and some turn them into action. Greendlinger and Byrne (1987) found among college men the likelihood to rape was correlated with coercive sexual fantasies in addition to rape-myth acceptance and aggressive tendencies. Abbey, Cozzarelli, McLaughlin, and Harnish (1987) found that the more revealing a woman's dress is, the more attractive and sexually desirable she is considered to be, but she is not regarded as "nice." In addition, males are likely to believe that females are more sexual than the women actually are and to overestimate the sexual intent of a woman they have contact with or merely observe (Abbey et al., 1987). Again, the pattern may be set early in their life. Eron and Huesmann (1984) reported that children who preferred watching violent television in elementary school took part in more violent behavior as adults than did those who had not had that preference when they were children.

Heilbrun and Loftus (1986) looked at this behavior in its extreme. They examined sexual sadism—in which the violence committed on the woman is itself sexually arousing to the man—among college males and found that "serious phenomena" of this kind were occurring among 30% of their subjects. Significantly, 60% of the men identified as attracted to sexual sadism had repeated episodes of unwanted sexual aggression.

A TYPICAL ACQUAINTANCE RAPE

In the course of researching *I Never Called It Rape,* Warshaw (1988) interviewed a woman whose story exemplifies how sex-role socialization contributes to rape between people who know each other. To protect their identities, the woman will be called Lori and the man who raped her, Eric. What follows is a narrative of her story, with some of her comments:

> Lori was 19 at the time of her rape; one year later, she talked with me about it. She knew Eric, who was in his mid-20s, because he was a customer at the restaurant where she worked. Eric's best friend wanted to date a friend of Lori's, but the young woman felt shy about dating alone and convinced Lori to join them and be Eric's date. Lori agreed.
>
> Unknown to Lori, her friend canceled the date the day before it was supposed to happen. Eric knew but didn't tell Lori. Instead he called her several times to make—and then change—their plans. Each time, he told her what they were going to do. Each time Lori agreed with his decision. Finally, he told her he was inviting some friends over to his house for a barbecue party. Again, she agreed with the plan.
>
> When they arrived at Eric's house, Lori asked about her friend and Eric's friend. Eric still didn't tell her they had canceled their date. "He kind of threw it off," Lori said of her attempt to bring up the subject of her friend's where-abouts. But that didn't raise her suspicions. "I didn't think anything of it," she said. "Not in my wildest dreams would I have thought he was plotting some-thing."
>
> The party broke up early. Lori thought that was odd, but she discounted her feelings of misgiving. "I've been known to overreact to things," she said, "so I ignored it." Even when Eric started to kiss her as they sat on his couch, she didn't think anything was wrong. In fact, she liked kissing him.
>
> Then the telephone rang and Eric answered it in another room. When he returned, Lori was standing up. He grabbed her from behind, put his hands across her eyes, and without saying a word, started walking her through his house. She didn't know what was happening. Moments later, he laid her down on what she discovered—as soon as he took his hands off her eyes—was a bed.
>
> "He starts taking off my clothes and I said, 'Wait—time out! This is not what I want.'" Eric told her that this was what she owed him because he made her dinner. Lori said, "This is wrong. Don't do this. I didn't go out with you with this intent."
>
> To which Eric said, "What do you call that on the couch?"
>
> "I call it a kiss, period," Lori replied.
>
> And Eric answered back, "Well, I don't."

Lori as a child was trained to be nice and to fulfill others' needs, so she had agreed to go out with Eric in order to help her friend. When Eric learned that Lori's friend had canceled her half of the double date, he decided not to tell Lori. He felt entitled to hide that information from her in order to get what he wanted—the date and sex. Eric also assumed that he was in charge of deciding where they would go and what they would do. Lori went along, thereby reinforcing Eric's belief in his right to control her. Eric ignored Lori's question. (Women's questions are unimportant to men, especially when they could create conflict with what men want.) Lori believed that men, especially men she dated or knew, were there to protect her. Like many women, Lori had learned to discount her own opinion and believed it's not nice to have misgivings about another person. Eric didn't ask Lori if she wanted to play this "game"; he was using his physical strength to take control. Lori didn't put up a fight. She didn't know what was happening, but it still didn't occur to her that the situation could be threatening. Eric felt entitled to take off Lori's clothes without her permission. He ignored Lori's clear statement that she didn't want him to undress her. Eric believed that since Lori kissed him she was agreeing to have intercourse. He rejected Lori's opinion again.

Soon things escalated even more. The two struggled a little and Lori managed to get free. She went into the bathroom.

"The whole time I'm thinking, 'I don't believe this is happening to me,'" she said. She walked out of the bathroom intending to ask Eric to take her home. Instead, he grabbed her, pushed her onto the bed, and started taking her clothes off again. Lori yelled, hit him, and tried to push him off her. Eric said, "I know you must like this because a lot of women like this kind of thing." Then he added, "This is the adult world. Maybe you ought to grow up some." Eric then raped her.

Afterward, he said, "Don't tell me you didn't like that." Lori said, "No."

She recalled, "By this time I'm crying because I don't know what else to do. I never heard of anybody having that happen to them." In the car headed back toward Lori's house, Eric asked her to go out with him again. When she stared at him in disbelief, he laughed.

For the next two weeks, Lori could barely function. She told no one about what happened because she blamed herself. Eric appeared in her restaurant one day and tried to hug her. When she pulled away, he said, "Oh, I guess you didn't get enough." Eventually Lori told her mother, decided not to press criminal charges against Eric, and moved several hundred miles away in order to avoid any further encounters with him.

In the second part of the narrative, Lori's sex-role socialization continued to affect the outcome of the incident. Despite all evidence, Lori still could not believe that the date was about to turn into a rape. Lori expected Eric to take care of her, even though she had just been physically struggling with him. Eric proved that Lori's wishes carried no weight with him. Eric believed that women always say "no" when they mean "yes" and that even physical resistance on the part of a woman is just part of the game women play. Lori was raised to trust men like Eric. She believed that only armed strangers commit rape. As far as Eric was concerned, Lori got what she deserved. "Nice" women don't get raped, Lori knew, so she must have somehow caused this thing to happen. It didn't occur to her to lay the blame where it belonged— with Eric. In Eric's mind, all he did was give Lori what *he* "knew she wanted." He also appeared to enjoy making degrading comments to her about their sexual relations. Lori felt powerless after the rape, especially because Eric remained in the community. Like most other acquaintance rape victims, she decided not to prosecute.

CONCLUSION

Messages we receive from family, the media, and peers socialize us to believe rape myths. Perhaps we can minimize acquaintance rape incidence by changing these socialization messages. Parent education on the dysfunction of current socialization and on how to socialize children in an egalitarian way is the first step. Letters to any television network, magazine, or paper that perpetuates these dysfunctional, rape-conducive myths and attitudes can express our disapproval. If the letters don't produce results, we can boycott the products that advertise in those media or boycott the media themselves.

Men and women are socialized to believe different messages. Men are socialized to think that they are supposed to have unquenchable sexual appetites, that they have a right to sex, and that women do not mean "no" when they say "no." A woman is socialized to think that nice men do not rape (and because she only dates nice men, she doesn't believe she will be raped); that if a woman is raped, it is her fault and she must have done something to bring it on; and that no one will believe her if she tells them that she was raped by someone she knows. Therefore, women are not likely to report an acquaintance rape—they think their assailant will not be arrested, will probably brag about the rape to his friends, and will probably rape other women—and the problem will continue. We need to create a society in which the sexual double standard is passé, men believe what women say, women say what they mean, women feel free to initiate sexually, and men are permitted to say "no" to sex without feeling that they have shirked their male duty and role. Only then will we stand a chance to reduce the incidence of acquaintance rape.

REFERENCES

Abbey, A. (1982). Sex differences in attributions for friendly behavior: Do males misperceive females' friendliness? *Journal of Personality and Social Psychology, 42,* 830–838.

Abbey, A., Cozzarelli, C., McLaughlin, K., & Harnish, R. (1987). The effects of clothing and dyad composition on perceptions of sexual intent: Do women and men evaluate these cues differently? *Journal of Applied Social Psychology, 17,* 108–126.

Barnett, N. J., & Feild, H. S. (1977). Sex differences in university students' attitudes toward rape. *Journal of College Student Personnel, 18,* 93–96.

Bart, P. B., & O'Brien, P. H. (1985). *Stopping rape: Successful survival strategies.* Elmsford, NY: Pergamon.

Burnstein, B. (1975, April). *Life history and current values as predictors of sexual behaviors and satisfaction in college women.* Paper presented at the meeting of the Western Psychological Association, Sacramento, CA.

Eron, L. D., & Huesmann, L. R. (1984). The control of aggressive behavior by changes in attitudes, values, and the conditions of learning. In R. Blanchard & C. Blanchard (Eds.), *Advances in aggression research, Vol. 1* (pp. 139–171). New York: Academic Press.

Greendlinger, V., & Byrne, D. (1987). Coercive sexual fantasies of college men as predictors of self-reported likelihood to rape and overt sexual aggression. *Journal of Sex Research, 23,* 1–11.

Gross, A. E. (1978). The male role and heterosexual behavior. *Journal of Social Issues, 34,* 87–107.

Heilbrun, Jr., A. B., & Loftus, M. P. (1986). The role of sadism and peer pressure in the sexual aggression of male college students. *Journal of Sex Research, 22,* 320–332.

Kanin, E. (1967). An examination of sexual aggression as a response to sexual frustration. *Journal of Marriage and the Family, 29,* 428–433.

Kanin, E. J. (1984). Date rape: Unofficial criminals and victims. *Victimology, 9,* 95–108.

Kirkpatrick, C., & Kanin, E. (1957). Male sexual aggression on a university campus. *American Sociological Review, 22,* 52–58.

Koss, M. P. (1988). Hidden rape: Incidence, prevalence, and descriptive characteristics of sexual aggression and victimization in a national sample of college students. In A. W. Burgess (Ed.), *Sexual Assault, Vol. II* (pp. 3–25). New York: Garland.

LaPlante, M. N., McCormick, N., & Brannigan, G. G. (1980). Living the sexual script: College students' views of influence in sexual encounters. *Journal of Sex Research, 16,* 338–355.

Levine-MacCombie, J., & Koss, M. P. (1986). Acquaintance rape: Effective avoidance strategies. *Psychology of Women Quarterly, 10,* 311–320.

Lewin, M. (1985). Unwanted intercourse: The difficulty of saying no. *Psychology of Women Quarterly, 9,* 184–192.

Mahoney, E. R., Shively, M. D., & Traw, M. (1986). Sexual coercion and assault: Male socialization and female risk. *Sexual Coercion & Assault, 1,* 2–8.

Makepeace, J. M. (1981). Courtship violence among college students. *Family Relations, 30,* 97–102.

Malamuth, N. M., & Check, J. V. P. (1980). Penile tumescence and perceptual responses to rape as a function of victim's perceived reactions. *Journal of Applied Social Psychology, 10,* 528–547.

Margolin, L., Miller, M., & Moran, P. B. (1989). When a kiss is not just a kiss: Relating violations of consent in kissing to rape myth acceptance. *Sex Roles, 20,* 231–243.

Muehlenhard, C. L., & Hollabaugh, L. C. (1988). Do women sometimes say no when they mean yes? The prevalence and correlates of women's token resistance to sex. *Journal of Personality and Social Psychology, 54,* 872–879.

Peplau, L. A., Rubin, Z., & Hill, C. T. (1977). Sexual intimacy in dating relationships. *Journal of Social Issues, 33,* 86–109.

Perry, D. G., Perry, L. C., & Weiss, R. J. (1989). Sex differences in the consequences that children anticipate for aggression. *Developmental Psychology, 25,* 1–8.

Peterson, S. A., & Franzese, B. (1987). Correlates of college men's sexual abuse of women. *Journal of College Student Personnel, 28,* 223–228.

Rapaport, K., & Burkhart, B. R. (1984). Personality and attitudinal characteristics of sexually coercive college males. *Journal of Abnormal Psychology, 93,* 216–221.

Russell, D. E. H. (1984). *Sexual exploitation.* Beverly Hills, CA: Sage.

Warshaw, R. (1988). *I never called it rape: The Ms. report on recognizing, fighting, and surviving date and acquaintance rape.* New York: Harper & Row.

Weis, K., & Borges, S. (1973). Victimology and rape: The case of the legitimate victim. *Issues in Criminology, 8,* 71–115.

CHAPTER 6

Alcohol and Acquaintance Rape

DEBORAH R. RICHARDSON and GEORGINA S. HAMMOCK

> We had been separated and I was still staying in the same apartment we had
> lived in. He came over one night real drunk. He can't handle drinking at all.
> He started bamming on the door, and broke it down. He wanted to have sex but
> I didn't want to. He pushed me, knocked me down, and tore all my clothes off.
> I was hollering and screaming and wouldn't keep still, so he just slapped me
> across the face and made me have sex.
>
> *(Russell, 1982, p. 166)*

The woman who told this story was raped by an acquaintance—her husband. She thought alcohol was a contributing factor in the rape. People often
assume that extenuating circumstances, such as the drunkenness of a perpetrator and/or a victim, provide explanations for violent incidents. The purpose of this chapter is to examine the extent to which alcohol plays a role in
acquaintance rape.

Alcohol is often consumed in situations that might involve sexual interaction, perhaps because people expect that alcohol will enhance their sexual
encounters (Athanasiou, Shaver, & Tavris, 1970; Rockwell, Ellinwood, &
Kantor, 1973). As Crowe and George (1989) stated, "Alcohol is considered
to be a tool of seduction, a measure of manhood, a giver of sexual courage,
and a trumpet against the walls of social restraint" (p. 374). Thus, we should
not be surprised to discover that alcohol may indeed play a role in sexual
aggression.

Three specific questions will guide our discussion of the role of alcohol in
acquaintance rape:

1. How often is the victim and/or perpetrator under the influence of
   alcohol when the rape occurs? We will report the incidence of alcohol-
   related acquaintance rape.
2. Is alcohol a cause of acquaintance rape? We will review some experimental investigations that examine the role of alcohol and alcohol
   expectancies in such incidents.
3. To what extent does drunkenness serve as an excuse for otherwise unacceptable behavior? We will consider the issue of alcohol as an excuse.

The cause-versus-excuse debate sets up a false dichotomy. Alcohol can, and often does, operate as both a facilitator of rape and as an excuse for it.

INCIDENCE

The first step in determining the role of alcohol in acquaintance rape is to establish the frequency with which the perpetrator and/or the victim are drinking alcohol at the time of or immediately preceding the incident. Because of the paucity of data on this topic, we will extrapolate from the few studies that present any relevant statistics. In addition, we will examine the strengths and weaknesses of the causal inferences made by the researchers.

To determine the incidence of and the risk factors associated with sexual aggression, Muehlenhard and Linton (1987) asked male and female college students to report on their sexual activities during dates. The researchers were particularly concerned with the incidence of "unwanted sexual activity," defined as "when the female does not want to engage in some sexual activity, and she makes this clear to the male either verbally or nonverbally, but he does it anyway. The unwanted sexual activity could be anything ranging from kissing to sexual intercourse" (p. 188). If the students indicated that they had experienced unwanted sexual activity at any time, they were asked to describe their worst experience. For comparison purposes, the students were asked to report on sexual activities during their most recent date. In each case, students indicated how much alcohol (or other intoxicating substance) they and their date had consumed. The researchers reported that the consumption of alcohol was related to the occurrence of unwanted sexual activity. Dates on which unwanted sexual activity had occurred were more likely than recent dates to have involved heavy use (acting or feeling moderately or extremely intoxicated) of alcohol or other drugs. The authors speculated that "alcohol reduces men's inhibitions against violence, provides an excuse for sexual aggression, and reduces women's ability to resist" (p. 194).

The prototype of acquaintance rape is forced sexual intercourse on a date; however, marital rape, another type of acquaintance rape in which husbands force intercourse on their wives, is a widespread occurrence. Two studies provide information about the extent to which alcohol is a factor in marital rape. Based on her interviews with women who had been raped by their husbands, Russell (1982) reported that 20–25% of the husbands had been drinking at the time they committed the rape (24% of the husbands were described as habitual drinkers). Frieze (1983) interviewed 137 battered women and a matched sample of women who had not reported battering by their husbands. Although Frieze did not report the actual frequency of alcohol use on the part of victims or their husbands, she indicated that 14% of the women who had been raped attributed the rape to their husband's drinking. She also reported that, when compared with the men who battered but did not rape their wives, the raping husbands were more likely to have been drunk when violent.

Scully and Marolla (1984) interviewed incarcerated convicted rapists of adult women, to determine their excuses and/or justifications for having committed the crime. Thirty-one percent of the rapists were acquainted with their victim; 75% mentioned in their account of the incident that they had consumed alcohol or other drugs; 44% reported that the victim had consumed alcohol or drugs. Unfortunately, because Scully and Marolla did not differentiate between acquaintance and stranger rapes, there is no way to determine whether alcohol was more or less likely to have been a factor in acquaintance or in stranger rapes.

Each of the studies mentioned above has some weakness that precludes a confident estimate of the extent to which alcohol is a factor in acquaintance rape. For example, Russell (1982) did not specifically ask the raped wives about alcohol consumption. She noted such information only if it was mentioned during the interview with the wife; therefore, Russell's 20–25% estimate may be conservative. Muehlenhard and Linton (1987) reported the incidence of heavy alcohol use among initiators and victims of *any* unwanted sexual activity; this general category does not allow us to determine whether forced *intercourse* was more or less likely to have involved consumption of alcohol or other drugs than were other unwanted sexual activities.

In general, the role of alcohol is not clear in these data; we cannot determine whether alcohol actually increases the probability of an acquaintance rape or whether it is only an excuse that people use to explain their own or another person's unusual or unacceptable behavior. Perhaps those involved in and those who observe an incident would be more likely to remember that someone was "under the influence" if an unpleasant or violent act occurred than if no such act took place. Indeed, people may be likely to remember the presence of alcohol only when they need to explain or find reasons for an unpleasant incident.

EXPERIMENTAL STUDIES

Studies in which the experimenter manipulates the consumption of alcohol and examines its effects on behavior have both advantages and disadvantages, when researchers are trying to understand acts of violence. The primary advantage is that such studies allow inferences about causation: With the ability to manipulate the amount of alcohol consumed by research participants, the researcher can determine whether alcohol facilitates aggressive behaviors. The major disadvantage of experimental approaches involves the extent to which researchers can reasonably generalize from behavior in the laboratory (under the watchful eyes of the experimenter) to behavior in the "real" world. Rape is a relatively infrequent behavior and one that most people would consider to be highly inappropriate. Certainly, it is not possible to set up laboratory situations in which subjects' likely response to being drunk would be to rape someone. Thus, experiments lack ecological validity because it is not possible to directly observe the specific behavior of interest in the setting in which it normally occurs. Nevertheless, by combining the results of experimental and nonexperimental investigations, we may be able to draw some useful conclusions regarding the role alcohol plays in acquaintance rape.

This section reviews experimental studies that address some aspect of sexual aggression—either the aggressive nature of such interactions and/or their sexual components.

Alcohol and Aggression Toward Women

Most laboratory studies that have examined levels of aggression directed toward male and female targets report that women are less likely to be targets of aggression (or are targets of lower levels of aggression) than are males (Baron, 1977). However, Richardson (1981) pointed out that the data from laboratory studies are not consistent with the incidence of real-world violence against women (especially rape and wife abuse), and she proposed that alcohol may be an important factor in reducing inhibitions against causing harm to women. To determine whether alcohol can serve as a facilitator of male aggression toward female targets, she gave alcohol (1.5 ounces per 40 pounds of body weight) to one-half of a group of male subjects; the other half consumed a drink without alcohol. (Neither group was told whether they had received alcohol.) The subjects then had an opportunity to aggress against a female target by delivering painful shocks during a reaction-time task. The results supported the notion that alcohol serves to remove constraints against harming women. The drunk males directed more aggression toward the female target than the sober males did.

We mentioned previously that a disadvantage of generalizing from laboratory studies is that the studies do not deal directly with acquaintance rape. The male subject and the female target in the Richardson study were acquainted only through their participation in the experiment, and there was no sexual aspect to their interaction. This "problem," however, does not invalidate the data or their relevance to real-world aggression against women. First, although acquaintance rape is a specific type of aggression, the behavior is nevertheless a form of sexual *aggression*. Second, considering that people are more likely to cause harm to people they know well than to people they do not know well (Berscheid & Walster, 1978), and considering the inhibitions that exist when behavior is public (as in a laboratory), the data from this study probably provide a conservative estimate of the influence of alcohol on males' aggression toward females.

Alcohol and Sexual Arousal

After reviewing the literature on alcohol and human sexuality, Crowe and George (1989) concluded that "alcohol disinhibits psychological sexual arousal and suppresses physiological responding" (p. 384). This conclusion is supported by the findings of many scientific investigations. Rather than review the evidence on the link between consumption of alcohol and general sexual arousal, we focus in this section on the relationship between alcohol and "deviant" sexual behavior. We are concentrating on studies that assessed responses to sexually aggressive stimuli (rather than merely sexual stimuli).

Most of these studies were designed to examine simultaneously the effect of expectancy and the effect of actual consumption of alcohol. This type of research design is particularly important for determining whether alcohol is a facilitator of sexual aggression or merely serves as a justification for otherwise unacceptable behavior. Expectancy refers to the subject's belief about whether he or she has consumed alcohol. In these studies, researchers are able to determine whether the alcohol itself (i.e., differences between those who have and those who have not consumed alcohol) or the subject's expectancies regarding the effect of alcohol (i.e., differences between those who believe they have consumed alcohol and those who believe they have not) influence behavior.

Briddell et al. (1978) argued that alcohol may not directly increase sexual arousal; rather, the expectancies associated with consumption of alcohol may be the most important factor in affecting sexual arousal. After manipulating alcohol consumption and expectancy as reviewed above, subjects were exposed to three different kinds of audiotaped erotic stimuli: mutually enjoyable intercourse, forcible rape (including use of physical force and a weapon), and sadistic aggression (without sexual activity). Physiological recordings that measured degree of penile erection indicated higher levels of sexual arousal when the males thought they had consumed alcohol than when they thought they had not. Actual consumption of alcohol did not have a significant effect on sexual arousal. The effect of expectancy occurred only when the males heard the rape and sadistic aggression tapes; neither consumption of alcohol nor alcohol expectancy affected response to the mutually enjoyable intercourse tape. When later asked to evaluate the effect of the beverage they had consumed, subjects who had actually consumed alcohol and those who believed they had consumed alcohol reported that their beverage had increased sexual arousal.

Citing evidence that rapists show more arousal to sexually deviant stimuli than do nonrapists (Abel, Barlow, Blanchard, & Guild, 1977), Briddell et al. (1978) concluded that "normal heterosexual males who have been drinking (or believe they have been drinking) may exhibit sexual arousal patterns indistinguishable from those patterns reported for identified rapists" (p. 427). They suggested that the effect of alcohol expectancy is to offer an excuse for otherwise unacceptable behavior.

The importance of alcohol expectancies has been demonstrated in other experimental investigations. Lang, Searles, Lauerman, and Adesso (1980) reported that alcohol expectancy increased interest in pornographic slides. George and Marlatt (1986) found that subjects who believed they had consumed alcohol watched erotic, violent, and violent–erotic stimuli longer than did subjects who believed they had not consumed alcohol.

These experimental studies do not allow us to settle definitively the issue of cause-versus-excuse. Whereas Richardson suggested that alcohol facilitates male aggression toward females, the studies in which expectancy has been manipulated suggest that alcohol may serve as an excuse for unacceptable sexual arousal (and perhaps for unacceptable sexual behavior). Crowe and George (1989) concluded that alcohol expectancies facilitate both physiological and self-reported arousal in men and that those expectancies provide "social permission or personal permission or both, to indulge in otherwise unacceptable behavior" (p. 380). The final section of this chapter examines the process by which alcohol may serve as both a facilitator and an excuse.

PERCEPTIONS OF RESPONSIBILITY

The studies we reviewed in the previous section demonstrated relationships between self-reported use of alcohol and incidence of rape, between controlled ingestion of alcohol and resultant aggressive behavior, and between alcohol expectancies and arousal by sexually deviant stimuli. Clearly, expectancies regarding the influence of alcohol affect responses of people who are consuming (or think they are consuming) alcohol. Crowe and George (1989) suggested that these expectancies disinhibit behavior in two ways. First, people who have consumed alcohol can blame their feelings or actions on that substance and thereby avoid accepting personal responsibility. Second, people can expect that others who observe their inappropriate behaviors will excuse them if they know they were drinking; that is, they expect others to attribute their behavior to the effect of alcohol. In this section, we consider the excuse-giving function of intoxication, by examining literature on the effect of victim and perpetrator drunkenness on judgments of responsibility and blame for rape. In essence, if individuals are held less accountable for a rape when they are drunk, then alcohol may be operating as an excuse.

This issue is not only relevant to the excuse-versus-cause debate; it also has general relevance to the study of how individuals "explain" or determine responsibility in cases of rape. Jurors, judges, family, police officers, friends, attorneys, and the victims and perpetrators themselves, often are motivated to determine accountability for rape. Any factor, such as intoxication of the victim and/or the rapist, that influences those judgments should be recognized. If such biases exist, their recognition could lead not only to more understanding of the plight of the rape victim but also to fairer legal proceedings and more helpful therapy.

Rapists' own perceptions of the effect of alcohol demonstrate how intoxication of the rapist and the victim can offer an excuse for socially deviant behavior by reducing the individual's own sense of personal responsibility. When Scully and Marolla (1984) interviewed convicted rapists, they collected data about both the actual use of alcohol or drugs prior to the rape and the rapists' perceptions of the effect of these substances. The rapists were classified by the researchers as either Admitters (those who acknowledged the action as rape) or Deniers (those who admitted sexual contact but denied rape). Admitters and Deniers considered the role of alcohol or drugs somewhat differently. Admitters were more likely than Deniers to suggest that alcohol consumption was a cause of or a contributing factor to their deviant behavior. They considered their intoxication an explanation for their behavior. Deniers, however, used alcohol consumption as an excuse: They accused their victims of being drunk or high when they raped them, and either denied taking any substances themselves or claimed they were unaffected by them. In this manner, the Deniers were able to increase the victim's responsibility for the act while lowering their own responsibility. Some even went so far as to suggest that the substances the victim had consumed aroused her. Thus, rapists apparently attempt to use their own or their victim's intoxication as an explanation or excuse.

To examine the perceptions of third parties (individuals other than the victim or the rapist), Richardson and Campbell (1982) asked male and female subjects to make judgments about the relative blame, the responsibility, and the character of a victim and a perpetrator in a rape case. Research participants read a scenario which described a rape incident in which a woman (who was drunk or sober) was raped by a man (drunk or sober) whom she had just met at a party she had given. Although the rapist received a majority of the blame overall, he was perceived to be less blameworthy and less responsible for the rape when he was drunk than when he was sober. The victim, on the other hand, was judged to be more responsible when she had been drinking than when she had not. In addition, a drunk rapist was rated less negatively on dimensions of character than a sober rapist, but victims were rated more negatively if drunk than if sober. As Richardson and Campbell (1982) predicted, alcohol served as an excuse *only for the rapist;* the victim was seen to be *more* responsible when she was drunk. This finding was explained in terms of perceivers' need to "make sense of" an unusual and unacceptable event. In the interest of trying to see the world as a fair or just place, perceivers may try to find excuses for the inappropriate behavior of the rapist and search for some reason to blame the seemingly blameless victim. Intoxication serves both of these needs well. It offers an excuse for the rapist and a reason to blame the victim.

Although Richardson and Campbell (1982) presented a situation in which the victim and the rapist were somewhat acquainted with one another, their study was not designed to deal specifically with acquaintance rape. One might expect that the degree of acquaintance between the rapist and the victim might moderate observers' judgments of the effects of intoxication—the closer the relationship between the victim and the rapist, the more difficult it might be to understand or explain how a rape could occur. Close relationships generally are not thought of as an appropriate context for violence or force. Thus, when the rapist and the victim have a relatively close relationship, perceivers should be even more inclined to use intoxication of the rapist and/or the victim as an excuse or reason for the occurrence of the incident.

Hammock and Richardson (1989) conducted a study to examine the effects of the degree of acquaintance between the victim and the rapist on observers' judgments of responsibility and blame. Again, the victim and rapist were each presented as being either intoxicated or sober. The rapist in this study was the victim's boyfriend (they had been dating for three years), her date (they had gone out three times before), or a relative stranger (they had just met at a party). Subjects were asked to assign percentages of blame (to total 100%) to the rapist, the victim, and the situation, and to evaluate the character of the victim and the rapist on several adjective scales. (The high correlations among the adjective ratings allowed use of a sum score to indicate *overall evaluation* of the rapist and victim.)

The effects for rapist intoxication replicated the effects found in the Richardson and Campbell (1982) study. Although the rapist generally was held more responsible and received more blame than either the victim or the situation, he was blamed less and held less responsible when drunk than when sober. And, he was perceived to be *most* responsible when both he and the victim were sober. Rapists also were evaluated less negatively when they were drunk than when they were sober.

Responsibility and blame to the victim were not affected by her degree of intoxication; rather, the nature of the relationship with the rapist and the *rapist's* degree of intoxication influenced assignment of responsibility and blame to the victim. She was seen as more responsible when the rapist was a relative stranger or a date than when he was her boyfriend. The victim also was seen to be more responsible for the rape if the man was drunk than if he was sober. On the evaluation measure, drunk victims were rated more negatively than sober victims.

Situational responsibility varied as a function of both the rapist's and the victim's intoxication. When either party was drunk, the situation was blamed more than when either was sober. Alcohol is the factor most frequently mentioned by research participants when they are asked to identify specific situational influences on a violent encounter (Richardson & Campbell, 1980, 1982). Thus, when either party was drunk, subjects considered that the alcohol consumed by the rapist and/or the victim deserved some blame for the occurrence of the rape.

The nature of the relationship between rapist and victim had little effect on subjects' perceptions. Date- or boyfriend-rapists were evaluated less negatively when they were drunk than when they were sober. Intoxication of a stranger-rapist did not affect the evaluation of him.

We had expected that the nature of the relationship between the victim and the rapist would moderate the effects of their intoxication on perceivers' judgments of responsibility and blame. This clearly did not happen. The fact that intoxicated boyfriend- and date-rapists were evaluated less negatively than sober ones lent some support to our predictions. The closeness of the relationship between the rapist and the victim, however, was not nearly as powerful an influence on observers' perceptions as we had expected.

Subjects' responses to questions about harm to the victim suggested that they considered the acquaintance rape to be just as much of a rape as the stranger rape. For example, regardless of the relationship between the parties, subjects recognized that violence had occurred in the interaction between the man and the woman. This may explain why we saw so few effects of victim–rapist relationship. As college students receive education about rape and its effects, they may be more likely to recognize forced intercourse for what it is; regardless of the relationship between the parties, rape is *rape.* Our data were collected at two campuses where efforts had been made to educate students about date rape. Perhaps those efforts had been successful (or, at least, the students recognized the "appropriate" responses to the questions we posed). Indeed, it might be interesting to compare the responses of "educated" and "uneducated" samples to determine the appropriateness of our explanation for these results.

In sum, it seems that the intoxication of a rapist and a victim influences both the degree to which they are considered to be responsible and blame-worthy and observers' general evaluations of them. Rapists are "excused" (by themselves and others) if they are intoxicated at the time of the event. They are also liked more if they are drunk when they commit the rape. The effects of victim intoxication vary as a function of whose perceptions are being measured. Convicted rapists who deny that they raped a woman consider her intoxication to have been a very important factor. Perceivers who were not directly involved in the incident do not seem to use the victim's degree of intoxication as a determinant of the extent of her responsibility for the event. However, they do evaluate the intoxicated victim more negatively than they evaluate the sober one.

Can we conclude that alcohol serves as an excuse in cases of rape? Clearly, rapists, regardless of their relationship with their victim, are held less accountable for the rape if they are intoxicated at the time they commit the crime; alcohol serves as a retroactive justification for the behavior of the male in these situations. However, *the excuse only works for the rapists.* To the extent that victim intoxication influences judgments, it operates to increase rather than decrease the victim's perceived responsibility for the event.

This effect of victim intoxication may be related to our society's sexual double standard, under which sexual behavior is riskier for women because of social norms and because of the possibility of pregnancy. Studies of the effect of alcohol expectancy on sexual arousal found that women do not show the same loss of inhibitions after low doses of alcohol that men do. These findings have been attributed to the fact that the greater sexual inhibitions of women can only be overcome by relatively powerful excuses (Crowe & George, 1989); the expectancy of relatively low doses of alcohol is simply too weak to overcome the women's strong inhibitions. The perceivers in the studies reported above may have been using similar reasoning: they may have expected that the victim should have been inhibited. In fact, she should have been so inhibited that the consumption of alcohol could not affect her behavior. Thus, intoxication could not decrease the amount of blame she received for the rape.

The results of these studies also have clear relevance for the experience of actual rapists and victims. First, intoxication of the perpetrator and/or the victim is likely to influence how they are viewed by attorneys and jurors. For example, Critchlow (1983) reported that drunk offenders are less likely to be brought to trial than are sober offenders. In addition, a bias against drunk rape victims might influence the responses of rape counselors and the experience of the victims themselves. A woman who was intoxicated at the time she was raped might hold herself more responsible for the rape or might fear a negative evaluation from others. In either case, she would be unlikely to report the crime to authorities or to seek help from a counselor.

HOW DOES ALCOHOL WORK?

We have reviewed a relatively wide variety of studies that have examined the probable role of alcohol in rape. As we suggested earlier, the effect of alcohol in these situations involves a relatively complex process that includes both cognitive and physiological responses.

Models of the effect of alcohol on social behavior offer explanations for the effect of alcohol in cases of rape (Crowe & George, 1989; Steele & Southwick, 1985; Taylor & Leonard, 1983; Wilson, 1981). Many social situations, especially those involving the possibility of sexual interaction, involve conflict that derives from the presence of both instigative and inhibitory cues; one may be simultaneously hesitant toward and interested in engaging in sexual activity. There is considerable evidence that intoxication leads to impairment of performance on relatively complex tasks that require central processing and integration of information (e.g., simultaneous attention to different stimuli, memory, complex problem solving). Because an intoxicated person has a lessened ability to attend simultaneously to multiple cues and to switch attention from one informational source to another, a relatively small number of situational cues will be attended to. Multiple cues from a variety of channels are typical of most interpersonal interactions. These multiple cues may be either internal (e.g., conflict between instigative and inhibitory cues) or external (e.g., verbal and/or nonverbal communication from the other person). Taylor and Leonard (1983) suggested that intoxicated individuals may deal with this confusion of multiple cues by focusing on the most salient aspects of the situation. They will be more responsive to immediate, apparent cues than to more subtle cues and they may have difficulty reading nonverbal cues.

In addition to the confusion of multiple cues, the intoxicated person is likely to be disinhibited because of his or her expectancies regarding the effect of alcohol. Also, the high degree of cognitive processing capacity demanded to initiate inhibition (Steele & Southwick, 1985) would not be available to the intoxicated individual; that is, the effect of the alcohol may disrupt the individual's ability to process the complexities of appropriate social behavior.

Crowe and George (1989) recognized the implications of these models for the occurrence of alcohol-related sexual aggression. Presumably, inhibitions against sexual aggression are stronger than the desire to engage in such behavior, unless "they are sufficiently weakened by such things as rape myths or belief in alcohol's excuse-giving qualities" (p. 383). Once weakened, the inhibitions might be overcome "simply by alcohol's general impairment of inhibition" (p. 383). Thus, both expectancies regarding the effect of alcohol and the actual effect of alcohol may contribute to the occurrence of sexual aggression.

This explanation may help us to understand how alcohol could operate in acquaintance rape situations. In the prototype of acquaintance rape, a rape during a date, a drunk male may be exposed to a variety of cues. He may have some expectation of sexual activity and of the influence of alcohol on his behavior; the female would presumably be responding to him in a relatively warm and friendly fashion, as would be typical on a date; and if he begins to initiate sexual activity in which she is not interested, her first communication of disinterest may be relatively subtle (e.g., removing his hands from her person, or moving away from him). When he is drunk, he is less likely to respond to subtle inhibitory cues and more likely to respond to more salient instigative cues (some of which may be provided by his imagination). His inability to deal with the complexity of multiple cues in the situation may increase the probability that he will use some form of coercion or force. This situation could be even more instigative if the female also is drunk, because she may be having difficulty reading cues from him; she may be slow to realize his intentions and therefore slow to offer inhibitory signals to discourage him.

This example is not intended to offer an excuse for a drunk male's pursuit of sexual activity beyond the point of the interest of his victim. Rather, we are trying to identify the process that may account for the presumed role of alcohol in acquaintance rape. There is considerable evidence for such a process in aggressive interactions (when the salient cues are hostile and threatening rather than sexual), and we might well expect similar processes in the case of acquaintance rape.

CONCLUSION

The data and model we have presented suggest that alcohol affects victims and perpetrators in a variety of ways that may enhance the probability that a rape will occur. Although the data do not allow us to determine conclusively that alcohol *causes* date rape, they suggest some steps that might be taken to decrease the probability that alcohol or other disinhibiting drugs will influence the behavior of a potential victim or perpetrator.

The most obvious step to take is education. Both males and females need to be made aware of the effect that alcohol might have on their sexual and aggressive behaviors. Private and public agencies have instituted public-education campaigns aimed at providing information about the effects of alcohol on activities such as driving or making business decisions. However, no major effort has been made to educate the public about the effects of intoxication on sexual and aggressive behavior. Instead, alcohol often is portrayed as a way to overcome shyness or social anxiety or as the means to a more pleasant sexual encounter. Perhaps this lack of information reflects a tendency to keep sexual matters in a shroud of secrecy. Educational programs directed toward increasing awareness of the effects of alcohol on judgments about the willingness of a person to engage in sexual behavior and on an individual's ability to understand subtle cues of interest and disinterest might help lead to a decline in the incidence of date rape. At the very least, they could result in a greater understanding of how the intoxication of victims and rapists affects perceptions of blame and responsibility. That education then might translate into a more supportive and less accusing environment for victims of acquaintance rape.

REFERENCES

Abel, G. G., Barlow, D. H., Blanchard, E. B., & Guild, D. (1977). The components of rapists' sexual arousal. *Archives of General Psychiatry, 34,* 895–908.

Athanasiou, R., Shaver, P., & Tavris, C. (1970, July). Sex. *Psychology Today,* pp. 37–52.

Baron, R. A. (1977). *Human aggression.* New York: Plenum.

Berscheid, E., & Walster, E. (1978). *Interpersonal attraction.* Reading, MA: Addison-Wesley.

Briddell, D. W., Rimm, D. C., Caddy, G. R., Krawitz, G., Sholis, D., & Wunderlin, R. J. (1978). Effects of alcohol and cognitive set on sexual arousal to deviant stimuli. *Journal of Abnormal Psychology, 87,* 418–430.

Critchlow, B. (1983). Blaming the booze: The attribution of responsibility for drunken behavior. *Personality and Social Psychology Bulletin, 9,* 451–473.

Crowe, L. C., & George, W. H. (1989). Alcohol and human sexuality: Review and integration. *Psychological Bulletin, 105,* 374–386.

Frieze, I. H. (1983). Investigating the causes and consequences of marital rape. *Signs, 8,* 532–553.

George, W. H., & Marlatt, G. A. (1986). The effects of alcohol and anger on interest in violence, erotica, and deviance. *Journal of Abnormal Psychology, 95,* 150–158.

Hammock, G. S., & Richardson, D. R. (1989). *The effect of rapist and victim intoxication and relationship on attributions of blame for rape.* Unpublished manuscript.

Lang, A. R., Searles, J., Lauerman, R., & Adesso, V. (1980). Expectancy, alcohol, and sex guilt as determinants of interest in and reaction to sexual stimuli. *Journal of Abnormal Psychology, 89,* 644–653.

Muehlenhard, C. L., & Linton, M. A. (1987). Date rape and sexual aggression in dating situations: Incidence and risk factors. *Journal of Counseling Psychology, 34,* 186–196.

Richardson, D. C. (1981). The effect of alcohol on male aggression toward female targets. *Motivation and Emotion, 5,* 333–344.

Richardson, D. C., & Campbell, J. L. (1980). Alcohol and wife abuse: The effect of alcohol on attributions of blame for wife abuse. *Personality and Social Psychology Bulletin, 6,* 51–56.

Richardson, D., & Campbell, J. (1982). The effect of alcohol on attributions of blame for rape. *Personality and Social Psychology Bulletin, 8,* 468–476.

Rockwell, K., Ellinwood, E., & Kantor, C. (1973). Drugs and sex: Scene of ambivalence. *Journal of the American College Health Association, 21,* 483–488.

Russell, D. E. H. (1982). *Rape in marriage.* New York: Macmillan.

Scully, D., & Marolla, J. (1984). Convicted rapists' vocabulary of motive: Excuses and justifications. *Social Problems, 31,* 530–544.

Steele, C. M., & Southwick, L. (1985). Alcohol and social behavior I: The psychology of drunken excess. *Journal of Personality and Social Psychology, 48,* 18–34.

Taylor, S. P., & Leonard, K. E. (1983). Alcohol and human physical aggression. In R. G. Geen & E. I. Donnerstein (Eds.), *Aggression: Theoretical and empirical reviews* (Vol. 2, pp. 77–102). New York: Academic Press.

Wilson, G. T. (1981). The effects of alcohol on human sexual behavior. In N. Mello (Ed.), *Advances in substance abuse* (Vol. 2, pp. 1–40). Greenwich, CT: JAI Press.

CHAPTER 7

Misperception as an Antecedent of Acquaintance Rape: A Consequence of Ambiguity in Communication Between Women and Men

ANTONIA ABBEY, PhD

The basic premise underlying the research described in this chapter is that in American society it is difficult to distinguish friendly cues from sexual cues. This ambiguity makes it difficult for people to decide whether certain words or actions are signs of platonic friendliness or of sexual attraction. How do people show liking? They smile, listen carefully, agree, and maintain eye contact (Heslin & Patterson, 1982). How do people display sexual interest? Again they smile, listen carefully, agree, and maintain eye contact (Muehlenhard, Koralewski, Andrews, & Burdick, 1986; Shotland & Craig, 1988). Many of the cues are similar, particularly those that occur early in the interaction sequence. This overlap in the cues used to convey friendliness and seduction insures that misperceptions of sexual intent will occur frequently.

For example, suppose a man asks to share a woman's table at a crowded delicatessen. To be polite, she asks him where he works and discovers that they both are in the same profession. They have a lively conversation about a variety of issues and laugh together several times. As she gets ready to go, he asks her if they could get together some evening after work. She blushes and tells him that she is married. He apologizes and leaves rather quickly. This example introduces several issues that are described in more detail in this chapter: (a) misperceptions of sexual intent occur frequently; (b) men more often misperceive women's attempts to be friendly as indicative of sexual interest than vice versa; (c) both parties may feel awkward and embarrassed when these misperceptions occur; and (d) most misperceptions are easily resolved.

Although many misperceptions are quickly corrected, some are not, and these can end in acquaintance rape. Consider an example of misperception involving a man and a woman who meet at a party. She is wearing tight jeans and a low-cut shirt. They both have several beers and dance and laugh together. She agrees to let him walk her home and come inside to talk. Later, when she resists his sexual advances, he gets angry, pushes her down, and forces her to have sexual intercourse with him. In this example, the male misperceived a series of cues throughout the evening (e.g., the woman's clothing, alcohol consumption, and willingness to be alone with him). He may have felt justified forcing sex because he felt he had been teased and led on.

Most Americans feel uncomfortable discussing sexual intentions and desires, particularly if they think their sexual interest may not be reciprocated. Consequently, people try to infer sexual intent from indirect verbal and nonverbal cues rather than through frank discussion. Such deductive strategies are bound to produce frequent errors. Bernard's (1969) observations about "the sex game," which were made more than 20 years ago, are unfortunately still true:

> Hints and innuendo, by communicating less than the whole truth, may be in effect forms of miscommunication . . . [they] may be ways of protecting oneself in case the reaction of the other person becomes threatening. . . . The girl hints that she will be receptive to his advances but does not commit herself because she is ready only if he is. An escape is needed in case he is not.
>
> *(p. 184)*

When people become used to "yes" being conveyed through subtle hints, it is not surprising that they frequently mistake a "no" for a "yes" and feel that it is appropriate to persist after being rebuffed.

A REVIEW OF THE EVIDENCE THAT MISPERCEPTIONS OF SEXUAL INTENT OCCUR

Frequency of Misperceptions of Sexual Intent

The few studies that have examined the prevalence of misperceptions of sexual intent suggest that they are very common. In this author's own research (Abbey, 1987a), two surveys were conducted with 985 college undergraduates. In both studies, approximately 60% of the students were in their first year of college; 96% were between the ages of 18 and 21; 60% were from small towns or rural areas; and 60% were female.

Study participants were asked: "Have you ever been friendly to someone of the opposite sex only to discover that she or he had *misperceived* your friendliness as a sexual come-on; you were just trying to be nice but she or he assumed you were sexually attracted to him or her?" Two-thirds of the students in the first survey reported that their friendliness had been mistakenly perceived as a sexual invitation on at least one occasion. Among students who had ever been misperceived, the average number of misperceptions was 4.8. Also, significantly more women (72%) than men (60%) had been misperceived.

Koss and Oros (1982) also found misperceptions of sexual intent to be common. Seventy percent of the college women and 53% of the college men they surveyed reported that, on at least one occasion, a member of the opposite sex had misinterpreted the level of sexual intimacy they desired.

Gender Differences in the Likelihood of Misperceiving Sexual Intent

Although both sexes frequently report misperceptions, these experiences are more common for women than for men. This author and her colleagues conducted a series of laboratory studies that further delineated this phenomenon (Abbey, 1982; Abbey, Cozzarelli, McLaughlin, & Harnish, 1987; Abbey & Melby, 1986; Harnish, Abbey, & DeBono, in press). In the first of these studies (Abbey, 1982), college undergraduates were scheduled for a psychology experiment in groups of four. Two males and two females were randomly paired with each other in male/female dyads and then each pair was randomly assigned to the actor or observer role. The actors were told that the study was designed to examine first impressions and the role that the topic of conversation played in how smoothly these interactions progressed. They were asked to talk with each other for five minutes about their impressions of the university. Unbeknown to them, the two observers and the experimenter watched and listened to their conversation from behind a hidden one-way mirror. After the conversation ended, all four participants completed a questionnaire on which they were asked to evaluate (a) how they thought both the female and the male actor were trying to behave during the interaction and (b) their own interest in developing a relationship with the opposite-sex actor. When they were done, everyone's roles and the purpose of the study were described to the study participants.

As expected, both sexes rated the female actors' friendliness equally high. Also as predicted, males rated the female actors as being more seductive and promiscuous than females did. Males were more sexually attracted to and eager to date the opposite-sex actor than females were. The female actors' self-ratings indicated that they intended to be friendly, not seductive. There is no way to determine whether their behavior was truly friendly or seductive. What is important is their own perception of their behavior. If these women were not trying to be seductive, then they were likely to be confused or offended if their partners had acted as if a sexual invitation had been offered.

Unexpectedly, males rated the male actors as being more flirtatious, seductive, and promiscuous than did females. Abbey (1982) interpreted these results as evidence that men view the world in a more sexualized manner than women do and, consequently, are more likely than women to interpret ambiguous cues emitted by women—or men—as evidence of sexual intent.

This study's basic findings were replicated in a second study of live interactions (Harnish, Abbey, & DeBono, 1989) and several studies in which respondents rated the behavior of videotaped actors (Johnson, Freshnock, & Saal, in press; Shotland & Craig, 1988; Sigal, Gibbs, Adams, & Derfler, 1988, Study 2). For example, Shotland and Craig (1988) videotaped pairs of male and female students acting in either a friendly or sexually interested manner toward each other. They found that college undergraduates who observed these videotapes could correctly distinguish between when the female and male actors were acting friendly and when they were acting sexually interested. They also found that in both the friendly and sexually interested scenarios, male observers perceived both female and male actors as being more flirtatious, seductive, promiscuous, and sexually interested in their partner than did female observers. This study's results indicated that both men and women are capable, in some circumstances, of distinguishing friendly from sexual cues but, regardless of the situation, males attribute more sexuality to other men and women than do females.

Commonly Misperceived Cues

Nonverbal Cues

It has long been this author's premise that misperceptions of sexual intent are most likely to occur when the verbal and nonverbal cues displayed in the setting are highly ambiguous. Attempts to confirm this hypothesis have shown that ambiguous cues are more likely to be misperceived and that, at every cue level, gender differences exist. In a study conducted by Abbey and Melby (1986), three nonverbal cues associated with liking and attraction were systematically varied in photographs of a young couple sitting at a table in a campus eatery: eye contact (yes, no); interpersonal distance (intimate, personal, social); and touch (no touch, hands near each other, male's hand touching female's hand, female's hand touching male's hand, holding hands). It was hypothesized that men's and women's perceptions of the sexual intent of the actors would be similar in the situations that were most clearly platonic (no eye contact; no touch; social distance) and the situations most clearly sexual (eye contact; hand-holding; intimate distance). In the more ambiguous situations (ambiguous form of touch; personal distance) men were expected to perceive more sexuality than were women.

In all situations, platonic, sexual, and ambiguous, male college undergraduates perceived the female actor as being more sexy, seductive, and promiscuous than did female undergraduates. Males were also more sexually attracted to the opposite-sex actor than females were. Close interpersonal distance and mutual or female-initiated touch led study participants of both sexes to perceive more sexual attraction and romantic involvement than did the other levels of distance and touch. Thus, nonverbal cues appeared to be used by both women and men to determine the likelihood that sexual attraction existed between members of a male-female dyad, but at each cue level, men's sexuality ratings were higher than were women's ratings of the opposite-sex target.

The nonverbal cues examined in the Abbey and Melby (1986) study are of particular interest because research suggests that, in general, it is more acceptable and common for women (than for men) to touch others, approach others closely, and make eye contact, perhaps because women are perceived as less threatening than men (Hall, 1984). Thus, women may have learned that it is appropriate for them to use these cues, without also learning that men are highly inclined to interpret their use of these cues as a sign of sexual interest. As Kanin (1969) observed:

> The typical male enters into heterosexual interactions as an eager recipient of any subtle signs of sexual receptivity broadcasted by his female companion. In some instances, however, these signs are innocently emitted by a female naive in erotic communication. He perceives erotic encouragement, eagerly solicits further erotic concessions, encounters rebuff, and experiences bewilderment.
>
> *(pp. 18–19)*

An outgoing, emotionally expressive woman may feel it is natural to hug a male friend or hold his hand. Unfortunately, he may interpret this behavior as a sexual overture and feel justified in expecting sexual touching to occur.

Clothing

Abbey et al. (1987) varied the revealingness of the clothing worn by male and female targets. It was hypothesized that women and men who were dressed in revealing clothes would be perceived more sexually than women and men in nonrevealing clothes. In Western culture, sexual availability is associated with clothing that exposes skin, particularly the chest or legs. Frequently people wear revealing clothing to attract the attention of a potential sexual partner. Given our society's emphasis on physical attractiveness, however, some people may dress in such a way simply to look their best, for the sake of their own self-esteem, and not to attract sexual partners (Goodchilds & Zellman, 1984).

To test these hypotheses, college students rated the sexual intent of a female and a male college student who were talking with each other after class. They examined photographs in which the revealingness of each member of the dyad's clothing was systematically varied. As in the studies previously described in this chapter, male study participants rated female targets as significantly more sexy, seductive, and promiscuous than did females, and males were more sexually attracted to opposite-sex targets than females were. This was true regardless of the revealingness of the women's clothing. As in the other study in which participants rated photographs (Abbey & Melby, 1986), consistent gender differences were not found in perceptions of the male targets' sexual intent. Abbey and her colleagues have suggested that men's sexuality schema is stronger for females than for males and requires more cues, perhaps verbal or interactive cues, in order to be triggered in response to other men. As will be discussed in greater detail in the next section of this chapter, American society emphasizes female sexuality and males are socialized from an early age to attend to women's physical attributes. Thus, men may be more attuned to cues of female, as opposed to male, sexuality.

The revealingly dressed woman (low-cut blouse, slit skirt, high heels) was perceived by both women and men as more sexy, seductive, and promiscuous and less kind, considerate, and sincere than the nonrevealingly dressed woman (blouse buttoned to neck, plain skirt, boots). Men were not perceived more sexually when dressed in revealing (top three buttons undone on shirt, tight pants) as compared to nonrevealing (shirt buttoned to neck, loose pants) clothing. Similarly, study participants rated the level of romantic involvement and sexual attraction higher when the female wore revealing clothes; the male's clothing had no effect on these judgments. Abbey et al. (1987) observed that it was difficult to achieve consensus regarding what type of male attire could be considered revealing. Informal pilot testing indicated that revealingly dressed males were viewed as either noncredible ("No guy would dress like that for class") or unappealing ("No one would talk to a guy dressed like that"). This may explain the lack of results regarding male attire, although it says something equally important about gender stereotypes. The fact that revealing clothes were seen as more acceptable attire for women than for men demonstrates society's emphasis on women as decorative, sensual beings.

Similar results were found by Goodchilds and Zellman (1984) in a study conducted with high school-age youth. They asked study participants to rate the likelihood that a number of different cues would be signs of a date's willingness to have sex. They found that females' ratings of revealing clothing worn by the male or female, the male's prior reputation, date locations such as a beach at night or the male's home, and activities like drinking alcohol together or complimenting a date were lower, or less indicative of a desire to have sex, than were males' ratings. There was only one cue that females perceived as a stronger sign than did males: the female's having a reputation of having sex frequently. Goodchilds and Zellman concluded that males are more likely than females to attach sexual meaning to a variety of activities that might occur on a date. They observed that their data help to explain the stereotype that immodest women encourage sexual advances.

Goodchilds and Zellman (1984) also emphasized the ease with which women's clothing can be misperceived: "Young men may receive what they interpret as a strong sexual signal, but in the view of the wearer and that of her girlfriends, she may simply be trying to keep up with the latest fashion trends" (p. 236). Imagine a young, somewhat insecure woman wearing a miniskirt on a first date. Her goal is to look sophisticated, but her choice of clothing may easily be interpreted by her date as a sign of sexual availability.

Women who choose to wear revealing clothing need to be aware of the message that this type of dress sends to others: Both women and men are likely to perceive them as sexual and unkind. Revealing clothing appears to evoke the prototype of woman as seductress (Scully & Marolla, 1984), which may or may not be the message intended.

Substance Use

The consumption of alcohol or other drugs also appears to be a cue that signals a woman's sexual availability. George, Gournic, and McAfee (1988) asked college undergraduates to read vignettes about a young couple on a date. The man always drank alcohol. The woman drank either alcohol or soda pop. The woman who had a few alcoholic drinks was perceived by both male and female study participants as more likely than the woman drinking soda pop to be responsive to a sexual come-on and more willing to be seduced. Descriptions of date rapes often include alcohol or drug use. Warshaw (1988) interviewed several date rape victims who were intoxicated at the time of the attack. Some reported that the rapist purposely tried to get them drunk or high on drugs; others became easy targets because of their diminished cognitive capacity. A date rape victim interviewed for a study by Abbey (1987b) described agreeing to date a man she was not particularly interested in, simply because he had asked her so many times that she decided to give him a chance. In retrospect, she felt that he had acted strangely all evening and that she should have known he had something planned. However, the marijuana she had smoked with him lulled her into complacency.

EXPLANATIONS FOR GENDER DIFFERENCES IN THE MISPERCEPTION OF SEXUAL INTENT

Traditional American sex roles and dating practices make misperceptions between the sexes almost inevitable. Women have traditionally been socialized to flirt and play hard-to-get (Berger, Searles, Salem, & Pierce, 1986; Bernard, 1969; Brodyaga, Gates, Singer, Tucker, & White, 1975; Medea & Thompson, 1974; Russell, 1975; Weis & Borges, 1973). Women are expected to express less overt interest in engaging in sexual activities than are men. Consequently, women are expected to initially resist men's sexual advances even when they find them desirable and plan on reciprocating. Women are also expected to set the limits on sexual activities and are held responsible when men overstep them (Grauerholz & Serpe, 1985). In a complementary fashion, men have traditionally been socialized to initiate all sexual encounters and to believe that women prefer lovers who are forceful, aggressive, and dominant. Despite the advances in women's opportunities that have been achieved in the past 25 years, research suggests that traditional gender-role stereotypes, especially those regarding the male role as initiator of dates and sexual activities, are still commonly endorsed by men and women (Burt,

1980; Grauerholz & Serpe, 1985; Green & Sandos, 1983; Peplau & Gordon, 1985; Ruble, 1983; Werner & LaRussa, 1985).

The Effects of Gender-Role Stereotypes on Men's Sexual Behavior

Gender differences in sexual and dating role socialization may cause some men to force sexual relations on dating partners, mistaking their partners' true lack of interest for flirtatious repartee. Although most date and acquaintance rapes appear to be planned (Kanin, 1969, 1985; Krasner, Meyer, & Carroll, 1976), some unknown percentage are at least partially due to misperception of sexual intent. Consider the common movie image of a man initiating an embrace with a reluctant female partner. At first the woman struggles to resist him, but gradually she stops and begins to reciprocate. Why shouldn't a man expect similar results with his date? A 1987 "Moonlighting" episode (described in Warshaw, 1988) perpetuated this stereotype. The two stars' longstanding sexual attraction was finally acted on after a serious, physical fight. Such an explicit association of physical force and sexual pleasure perpetuates the stereotype that women find forced sex enjoyable and aggressive men arousing (Burt, 1980; Hall, Howard, & Boezio, 1986).

Research by several investigators, as well as consideration of the mass-media depiction of women and men (Cash, 1981; Goffman, 1976; Miller, 1975; Umiker-Sebeok, 1981; Venkatesan & Losco, 1975), suggest that women are more often perceived as sexual objects than are men. In American society, women's physical appearance is emphasized more than men's, and women's clothing is more overtly designed to be sexually revealing. Companies that try to sell a product by promoting the sex appeal of its users almost always depict a female as the object of sexual interest (Belkaoui & Belkaoui, 1976; Umiker-Sebeok, 1981).

It is not surprising that boys raised in this climate develop an orientation toward women that emphasizes female sexuality. Every day, boys can observe advertisements in which automobiles and alcohol are sold by revealingly dressed women; *Playboy* and *Penthouse* are prominently displayed on magazine racks at their local drugstore; and large sections of department stores are devoted to women's lingerie, with no equivalent for men. Newspapers have traditionally portrayed women principally in the roles of spouse, fashion model, and bride-to-be (Miller, 1975). The disproportionate societal emphasis on women's (as compared to men's) sexual appeal may lead men to minimize women's other capacities and to develop a schema about women that focuses on their sexuality. Once men develop this sexual gender schema, it may act as a generalized expectancy that colors their perceptions of others' behaviors. Events that fit existing schemata are remembered better than those that do not, and ambiguous evidence is likely to be interpreted in such a way that it confirms existing schemata (Bem, 1981).

Thus, once males develop a sexual schema about women, they are likely to interpret ambiguous evidence as confirming their preexisting beliefs. As the literature on stereotypes and self-fulfilling prophecies demonstrates (Darley & Fazio, 1980; Ross, Lepper, & Hubbard, 1975; Snyder, Campbell, & Preston, 1982), people typically perceive experiences as fitting their existing conceptions. Thus, over time, schemata become strengthened and more impervious to contradictory evidence.

Gross (1978) carefully described how the socialization experiences of women and men cause sexuality to be a more central component of men's gender identity than of women's. In American society, sex is perceived as more important and enjoyable for men than for women (Ruble & Ruble, 1982). It is commonly believed that men have stronger sex drives than women do, and that they are difficult for men to control once aroused (Goodchilds & Zellman, 1984; Jackson, 1978). This belief, combined with the role as initiator of sexual interactions, can cause men to force sexual intercourse on an unwilling female partner.

The Effects of Gender-Role Stereotypes on Women's Sexual Behavior

Women's socialization as reluctant, passive participants in sexual activities and their awareness of stereotypes about the forcefulness of men's sexual drives lead them to act in ways that reinforce males' sexual schemata (Berger et al., 1986). Based on female college students' responses to a hypothetical scenario in which their date wanted to have sexual intercourse but they did not, Lewin (1985) argued that for many women it is preferable to accept unwanted intercourse rather than to risk antagonizing a date. She suggested that norms about women's empathic role and men's dominant role lead some women to accept unwanted sex after their initial attempts to alter the situation are unsuccessful.

Muehlenhard and Hollabaugh (1988) asked 610 female Texas college undergraduates if they had ever told a man they did not want to have sex even though they were willing; that is, had they ever said "no" when they meant "yes"? Thirty-nine percent of these women had said "no" when they meant "yes," at least once. The women reported three types of reasons for refusing agreeable sexual offers: practical reasons such as not wanting to appear too eager or easy, inhibitive reasons such as moral concerns or embarrassment, and manipulative reasons such as wanting their date to try harder or wanting to get back at him. Muehlenhard and Hollabaugh argued that "given society's sexual double standard, token resistance may be a rational behavior" (p. 872). Women who willingly engage in sexual activities outside of marriage risk being labeled as promiscuous (Garcia, 1982). Thus, some women may act disinterested to preserve their self-image and reputation. Unfortunately, token resistance perpetuates miscommunication between the sexes and encourages date rape. It is easy to see how a man who has previously turned a "no" into a "yes" might force sexual intercourse on a date who says "no" and means it.

Goodchilds and Zellman (1984) asked the high school-age youths who participated in their study whether males had the right to force sexual intercourse on females in nine different situations. Twenty-seven percent of the women said force was always unacceptable, while only 15% of the men did. Both sexes agreed that force was most acceptable if a woman got a man sexually excited, if she led him on, or if they had dated a long time. These results indicated that most adolescents perceive sexual relationships as adversarial and forced sex as acceptable if the man's sexual passions are aroused by the woman.

HOW ARE MISPERCEPTIONS OF SEXUAL INTENT RESOLVED?

As noted earlier, Abbey (1987a) surveyed 985 college undergraduates about their experiences with misperception of sexual intent. The 764 students who had ever been misperceived described their most recent experience in detail. Students' typical relationship to the misperceiver was casual friend or acquaintance. Misperceptions most commonly occurred at parties at which alcohol was freely available. The most common way that these students became aware that their friendliness had been misperceived was when they were touched or kissed by the misperceiver. The women in the survey were much more likely than the men to say that they were touched or kissed when they did not want to be. Suggestive remarks, an explicit request for sex, and attentiveness were also commonly mentioned signs of misperception. Men more often than women learned of the misperception indirectly through a friend rather than directly through the misperceiver.

The single technique most frequently used by these students to cope with being misperceived involved simply telling the person that they were not interested (41%). However, 46% of these students used an indirect strategy such as trying to get away, making excuses, and acting as if nothing had happened. Common reactions from the misperceiver included continuing to try to interest the individual, acting angry, and being understanding. Strangers were most likely to keep trying, while friends were most likely to be either understanding or upset. Sometimes friends talked it over and felt that they understood what had happened; at other times, friends became hostile and accusatory when misperception occurred. It seems likely that the previous quality of the relationship determined whether a friendship could withstand sexual misperception.

After being misperceived, women were more likely than men to feel upset, angry, and embarrassed; men were more likely than women to feel happy and amused. This indicated that men and women frequently perceived the event quite differently: men were flattered and women were upset.

Very few of these misperceptions ended in forced sexual intercourse. (Students were asked to describe the most recent event, not the most violent.) One woman reported being raped by an acquaintance at a fraternity party. He convinced her that he wanted to talk with her in a quiet place, and when he succeeded in getting her there he raped her. She felt partially responsible because she had been drunk enough to believe him. Another woman described being raped by a coworker. She agreed to go to his apartment after work, for pizza. She thought his roommates would be there but the apartment was empty. After eating pizza and drinking a beer, he forced her to have sex with him.

Being in an early year in school positively related to experiencing forced sex. Many women commented on doing things when they were in their first year of college that they would never do afterward because they had learned that men would misinterpret such behavior (e.g., going upstairs in a fraternity house, going to a man's room or apartment, getting drunk at a party).

In summary, the results of this study suggested that most misperceptions occur during brief, relatively nontraumatic encounters but that some end in forced sex. The fact that almost half of these students responded to being misperceived by acting as if nothing had happened helps to explain how simple misperceptions can escalate into forced sexual encounters. Norms of politeness and indirectness appear to be so strong that, even when aware of being misperceived, many people choose not to directly correct their misperceiver's perceptions. Consequently, the misperceiver continues to interpret ambiguous words and actions as evidence of sexual interest. The longer the misperception lasts, the more likely it is that the misperceiver will feel justified in expecting sexual intercourse to occur.

Muehlenhard and Linton (1987) asked 635 college undergraduates about their worst experience with sexual assault on a date. Approximately three-quarters of the women had experienced some level of sexual aggression on a date; 15% of the women had experienced forced sexual intercourse. Approximately half of the men reported engaging in sexual aggression on a date; 7% acknowledged forcing sexual intercourse. [By asking about students' worst experience, these researchers found evidence of more forced sex than did Abbey (1987a).] Muehlenhard and Linton found that (a) miscommunication of sexual intent, (b) the male's having traditional sex role beliefs, and (c) the male's initiating the date, paying the expenses, and driving were all associated with occurrence of sexual assault on a date. When misperception occurred, both women and men agreed that the man felt led on; however, women more often than men felt that this was unintentional.

It is easy to see how a traditional male might interpret a series of ambiguous cues that take place on a date as signs of sexual interest and, consequently, feel led on when the woman repels his advances. Consider the scenario in which a woman wears a stylish, short skirt and tight sweater on a date. She has several alcoholic drinks. She smiles, laughs, sits close, and allows her date to hold her hand. She agrees to come into his apartment for a cup of coffee. She willingly kisses him but wants to stop there. He thinks she must be saying "no" just as a formality. He thinks he has the right to feel led on and to take what he deserves after paying for an expensive evening and becoming sexually aroused by looking at her clothing and kissing her. In cases where the man then forces sex, the woman may feel guilty because she was unable to control the situation—and she is unlikely to tell anyone about what happened (Koss, Gidycz, & Wisniewski, 1987).

The resolution to this problem seems obvious, although achieving it is by no means simple. Men need to know that when a woman says "no" she means it and that her desires must be respected, regardless of what she has said or done previously. For this to occur, women must say "no" only when they genuinely mean it and must be more aware of the way in which their behaviors are perceived by men. Certainly women have the right to dress as they choose or to drink alcohol on a date, but they need to realize how some men are likely to interpret these cues and counteract those assumptions by verbally making their intentions clear.

Gaps in the Existing Knowledge About Misperception

There are many gaps in the existing knowledge about misperceptions of sexual intent. Most of the available research has been conducted with white, middle-class, unmarried college students 18 to 21 years old. It seems likely that misperceptions most commonly occur between young, single people who are actively dating. It is also possible for middle-age, married career women to be misperceived, even by colleagues. For example, one woman tried to be direct and clear when she thought a male coworker who asked her to join him for dinner might have been interpreting her friendliness as a sexual invitation. She said she would like to go with him but wanted to be sure he knew that she was married. From her monogamous mindset, mentioning that she was married clearly indicated that she was only interested in platonic interaction. Only later, when her colleague made sexual advances, did she realize that from his perspective her intentions were still unclear.

It is also important that studies similar to those done by Abbey (1987a) and Muehlenhard and Linton (1987) be conducted with individuals from a variety of ethnic and socioeconomic backgrounds. Misperceptions are likely to be particularly common among cultural groups that emphasize nonoverlapping gender roles and characterize men's sexual desires as insatiable.

More information is also needed about personality traits and life experiences associated with misperception. Are men and women with traditional gender roles most likely to be in relationships in which misperception occurs? Are shy women most likely to experience forced sex as a result of misperception? Are sexually inexperienced men most likely to misinterpret their dates' cues? Men who are hostile toward women, desire to dominate women, and believe violence toward women is acceptable are most likely to behave aggressively toward women (Malamuth, 1985). It has not been documented whether the cues mentioned in this chapter as commonly mis-perceived (e.g., clothing, drinking alcohol, date location, touch) enhance the likelihood that these men will behave aggressively.

Research examining the long-term impact of misperception would also be of value. Although the study conducted by Abbey (1987a) indicated that most misperceptions were quickly resolved and not associated with strong negative affect, those that involved forced sex of any type were associated with greater feelings of guilt, anger, upset, embarrassment, being used, and insult. More needs to be learned about how long these negative feelings last and what effects they have on these individuals' future interactions with members of the opposite sex. Acquaintance rape frequently destroys the victim's capacity to trust men (Burgess & Holmstrom, 1979; Koss & Burkhart, 1989). A certain amount of distrust may be adaptive in terms of preventing future victimiza-tion, but too much distrust can ruin these women's ability to develop positive, supportive relationships.

CONCLUSIONS

The studies reviewed in this chapter, and in other chapters in this book, indicate that acquaintance rape is very common and that misperception is a frequent contributory factor (Koss, Dinero, Seibel, & Cox, 1988; Muehlen-hard & Linton, 1987). Educational programs need to be implemented to teach dating-age youth how to honestly and clearly convey their intentions and impute the intentions of their dates rather than to rely on indirect cues such as clothing, alcohol, and date location. These lessons might be added to existing social skills curricula (Bellack & Hersen, 1979). These efforts are likely to be more effective if parents become involved. If parents are made aware of the implicit messages their lessons about proper dating roles convey, they might change their messages and reevaluate their own gender stereotypes. Reeduca-tion of the writers and producers of television shows and commercials could lead to less reinforcement of traditional sexual stereotypes in media portray-als of women and men. Future generations of American youth will learn that "no" means "no" and "yes" means "yes" only if they consistently receive this message from peers, parents, teachers, the media, and, most importantly, their dates.

REFERENCES

Abbey, A. (1982). Sex differences in attributions for friendly behavior: Do males misperceive females' friendliness? *Journal of Personality and Social Psychology, 42*, 830–838.

Abbey, A. (1987a). Misperceptions of friendly behavior as sexual interest: A survey of naturally occurring incidents. *Psychology of Women Quarterly, 11*, 173–194.

Abbey, A. (1987b). Perceptions of personal avoidability versus responsibility: How do they differ? *Basic and Applied Social Psychology, 8,* 3–20.

Abbey, A., Cozzarelli, C., McLaughlin, K., & Harnish, R. J. (1987). The effects of clothing and dyad sex composition on perceptions of sexual intent: Do women and men evaluate these cues differently? *Journal of Applied Social Psychology, 17,* 108–126.

Abbey, A., & Melby, C. (1986). The effects of nonverbal cues on gender differences in perceptions of sexual intent. *Sex Roles, 15,* 283–298.

Belkaoui, A., & Belkaoui, J. M. (1976). A comparative analysis of the roles portrayed by women in print advertisements: 1958, 1970, 1972. *Journal of Marketing Research, 13,* 168–172.

Bellack, A. S., & Hersen, M. (1979). *Research and practice in social skills training.* New York: Plenum.

Bem, S. L. (1981). Gender schema theory: A cognitive account of sex typing. *Psychological Review, 88,* 354–364.

Berger, R. J., Searles, P., Salem, R. G., & Pierce, B. A. (1986). Sexual assault in a college community. *Sociological Focus, 19,* 1–26.

Bernard, J. (1969). *The sex game.* London: Leslie Frewin.

Brodyaga, L., Gates, M., Singer, S., Tucker, M., & White, R. (1975). *Rape and its victims: A report for citizens, health facilities, and criminal justice agencies.* U.S. Department of Justice. Washington, DC: U.S. Government Printing Office.

Burgess, A. W., & Holmstrom, L. L. (1979). Adaptive strategies and recovery from rape. *American Journal of Psychiatry, 136,* 1278–1282.

Burt, M. R. (1980). Cultural myths and supports for rape. *Journal of Personality and Social Psychology, 38,* 217–230.

Cash, T. F. (1981, August). *The interface of sexism and beautyism.* Paper presented at the annual meeting of the American Psychological Association, Los Angeles.

Darley, J. M., & Fazio, R. H. (1980). Expectancy confirmation processes arising in the social interaction sequence. *American Psychologist, 35,* 867–881.

Garcia, L. T. (1982). Sex-role orientation and stereotypes about male-female sexuality. *Sex Roles, 8,* 863–876.

George, W. H., Gournic, S. J., & McAfee, M. P. (1988). Perceptions of postdrinking female sexuality: Effects of gender, beverage choice, and drink payment. *Journal of Applied Social Psychology, 18,* 1295–1317.

Goffman, E. (1976). *Gender advertisements.* New York: Harper & Row.

Goodchilds, J. D., & Zellman, G. L. (1984). Sexual signaling and sexual aggression in adolescent relationships. In N. M. Malamuth & E. Donnerstein (Eds.), *Pornography and sexual aggression* (pp. 233–243). Orlando, FL: Academic Press.

Grauerholz, E., & Serpe, R. T. (1985). Initiation and response: The dynamics of sexual interaction. *Sex Roles, 12,* 1041–1059.

Green, S. K., & Sandos, P. (1983). Perceptions of male and female initiators of relationships. *Sex Roles, 9,* 849–852.

Gross, A. E. (1978). The male role and heterosexual behavior. *Journal of Social Issues, 34,* 87–107.

Hall, E. R., Howard, J. A., & Boezio, S. L. (1986). Tolerance of rape: A sexist or antisocial attitude? *Psychology of Women Quarterly, 10,* 101–118.

Hall, J. A. (1984). *Nonverbal sex differences: Communication accuracy and expressive style.* Baltimore: The Johns Hopkins University Press.

Harnish, R. J., Abbey, A., & DeBono, K. G. (in press). Toward an understanding of the "sex game": The effects of gender and self-monitoring on perceptions of sexuality and likability in initial interactions. *Journal of Applied Social Psychology.*

Heslin, R., & Patterson, M. L. (1982). *Nonverbal behavior and social psychology.* New York: Plenum.

Jackson, S. (1978). The social context of rape: Sexual scripts and motivation. *Women's Studies International Quarterly, 1,* 27–38.

Johnson, C. B., Freshnock, N., & Saal, F. E. (in press). Friendliness or sexual come-on: A clue to understanding sexual harassment? *Psychology of Women Quarterly.*

Kanin, E. J. (1969). Selected dyadic aspects of male sex aggression. *The Journal of Sex Research, 5,* 12–28.

Kanin, E. J. (1985). Date rapists: Differential sexual socialization and relative deprivation. *Archives of Sexual Behavior, 14,* 219–231.

Koss, M. P., & Burkhart, B. R. (1989). A conceptual analysis of rape victimization: Long-term effects and implications for treatment. *Psychology of Women Quarterly, 13,* 27–40.

Koss, M. P., Dinero, T. E., Seibel, C. A., & Cox, S. L. (1988). Stranger and acquaintance rape: Are there differences in the victim's experience? *Psychology of Women Quarterly, 12,* 1–24.

Koss, M. P., Gidycz, C. A., & Wisniewski, N. (1987). The scope of rape: Incidence and prevalence of sexual aggression and victimization in a national sample of higher education students. *Journal of Consulting and Clinical Psychology, 55,* 162–170.

Koss, M. P., & Oros, C. J. (1982). Sexual experiences survey: A research instrument investigating sexual aggression and victimization. *Journal of Consulting and Clinical Psychology, 50,* 455–457.

Krasner, W., Meyer, L. C., & Carroll, N. E. (1976). *Victims of rape.* Washington, DC: U.S. Government Printing Office.

Lewin, M. (1985). Unwanted intercourse: The difficulty of saying no. *Psychology of Women Quarterly, 9,* 184–192.

Malamuth, N. M. (1985). Predictors of naturalistic sexual aggression. *Journal of Personality and Social Psychology, 50,* 953–962.

Medea, A., & Thompson, K. (1974). *Against rape.* New York: Farrar, Straus, & Giroux.

Miller, S. H. (1975). The content of news photos: Women's and men's roles. *Journalism Quarterly, 52,* 70–75.

Muehlenhard, C. L., & Hollabaugh, L. C. (1988). Do women sometimes say no when they mean yes? The prevalence and correlates of women's token resistance to sex. *Journal of Personality and Social Psychology, 54,* 872–879.

Muehlenhard, C. L., Koralewski, M. A., Andrews, S. L., & Burdick, C. A. (1986). Verbal and nonverbal cues that convey interest in dating. *Behavior Therapy, 17,* 404–419.

Muehlenhard, C. L., & Linton, M. A. (1987). Date rape and sexual aggression in dating situations: Incidence and risk factors. *Journal of Counseling Psychology, 34,* 186–196.

Peplau, L. A., & Gordon, S. L. (1985). Women and men in love: Gender differences in close heterosexual relationships. In V. E. O'Leary, R. K. Unger, & B. S. Wallston (Eds.), *Women, gender, and social psychology* (pp. 257–292). Hillsdale, NJ: Erlbaum.

Ross, L., Lepper, M. R., & Hubbard, M. (1975). Perseverance in self-perception and social perception: Biased attributional process in the debriefing paradigm. *Journal of Personality and Social Psychology, 23,* 880–892.

Ruble, D. N., & Ruble, T. L. (1982). Sex stereotypes. In A. G. Miller (Ed.), *In the eye of the beholder* (pp. 188–251). New York: Praeger.

Ruble, T. L. (1983). Sex stereotypes: Issue of change in the 1970's. *Sex Roles, 9,* 397–402.

Russell, D. E. H. (1975). *The politics of rape.* New York: Stein & Day.

Scully, D., & Marolla, J. (1984). Convicted rapists' vocabulary of motive: Excuses and justifications. *Social Problems, 31,* 530–544.

Shotland, R. L. & Craig, J. M. (1988). Can men and women differentiate between friendly and sexually interested behavior? *Social Psychology Quarterly, 51,* 66–73.

Sigal, J., Gibbs, M., Adams, B., & Derfler, R. (1988). The effect of romantic and nonromantic films on perception of female friendly and sexual behavior. *Sex Roles, 19,* 545–554.

Snyder, M., Campbell, B. H., & Preston, E. (1982). Testing hypotheses about human nature: Assessing the accuracy of social stereotypes. *Social Cognition, 1,* 256–272.

Umiker-Sebeok, J. (1981). The seven ages of women: A view from American magazine advertisements. In C. Mayo & N. M. Henley (Eds.), *Gender and nonverbal behavior* (pp. 209–252). New York: Springer-Verlag.

Venkatesan, M., & Losco, J. (1975). Women in magazine ads: 1959–71. *Journal of Advertising Research, 15,* 49–54.

Warshaw, R. (1988). *I never called it rape: The Ms. report on recognizing, fighting, and surviving date and acquaintance rape.* New York: Harper & Row.

Weis, K., & Borges, S. (1973). Victimology and rape: The case of the legitimate victim. *Issues in Criminology, 8,* 71–115.

Werner, P. D., & LaRussa, G. W. (1985). Persistence and change in sex role stereotypes. *Sex Roles, 12,* 1089–1100.

PART 4

Types of Acquaintance Rape

CHAPTER 8

Nonviolent Sexual Coercion

CHARLENE L. MUEHLENHARD, PhD and JENNIFER L. SCHRAG

Many women are coerced into having unwanted sexual intercourse by being violently raped. Even more women are coerced into having unwanted sexual intercourse in numerous, more subtle ways. This chapter discusses types of sexual coercion that would not be legally classified as "rape" but nevertheless have a powerful, insidious effect on women in our society.

We believe that it is important to consider all forms of sexual coercion, ranging from violent assaults to more subtle and socially acceptable forms of coercion. We are aware that some researchers believe that there is so much yet to be learned about forceful rape that it is somewhat frivolous to focus on other forms of coercion. We disagree. For women to be truly free and autonomous, we must be free from all forms of coercion. Our view of sexual coercion is analogous to Gelles and Straus's (1988) view of family violence. In their definition of *violence*, they included a continuum of violent behaviors ranging from slaps and spankings to attacks with weapons. They stated:

> We are frequently criticized that such a broad definition dilutes our message and the possible impact of our research and recommendations. For our part, we think such criticisms are not only incorrect, but potentially harmful. Claiming that only outrageous and unusual acts represent violence serves to license the more normal slaps, spankings, and pushes. As we have said again and again, violence is possible if we fail to define it as wrong or improper.
>
> *(p. 54)*

Similarly, we choose not to limit our discussion of sexual coercion to "outrageous and unusual acts." Instead, we focus on nonviolent sexual coercion, in the hope that labeling it as coercive may be a step toward change.

Some forms of nonviolent coercion, such as a man's coercing a woman into having sex through the use of continual arguments, are sometimes included in studies of rape done by psychologists and sociologists (Koss, Gidycz, & Wisniewski, 1987). Other forms of coercion, such as compulsory heterosexuality, are discussed in feminist literature (Rich, 1980). In this chapter, we integrate psychological, sociological, and feminist literature.

115

Because of the focus of this book and space limitations, our discussion is limited to adult women's being nonviolently coerced into engaging in unwanted sexual activities. Topics such as child sexual abuse, obscene phone calls, flashing, nonsexual domestic violence, sexual pressure experienced by men, and physically violent sexual coercion are outside the scope of this chapter. Instead, our focus is on more subtle ways in which women are coerced into having sex. These forms of sexual coercion occur almost exclusively between acquaintances.

FORMS OF SEXUAL COERCION

Women face two general types of nonviolent sexual coercion. One is the pressure to be in male–female relationships that implicitly involve sex with men, such as heterosexual dating relationships or marriage. We refer to this as *indirect sexual coercion.* The other type of coercion involves specific pressures to engage in unwanted sexual activity within a relationship. We refer to this as *direct sexual coercion.* Those types of sexual coercion—especially indirect sexual coercion—are often so subtle and insidious that women may not realize that they are being coerced.

COMPULSORY HETEROSEXUALITY

One of the most subtle forms of coercion women face is the pressure to be heterosexual. It is often assumed that people are innately heterosexual, but this assumption has been challenged by some feminists (Rich, 1980) and sexual scientists (Van Wyk & Geist, 1984).

> In this viewpoint, sexuality is considered to be primarily a learned phenomenon. Proponents of this view believe that the psychological conditioning associated with the reinforcement or punishment of early sexual behavior (and sexual thoughts and feelings) largely controls the process of sexual orientation.
>
> *(Masters, Johnson, & Kolodny, 1986, p. 352)*

Rich (1980) hypothesized that girls and women are socialized to be heterosexual. She labeled this process "compulsory heterosexuality," which she described as "the enforcement of heterosexuality for women as a means of assuring male right of physical, economical, and emotional access" (p. 647). In other words, as long as women are socialized to be heterosexual, men will have access to and control over women.

Heterosexuality is taught and enforced in a multitude of ways. Some are subtle, such as when children's books and television shows portray marriage as the ultimate goal in women's lives (Weitzman, 1979). Some are blatant, such as discrimination against lesbians (Weitz, 1989). This chapter discusses several additional types of pressure that women face to be in relationships with men. Although psychologists and sociologists typically do not think of such pressure as related to sexual coercion, we argue that pressure on women to be in sexual relationships with men is a form of sexual coercion.

GENDER ROLES

Every society has some division of labor based on sex. Because the nature of these divisions differs dramatically from one society to another, the purpose of these divisions clearly is not to tailor gender roles to women's and men's biological capabilities (Rubin, 1984). It has been argued that the actual purpose of this division of labor is to make women and men dependent on each other, in that the smallest viable economic unit typically must contain at least one man and one woman (Rubin, 1984). Thus, gender roles are a subtle source of pressure for women to be in relationships with men.

ASSUMPTIONS ABOUT THE NATURE OF SEX

"Sex" is typically assumed to be synonymous with penile–vaginal intercourse (Zilbergeld, 1978). What is regarded as legitimate sex is a more political than a biological decision: "Hunger is hunger, but what counts as food is culturally determined and obtained. . . . Sex is sex, but what counts as sex is equally culturally determined and obtained" (Rubin, 1984). Assuming that penile–vaginal intercourse is the only legitimate form of sex means that having "sex" requires a man and a woman. This assumption can be a source of pressure on women to be in relationships with men.

How society defines "sex" also has numerous repercussions for women who freely choose to be heterosexual. Behaviors other than penile–vaginal intercourse are devalued and labeled as "foreplay." Intercourse is the ultimate goal (Zilbergeld, 1978). Penile–vaginal intercourse serves society's need for reproduction and often satisfies men's sexual desires, but it is less likely to satisfy women's sexual desires (Shulman, 1983). Penile–vaginal intercourse stimulates men's most sensitive organ—the penis—but is less likely to stimulate women's most sensitive organ—the clitoris. An estimated 50% to 70% of women do not regularly reach orgasm through penile–vaginal intercourse (Hite, 1976; Masters et al., 1986). It is no wonder that more women than men are labeled as having "inhibited orgasm," which involves the ability to become sexually aroused but the inability to reach orgasm (American Psychiatric Association, 1987). Yet, because of the way in which sex is defined, many women continue to engage in penile–vaginal intercourse, feel inadequate, fake orgasms (Hite, 1976), and refrain from asking for other forms of sexual stimulation.

Our sexual norms also include the assumption that sex is supposed to proceed linearly from kissing to petting to intercourse. If a woman pets but does not desire intercourse, she is often labeled as a "tease" or as "leading the man on," which many people regard as justification for rape (Giarrusso, Johnson, Goodchilds, & Zellman, 1979). "Many a woman accepts that she has 'asked for it' if she has allowed herself to engage in what might be for her a preferred way of being sexual: cuddling and petting not necessarily culminating in sexual intercourse" (Russell, 1984, p. 163). Thus, society's sexual norms can lead a woman to agree reluctantly to have sexual intercourse to avoid feeling like a "tease." These sexual norms can also result in forced sex if a man feels entitled to sexual intercourse because a woman has petted with him.

ASSUMPTIONS ABOUT THE NATURE OF MARRIAGE

Social customs, religion, and the law have promoted the idea that wives owe sex to their husbands and have no right to refuse (Daly, 1978). Monsignor S. J. Adamo (1984) wrote, "I was taught to instruct wives in particular that it was sinful to deny the husband sex except for serious reasons, and that an unloving wife could drive her husband to drink or masturbation or adultery—and those sins would be on her soul" (p. 43). Rape laws codified the idea that wives owe sex to their husbands by defining rape as a man's engaging in sexual intercourse "with a woman *not his wife* [italics added]; by force or threat of force; against her will and without her consent" (Estrich, 1987, p. 8). Chapter 9 shows how, in 1990, most states have retained some variation of this marital exclusion. These assumptions about the nature of marriage make it difficult for wives to refuse sex and thus are a form of sexual coercion.

FEAR OF MALE VIOLENCE

Society conditions women to fear living alone and going out alone at night, and it teaches women that they need men to protect them from other men (Stanko, 1988). Although women are actually more likely to be assaulted, raped, or murdered by their dates and husbands than by strangers (Koss, Dinero, Seibel, & Cox, 1988; Russell, 1984; Stanko, 1988), the fear of such violence from strangers pressures women to be in relationships with men.

Fear of male violence can also lead to direct sexual coercion. For example, Walker (1984) found that some battered women engaged in—or even initiated—unwanted sex for reasons related to fear of their husbands' violence. The women reported "initiating sex to prevent a beating, sex occurring right after a beating to calm him down, and having sex after he beat the baby due to fear he might do so again" (Walker, 1984, p. 49). Even when the women initiated sex, sex in such cases is clearly coercive.

STATUS COERCION

The status that relationships with men convey to women can be another source of pressure for women to be in sexual relationships with men.

Status can be a motive for dating and for engaging in unwanted sex in dating relationships. In a recent pilot study, for example, several women described having sex with a man to keep him in the relationship because of the status he conveyed. One woman wrote about her experience in high school:

> The guy was someone who every girl in school wished she could have. Most every girl envied me. . . . When the situation got real heavy, I told him that we needed to cool off. He told me that he was sick of my childishness and that he didn't have to be there. He implied that he could have anybody he wanted. (I knew it was true) . . . I hesitated because I was scared that he really might leave me this time and go find someone else. I let him go ahead.
>
> *(Schrag & Muehlenhard, 1989)*

Status can also be a motive for marriage. Single women are regarded more negatively than married women (Bernard, 1973; Caplan, 1985; Johnston & Eklund, 1984; Rich, 1980). A wife's status parallels that of her husband (Nilson, 1978). Physicians' wives are held in higher esteem than are wives of elevator operators; in fact, physicians' wives are held in higher esteem than are female veterinarians, pilots, and architects, and are held in almost as high esteem as are female physicians (Eichler, 1977). "A woman gains only 7 social standing points by becoming a physician herself over marrying one" (Nilson, 1978, p. 546).

ECONOMIC COERCION

Sexual Harassment

Women face economic coercion when they are sexually harassed in the workplace. Sexual harassment can be defined as sexual pressure imposed on someone who is not in a position to refuse it (MacKinnon, 1987). Because of the power that men in positions of authority have over women, sexual harassment is a problem faced almost exclusively by women (Benson & Thomson, 1982). Women may have to choose between either submitting to unwanted sexual advances or losing their jobs. Some women, unable to afford the loss of a job, may "choose" to endure the unwanted sexual advances.

Dating

In the American dating system, it is still expected that sex will be exchanged for money (Weis & Borges, 1973). Men typically pay all the dating expenses (Muehlenhard & Linton, 1987). College students think that a woman is more likely to want to have sex with the man she is dating if he, rather than she, pays for her concert ticket; furthermore, if she does not want to have sex, they regard rape as more justifiable if he, rather than she, has paid for her ticket (Muehlenhard, 1988; Muehlenhard, Friedman, & Thomas, 1985). A survey of high school students revealed that 39% of the boys and 12% of the girls felt that it is acceptable for a boy to force a girl to have sex if he spends a lot of money on her (Giarrusso et al., 1979). Dates involving sexual aggression are more likely than typical dates to have involved the man's paying all the dating expenses (Muehlenhard & Linton, 1987).

A man's paying the dating expenses may lead to forceful sexual aggression because he feels entitled to sex in exchange for his expenditures. Or, nonviolent sexual coercion may occur because the woman feels obligated, either because she has incorporated society's norms or because the man persuades her that she is obligated to him. A survey of college women found that at least 10% of the female subjects had engaged in unwanted sexual intercourse because they felt obligated due to the money, time, or effort the man had spent (Muehlenhard & Long, 1989). A survey of college men found that 19% had given a woman expensive drugs so that she would feel sexually obligated to them (Mosher & Anderson, 1986).

Marriage

Exchanging sex for money is often regarded as a basis for marriage, in which women exchange sex and housework for men's financial support (DeBeauvoir, 1953; Friedan, 1963). "In the process of learning the female role, [a girl] is taught to value her sexual favors as an important item of exchange, to be used, ideally, to transact a marriage contract. As has been frequently pointed out, sex and love for her is a job" (Weis & Borges, 1973, p. 81). "Once a man enters into a long-term relationship with a woman, he has in a sense recognized her as his social equal and thus must 'pay' more (e.g., a house, a car, clothes, and so on) for the same sexual service" (James, 1978, p. 182).

Economic need may pressure women into marriage. In the United States, women who work full-time earn only 70% of men's earnings (Pear, 1987). Women with greater financial resources are less likely to marry than other women, whereas men with greater financial resources are more likely to marry than other men (Gerstel & Gross, 1989).

Economic need can also pressure women to remain in unhappy marriages. Weitzman (1985) described the fate of many divorced American women: After divorce, men's standard of living increases 42%, on the average, whereas women's and children's standard of living decreases 73%. Only about 5% to 10% of divorced women receive alimony, and two-thirds of custodial mothers receive no child support from their ex-husbands (Hewlett, 1986). This is devastating for most women, given that a significant number of married women are not employed outside the home, and married women who are employed full-time earn less than half of what married men earn (Hewlett, 1986).

These economic realities make it difficult for women to leave unhappy marriages and can pressure women into engaging in unwanted sex with husbands whom they cannot afford to leave. For example, Bolling (1988) reported that many of his female patients engaged in anal sex without condoms with husbands or lovers who were at high risk for AIDS (e.g., IV drug users) because the men refused to use condoms and the women were economically dependent on the men. Many wives of middle- and upper-class men also engage in unwanted sex with husbands on whom they are economically dependent (Joseph & Lewis, 1981).

Prostitution

Some women exchange sex for money in a more direct way, engaging in prostitution because it is the most lucrative job they can find, given the level of pay that women's work typically gleans (James, 1978). "The economic rewards of prostitution are normally far greater than those of most other female occupations" (Benjamin & Masters, 1964, p. 93). Because traditionally women's roles and occupations (wife and mother, secretary, waitress, and so on) have involved service or sexual attractiveness (James, 1978), and because even in the same occupation women earn less today than men do (Pear, 1987), many women—especially those who are unskilled or low-skilled—may see prostitution as their only option for economic survival.

DISCRIMINATION AGAINST LESBIANS

In addition to gender roles, fear of male violence, and status and economic coercion, discrimination against lesbians is one more source of pressure for women to be in sexual relationships with men. For women who might prefer not to be in heterosexual relationships, discrimination against lesbians continues as a form of indirect sexual coercion.

The individual who identifies herself as a lesbian—or who is so labeled by others—may face severe social, economic, and legal sanctions. Along with communists, the diseased, and the insane, persons who openly acknowledge their homosexuality may be denied admission to the United States. In most U.S. jurisdictions, discrimination against homosexuals in housing, employment, child custody, and other areas of life is legal, while homosexual behavior is illegal. . . . Most court decisions have held that [homosexuals] are not covered under the equal-protection clause of the United States Constitution.

(Weitz, 1989, p. 446)

Such intolerance pushes women who might not prefer heterosexual relationships toward unwanted—that is, coercive—heterosexual relationships.

VERBAL SEXUAL COERCION

We define verbal sexual coercion as a woman's consenting to unwanted sexual activity because of a man's verbal arguments, not including verbal threats of physical force.

Verbal sexual coercion is prevalent. For example, in a national study of over 6,000 higher education students, Koss et al. (1987) found that 44% of the women had engaged in unwanted intercourse because they had been overwhelmed by a man's continual arguments and pressure; 10% of the men had obtained sexual intercourse with unwilling women using this strategy.

Men use many types of verbal coercion to obtain sex: threatening to end the relationship or to find someone else to satisfy their sexual needs (Kanin, 1967; Mosher & Anderson, 1986; Muehlenhard & Cook, 1988); telling a woman that her refusal to have sex was changing the way they felt about her (Mosher & Anderson, 1986); asserting that "everybody does it" or questioning the woman's sexuality (e.g., implying that she is "frigid") (Muehlenhard & Cook, 1988); making the woman feel guilty (Muehlenhard & Cook, 1988); falsely promising love or marriage or using other lies (Kanin, 1967; Mosher, 1971; Muehlenhard & Falcon, in press); telling a woman with whom they were petting that she could not stop and leave them with "blue balls" (an uncomfortable condition involving testicular congestion resulting from sexual arousal without orgasm) (Mosher & Anderson, 1986); calling a woman a name angrily and pushing her away when she would not have sex (Mosher & Anderson, 1986); and threatening to do bodily self-harm (Muehlenhard & Cook, 1988).

Many verbally coercive college men had engaged in such behavior while they were still in high school (Kanin, 1967). Men who engage in verbal sexual coercion are characterized by traditional gender-role attitudes, calloused sexual attitudes toward women, and the acceptance of male sexual dominance over women (Mosher, 1971; Muehlenhard & Falcon, in press). Verbally coercive men are also likely to be socially skilled—that is, they find it easy to initiate conversations and dates with women (Muehlenhard & Falcon, in press).

Cultural norms might account for the high prevalence of verbal sexual coercion in our society. One such cultural norm is the ideology of male supremacy, in which sex is viewed as a demonstration of male superiority and dominance and female inferiority and submission (Lewin, 1985). It is harder to be assertive with a higher status person than with a subordinate (Lewin, 1985).

Women are socialized to believe that men's needs are more important than their own needs (Lewin, 1985). When Lewin asked women to react to scenarios in which a woman refused a man's sexual advance, the women's most common reaction was concern that they had hurt the man's feelings. This can make women vulnerable to verbal sexual coercion.

Society also perpetuates the myth that women who "lead men on" deserve what they get. Women who believe this myth are more likely to be sexually coerced verbally than women who do not believe it (Muehlenhard & Mac-Naughton, 1988). If a woman believes that she has "led a man on," she might believe that she has forfeited her right to refuse sex.

Low self-esteem might work in conjunction with cultural norms to increase a woman's vulnerability to sexual coercion. A woman with low self-esteem might fear that if she refuses her partner's sexual advances, she will lose him, and her value will be lessened because she is no longer associated with him (Parrot, 1985). This fear relates to both compulsory heterosexuality and status coercion (discussed earlier in this chapter), wherein women derive status from their relationships with men.

SEXUAL COERCION AND ALCOHOL AND DRUG INTOXICATION

The legal definition of rape in most states includes "intercourse completed when the woman was drugged, unconscious, asleep, or otherwise totally helpless and hence unable to consent" (Russell, 1984, p. 35), even if no violence was used to obtain intercourse.

Under what circumstances is it coercive for a man to have sex with an intoxicated woman? This question is controversial. One could imagine a continuum of sex due to intoxication. At one extreme, imagine a woman who gets intoxicated of her own volition, meets a man, and makes a sexual advance toward him, which he accepts. Even if she subsequently regrets her behavior, few people would regard this situation as sexual coercion. At the other end of the continuum, imagine a woman who attends a party and is told that the punch is nonalcoholic, when in fact it is not. She has several drinks and begins to feel dizzy. She is told that she can lie down in an upstairs bedroom. She passes out on the bed, and several men have sex with her while she is unconscious. This situation would clearly be defined as rape.

Between these two extremes lie numerous situations that vary with respect to how willing the woman was to have sex and how coercive the man was. Giarrusso et al. (1979) found that 39% of high school boys and 18% of high school girls said it is justifiable for a boy to force a girl to have sex if she is drunk or stoned; a girl who believes this myth might reluctantly agree to have sex, feeling that she has forfeited her right to refuse sex if she is intoxicated. A survey of college women revealed that 19% reported engaging in sexual intercourse when they were intoxicated (drunk or stoned) and later wishing they had not; 11% reported engaging in unwanted sexual intercourse because the other person got them intoxicated and took advantage of the situation; 13% reported engaging in unwanted sexual intercourse because they were so intoxicated that they were either unaware of what was happening or unable to stop the situation (Muehlenhard & Cook, 1988). A nationwide study of higher education students revealed that 8% of the women answered yes to the question, "Have you had sexual intercourse when you didn't want to because a man gave you alcohol or drugs?" (Koss et al., 1987).

Ehrhart and Sandler (1985) identified over 50 cases of gang rape occurring on college campuses. Every one of these gang rapes involved alcohol. Sometimes the woman was so intoxicated that she was unable to give consent—thus fulfilling the legal definition of rape. In some cases, the men may not have thought of their behavior as rape; instead, they may have regarded their behavior as group sex with a willing woman (Ehrhart & Sandler, 1985). Although Ehrhart and Sandler did not estimate the prevalence of gang rape, Mosher and Anderson (1986) found that 10% of a sample of college men reported waiting their turn in line with other men who were sharing a "party girl" (Mosher & Anderson, 1986).

Many men report using alcohol or drugs to obtain sex with unwilling women. Mosher and Anderson (1986) found that 75% of college men reported using alcohol or drugs in an attempt to obtain sex: 66% had gotten a woman high on alcohol, and 42% had gotten a woman high on marijuana or pills, in an attempt to get her to have sex. Men who obtain sex with unwilling women by getting them intoxicated are characterized by the acceptance of traditional gender roles and male sexual dominance over women, calloused sexual attitudes toward women, and social skill in initiating conversations and dates with women (Mosher & Anderson, 1986; Muehlenhard & Falcon, in press).

RAPE WITHOUT "FORCE"

Another type of sexual coercion is rape that does not involve "force"—that is, situations in which the woman does not want to engage in sex, she makes this clear to the man, and sex occurs anyway, without the man's using or threatening force. Because it does not involve force, this type of sexual coercion would not be defined as rape under most rape laws or in studies that use the legal definition of rape (Koss et al., 1987). It seems to be common, however. Muehlenhard and Linton (1987) asked college students about situations in which the woman did not want to engage in sexual intercourse, she made this clear to the man either verbally or nonverbally, and he did it anyway. Both women and men reported that men's most common strategy was "just doing it," even after the woman said no. This strategy was checked more often than such strategies as threats, physical coercion, or using a weapon. Similarly, Rapaport and Burkhart (1984) found that men's most common strategy for obtaining sex with an unwilling woman was ignoring her protests, rather than using more violent behavior.

There could be many reasons why a woman might not resist a man's advances so that unwanted intercourse could occur without force. The woman may fear that resisting will make the man violent. She may be confused. Her socialization may make it difficult for her to resist. One woman recalled, "Even as I say this now it sounds crazy to me, after what he did to me, . . . but I didn't scream. Not because I didn't think to scream. . . . I decided not to scream because I didn't want to embarrass him" (Meyer, 1984, p. 1). The reason that a woman does not resist should not be important, however; what should be important is that she did not consent and that she expressed this to the man. Saying no should be sufficient. Unfortunately, a woman's not consenting to sex is not enough in the eyes of most jurors, especially if the rapist was acquainted with the victim and did not use a weapon.

Court decisions have generally held that the issue in rape cases is not one of consent; it is one of force (Estrich, 1987). Force by a man is usually defined in terms of the amount of resistance used by a woman. If the woman did not physically resist, the courts see the man as not having used force, even if the woman did not consent. Estrich (1987) discussed a 1984 case, *State v. Alston*, (310 N.C. 399, 312 S.E.2d 470), in which the court acknowledged that sexual intercourse had occurred without the woman's consent and against her will. Even though the defendant had abused the woman during the course of their relationship, and even though he had threatened her shortly before intercourse occurred, the court ruled that no force was used and the act was not rape because the woman did not resist.

> The definition of force . . . protects male access to women where guns and beatings are not needed to secure it. The court . . . made clear that, at least in "social" contexts like this one with appropriate victims, a man is free to proceed regardless of verbal consent.
>
> *(Estrich, 1987, pp. 62–63)*

The court requires that a woman use a "reasonable" amount of resistance. Commenting on how much resistance a "reasonable" woman is required to put forth, Estrich stated:

> Their version of a reasonable person is one who does not scare easily, one who does not feel vulnerable, one who is not passive, one who fights back, not cries. The reasonable woman, it seems, is not a schoolboy "sissy"; she is a real man.
>
> *(Estrich, 1987, p. 65)*

Clearly, changes in the law and in the courts' interpretation of the law are needed.

CONCLUSION

Women clearly face numerous sources of sexual coercion. Some of these sources of coercion are obvious; others are so embedded in the structure of society that they are rendered almost invisible. Any situation in which women are not free to choose is coercive. As long as women are pressured into sexual relationships or sexual behaviors that they do not truly want, women cannot be free and autonomous. A recognition of the problem is the first step toward change.

REFERENCES

Adamo, S. J. (1984, December 7). Time for a new definition of wifely obedience. *Philadelphia Daily News,* p. 43.

American Psychiatric Association. (1987). *Diagnostic and statistical manual of mental disorders* (3rd ed. rev.). Washington, DC: Author.

Benjamin, H., & Masters, R. (1964). *Prostitution and morality.* New York: Julien Press.

Benson, D. J., & Thomson, G. E. (1982). Sexual harassment on a university campus: The confluence of authority relations, sexual interest and gender stratification. *Social Problems, 29,* 236–251.

Bernard, J. (1973). *The future of marriage.* New York: Bantam.

Bolling, D. (1988, March). *Heterosexual anal intercourse (HAI): Patient denial and patterns of exposure.* Paper presented at the western regional meeting of the Society for the Scientific Study of Sex, Dallas, TX.

Caplan, P. J. (1985). Single life and married life. *International Journal of Women's Studies, 8,* 6–11.

Daly, M. (1978). *Gyn/ecology: The metaethics of radical feminism.* Boston: Beacon Press.

DeBeauvoir, S. (1953). *The second sex.* New York: Knopf.

Ehrhart, J. K., & Sandler, B. R. (1985). *Campus gang rape: Party games?* Washington, DC: Association of American Colleges.

Eichler, M. (1977). The prestige of the occupation housewife. In P. Marchak (Ed.), *The working sexes* (pp. 151–175). Vancouver, Canada: University of British Columbia.

Estrich, S. (1987). *Real rape: How the legal system victimizes women who say no.* Cambridge, MA: Harvard University Press.

Friedan, B. (1963). *The feminine mystique.* New York: Norton.

Gelles, R. J., & Straus, M. A. (1988). *Intimate violence.* New York: Simon & Schuster.

Gerstel, N., & Gross, H. E. (1989). Women and the American family: Continuity and change. In J. Freeman (Ed.), *Women: A feminist perspective* (pp. 89–120). Mountain View, CA: Mayfield.

Giarrusso, R., Johnson, P., Goodchilds, J., & Zellman, G. (1979, April). Adolescents' cues and signals: Sex and assault. In P. Johnson (Chair), *Acquaintance rape and adolescent sexuality.* Symposium conducted at a meeting of the Western Psychological Association, San Diego, CA.

Hewlett, S. A. (1986). *A lesser life: The myth of women's liberation in America.* New York: William Morris.

Hite, S. (1976). *The Hite report: A nationwide study on female sexuality.* New York: Macmillan.

James, J. (1978). The prostitute as victim. In J. R. Chapman & M. Gates (Eds.), *The victimization of women* (pp. 175–201). Beverly Hills, CA: Sage.

Johnston, M. W., & Eklund, S. J. (1984). Life-adjustment of the never-married: A review with implications for counseling. *Journal of Counseling and Development, 63,* 230–231, 234–236.

Joseph, G. I., & Lewis, J. (1981). *Common differences: Conflicts in black and white feminist perspectives.* Garden City, NY: Doubleday.

Kanin, E. J. (1967). An examination of sexual aggression as a response to sexual frustration. *Journal of Marriage and the Family, 29,* 428–433.

Koss, M. P., Dinero, T. E., Seibel, C. A., & Cox, S. L. (1988). Stranger and acquaintance rape: Are there differences in the victim's experience? *Psychology of Women Quarterly, 12,* 1–24.

Koss, M. P., Gidycz, C. A., & Wisniewski, N. (1987). The scope of rape: Incidence and prevalence of sexual aggression and victimization in a national sample of higher education students. *Journal of Consulting and Clinical Psychology, 55,* 162–170.

Lewin, M. (1985). Unwanted intercourse: The difficulty of saying no. *Psychology of Women Quarterly, 9,* 184–192.

MacKinnon, C. A. (1987). *Feminism unmodified: Discourses on life and the law.* Cambridge, MA: Harvard University Press.

Masters, W. H., Johnson, V. E., & Kolodny, R. C. (1986). *Masters and Johnson on sex and human loving.* Boston: Little, Brown.

Meyer, T. J. (1984, December 5). "Date rape": A serious campus problem that few talk about. *Chronicle of Higher Education, 29,* 1, 12.

Mosher, D. L. (1971). Sex callousness toward women. In *Technical reports of the Commission on Obscenity and Pornography, Vol. 8,* (pp. 313–325). Washington, DC: U.S. Government Printing Office.

Mosher, D. L., & Anderson, R. D. (1986). Macho personality, sexual aggression, and reactions to guided imagery of realistic rape. *Journal of Research in Personality, 20,* 77–94.

Muehlenhard, C. L. (1988). Misinterpreted dating behaviors and the risk of date rape. *Journal of Social and Clinical Psychology, 6,* 20-37.

Muehlenhard, C. L., & Cook, S. W. (1988). Men's reports of unwanted sexual activity. *Journal of Sex Research, 24,* 58–72.

Muehlenhard, C. L., & Falcon, P. L. (in press). Men's heterosocial skill and attitudes toward women as predictors of verbal sexual coercion and forceful rape. *Sex Roles.*

Muehlenhard, C. L., Friedman, D. E., & Thomas, C. M. (1985). Is date rape justifiable? The effects of dating activity, who initiated, who paid, and men's attitudes toward women. *Psychology of Women Quarterly, 9,* 297–309.

Muehlenhard, C. L., & Linton, M. A. (1987). Date rape and sexual aggression in dating situations: Incidence and risk factors. *Journal of Counseling Psychology, 34,* 186–196.

Muehlenhard, C. L., & Long, P. J. (1990). *A gender role analysis of men's versus women's reports of pressure to engage in unwanted sexual intercourse.* Manuscript submitted for publication.

Muehlenhard, C. L., & MacNaughton, J. S. (1988). Women's beliefs about women who "lead men on." *Journal of Social and Clinical Psychology, 7,* 65–79.

Nilson, L. B. (1978). The social standing of a housewife. *Journal of Marriage and the Family, 40,* 541–548.

Parrot, A. (1985, April). *Relationship between self-esteem, locus of control, and acquaintance rape victimization.* Paper presented at the eastern regional meeting of the Society for the Scientific Study of Sex, Philadelphia, PA.

Pear, R. (1987, September 3). Women reduce lag in earnings but disparities with men remain. *New York Times,* pp. 1, 7.

Rapaport, K., & Burkhart, B. R. (1984). Personality and attitudinal characteristics of sexually coercive college males. *Journal of Abnormal Psychology, 93,* 216–221.

Rich, A. (1980). Compulsory heterosexuality and lesbian existence. *Signs: Journal of Women in Culture and Society, 5,* 631–660.

Rubin, G. (1984). The traffic in women: Notes on the "political economy" of sex. In A. M. Jagger & P. S. Rothenberg (Eds.), *Feminist frameworks* (pp. 155–171). New York: McGraw-Hill.

Russell, D. E. H. (1984). *Sexual exploitation: Rape, child sexual abuse, and workplace harassment.* Beverly Hills, CA: Sage.

Schrag, J. L., & Muehlenhard, C. L. (1989). [Pilot study on women's unwanted sexual experiences]. Unpublished data.

Shulman, A. K. (1983). Sex and power: Sexual bases of radical feminism. In M. W. Zak & P. A. Moots (Eds.), *Women and the politics of culture* (pp. 274–282). New York: Longman.

Stanko, E. A. (1988). Fear of crime and the myth of the safe home: A feminist critique of criminology. In K. Yllo & M. Bograd (Eds.), *Feminist perspectives on wife abuse* (pp. 75–88). Newbury Park, CA: Sage.

Van Wyk, P. H., & Geist, C. S. (1984). Psychosocial development of heterosexual, bisexual, and homosexual behavior. *Archives of Sexual Behavior, 13,* 505–544.

Walker, L. E. (1984). *The battered woman syndrome.* New York: Springer.

Weis, K., & Borges, S. S. (1973). Victimology and rape: The case of the legitimate victim. *Issues in Criminology, 8,* 71–115.

Weitz, R. (1989). What price independence? Social reactions to lesbians, spinsters, widows, and nuns. In J. Freeman (Ed.), *Women: A feminist perspective* (4th ed., pp. 446–456). Mountain View, CA: Mayfield.

Weitzman, L. J. (1979). *Sex role socialization: A focus on women.* Palo Alto, CA: Mayfield.

Weitzman, L. J. (1985). *The divorce revolution: The unexpected social and economic consequences for women and children in America.* New York: Free Press.

Zilbergeld, B. (1978). *Male sexuality: A guide to sexual fulfillment.* New York: Bantam.

CHAPTER 9

Wife Rape*

DIANA E. H. RUSSELL, PhD

*I cannot say that I think you very generous to the Ladies, for whilst you are pro-
claiming peace and good will to men, Emancipating all Nations, you insist upon
retaining an absolute power over Wives. But you must remember that Arbitrary
power is like most other things which are very hard, very liable to be broken.* . . .

Abigail Adams to John Adams, 1776;
Familiar Letters of John Adams and His Wife, Abigail Adams,
During the Revolution, *Charles Francis Adams (Ed.), 1876*

The marriage license [is] a raping license.

David Finkelhor and Kersti Yllo, License to Rape, *1985*

HISTORY OF WIFE RAPE AND THE LAW

The laws relating to rape in some states of this nation, and in most countries
of the world, include what is commonly referred to as "the marital exemption." Until very recently, these laws defined rape as the forcible penetration
of the body of a woman who was not the wife of the perpetrator. Accordingly, rape in marriage was a legal impossibility in the majority of states that
used this definition. Even in 1990, wife rape remains a legal impossibility in
seven states.

The origin of the marital exemption is invariably traced to a pronouncement by Matthew Hale, Chief Justice in England in the 17th century. As
published in *History of the Pleas of the Crown* in 1736, it reads as follows:

But the husband cannot be guilty of a rape committed by himself upon
his lawful wife, for by their mutual matrimonial consent and contract the

---

* Adapted, with minor revisions, from Diana E.H. Russell, *Rape in marriage* (expanded and
revised edition), Chap. 2. Bloomington, IN: Indiana University Press, 1990. Reprinted by
permission. References reproduced from original.

wife hath given up herself in this kind unto the husband which she cannot retract.

(Geis, 1978)

There has been considerable reluctance to change the laws condoning wife rape. One explanation for this reluctance may be that wife rape is "too close for personal comfort for the well-placed, married males who make up the vast majority of the membership of American state legislatures" (Geis, 1978). Some of the arguments that have greeted legislative efforts to outlaw rape in marriage give strong support to this thesis. The following are examples of such arguments described as "typical" by the National Center on Women and Family Law:

The State of Florida has absolutely no business intervening into the sexual relationship between a husband and a wife. . . . We don't need Florida invading the sanctity and intimacy of a relationship.

(Rep. Tom Bush, May 29, 1980)

[T]he Bible doesn't give the state permission anywhere in that Book for the state to be in your bedroom, and that is just exactly what this bill has gone to. It's meddling in your bedroom; the State of Florida, as an entity, deciding what you can do and what you can't do.

(Rep. John Mica, May 29, 1980)

But if you can't rape your wife, who can you rape?

(California State Senator Bob Wilson, addressing a group of women lobbyists,
Spring 1979) (Schulman, 1980).

The *Rideout* Case in Oregon

The spousal immunity clause was deleted from Oregon's rape statute in 1977. A year later in that state, John Rideout was indicted for raping his wife, Greta, and he thus became the first husband charged with marital rape to be criminally prosecuted while still living with his wife. Although there have been many other cases of husbands charged with rape in various states since then, the *Rideout* case is the most notorious. Despite the publicity about this case, which was often critical of Greta Rideout and of the fact that a husband could be accused of raping his wife, the *Rideout* case has done more than any other to raise consciousness about the issue of wife rape. This is how the case was described in the media at the time:

A twenty-three-year-old woman who'd been physically and psychologically abused by her husband for over two years, [Greta Rideout] found that as soon as she quit submitting to his desires, her husband's sexual aggression became so violent she could label it nothing less than rape. . . .

She had met John Rideout four years ago (in 1974) in Portland. . . . Before they were married (shortly after their two-and-a-half-year-old daughter, Jenny, was born), Greta said he'd slapped her face and "demolished" the house they were living in. She left him then—the first of three times.

"Two months after we were married, he began the mental abuse—calling me a dumb bitch, accusing me of being with someone else," she said, "but I was trying to deal with it. I wanted the marriage to work out, for better or worse. And believe me, most of it was worse."

Slowly she began to see a change taking place. The first time he gave her a black eye was a year and a half ago (in 1976). Aggressive sex, too, began to be a part of the pattern, according to Greta. "He was highly obsessed with sex; he wanted it two or three times a day. No matter what I gave him, he was never totally satisfied."

What seemed to give him the most pleasure, she reflected, was the violent sex which became a once-a-week occurrence. "And the more riled I got, the more he seemed to enjoy it."

Like most battered women, Greta Rideout had been afraid to fight back. The relationship became one of "love-hate, love-hate." John even threatened to sexually manipulate their daughter and told his wife he would show Jenny "what sex is all about" when she became an adolescent. . . .

She left him for the third time in July but returned for the same reason she had done so before. She couldn't support her daughter on the part-time minimum wages of her cashier's job or on welfare. She said she considered leaving Jenny with friends while she got on her feet financially, but thought John would accuse her of abandoning the child and try to take Jenny from her. Many of their arguments had been over money; John's work as a gas station attendant plus her meager wages "barely covered essentials," she said.

When she returned for the last time, her plan was to save up enough money to be able to leave for good.

"Before this point I had submitted. Now I was swimming to the surface to get out of the gutter, and he knew it. He saw the strength rising in me. . . ." It was around this time that his violence toward her seemed to intensify. "At times I'd be laying watching TV, and he'd walk up and kick me. I started feeling, God, he's weird." But he told her, "You're my wife; I can do what I want."

"He was in love with me when I was weak, but when I showed any strength, he hated my guts," she recalled. At the same time, she now realizes, he both loathed and was excited by strong women.

"He would see pretty women, strong career women, on TV or in magazines, and they seemed 'prudish' to him. He'd get worked up and say, 'Jeez, I'd like to rape that bitch's ass.'"

On October 10 (1978), John and Greta had an argument over money. He'd quit his job to return to school on the GI Bill and she thought he was squandering money at bars, playing pool—and not attending classes. She ran away from him, but he chased her, locked her in the apartment and started demanding sex. When she refused, he beat her until finally, she testified in court, she submitted for fear he would break her jaw.

John Rideout and his attorney never denied that he beat her that day, or that they had sexual intercourse. Their marriage had a pattern of fight, make up, and make love, the men said. (By the time their fights were over, said Greta, she often just submitted to sex. On the day of the rape, she said she was "totally repulsed" by the idea of having sex with John.)

Greta's rape story was confirmed by the doctor who examined her afterward and the Crisis Center worker who'd answered her call. "She was so scared that I was shaking; she had me scared to death," remembered volunteer Wanda Monthey. (Celarier, 1979)

On December 27, 1978, John Rideout was acquitted of the charge of first degree rape of his wife by a jury of eight women and four men.

On January 6, 1979, less than two weeks after John was found not guilty, the Rideouts announced their reconciliation. Their faces beamed out from the pages of newspapers across the nation. "The law is right," John Rideout was quoted as saying. "It's a hard thing for a person like me to come back and say he believes the law is right when the law was used on me."

In March 1979, the couple separated again. Greta was quoted as saying, "I was going to go mad if I stayed there any longer. He has some pretty wild ideas about marriage." She added, "He also said that the things he told me about women's rights after the trial were wrong." Jean Christensen, Greta's attorney, obtained a divorce for her. Greta resumed her maiden name.

A few months later, John Rideout was back in court. On September 4, 1979, he pled guilty to a charge of criminal trespass for breaking into his ex-wife's home on August 27. He was given a nine-month suspended jail sentence, put on two years' probation, and required to pay $15 for the door he damaged and to submit to psychiatric evaluation. In February of this year, John Rideout was sentenced once again to nine months in jail for harassing his ex-wife; probation would be considered if Rideout consented to mental counseling.

Rideout's continuing attacks upon his ex-wife [after the rape trial] did not receive the sensational headlines that had attended the trial and reconciliation, so people still remember the Rideouts when they announced they were back together. Reporter Rae Nadler, writing in the *Hartford Courant*, described them at the time: "They posed together, a handsome couple, while the headlines declared 'Rideouts Will Ride It Out.' The world grinned and shook its head."

(Griffen, 1980)

Wife Rape and the Law

Those who opposed striking the marital exemption from Oregon's rape laws saw the brief reconciliation of John and Greta Rideout as conformation that the state had no business meddling in the private affairs of married couples. Those who favored the legal reform and/or believed Greta's account of being raped by John perceived their reconciliation as a terrible blow. Though Greta may have been raped, the argument went, her experience could not have been that traumatic or she would not have reconciled with her husband. Such a conclusion shows little understanding of the dynamics of relationships, particularly those in which women are battered; and Greta was not only a victim of wife rape but a battered wife as well.

The issues of battered women and rape victims emerged as public concerns at different times and have developed in this and other countries as if they were two totally different problems. Separate literatures have developed around each, different institutions have been developed for handling them, and different people have been attracted to working with either rape victims or battered women, each often remaining quite ignorant of the other problem.

The *Rideout* case is one of many in which it is impossible to separate these two forms of male violence. But although ongoing intimate heterosexual relationships that are violent often involve both rape and beating, it is also important to recognize that the issues of wife rape and wife beating can be quite separate in many marriages, and that wife rape is not merely one more abuse suffered by the already battered woman.

MARITAL RAPE LEGISLATION AND COURT DECISIONS: THE CONTEMPORARY SCENE IN THE UNITED STATES

In July 1980 only Oregon, Nebraska, and New Jersey had completely abolished the marital rape exemption, and California, Delaware, Hawaii, Minnesota, and Iowa had partially striken it. Nine years later in July 1989, husbands could be prosecuted for raping their wives in forty-two states, the District of Columbia, and on all federal land. This represents an extraordinary achievement on the part of many feminists and their allies who have had to work very hard to break through the resistance on the part of mostly male legislators. These forty-two states are listed in the two left-hand columns of Table 9.1.

The seventeen states in the far left column of the chart are those that no longer permit a marital rape exemption. This is to say that wife rape is a crime in these states, regardless of whether the couple lives together or apart.

In the twenty-six states in the middle column of the chart, husbands can be prosecuted for raping their wives in some circumstances, but they are totally exempt from prosecution in others that are prosecutable for nonmarital rape. For example, in some states, so-called lower degrees of rape are not considered crimes in cases of wife rape: for instance, rape imposed

TABLE 9.1.   State Law Chart*

Husbands Can Be Prosecuted for Raping Their Wives		Husbands Cannot Be Prosecuted Unless Couple Living Apart or Legally Separated or Filed for Divorce or Order of Protection
No Exemptions	Some Exemptions	
N-17	N = 26	N = 7
Alabama	Arizona	Kentucky
Alaska	California	Missouri
Arkansas	Connecticut	New Mexico
Colorado	Delaware	North Carolina
Florida	Hawaii	Oklahoma
Georgia	Idaho	South Carolina
Indiana	Illinois	Utah
Maine	Iowa	
Massachusetts	Kansas	
Nebraska	Louisiana	
New Jersey	Maryland	
New York	Michigan	
North Dakota	Minnesota	
Oregon	Mississippi	
South Dakota	Montana	
Vermont	Nevada	
Wisconsin	New Hampshire	
(District of	Ohio	
Columbia, and	Pennsylvania	
federal lands in	Rhode Island	
any state)	Tennessee	
	Texas	
	Virginia	
	Washington	
	West Virginia	
	Wyoming	

* This is an adaptation of an updated chart prepared by the National Clearinghouse on Marital and Date Rape, Berkeley, California, February 1990. Adapted by permission.

by force but without the wife's suffering additional degrees of violence such as kidnapping or being threatened with a weapon; and nonforceful rape that is imposed when the woman is unable to consent because she is unconscious, drugged, asleep, ill, or physically or mentally helpless in some other way.

California's spousal rape law still requires that the victim report the crime within 90 days of its occurrence. One reason for this provision is to protect men from the assumed-to-be-numerous vindictive and dishonest wives who are by this provision rendered less able to fabricate a charge of marital rape in divorce cases. For instance, this provision attempts to prevent a woman from being able to report during divorce proceedings or custody battles that her husband raped her throughout her marriage. Or, if she does make such a charge, these rapes are not prosecutable offenses. There are numerous other such exemptions built into the California spousal rape law,* as in many of the other 25 states in the middle column of the chart.

In the seven remaining states (those on the far right of the chart), wife rape is not a crime. If a husband rapes his wife when they are living apart or have obtained a legal separation, or when one of the parties has filed for a divorce or for an order of protection, the couple is defined as unmarried for the purposes of prosecution. As marital rape expert Laura X states: "The seventeenth century legal definition of 'married' (i.e., a wife gives up her right to consent) is thus reinforced in these states" (National Clearinghouse on Marital and Date Rape, 1990). She goes on to point out that the husband in these seven states can continue to rape his wife until *she* takes action; the burden is on her to leave him or to file for divorce—sometimes life-threatening steps for her to initiate—instead of it being the state's responsibility to remove him from her, and from society, for raping her (National Clearinghouse on Marital and Date Rape, 1990).

The National Clearinghouse on Marital and Date Rape is the only source for national statistics on the outcome of wife rape cases that have been reported to the police. The Clearinghouse staff followed up information obtained from a newspaper clipping service and a vast network of contacts at rape crisis centers and battered women's shelters, with phone calls to the prosecutors, court officials, attorneys, and journalists—in short, anyone who could supply them with further information about the outcome of the cases they had learned about. Unfortunately, the Clearinghouse data cover only the period 1978 (after the acquittal of John Rideout) to 1985, when lack of funding prevented the continuation of this project. Although it can be assumed that their method of acquiring information did not enable the staff to draw up a complete compendium of all the wife rape cases reported in the

---

* 1. Other circumstances in which wife rape in California is not a crime are as follows:
  a) The wife is incapable of giving consent because of a mental disorder, developmental or physical disability about which her husband is or should be cognizant.
  b) The wife is prevented from resisting due to intoxicating, anesthetic or controlled substances (illegal drugs, mostly narcotics, and others such as barbiturates) administered by her husband or about which he is cognizant.
  c) The wife is unconscious of the nature of the act at the time it occurred.
  d) Intercourse is forced on the wife by threat of deportation or incarceration (for example) by a husband who is a public official such as a policeman or immigration official—or who poses as such—when the wife has reason to believe that her husband has such authority. (This circumstance is particularly endemic in Los Angeles and other areas where brides are imported as sex slaves either by United States GIs or by men of their own or other cultures. In these cases the woman is often kept at home, terrorized, and because she does not understand the language, she cannot learn the truth about her husband's occupation.)
  2. The convicted husband/rapist does not have to report as a sex offender.
  3. Husband/rapists are the only rapists who can be charged with a misdemeanor instead of a felony for the crime of rape.
Source: National Clearinghouse on Marital and Date Rape, document prepared by Laura X, 1989.

United States between 1978 and 1985, it is nevertheless the most complete data available on the outcome of wife rape cases.

An adapted version of the National Clearinghouse's table on arrest, prosecution, and conviction statistics for marital rapists appears in Table 9.2.

The 88% conviction rate for victims of wife rape whose reports to the police resulted in arrest is strikingly high. It is considerably higher than many people either anticipated or currently realize. It is also significantly higher than the conviction rate for *non*marital rapes. This is surprising because it is generally true that the more intimate the relationship between the victim and the rapist, the less likely are reporting, arrest, and conviction (Russell, 1984).

One reason for the high conviction rate for wife rape is probably that—contrary to the fears of many legislators—the wives who charge their husbands with rape have often been subjected to particularly brutal and/or deviant experiences. The thousands of women who are raped by their husbands in more "ordinary" ways, without the employment of tire irons, dogs, strangulation, or death threats, are simply not reporting their experiences to the police. And it is doubtful that the vast majority ever will. Given the continuing misogyny of the legal and law enforcement systems, we should not delude ourselves that this is a problem that will be solved by having every victim of wife rape report her attack to the police.

I believe that the next steps in the campaign for the rights of wife rape victims (and all married women are potential wife rape victims) are for concerned women and men to mobilize for the pursuit of the following goals:

1. The criminalization of wife rape is the seven holdout states that have so far been unwilling to institute this reform.
2. The passing of laws in the 26 states that still treat some forms of rape by husbands as noncriminal, the implicit assumption being that wife rape is less serious than rape by other perpetrators.

Feminist legal theorists, such as Joanne Schulman (formerly the staff attorney of the National Center on Women and Family Law), Sarah Wunsch and Anne Simon (formerly at the Center for Constitutional Rights), have

TABLE 9.2. Outcome of Wife Rape Cases Reported to the Police: 1978–1985

Outcome	Number of Cases
Husband Arrested	210
Charge Dropped	48
Case Still Pending (as of 1985)	44
Prosecution Ended with Acquittal	14
Prosecution Ended with Conviction	104
Total Prosecuted Cases	118
Convictions as a Percentage of Prosecuted Cases	88%

noted that proposed marital rape laws are often butchered by amendments before becoming law. This is what has happened in 26 states. In contrast, the highest courts in several states have simply struck down the marital rape exemption as an unconstitutional denial of equal protection for wives. Because the rape of unmarried women is considered a crime, some of them have argued that equity requires that it also be so for married women. The courts have not followed the practice of many legislatures in maintaining that wife rape is different from rape by other perpetrators.

These feminist attorneys therefore have proposed that the wives in the 34 states that either do not have a law against wife rape or that do not have a satisfactory law, should organize a class action suit in each of these states to have the exemptions struck down by the courts as unconstitutional.

3. Courts can also strike down the exemptions for husbands as unconstitutional if they agree, as in *Liberta* (New York) (Wunsch, 1986), with Friend of the Court briefs requesting such a decision.

Sarah Wunsch of the Center for Constitutional Rights has summarized the significance of the 1984 New York State Court of Appeals' case called *People of the State of New York v. Mario Liberta* in a pamphlet first published in July 1986. The Court of Appeals demolished "the excuses for not having laws to protect women against marital rape" by offering the following arguments:

Marriage does not give a husband a right to forced sex; rape is not part of the marriage contract. While it is understood that sex is a part of marriage, a woman has no "duty" to provide sex on demand whenever and in whatever way the husband desires it; and often, rape has nothing to do with sex.

Accusing angry wives of making up charges of rape is just another example of discrimination against women. In states where marital rape is treated as rape, there is no evidence that wives are making up charges. In fact, rape is one of the most underreported of all crimes.

Just because a crime may be hard to prove in some cases doesn't mean that prosecutors should be unable to ever present such a case. Actually, there is a high conviction rate in marital rape cases that have gone to trial.

Marital privacy is meant to protect the privacy of husbands and wives to engage in activities they both agree to; it is not a shield for violent, brutal acts.

Making marital rape a crime does not make it harder to keep a marriage going. By making rape in marriage a crime, some rapes can be prevented and the institution of marriage may be strengthened by the respect for women it conveys.

(Wunsch, 1986, pp. 8–9)

4. Wives who reside in states where wife rape is still legal can sue their husbands for damages in civil court, as pioneering rape law analyst Camille Le Grand proposed in the 1970s. However, she also pointed

out that it would be easier to sue one's husband civilly in a state where wife rape was taken seriously enough to be considered criminal.

On the other hand, it is equally important for all of us to recognize that wife rape is not a problem that will ever be solved by turning to the law. As long as men are the ones to make and implement the laws, there will be little justice for women. The primary dedication of male legislators is to their own interests, not to women's. Taking their husbands to court is not an option that many wives will consider, for economic, social, and psychological reasons. In addition, many women realize that the system is unlikely to be fair to them. For some it would also be highly dangerous to report sexual assault by their husbands because of the vindictive and sometimes lethal violence to which they might then be subjected.

The solution to the problem of wife rape starts with breaking silence about it. Women must realize that rape in marriage is common, but illegal, and married women need to know that they have a *right* to decline their husbands' sexual advances whenever they want to. For these goals to be achieved, feminists—particularly those who work in battered women's shelters and rape crisis centers—must acknowledge the significance and seriousness of wife rape in the United States, and place it on their agenda of issues that must be confronted and remedied. Service workers must extend their services to the victims of wife rape, and include wife rape in their efforts to educate the community. These are some of the first steps toward creating new norms for men's behavior in marriage. New remedies will emerge once these norms have been established. This may involve publicly shaming men, as the Chinese battered wives did in their "speak bitterness" sessions after the Communist revolution. Whatever the method, one thing is clear. True gender equality in and outside of marriage is necessary before all wives will be free from the risk of rape by their husbands.

REFERENCES

Adams, C. F. (Ed). (1875). Abigail Adams to John Adams, 1776. *Familiar Letters of John Adams and His Wife, Abigail Adams, During the Revolution.* Boston: Houghton Mifflin.

Celarier, M. (1979, January 10–16). I kept thinking maybe I could help him. *In These Times.* Chicago: Institute for Public Affairs.

Finkelhor, D., & Yllo, K. (1985). *License to rape: Sexual abuse of wives.* New York: Holt, Rinehart, & Winston.

Geis, G. (1978). Rape in marriage: Law and law reform in England, the United States, and Sweden. *Adelaide Law Review, 6*(2).

Griffen, M. K. (1980, September). In 44 states, it's legal to rape your wife. *Student Lawyer, 9*(1).

National Clearinghouse on Marital and Date Rape. (1990, January 1). State law chart. Unpublished sheet.

Russell, D. E. H. (1984). *Sexual exploitation: Rape, child sexual abuse, and workplace harassment.* Beverly Hills, CA: Sage Publications.

Schulman, J. (1980, October). The marital rape exemption in the criminal law, *Clearinghouse Review, 14*(6).

Wunsch, S. (1986). *Stopping sexual assault in marriage: A guide for women, counselors and advocates.* New York: Center for Constitutional Rights.

CHAPTER 10

Acquaintance Gang Rape on Campus

CHRIS S. O'SULLIVAN, PhD

In the Spring of 1984, two "gang rape" trials were in progress. One received a great deal of national publicity. Six men were charged with aggravated rape of a woman at Big Dan's Tavern in New Bedford, Massachusetts. Four were convicted. The other trial received only local attention and sent a different message. Seven college students were tried for third-degree sexual assault of a 17-year-old Michigan State University (MSU) student in a dormitory. After a three-week trial, in the course of which the five defense lawyers each displayed the victim's jeans and football jersey before the court and asked her why she wasn't wearing a bra when she went to the midnight dorm party, the students were acquitted. Questioned about the verdict, an MSU senior was quoted in the local paper as saying, "I don't believe she was raped . . . I believe they ran a train on her" (Pierson, 1984, p. 1B). A notable similarity between the two trials—and others—was the community support given to the defendants.

In New Bedford, over 6,000 citizens gathered outside the City Hall to protest the conviction of four of the men (Chancer, 1987). In a similar demonstration, when five Kentucky State University students were arrested on charges of raping and sodomizing a fellow student, 200 students held an angry rally in their support. In both instances, the protesters not only defended the men but also attacked the woman, maintaining she should be punished. This pattern of sympathy suggests that such sexual behavior is acceptable for men.

As further evidence that such behavior is tolerated in "decent" young men, the character witnesses for the Michigan State defendants included a minister and a girlfriend who testified that the men were incapable of rape. The defense argument was that the woman had consented or had not clearly expressed her objection. Because the defendants in these cases did not deny having sex with the same woman sequentially or simultaneously, the testimony of the character witnesses and community support for the defendants implied that exemplary moral character is consistent with having sex with a young woman in tandem with several buddies.

The thesis of this review is that group sexual assault is considered normal behavior for some groups of young men in our society. I will attempt to

140

provide some preliminary answers to the fundamental questions of what the practice is, how often it occurs, who does it, to whom, and why. A brief discussion of the difficulties of prosecuting such cases is included as are suggestions for societal change.

THE GANG RAPE PHENOMENON

Although considerable attention has been devoted to rape in psychological and sociological literature over the past decade, group rape has rarely been discussed as a distinct phenomenon. While the existing literature is extremely helpful in understanding the sociocultural context that supports sexual aggression, there may be important differences between single- and multiple-perpetrator rape, especially in regard to motivation and situational characteristics. Other differences may include offender characteristics and psychological consequences for victims. The primary focus here is on perpetrators rather than victims.

To term it "gang rape" when many men have sex with the same woman and the men deny coercion, is to prejudice the issue. Many of the cases discussed in this chapter as instances of gang rape were not determined to be rapes in judicial proceedings. Aside from the fact that many rapists and their victims do not recognize the crime that has been committed, difficulties of proving rape charges are compounded when there are multiple perpetrators. Because prosecutions and convictions are so rare, any case in which a woman alleged that her participation in sex with a group of men was involuntary is considered an instance of group rape for purposes of this discussion. Cases in which we do not know the woman's view of the incident and there are no allegations of force will be termed "trains," in the common vernacular of the subcultures in which such sex is practiced.

A group is considered here to consist of three or more men. There are two reasons for adopting this criterion. First, although two persons are often considered a group in social psychology, most of the group dynamics relevant to gang rape are not activated unless there are at least three group members. Second, several female college students in my samples reported soliciting sex with two men, preferring it to sex with one man, but none reported voluntarily engaging in or enjoying sexual encounters with more than two men. The mean number of male participants in the cases I have studied is five.

Campus gang rapes are emphasized here. That street gangs (Amir, 1971) or motorcycle gangs (Fort, 1971) have sex with a single female ritualistically, for example, as an initiation rite, is known and is typically accounted for by the social deviance of these groups. That group rapes may be a common practice among college students is the basis of the claim that they are normative and of the hypothesis that they are an outgrowth of conventional sex roles. Campus gang rapes are also usually acquaintance rapes, occurring during social get-togethers.

Because of the lack of existing literature on campus gang rapes, most of the following observations are based on two trials attended by the author and 22 other incidents during the past 10 years, documented in newspapers, in Warshaw's report (1988), and in materials published by the Project on the Status and Education of Women of the Association of American Colleges.

INCIDENCE OF GROUP SEXUAL ASSAULTS ON COLLEGE CAMPUSES

Because there have been no systematic attempts to collect data on the incidence and prevalence of gang rapes in particular, estimates of their occurrence must be extrapolated from the rape literature or from anecdotal evidence and media reports.

Koss (1987), in a study of the national incidence of acquaintance rape among college students, found that 15% of the women (as victims) and 4% of the men (as perpetrators) had been involved in forced intercourse. The mean number of rapes reported by these subjects was above two. Five percent of the women who reported having been raped and 16% of the men who reported having raped said that their most serious incident involved more than one offender. Thus, in Koss's sample, nearly 1% of the men and women at colleges across the United States identified their most serious experience with sexual aggression as involving two or more men and one woman. These data may provide an underestimate of the occurrence of gang rapes because subjects were asked to report the number of men involved in only their single most serious experience. On the other hand, Koss's data may provide an overestimate because cases involving two men are included but do not meet the criterion for group rape here.

Using a more restricted sample, Rivera and Regoli (1987) mailed surveys to 400 randomly selected sorority women at a southwestern university. Two percent of their 174 respondents reported having been raped by two or more men while at the university. Drawing on a different population, Amir's (1971) study of rape in Philadelphia showed a much higher percentage of gang rape: 26% of the 646 rapes he identified were perpetrated by three or more men, and 55% of the rapists were involved in group rapes. Similarly, of the 81,030 rapes in 1986 on which the Bureau of Justice Statistics had data, 25% involved group rape offenders (Flanagan & Jamieson, 1988).

Anecdotal evidence of collegiate gang rapes is consistent with the frequency level suggested by Koss's data. Bernice Sandler of the Association of American Colleges reported that she had been told of 80 cases of group sexual assaults at colleges across the country (personal communication, May 16, 1988). She described the phenomenon as occurring among students at all types of institutions, from private religious colleges to large state universities and Ivy League colleges (Ehrhart & Sandler, 1985).

An article by a *Chicago Tribune* reporter (Schmich, 1988) listed the following group sexual assaults at universities. Eight men sexually assaulted a woman at a fraternity party at the University of Rochester in February 1988; a similar incident took place at Stetson University in Florida that Spring; 29 men were disciplined for the rape of a sorority pledge by several men at a fraternity party while other men took photographs, at San Diego State University in 1985; six fraternity brothers at the University of Florida allegedly raped a "little sister" at a rush party in 1983 (this fraternity advertised its rush parties with a train on the posters). The indictment of three University of Minnesota basketball players for sexually assaulting a local college student at a motel while playing in Wisconsin was reported in *Sports Illustrated* (Neff & Sullivan, 1986). A gang rape case at the University of California at Berkeley in 1986 generated much publicity ("UC Women," 1986).

In May 1989, groups of students at three different universities were defending themselves in court against charges of collectively raping a visitor to their campus residence. Media attention at that time, however, was focused on two sexual assaults by groups of high school students. New York City was in an uproar over the multiple rape and beating of a woman jogging in Central Park (Wolff, 1989), and five teenagers in suburban New Jersey had been arrested for sexually assaulting a mildly retarded teenage acquaintance ("Five youths held," 1989).

CHARACTERISTICS OF ASSAILANTS

Those most likely to rape or be raped, respectively, are men and women 20 to 24 years old; the next most likely group is 16 to 19-year-olds (Russell, 1982). Thus, sexual assault is most commonly committed by college-age men against women of college age. In their study of men convicted of sexual assault of adults, Groth and Birnbaum (1979) reported that the majority of the gang rapes were peer rapes between young adults; the mean age of the rapists was 23 and of the victims, 22.

Although some researchers (Amir, 1971; Schwendinger & Schwendinger, 1983) contended that the tendency to be sexually aggressive is associated with social deviance and low socioeconomic status (SES), Smith and Bennett (1985) maintained that sexual aggression is predicted by conflict between the sexes, across class and economic lines. As with other forms of criminal behavior, particularly abuse within relationships (child and spouse abuse), it may be that low SES individuals are more likely to be detected, prosecuted, and convicted than high SES perpetrators.

In fact, in parallel to the groupthink phenomenon (Janis, 1982), membership in a *privileged* group may protect a perpetrator from doubts about the propriety of his behavior, as well as from the perception of criminality by others. Janis proposed the concept of groupthink to explain disastrous decisions by elite groups, such as the decision by Kennedy's cabinet to invade Cuba. Impressed by each other, Janis suggested, members of such high status groups become convinced of the group's moral superiority, invulnerability, and consensus.

Consideration of publicized cases suggests that elite groups on campus are most likely to engage in group sexual assault. Football and basketball players enjoy more prestige than soccer or baseball players, and are more often accused of gang rape. The men charged with sexual assault at Florida State, San Diego State, and Stetson were "Pikes," members of the Pi Kappa Alpha fraternity. According to a reporter investigating the Florida State case, the national adviser to this fraternity said that "Pikes are a cut above most students on this campus. They have more money. They are better dressed. They drive better cars," (Hull, 1988, p. 6F). Although his point was that these young men are too high-class to commit a gang rape, this sort of group identity may discourage moral self-scrutiny. If the public also assumes that only "low life" would commit such a crime, social class may constitute an effective defense. Thus, lawyers for the seven Michigan State students emphasized their clients' middle-class background (they arrived at court in limousines), while depicting the victim as a streetwise ghetto kid.

Cohesive Groups

Of the 24 documented cases of alleged gang rape by college students in the past 10 years, 13 were perpetrated by fraternity men, four by groups of basketball players, four by groups of football players, one by lacrosse players, and only two by men unaffiliated with a formal organization. Fraternities have houses where they can have unsupervised parties, serve alcohol, and enjoy privacy from nonmembers in their bedrooms and living rooms. College football and basketball players often live in their own dormitory and have motel rooms when on the road (the University of Minnesota basketball players assaulted their victim in a motel). Thus, these groups are more likely than others on college campuses to have facilities and opportunities for illicit activities.

Their living situation may facilitate gang rape, but other evidence suggests that the cohesiveness of these groups is an equally important factor. First, several of the known gang rapes by college athletes and fraternity brothers have taken place not in reserved residences but in regular campus housing. Second, other tightly knit groups of men, such as members of a rock band (Blakely, 1984), have been implicated in gang rapes. Although only two of the prosecuted campus gang rapes did not involve football or basketball players or fraternity members, a participant in one of these incidents referred to his codefendants as "the other members," although they did not belong to any known organization. That is, the assault was perpetrated by such a tightly knit group of friends that they saw themselves as "members." Often, some of the team members who rape together come from the same hometown and grew up together.

Another group that has been identified as having participated in group sexual assaults are soldiers in combat. Brownmiller (1975) reported that gang rapes were committed in World War II by German soldiers as they marched through France and Belgium, by Japanese soldiers in China, by Moroccan soldiers in Italy, and by American soldiers in France and Germany. She provided vivid second-hand accounts of repeated group sexual assaults followed by murder and mutilation of their victims by Americans fighting in Vietnam. Combat soldiers tend to fall into the same age range as college students or street gang members, and belong to a formal single-sex organization.

Differential association theory (DeFleur & Quinney, 1966) is helpful in formulating predictions. This theory postulates that criminal behavior is learned through symbolic interactions within intimate social groups. Which segments of the population of American men aged 16 to 24 are likely to participate in group sexual assaults? The theory suggests that fraternity members and members of athletic teams may participate in group assaults not only because they have the facilities and are already organized, but also because the behavior is *learned* within these primary groups and is passed down along with other traditions. In some cases, there seems to be a ritualistic aspect to the assaults.

Research on campus rape also shows that athletes and fraternity men are more likely to be sexually aggressive individually than other college students. Garrett-Gooding and Senter (1987) found that more fraternity men (35%) reported having forced intercourse than did members of other organizations, such as student government (9%), or men not affiliated with any organization (11%). A *Philadelphia Daily News* investigation (Hoffman, 1986) reported:

> Football and basketball players representing NCAA-affiliated schools were reported to police for sexual assault approximately 38% more often than the average male on a college campus, as measured by an FBI survey.
>
> *(p. 104)*

Furthermore, men who would *not* rape alone may become rapists in the company of their sexually aggressive buddies. Groth and Birnbaum (1979) noted that the majority of those convicted of group rape in their sample, whom they identified as "followers" rather than instigators, had raped only in groups prior to their conviction. One of the Kentucky State defendants told police that he left the woman alone when he found her partially clothed in his room because she was unwilling to have sex with him. When he returned and found his friends assaulting her, he joined in.

MOTIVATIONS FOR GROUP SEXUAL ASSAULT

One of the most interesting aspects of group sexual assault is that it is a *group* activity, implying that the discussion of motivation must take into account the fact that there is, in some sense, an audience and that something is being shared. One source of hypotheses about motives is Scully and Marolla's (1985) study of convicted rapists' accounts of the rewards of rape, with particular attention to the responses of gang rapists, who were mostly in their late teens or early twenties. Brownmiller's (1975) review of gang rape provided confirmation of the motives identified by Scully and Marolla (1985), and Farr's (1988) study of "Good Old Boys Sociability groups" (GOBS), men who maintained a group affiliation from adolescence into adulthood, provided a helpful picture of the activities of middle-class "gangs."

Excitement and Belonging

The most common description of the rewards of rape by the incarcerated gang rapists interviewed by Scully and Marolla (1985) fell into the category of recreation and adventure. Farr (1988) stated that "fun and trouble enjoy a symbiotic relationship as sociability themes" (p. 271). One activity that fits this description, Farr continued, is fooling around with a "bad woman," defined as any woman who is not the wife or girlfriend of a member.

A unique reward of gang rape described by Scully and Marolla's (1985) respondents was the camaraderie among the men. A reporter interviewed by Brownmiller (1975, p. 98) believed that American soldiers, unlike South Vietnamese soldiers, preferred gang rape to solitary rape because our soldiers were trained in the buddy system. I would suggest that the fact that American soldiers did not share a language with their victims, who resembled the enemy, also provided a motive for sharing the rape with friends. Similarly, Groth and Birnbaum (1979) listed rapport, fellowship, and cooperation as unique benefits of gang rape.

Also viewed positively, by Scully and Marolla's respondents and American soldiers (Brownmiller, 1975, p. 107), was the challenge of performing in the group situation. Farr (1988) noted that, just as fun and trouble go hand-in-hand, so are competition and camaraderie intertwined in male sociability groups. Geis (1971) also maintained that a primary motive in group sexual assault, especially for group leaders, is to sustain an image with the group. For followers, Groth and Birnbaum (1979) added, participation seems to stem in part from indebtedness to or emotional dependency on the leader.

In part, then, participation in a group sexual assault is motivated by the relationships among the men, for the purpose of maintaining or creating images and roles within the group. Certainly, providing a woman to the group, as in several of the documented campus cases where a college student offered his date to his friends, falls in the category of motives related to intragroup acceptance. An intriguing possibility is suggested by the presence in both the Florida State and Michigan State cases of a visiting friend from another college. Does an outsider intensify the competition and need to create a masculine image?

Sex

It appears that part of the appeal is the shared experience with one's buddies. Earlier studies of gang rape posited that the men were latent homosexuals and sharing the woman was a way of sharing sex covertly. The same authors (e.g., Blanchard, 1959) often alleged at the same time that women wanted to be raped. We reject the latter reading of the unconscious, and contemporary social science has rejected the former as requiring unnecessary and unsupported assumptions. The men are sharing an experience of heterosexual sex. That does say something about their social and emotional relationships with their own sex, but does not in itself inform us that they would rather have sex with each other. Groth and Birnbaum (1979) concurred: "Men do not rape women out of sexual desire for other men, but they may rape women, in part, as a way to relate to men" (p. 116). To further this point, these authors used the analogy of two men robbing a store together: they are not covertly expressing a desire to rob each other.

One motive that should not be overlooked in this age group, however, is simply the opportunity to have heterosexual intercourse. One offender who was interviewed by Scully and Morolla (1985) had been involved in 20–30 group rapes. He stated that he had participated in gang rapes because his driver's license had been revoked, depriving him of the opportunity to take women out alone. A college student interviewed by Gianturco and Smith (1974) about his participation in a "train" during Spring break in Florida seemed to be delighted by the unusual sexual availability of college women. He did not know the other men, thus apparently relations among the men played little or no role in his participation.

A related enticement of group rape for young men who are unable to make relationships with women on their own is that it allows for sexual intercourse without responsibility toward the sexual partner. Solitary rapists sometimes seek reassurance from their victims that they were also sexually satisfied, as Brownmiller (1975, p. 196) and Russell (1974, p. 111) noted. Conversely, Scully and Marolla (1985) were told that a reward of group rape was that no individual had to be concerned about or relate to the woman.

AGGRESSION IN GROUPS

It is well-established that individuals are more aggressive in groups than they would be when acting alone. Such group processes are probably what participants in group sexual assaults and their defenders have in mind when they attempt to deflect blame by explaining, "Things got out of hand" (as several "enlightened" male students have confided to me about group sexual assaults). Three factors identified by social psychologists to explain why groups are so easily ignited to aggression can be applied to gang rape.

An individual in a group is less likely to behave altruistically and more likely to harm others than if the same individual were alone. One reason for these tendencies is that responsibility for the welfare of a victim is diluted by the presence of others, who share the blame. The term *diffusion of responsibility* is applied to situations in which the presence of others acting in a similar fashion diminishes the feeling of responsibility any individual feels for the harmful consequences of his or her own behavior.

A slightly different concept, *deindividuation,* refers to a state of loss of self-awareness, including awareness of one's beliefs, attitudes, and self-standards. (In contrast, diffusion of responsibility does not entail forgetting oneself or what one considers proper behavior, but only feeling it is not one's job to uphold these standards all alone. Deindividuation connotes irrationality.) This loss of self is sometimes encouraged to promote group spirit, as in a pep rally, or to facilitate behavior that is otherwise unacceptable. For example, soldiers' uniforms are deindividuating in that they remove signs of individuality and are thought to make it easier for them to adopt the alien role of killer. Alcohol promotes deindividuation by allowing escape from one's conscience and self-consciousness. Group cohesion and loyalty can produce deindividuation by substituting a group identity, with a group history and mores, for individual identities with unique, personal histories and beliefs.

Finally, in a group setting, particularly when group identity produces conformity, *modeling* of aggression also occurs. Not only would watching peers rape and sodomize a woman indicate the appropriateness of such behavior, it would also demonstrate how it is done.

Medea and Thompson (1974), reporting an incident in which up to 40 fraternity brothers raped and sexually humiliated a woman who was developmentally disabled, speculated about the men's motivation. They attributed the students' behavior to group membership, illustrating how diffusion of responsibility, deindividuation, and modeling might come together to render a grotesque act not only tolerable but pleasurable:

Who can doubt that these same young men would . . . have had considerable qualms about doing these things to a woman by themselves? They would probably have felt that what they were doing was perverse and shameful. It was the presence of other men that made the act acceptable; in fact, it was probably the presence of the other men that made it attractive . . . it was the sort of appeal that baiting a dog, or watching a hanging holds.

(p. 35)

SOCIAL FOUNDATIONS OF GANG RAPE

The victims of the majority of gang rapes by students are women. This behavior simply cannot be understood—although the volumes of commentary and analysis generated about the Central Park gang rape case in the Spring of 1989 (O'Sullivan, 1990) have attempted to do so—without consideration of the perpetrators' attitudes toward women and of women's roles in the society and subcultures in which group sexual assaults are practiced and tolerated.

Attitudes

A large number of recent studies of college students have identified the relationship between traditional sex-role attitudes and the prevalence of rape. Hall, Howard, and Boezio (1986) found sexist attitudes to be more strongly correlated than antisocial personality with tolerance of rape. Berger, Searles, Salem, and Pierce (1986) concluded from a review of recent literature that traditional gender-role orientations are associated with rape-tolerant attitudes, and traditional attitudes toward female sexuality are associated with higher levels of sexual aggression. Garrett-Gooding and Senter (1987) suggested that their finding that fraternity men are more sexually aggressive than other college men was due to a combination of selection (fraternities disproportionately select men with traditional sex-role attitudes) and socialization.

Cultural Correlates

Perhaps more helpful in explaining group sexual assault as normative was an anthropological study by Sanday (1981), who reviewed anthropological records to classify 156 tribal societies as rape-free or rape-prone. Most of the rape-prone cultures she described had prescriptions for gang rape, rather than individual rape. A few of the correlations she identified as uniquely characterizing rape-prone cultures seem especially applicable to the population under consideration here.

One cultural characteristic that was strongly associated with the prevalence of rape was having special places for men and special places for women (Sanday, 1981). Among the Mundurucu of Brazil, for example, each village has a men's house, where all the men live together; women and children live in separate dwellings (Murphy, 1959). Thus, it is postulated here that group sexual assaults are most likely to occur in sex-segregated men's housing on college campuses. Perhaps recognition of this pattern motivated Bowdoin College to require admission of women to fraternities ("Bowdoin Fraternities Assailed," 1988), to reduce aggressive and antisocial behavior.

In rape-prone societies, the sexes are separated not only physically but also by rigid sex-role differentiation in which the male role is more valued. Thus, we might expect gang rapes to be most common among men who not only live apart from women but also perform roles closed to women (e.g., football players and fraternity members).

In such societies, which Sanday (1981) labeled male-dominated, a woman's violation of her prescribed sex role may be punished by rape or the threat of rape. One of these prescriptions is that women are supposed to be sexually naive and inexperienced. Gang rape is a punishment for promiscuity and can be seen as a means of controlling women's sexuality. Adulterous or promiscuous women are punished with gang rape among the Cheyenne, Omaha, and Mundurucu. According to Mead, as cited by Webster (1978), cultures must discipline female receptivity to maintain the family structure.

Parallels may be seen in accounts of gang rape in our own culture. A male student attempted to explain to me why a woman who charged several football players with rape and assault had not in fact been raped. His explanation was that, by dating two of the men who were close friends and having sex with each, she had hurt their feelings. They were angry at her for being sexually indiscriminate and, joined by other players, "ganged up" on her in revenge when she came to visit. The norm is that women are supposed to be sexually selective. If they are not, they may be "fair game," or worse. A student at another college told me of plans his fraternity made for "running a train." The woman was selected weeks in advance. They believed she was sexually promiscuous and therefore wouldn't "mind." Such beliefs bear a resemblance to those of the Canela in Brazil. If a young unmarried woman in Canela society takes a lover, she is supposed to be available to all men. If she refuses, she will be gang raped (Webster, 1978).

A particular woman's reputation for promiscuity may be a misperception, yet her gang rape victimization can itself contribute to the fallacy. Groth and Birnbaum (1979) gave accounts of group assaults in which, as the victim was raped by each successive man, she was increasingly seen as "a whore" who deserved to be raped. Her "promiscuity" angered the men, who became increasingly abusive. Similarly, bachelors in Eastern Bororo gang rape a selected female who then becomes the men's house prostitute (Webster, 1978).

Characteristics of Gang-Rape Victims

The mean age of the victims in the 24 cases of campus gang rapes discussed in this review was 18; usually they were first-year students who were inexperienced with campus life. Victims of group assaults by acquaintances at fraternities and men's dorms tend to have two characteristics: They are naive, but they have somehow gained a reputation among the men for being promiscuous. A "perfect victim," from that point of view, was the complaining witness in the Kentucky State case. At the age of 20, she was divorcing the man she had dated from the age of 14; she had been at the university for a few weeks. To the 18- and 19-year-old men she accused, she seemed a racy character. Not only was she older and a divorcée, but also she had sneaked into the men's dorm on a prior occasion. One man told the others, as they rode a bus to a football game, that he had had sex with her that first evening, within hours of meeting her. (She denied it.)

Generally, women who habitually socialize with a group of men, and therefore are more often available to them, are no more likely to be victims of a group sexual assault than social outsiders are (Garrett-Gooding & Senter, 1987). The reason seems to be that social insiders are cognizant of the group mores. Sorority women learn from their sisters what different behaviors "mean" within the system. For example, they learn not to go upstairs to the bathroom at a fraternity party unless accompanied by another woman

(Ehrhart & Sandler, 1985) and that getting drunk is taken by the men as a signal of availability. Women who are not part of the same social set as the men may be ignorant of such rules. Consequently, they may miscommunicate their intentions by violating the norms or may unknowingly take risks, and become targets of sexual assault. Despite their knowledge of these rules, several of the victims in the 24 cases were girlfriends or long-term friends of the perpetrators who were lulled into trust, thought they were protected in violating the rules, and found themselves betrayed.

DIFFICULTIES OF PROSECUTING ACQUAINTANCE GANG RAPES

Nineteen of the 24 documented campus cases were reported to the police. Eight of these reported cases did not proceed to prosecution, most often because the district attorney or the grand jury felt there was insufficient evidence that a crime had been committed. Of the 11 cases in which the accused men were indicted, three did not go to a jury because the men pleaded guilty to lesser charges (misdemeanor sexual assault) or pleaded no contest to rape. In five of the six cases that have been tried, all of the men were acquitted. In the sixth case, two of three defendants were convicted (the only finding of guilt in the 24 cases studied). In many cases, even those unsuccessfully prosecuted in criminal court, the women have filed, and occasionally won, civil suits against the men and/or the university.

Criminal proceedings in acquaintance group sexual assault cases where the woman has not received severe physical injuries are embedded in a context of injudicious assumptions about male and female sexuality, interactions between young men and women, and the relative veracity of a disturbed young woman vs. confident young men. Nevertheless, some of the more easily isolated reasons for the difficulty of prosecuting such cases are outlined below.

Her Word Against Theirs

Because campus gang rapes are likely to occur among acquaintances, they share the underreporting problem of date rapes. When acquaintance gang rapes are reported, conviction is difficult because multiple defendants provide counter-testimony to that of the victim, who may be the sole eyewitness for the prosecution.

As with other forms of acquaintance rape, the defense argument is usually consent. It seems impossible to get a conviction unless one of the participants, or an eyewitness other than the victim, testifies for the prosecution. To take the extreme example of a case recently tried in Texas ("Suspended term," 1989), even though the woman was abducted and alleged she was raped on the hood of a truck by 20 men at a cock fight, the prosecution was losing its case—the many witnesses claimed the woman was laughing and enjoyed it—until a 14-year-old defendant was moved by the courtroom attack on the woman to testify for the prosecution. It was this boy's testimony, not the victim's, that secured convictions of the first nine defendants. In campus gang rape cases, the group bonds among the participants and witnesses, and their common living quarters, discourage such testimony. It may be necessary for the prosecutor to offer a deal to one of the participants in a gang rape in order to persuade a jury beyond a reasonable doubt that the woman did not consent.

Consent

The legalistic difficulty, as pointed out by Snelling (1975), is that each act must be considered individually as well as in context. Snelling maintained that, unless the woman is overcome with terror or fatigue (which also must be established by evidence, another difficulty), she must make her objection clear to each actor for his act to be considered rape. A victim, however, may view her serial rapes as a single incident. Responding to the men as a group, she may not voice her objections or resist anew with each man. Men may perceive a decline in her objections as a change from nonconsent to consent. Scully and Marolla (1985) quoted a convict who admitted to participating in more than 20 gang rapes as saying, "It might start out as rape but, then, they [the women] would quiet down and none ever reported it to the police" (p. 260).

Protection from Self-Incrimination

The smartest decision made by the defense attorneys in the Kentucky State case was to abide by their pact that none of their clients would take the stand unless all the defendants did (personal communication, Robert Bowman, May 5, 1989). None of them did, relying on the right not to testify against oneself. The victim, whose standing in court is merely that of a witness for the state, has no such rights because she is not on trial, legally. As a result, inconsistencies in her accounts, from her initial statement to the police, to the preliminary hearing, her grand jury testimony, and her testimony at the trial persuaded the jury in the Kentucky State case that she was unreliable, but inconsistencies in the men's stories were not subject to examination.

The fundamental right not to incriminate oneself that can keep a group of alleged rapists off the stand is problematic for the prosecution, even if consent is not at issue because the woman was unconscious during the rape. In such cases, we know that a crime has occurred, but the victim is unable to identify her assailants in court, at least not in regard to specific criminal acts by specific individuals.

CONCLUSION

This review suggests that the measures being taken on college campuses to reduce the frequency of sexual assault may not ameliorate the problem of acquaintance gang rapes. Such measures include having separate dorms for men and women, restricting visitation, and having better campus lighting (Carmody, 1989; Herzog, 1989). These policies and practices admittedly are designed to prevent sexual interactions among college students altogether (Herzog, 1989) or are oriented toward reducing the incidence of stranger rape. The cultural and attitudinal correlates of group sexual assault and the conditions under which campus gang rapes have occurred demonstrate that restricted access between the sexes will not remedy the problem. Profound attitude change is necessary.

With a few notable exceptions, educational efforts to reduce rape are primarily directed at or attended by college women rather than men. Although such education may help women to recognize when they have been raped, it will be less effective in reducing group assault than would educating those who have a choice about engaging in it. Prevention must begin with education of young men, particularly those who belong to male groups.

Attitude change in two areas will be necessary for men in groups to desist from joining in sexual assaults. The first such needed change is in attitudes toward women and understanding of women's sexuality. It seems to be particularly important to convey that a woman who chooses to be sexual, perhaps with several different individuals, is still sexually selective and is not available to the population at large. A related misconception common among college men is revealed by responses to Burt's (1980) Rape Myth Scale: Any woman who dresses or behaves "provocatively" is thought to be directing her seduction at all men who happen to see her and not at a particular man.

An even more difficult area of change that would effectively reduce sexual assault is men's attitudes toward themselves and their own sexuality. It is instructive to consider how men involved in group sexual assaults or "trains" may differ from those who find the practice unappealing and would not participate. My interviews have yielded two characteristic attitudes of men who are repulsed by the notion. They feel that sex is private (they reject sex as an arena for "cooperation and competition"); and they feel that sex is intimate (they reject sex without caring about their partner).

In contrast, a witness in the Kentucky State case who left the victim alone in the room of two of her assailants testified that he had no respect for the victim and didn't care what happened to her because she had had oral sex with him (Baker, 1989). What was striking in his statement, in addition to his disregard for the woman, was his attitude toward his own body and sexuality. That, according to his own account, he had oral intercourse with a person who disgusted him suggests a lack of self-respect and self-integration. That she became worthless because of it suggests a revulsion for his own sexuality.

Although attitude change at the individual level might reduce the campus acquaintance rape rate, it does not address the problem of group norms and group pressure. Yet, attempts to educate the groups as such will probably succeed only when the perspective presented is endorsed by highly regarded group members. In the absence of such leadership, an alternative is to diminish group cohesion and decrease opportunities for group assaults by dispersing members throughout campus residences. Comparing practical strategies, breaking up male groups would probably be more effective in reducing group assault than attempting to keep women out of men's dorms.

REFERENCES

Amir, M. (1971). *Patterns in forcible rape.* Chicago: University of Chicago Press.

Baker, A. B. (1989, May 3). Rape case testimony allowed on previous sexual activity. *Lexington Herald-Leader,* pp. A1, A7.

Berger, R. J., Searles, P., Salem, R. G., & Pierce, B. A. (1986). Sexual assault in a college community. *Sociological Focus, 19,* 1–26.

Blakely, M. K. (1984, July). The New Bedford verdict. *Ms.,* p. 116.

Blanchard, W. H. (1959). The group process in gang rape. *Journal of Social Psychology, 49,* 259–266.

Bowdoin fraternities assailed (1988, May 1). *New York Times,* p. 25.

Brownmiller, S. (1975). *Against our will: Men, women, and rape.* New York: Simon & Schuster.

Burt, M. R. (1980). Cultural myths and supports for rape. *Journal of Personality and Social Psychology, 38,* 217–230.

Carmody, D. (1989, January 1). Increasing rapes on campus spur colleges to fight back. *New York Times,* pp. 1, 10.

Chancer, L. S. (1987). New Bedford, Massachusetts, March 6, 1983–March 22, 1984: The "before and after" of a group rape. *Gender and Society, 1,* 239–260.

DeFleur, M. L., & Quinney, R. (1966). A reformulation of Sutherland's differential association theory and a strategy for empirical verification. *Journal of Research in Crime and Delinquency, 3,* 1–22.

Ehrhart, J. K., & Sandler, B. R. (1985). *Campus gang rape: Party games?,* Washington, DC: Association of American Colleges.

Farr, K. A. (1988). Dominance bonding through the Good Old Boys Sociability group. *Sex Roles, 18,* 259–277.

Five youths held in sex assault on mentally impaired girl, 17. (1989, May 25). *New York Times,* pp. 1, B17.

Flanagan, T. J., & Jamieson, K. M. (1988). (U. S. Department of Justice Bureau, of Justice Statistics.) *Sourcebook of criminal justice statistics—1987.* Washington, DC: U.S. Government Printing Office.

Fort, J. (1971, February). Sex and youth: Normal, hippie, radical, and Hell's Angel. *Medical Aspects of Human Sexuality,* 18–29.

Garrett-Gooding, J., & Senter, R. (1987). Attitudes and acts of sexual aggression on a university campus. *Sociological Inquiry, 59,* 348–371.

Geis, G. (1971, May). Group sexual assaults. *Medical Aspects of Human Sexuality,* 101–113.

Gianturco, D. T., & Smith, H. L. (1974). *The promiscuous teenager.* Springfield, IL: Thomas.

Groth, A. N., & Birnbaum, H. J. (1979). *Men who rape.* New York: Plenum.

Hall, E. R., Howard, J. A., & Boezio, S. L. (1986). Tolerance of rape: A sexist or antisocial attitude? *Psychology of Women Quarterly, 10,* 110–118.

Herzog, K. (1989, May 14). Rape trial over, sex debate isn't. *Frankfort State Journal,* pp. A1, A12.

Hoffman, R. (1986, March 17). Rape and the college athlete: Part one. *Philadelphia Daily News,* p. 104.

Hull, A. V. (1988, May 29). A Greek tragedy. *St. Petersburg Times,* pp. 1F, 6F.

Janis, I. L. (1982). *Groupthink,* 2nd Ed. Boston: Houghton-Mifflin.

Koss, M. P. (1987). *Hidden rape: A national survey of psychopathological consequences.* Progress report, 2R01MH31618-04 to National Institute of Mental Health.

Medea, A., & Thompson, K. (1974). *Against rape.* New York: Farrar, Straus, & Giroux.

Murphy, R. F. (1959). Social structure and sex antagonism. *Southwestern Journal of Anthropology, 15,* 89–98.

Neff, C., & Sullivan, R. (1986, February 3). A basketball program in turmoil. *Sports Illustrated,* p. 21.

O'Sullivan, C. S. (1990, April). *What's rape? A content analysis of coverage of the 1989 Central Park assault.* Paper presented at the meeting of the Eastern Psychological Association, Philadelphia.

Pierson, D. K. (1984, April 1). Mixed bag of reactions follows rape trial verdict. *Lansing State Journal,* 1B-2B.

Rivera, G. F., Jr., & Regoli, R. M. (1987). Sexual victimization experiences of sorority women. *Sociology and Social Research, 72,* 39–42.

Russell, D. E. H. (1974). *The politics of rape.* Briarcliff Manor, NY: Stein and Day.

Russell, D. E. H. (1982). The prevalence and incidence of forcible rape and attempted rape of females. *Victimology: An International Journal, 7,* 81–93.

Sanday, P. R. (1981). The socio-cultural context of rape: A cross-cultural study. *Journal of Social Issues, 37,* 5–27.

Schmich, M. T. (1988, May 15). Fraternity gang rapes now all too common at colleges. *Lexington Herald-Leader,* p. A11.

Schwendinger, J., & Schwendinger, H. (1983). *Rape and inequality.* Beverly Hills: Sage.

Scully, D., & Marolla, J. (1985). Riding the bull at Gilley's: Convicted rapists describe the rewards of rape. *Social Problems, 32,* 251–263.

Smith, M. D., & Bennett, N. (1985). Poverty, inequality, and theories of forcible rape. *Crime and Delinquency, 31,* 295–305.

Snelling, H. A. (1975). What is non-consent (in rape)? In L. G. Schultz (Ed.), *Rape victimology* (pp. 157–163). Springfield, IL: Thomas.

Suspended term for gang rapist (1989, February 19). *New York Times,* p. 20.

UC women object to settlement of group rape case. (1986, November 28). *Los Angeles Times,* p. 38.

Warshaw, R. (1988). *I never called it rape: The Ms. report on recognizing, fighting, and surviving date and acquaintance rape.* New York: Harper & Row.

Webster, P. (1978, Summer). Politics of rape in primitive society. *Heresies, 6,* pp. 16–18, 20, 22.

Wolff, C. (1989, April 21). Youths rape and beat Central Park jogger. *New York Times,* p. B1, B3.

PART 5

Victims

CHAPTER 11

Factors That Increase the Likelihood of Victimization

PATRICIA A. HARNEY, MA, and CHARLENE L. MUEHLENHARD, PhD

Many investigators are rightly concerned with the use of risk research for victim-blaming. In the past, research about risk factors for rape has been interpreted in ways that blame women for their victimization. One example of victim-blaming is in Amir's (1971) work, in which he investigated the characteristics and behaviors of rape victims and concluded that 19% of the reported forcible rapes he examined were "victim precipitated":

> The term "victim precipitation" describes those rape situations in which the victim actually, or so it was deemed, agreed to sexual relations but retracted before the actual act or did not react strongly enough when the suggestion was made by the offender(s). The term applies also to cases in risky situations marred with sexuality, especially when she uses what could be interpreted as indecency in language and gestures, or constitutes what could be taken as an invitation to sexual relations. . . . Victim behavior consists of acts of commission (e.g., she agreed to drink or ride with a stranger) and omission (e.g., she failed to react strongly enough to sexual suggestions and overtures). . . . These results point to the fact that the offender should not be viewed as the sole "cause" and reason for the offense, and that the "virtuous" victim is not always the innocent and passive party. Thus, the role played by the victim and its contribution to the perpetration of the offense becomes one of the main interests of the emerging discipline of victimology. Furthermore, if penal justice is to be fair it must be attentive to these problems of degrees of victim responsibility for her own victimization.
>
> *(Amir, 1971, pp. 261, 266, 275, 276)*

Such interpretations and conclusions suggest that women, rather than men or the larger culture, are responsible for preventing rape.

The same data, however, when discussed within a different context, may have potential to empower women. Following an experience of rape, women often ask, "Why did this happen to me?" or, "What can I do to make sure that this never happens again?" Feelings of powerlessness are reflected in such questions. While rape can happen to any woman, anywhere, anytime, the probability of rape does vary, more or less, in relation to the presence of the risk factors discussed here. Some factors, such as situational factors (e.g., alcohol intoxication) might be partially within a woman's control. Others, such as cultural factors (e.g., male dominance) and personal factors (e.g., age or history of child sexual abuse), are not within a woman's control. Accordingly, societal changes are necessary to alter these risk factors and to reduce the occurrence of rape.

CULTURAL FACTORS THAT INCREASE THE RISK OF VICTIMIZATION

Cross-Cultural Research

As Brownmiller (1975) asserted, rapists have power that is more than physical. The institutionalized context within which rape occurs works for rapists by providing them with a set of interactive economic, ideological, legalistic, and political systems that support their power. The same systems work against rape victims by weakening their power. Results from several studies are consistent with the contention that rape occurs most frequently amid cultural belief systems that ascribe to an ideology of male dominance and that are rife with intergroup and interpersonal violence.

Sanday (1981), for example, examined differences between cultures that she classified as "rape-prone" and "rape-free." From the standard cross-cultural sample published by Murdock and White (1969), Sanday coded information on rape for 156 tribal societies, dating from 1750 B.C. to the late 1960s. Sanday classified as rape-prone those societies in which rape served as a threat to control women, men raped women in warfare, and rape was used as a ceremonial act. In rape-prone societies, Sanday found that men comprised the dominant social group, men used women as a means of economic exchange, and women had little or no political power or voice in public decision making. Special places set aside only for men were more common in rape-prone than in rape-free societies. Additionally, Sanday found that rape-prone societies were characterized by a high degree of intergroup and interpersonal violence and more frequent warfare. Finally, Sanday found that rape-prone societies were more likely to ascribe to an ideology that encouraged men to be tough and aggressive.

The validity of the categories *rape-prone* and *rape-free* remains somewhat ambiguous (e.g., some of the evidence for a rape-free classification included such quotes from male villagers as, "We have no crimes of this nature here. Our women never resist" [p. 16]). Whether men never rape or women do not fight back when they are raped remains unclear from Sanday's description. Nevertheless, Sanday's results suggest that the risk of rape for women may vary with the extent to which cultures legitimize violence and an inequality of power exists between men and women.

Research on tribal societies may appear to present an irrelevant comparison to today's Western culture. A closer examination, however, reveals many similarities. As in Sanday's rape-prone cultures, women in American culture have little political power. For example, no woman, to date, has served as president or vice president of the United States. Women comprise approximately 7% of the U.S. House of Representatives (Davies, 1988) and 2% of the U.S. Senate (Hoffman, 1989). The economic power wielded by women is still quite lean; women employed full-time earn approximately 70% of men's earnings (Pear, 1987). Religious institutions provide another instance of inequality. Approximately 6.5% of leaders of U.S. religious groups are women (Hoffman, 1989). In one of the more "progressive" Christian churches, the Episcopal Church, only one woman has ever been appointed to the position of bishop. Women are also barred from becoming Catholic priests, bishops, or popes.

Sanday (1981) reported that the presence of special, all-male places typifies rape-prone cultures. Many such places exist in American culture. Ehrhart and Sandler (1985) cited the fraternity as a social context at high risk for the occurrence of rape. The very purpose of fraternities is to encourage male bonding; Warshaw (1988) described how such bonding in fraternities occurs, often at the expense of women. Kanin (1967) found that men in fraternities were more likely to be sexually aggressive than men who were not in fraternities. Ehrhart and Sandler (1985) identified over 50 cases of campus gang rape; almost all of these occurred in fraternities.

American culture ascribes higher status to special places set aside for men than to women-only spaces. Sports teams, for example, serve as ground where men congregate separately from women and have higher status than women. Lest one cite the existence of women's sports teams as "equal play," the sports page of any newspaper will prove that male sports figures garner special power in the public eye. At some universities, admission to women's sporting events is free to the public; rarely is admission free to male sporting events. Rarely, too, do all-women's philanthropic groups (e.g., the Junior League) wield the same degree of economic and political power as all-men's groups (e.g., the Masons). To the extent that economic value, media attention, and public adulation differ between male and female organizations, such groups serve as further support of the power differential between men and women.

Because women have second-class status due to the denial of equal representation in positions of power, the denial of equal access to economic resources, and the reinforcement of subordination to men, Sanday's research suggests that the culture maintains an increased risk of rape for women. Consequently, people working for and within these cultural institutions have the power and the responsibility to decrease the risk of sexual victimization.

Individual Differences Within Our Culture

Within-culture variability in the acceptance of traditional gender roles and rape-supportive beliefs provides another way to investigate the effects of ural beliefs on the risk of rape. Accordingly, the relationship between the internalization of traditional cultural norms and the acceptance of rape myths has been explored. Researchers have typically measured traditional gender role attitudes using Spence and Helmreich's (1972) Attitudes Toward Women Scale (e.g., "Wifely submission is an outworn value," and "The initiative in dating should come from the man") or Burt's (1980) Sex Role Stereotyping Scale (e.g., "A woman should be a virgin when she marries," and "It is acceptable for the woman to pay for the date").

Feild (1978) and Burt (1980) were among the first investigators to document rape myths in the general population. Examples of rape myths are beliefs that portray women as secretly desirous of rape, as responsible for inciting or preventing rape, and as promiscuous if they are raped. Both Burt (1980) and Feild (1978) found that people with greater acceptance of and adherence to traditional gender roles were more likely to support rape myths than were people who had more liberal attitudes toward gender roles. Recent researchers have replicated the finding that traditionality significantly predicts the likelihood of supporting rape myths (Check & Malamuth, 1983; Costin & Schwarz, 1987; Shotland & Goodstein, 1983). Similarly, people with traditional beliefs are more likely to blame the victim for the rape and to denigrate the victim and are much less likely to label acquaintance rape as "rape" (Acock & Ireland, 1983; Muehlenhard & MacNaughton, 1988; Shotland & Goodstein, 1983). Traditional men are more likely than nontraditional men to regard rape as justifiable (Muehlenhard, 1988) and to report having committed rape (Muehlenhard & Falcon, in press).

Just as Sanday (1981) found that the acceptance of intergroup and interpersonal violence was indicative of rape-prone societies, researchers have found that people who accept interpersonal violence and adversarial relations between men and women in contemporary American culture are more likely to endorse rape myths (Burt, 1980) and to view male aggressive behavior as "normal" (Shotland & Goodstein, 1983). Furthermore, sexually aggressive men are more likely than nonaggressive men to regard rape as justifiable (Kanin, 1967).

Other research provides evidence for the links among traditionality, likelihood to rape, and sexual arousal. Results from a study by Check and Malamuth (1983) revealed that male subjects who scored high on measures of gender-role stereotyping became equally aroused by depictions of acquaintance rape and consensual sex. This arousal pattern of male subjects high in gender-role stereotyping was much like that of convicted rapists. Additionally, men who scored high on gender-role stereotyping measures reported a greater likelihood of committing acquaintance rape than men low in gender-role stereotyping.

Given the ample evidence that the acceptance of traditional gender-role norms relates, at the individual level, to rape-conducive attitudes and men's propensity to rape, it is quite likely that societies with clearly delineated gender norms that restrict the rights and roles of women will also, on the whole, support rape-facilitative attitudes. Cultural norms that maintain a higher status for men than for women can increase in several ways the risk of victimization for women living in the culture. As is evidenced from the research presented above, men who internalize such norms report a higher probability of raping women than men who do not. Cultural norms can increase women's risk of victimization even further if women inculcate these norms through socialization. For example, if women are socialized to put men's needs ahead of their own, they could be at greater risk of victimization. The relationship between women's traditionality and risk of victimization is discussed further in the section on personal characteristics.

Media Violence and Pornography

To bridge the relationship between cultural beliefs and individuals who endorse rape myths, the channels through which general cultural beliefs are transmitted to a society's members must be identified. Media violence and pornography are two such channels available in Western culture. If media violence and pornography act as cultural tools through which rape myths are funneled, the probability of raping may be greater for men who have been exposed to these materials, and the probability of being raped may be greater for women who must live in the same society as these men.

Cross-cultural studies investigating the association between pornography and rape could assess women's risk of rape as a function of the prevalence of pornography. Green (1987) compared the rates of reported rapes in Western cultures before and after those countries legalized pornography and concluded that there is no cross-cultural evidence that the increased availability of pornography affects the rates of rape.

Several problems exist with Green's analysis. First, stranger rape is much more likely to be reported than acquaintance rape (Koss, Dinero, Seibel, & Cox, 1988; Russell, 1984). Therefore, Green's analysis of reported rape reveals little about the effects of pornography on acquaintance rape, which in the United States comprises 80% to 90% of all rapes (Koss et al., 1988; Russell, 1984). Second, it is possible that pornography was available in these countries before it was legalized. A stronger test of the effects of pornography would include a comparison between countries in which pornography was never available and countries in which it was. Such an empirical test would be difficult, of course, because one might not be able to determine whether pornography existed illegally. Third, the effects of pornography may be seen in phenomena other than the rate of sexual assault. For example, pornography might influence the types of sexual assaults committed, rather than the rates of those assaults. Fourth, Green does not differentiate among erotica (e.g., depictions of egalitarian, mutually consenting, nonviolent sex), degrading or dehumanizing pornography, and violent pornography.

Other research has attempted to separate the effects of erotica, dehumanizing pornography, and violent pornography. In their review of the literature, Linz, Donnerstein, and Penrod (1987) demonstrated that the effects of violent stimuli are far more pernicious than the effects of sexually explicit stimuli. Malamuth and Check (1981) found that males, but not females, were more accepting of interpersonal violence and were more likely to endorse rape myths after viewing R-rated, violent films that depicted women as reacting positively to being raped. If exposure to media violence and violent pornography increases the likelihood that male viewers will accept interpersonal violence and rape myths (Malamuth and Check, 1981), and if the acceptance of interpersonal violence and rape myths relates to a male's likelihood to aggress sexually (Malamuth, 1981; Muehlenhard & Linton, 1987; Rapaport & Burkhart, 1984), then the inference that frequent exposure to violent pornography increases the likelihood that a male will aggress sexually requires only a small leap.

Institutions That Promote Traditional Gender Roles

As reviewed previously, there is abundant evidence demonstrating the relationships among traditional gender-role attitudes, rape-conducive attitudes, and sexually aggressive behavior. Consequently, institutions that promote traditional gender roles might also promote a rape-conducive environment. A list of such institutions would be lengthy—for example, traditional gender roles and male dominance are promoted by the following: the socialization of infants, children, and adolescents by parents and teachers (Lips, 1989); the socialization of college and graduate students by professors (Fox, 1989); dating rituals (Peplau & Campbell, 1989); marriage (Steil, 1989); women's position in the workplace (Blau & Winkler, 1989; Glenn & Feldberg, 1989); the English language (Adams & Ware, 1989); nonverbal interpersonal behavior (Henley & Freeman, 1989); and the depiction of women in television shows, commercials, cartoons, children's books, magazines, newspapers, films, and textbooks (Basow, 1986). These institutions promote traditional gender-role attitudes and male dominance, which Sanday (1981) found to characterize rape-prone societies. Compared with the effects of violent pornography, the effects of these institutions on rape are probably more subtle—and thus more insidious.

SITUATIONAL FACTORS THAT INCREASE THE RISK OF SEXUAL VICTIMIZATION

Dating Rituals

Brownmiller (1975) discussed the myriad ways in which, centuries ago, marriage served as a license to rape. While courtship rituals have changed since the time when "fathers sold to prospective bridegrooms the title to his daughter's unruptured hymen" (Brownmiller, p. 10), the legacy of culturally appropriate gender roles is played out quite clearly in present dating relationships.

Contemporary dating "scripts" (Check & Malamuth, 1983) follow traditional gender-role norms in various ways. Men are encouraged to be active and to initiate dates; women are supposed to remain passive and wait to be asked. Men's control over economic resources is reinforced by the expectation that men will pay for all the expenses on dates; the presumption that men will receive sex in return is then set into motion. As rape has been related to power differences between men and women (Russell, 1975; Sanday, 1981), these elements of dating situations have been hypothesized as related to power (Peplau & Campbell, 1989). Consequently, it has been hypothesized that traditional dating scripts may increase the risk of rape (Check & Malamuth, 1983).

Research reveals that the risk of rape varies according to the presence of these factors in the dating situation. Muehlenhard and Linton (1987) found that sexual aggression was more likely to occur on dates initiated and paid for by men, and on dates for which men did the driving. Moreover, the researchers found that men were more likely to report feeling "led on" during sexual aggression dates than on typical dates.

Several possibilities exist to explain why sexual aggression dates are characterized by the man's control over initiation, expenses, and transportation. Men might misperceive a woman as willing to engage in sex when she is not. Men are more likely to believe women want sex on dates for which men pay the expenses than on dates for which the couple goes "dutch" (Muehlenhard, 1988). For this reason, perhaps, men are more likely to feel led on during sexual aggression dates (Muehlenhard & Linton, 1987).

Alternatively, men might feel entitled to sex in exchange for the effort and money they expend by initiating and paying for the date. Consistent with this hypothesis, men—especially traditional men—rated rape as significantly more justifiable when the man paid than when the woman paid (Muehlenhard, 1988). Muehlenhard's results are consistent with traditional gender roles in which it is expected that sex and financial support will be exchanged (Weis & Borges, 1973).

Practical considerations make dates for which the man initiates, pays, and drives high-risk dates. The person who initiates the date often chooses the activity and location. The person might choose an isolated location; as discussed subsequently, rapes are more likely to occur in isolated places. Furthermore, a woman's vulnerability is heightened when the man controls transportation because she may have no other means to leave a threatening situation. Because women are taught to fear being alone without a man to "protect" them (Stanko, 1988), women may perceive the option to walk home alone at night as equally or more dangerous than remaining with their date.

These findings support the hypothesis that men's beliefs about women's sexual desires and about the justifiability of rape relate to their internalization of traditional gender roles. Traditional men are more likely than nontraditional men to feel entitled to sexual contact after they pay for dating expenses. Clearly, traditional dating scripts need to change in such a way that the balance of power between men and women is righted. In the meantime, men need to be clear about their own intentions and their date's level of sexual interest. Further research might focus on the various ways in which men ascribe meaning to women's behavior and the relationship between men's misattributions and their risk of raping their dates.

Sexual Activity

Researchers examining situational factors influencing the risk of rape have suggested that the likelihood of rape increases with the amount of exposure a woman has to potential perpetrators (Koss & Dinero, 1989). While some studies showed no differences between the sexual experience of victimized and nonvictimized women (Kanin, 1957; Kanin & Parcell, 1977), more recent research revealed that victimized women tend to have had a greater number of dating and sexual partners, to experience first sexual intercourse at a younger age, and to have more liberal sexual values than nonvictimized women (Amick & Calhoun, 1987; Koss, 1985; Koss & Dinero, 1989). Koss and Dinero (1989) found that victimized women had a greater number of sexual partners prior to being raped.

Several explanations have been offered for these results. Women may experience punishment by their dates for espousing liberal values (Korman & Leslie, 1982). Child sexual abuse may influence both sexual behavior and later revictimization (Russell, 1986); this relationship is discussed subsequently. Finally, the probability rationale predicts that the more men a woman dates, the greater are her opportunities to meet a date rapist (Koss & Dinero, 1989). Empirical support for these explanations is scanty; thus, further research is needed to identify the various processes at work behind the relationships among sexual activity, exposure, and victimization.

Victim–Offender Relationship

Although the stereotypical rape involves a stranger jumping out of the bushes, research reveals that 80–90% of all rapes are committed by men acquainted with the victims—boyfriends, husbands, nonromantic acquaintances, and authority figures (Koss et al., 1988; Russell, 1984). Koss et al. (1988) found that most rapes occurred between dating partners and more women were raped by steady dates than by casual dates.

While rape by a romantic acquaintance is more likely than rape by a nonromantic acquaintance or a stranger, it is less likely to be labeled by the woman as rape (Koss, 1985). Women also seem to be less successful in resisting rape attempts by dating partners than attempts by strangers or nonromantic acquaintances (Amick & Calhoun, 1987; Bart & O'Brien, 1985). Ironically, in American culture, women are encouraged to turn to men for protection when they are actually at greater risk of sexual assault by their boyfriends and husbands than by strangers.

Victimization Sites

The risk of rape varies with location. In instances of date rape, victimization sites are typically the offender's home, a car, or an isolated location (Amick & Calhoun, 1987; Muehlenhard & Linton, 1987). More rape attempts occur indoors than outdoors, and women are more likely to thwart rape attempts when they are outside rather than inside (Bart & O'Brien, 1985). Fraternity parties, especially those serving alcohol, are particularly conducive to gang rapes (Ehrhart & Sandler, 1985).

One explanation offered for these results is the issue of territoriality. Men are more likely to assert their desires and feel entitled to gratification when they are on their own "turf," whereas women may feel less able to assert themselves when in "foreign" territory (Abarbanel, personal communication, March 24, 1986). Researchers have considered other factors as well. Muehlenhard (1988) presented to male and female subjects a dating scenario in which location of dating activity varied; the subjects were then asked to rate the woman's willingness to have sex. Both male and female subjects perceived the woman as more likely to want sex when the couple went to the man's apartment rather than to a movie, suggesting that people use dating locations to make attributions about women's sexual intent. Male subjects' ratings of how much the woman wanted sex were significantly higher than female subjects' ratings, suggesting that misunderstandings about sexual intent are likely. Regarding isolated locations, women simply have difficulty leaving the situation (Amick & Calhoun, 1987). Apparently, it is not always the location per se that contributes to the risk of rape, but the meaning ascribed to the woman's presence in the particular location. When investigating other locations that might increase the risk for victimization, researchers would do well to examine further the ways in which men perceive, or misperceive, women's motivation for being in any given location.

Alcohol Use

A number of studies have revealed that between one third and two thirds of offenders and victims were intoxicated at the time of the assault (Amir, 1971; Koss & Dinero, 1989; Muehlenhard & Linton, 1987; Rada, 1975; Russell, 1984; Wilson & Durrenberger, 1982). Although alcohol is frequently consumed in social contexts, one study in particular found that heavy alcohol use is more characteristic of sexual aggression dates than of typical dates (Muehlenhard & Linton, 1987). While alcohol may have physiological disinhibitory effects, results from recent research revealed that alcohol expectancy heightens aggression and sexual aggression over and above the effects of actual alcohol content (Briddell et al., 1978; George & Marlatt, 1986). Furthermore, differential social meanings are ascribed to men and women who drink. Studies have demonstrated that the male offender is frequently attributed less responsibility for sexual aggression when he is drunk, whereas the female victim is often ascribed more responsibility when she is drunk, and her character is devalued (Richardson & Campbell, 1982; Sharp, 1987). Clearly, the consumption of alcohol by both the man and the woman works in conjunction with a multitude of other, socially constructed factors to facilitate sexual aggression between acquaintances.

PERSONAL CHARACTERISTICS THAT MAY INCREASE THE RISK OF VICTIMIZATION

"Victim-precipitation" models regard the personal characteristics of rape victims as causal factors in rape occurrence (Amir, 1971). However, as Finkelhor (1984) stated, four preconditions are necessary for sexual abuse to occur: (a) There must be an offender with the motivation to sexually abuse, (b) the offender must overcome internal inhibitions against abusing, (c) the offender must overcome external obstacles against abusing, and (d) the offender must overcome resistance by the victim. For sexual aggression to be explained fully, one must account for the presence of all four of these preconditions (Finkelhor, 1986).

Exploration of the personal characteristics that distinguish victims from nonvictims can be helpful in identifying factors that may increase the likelihood that an offender can overcome both external obstacles and resistance by the victim. Because the responsibility for sexual aggression lies with the aggressor, in no way do we view victim characteristics that increase the likelihood of the offender's overcoming obstacles and resistance as factors that *cause* rape and sexual aggression. It is important to examine victim characteristics within a situational and sociocultural context; a personal characteristic can be regarded as a risk factor only if there is something for which a risk exists. Shotland's (1989) analogy to Nazi Germany clarified this point. Although being Jewish in the 1930s was a personal characteristic that increased the risk of extermination in concentration camps, in no way did a Jewish identity necessitate extermination. The responsibility for the Holocaust lay with the social–political context that supported antisemitism and genocide and with the individuals who perpetrated the violence against Holocaust victims. In the same vein, the victim characteristics reviewed here are regarded not as factors that act as causal agents of rape, but as factors that, in interaction with the cultural and situational contexts previously described, increase the risk of victimization.

Demographic Characteristics

Girls and women are significantly more likely to experience sexual aggression than boys and men (Finkelhor, 1986; Koss, 1985; Koss, Gidycz, & Wisnieski, 1987; Russell, 1982, 1984, 1986). Clearly, females born into a rape-prone culture (Sanday, 1981) are at greater risk of victimization than are males born into the same culture.

Two studies drawing from probability samples found equal prevalence rates of rape between black women and white women (Koss et al., 1987; Russell, 1984). The same studies found an especially high prevalence of victimization among Native American women and a low prevalence among Asian-American women (Koss et al., 1987; Russell, 1984). Because cultural biases may have affected disclosure in the two studies cited, further research is needed to examine the validity of and the possible reasons for the reportedly high rates of rape for Native American women and the reportedly low rates of rape for Asian-American women.

Women of various ages experience different degrees of vulnerability to victimization. Russell (1984) found that the highest risk of rape occurs for women between the ages of 13 and 26. Katz and Mazur (1979) concluded that the ages between 13 and 24 constitute a high-risk period. A number of reasons may account for the increased vulnerability of this age group. These ages correspond to the ages at which dating frequency is highest; thus, women in this age group may be exposed to a larger number of possible perpetrators than at other times in their lives. The age of rapists tends to fall within a similar range (Russell, 1984). Men are more likely to rape women with whom they associate, and the women with whom they associate are most likely to be in their same age group. Finally, culture tends to dictate when women should be ready for sex rather than to allow women to decide for themselves when they feel ready for sex.

Altogether, however, few demographic variables distinguish between women who are sexually victimized and those who are not. Further investigation is required to assess the validity of the few differences found.

Belief Systems and Personality Factors

It has been hypothesized that socialization trains women to be rape victims (Brownmiller, 1975) and that women who internalize traditional gender-role norms are a greater risk for victimization (Amick & Calhoun, 1987; Koss, 1985; Selkin, 1978). There is mixed support for this assertion in the literature. Muehlenhard and Linton (1987) found that women who had experienced sexual aggression on dates were slightly less traditional than women who had not experienced sexual aggression. Koss (1985) and Koss and Dinero (1989) found that victimized women were not significantly different from nonvictimized women on measures of traditionality.

Alternatively, Amick and Calhoun (1987) and Selkin (1978) found that women who successfully resisted rapists scored higher on the California Personality Inventory scales of dominance and social presence than women who resisted unsuccessfully. Bart and O'Brien (1985) found that women who used traditionally "feminine" forms of resistance (e.g., pleading and crying) were more likely to be raped than women who used physical forms of resistance and that women who avoided rape were more likely to have a nontraditional image of their future, adult selves.

It is possible that no differences exist in degree of traditionality between women who experience sexual assault and those who do not, but that the presence of some personality factors (e.g., dominance) might help to thwart a rape attack. Future research might help to understand the role of such personality factors in the risk of victimization; at the present time, however, very little can be concluded about the role of the victim's personality in the risk of victimization.

Child Sexual Abuse: Its Impact on Risk of Rape

Significant associations between childhood sexual abuse and sexual victimization in adulthood have been observed in recent research (Koss & Dinero, 1989; Miller et al., 1978; Murphy, 1987; Russell, 1986). Estimates vary between studies, depending on the sample used and the methodology employed. Russell (1986) found that 65% of incest victims in her probability sample experienced rape or attempted rape in adulthood, compared with 35% of women who never experienced child sexual abuse. Koss and Dinero (1989) found that child sexual abuse was one of the best predictors of rape victimization in adulthood, over and above personality, attitudinal, and situational variables, although even this variable did not predict very well who would be victimized in adulthood. Accordingly, researchers are seeking to understand the long-term effects of child sexual abuse and the processes by which such traumatic early experiences increase the risk of later victimization.

In Browne and Finkelhor's (1986) review of the literature on initial and long-term effects of child sexual abuse, they noted that adults who survived sexual abuse as children were significantly more likely than adults not victimized as children to experience depression, very low self-esteem, feelings of isolation, interpersonal problems, and substance abuse. Because heavy alcohol use has been associated significantly with acquaintance rape situations, substance abuse may be one intervening variable linking child and adult experiences of sexual victimization. Browne and Finkelhor concluded that the long-term effects of child sexual abuse may impact upon the adult survivor in such a way as to heighten her vulnerability to abuse in adulthood.

Russell (1986) offered several possible explanations for the association between child and adult sexual victimization. One possibility is that child sexual abuse specifically increases the risk of adult sexual abuse. Russell cited Finkelhor and Browne's (1985) model of "Traumagenic Dynamics" of child sexual abuse, which referred to a process by which a child's self- and sexual esteem are damaged by the abuse. Behavioral manifestations of the child's low self- and sexual esteem may include early promiscuity and drug/ alcohol abuse, both of which can increase the risk of later sexual victimization. Results from a study by Burnam et al. (1988) revealed that sexual assault predicted the onset of depressive episodes, alcohol and drug dependence disorders, and anxiety disorders. Additionally, depression was identified as a risk factor for later sexual abuse. Another possibility, however, is that child sexual abuse does not increase the risk of adult sexual abuse; instead, adult women who are raped might be more likely to remember and report child sexual abuse experiences than adult women who are not raped.

Russell's hypotheses, as well as the other ideas presented here, will best be tested empirically by prospective, multimethod, multifactorial designs to observe and document the process of revictimization. It should be emphasized that, regardless of processes by which revictimization occurs, the responsibility of abuse lies solely with the abuser. The ability to identify high-risk situations, however, can help women who ask "Why does this keep happening to me?" to understand the insidious effects of incest, child sexual abuse, and previous rape victimization, and to change the factors within their control that may help reduce their chances of later victimization.

CONCLUSIONS AND RECOMMENDATIONS FOR CHANGE

The research reviewed here presents a multitude of factors that heighten women's vulnerability to sexual victimization. The task of reducing the prevalence of rape confronts people from a number of sectors: clinicians, educators, policy makers, and researchers, as well as the general public. The following recommendations are suggested.

Researchers cannot fully explain the phenomenon of rape without acknowledging the cultural and situational context in which the rapist and victim are embedded. Exploration of cultural meanings may help explain some of the factors that cause the rapist to rape and that contribute to the victim's likelihood of victimization. Furthermore, research that focuses exclusively on the victim must be interpreted keeping in mind that the cause of a sexually aggressive act lies always with the aggressor. Otherwise, researchers may do further harm to those women whom investigators aim to help.

Clinicians working with women who have experienced sexual victimization need to recognize the stigma assigned to victims and the way in which stigmatization further exacerbates feelings of powerlessness. Women always need to be supported for their coping and survival, not blamed for their victimization. Clinicians can also help women increase their personal power by helping them identify factors over which they have control, so as to decrease their chances of being victimized again.

None of the above recommendations will yield marked change, however, until societal changes take place. The most effective way to reduce the chances of victimization is to rectify the imbalance of power between men and women. Consequently, equal representation of women and men in positions of power is necessary. People who currently promote gender stereotypes (e.g., advertisers, educators, filmmakers) could all effect change by debunking those stereotypes. Programs that educate high-risk groups (Warshaw, 1988) about acquaintance rape should be adopted by junior high schools, high schools, and universities. Social policies are needed to eradicate the sexual victimization of children as well as of adults. A significant reduction in the incidence of rape will not occur as a result of behavioral changes made by individual women. Instead, changes in the socialization of men and the relative status of women are necessary to reduce the likelihood that women will be sexually victimized.

REFERENCES

Acock, A. C., & Ireland, N. K. (1983). Attribution of blame in rape cases: The impact of norm violation, gender, and sex-role attitude. *Sex Roles, 9,* 179–193.

Adams, K. L., & Ware, N. C. (1989). Sexism and the English language: The linguistic implications of being a woman. In J. Freeman (Ed.), *Women: A feminist perspective* (pp. 470–484). Mountain View, CA: Mayfield.

Amick, A., & Calhoun, K. (1987). Resistance to sexual aggression: Personality, attitudinal, and situational factors. *Archives of Sexual Behavior, 19,* 153–163.

Amir, M. (1971). *Patterns in forcible rape.* Chicago: University of Chicago Press.

Bart, P. B., & O'Brien, P. H. (1985). *Stopping rape: Successful survival strategies.* Elmsford, NY: Pergamon.

Basow, S. A. (1986). *Gender stereotypes: Traditions and alternatives* (2nd ed.). Monterey, CA: Brooks/Cole.

Blau, F. D., & Winkler, A. E. (1989). Women in the labor force: An overview. In J. Freeman (Ed.), *Women: A feminist perspective* (pp. 265–286). Mountain View, CA: Mayfield.

Briddell, D. W., Rimm, D. C., Caddy, G. R., Krawitz, G., Sholis, D., & Wunderlin, R. J. (1978). Effects of alcohol and cognitive set on sexual arousal to deviant stimuli. *Journal of Abnormal Psychology, 87,* 418–430.

Browne, A., & Finkelhor, D. (1986). Impact of child sexual abuse: A review of the research. *Psychological Bulletin, 99,* 66–77.

Brownmiller, S. (1975). *Against our will: Men, women and rape.* New York: Simon & Schuster.

Burnam, M. A., Stein, J. A., Golding, J. M., Siegel, J. M., Sorenson, S. B., Forsythe, A. B., & Telles, C. A. (1988). Sexual assault and mental disorders in a community population. *Journal of Consulting and Clinical Psychology, 56,* 843–850.

Burt, M. R. (1980). Cultural myths and supports for rape. *Journal of Personality and Social Psychology, 38,* 217–230.

Check, J. V., & Malamuth, N. M. (1983). Sex role stereotyping and reactions to depictions of stranger versus acquaintance rape. *Journal of Personality and Social Psychology, 45,* 344–356.

Costin, F., & Schwarz, N. (1987). Beliefs about rape and women's social roles: A four-nation study. *Journal of Interpersonal Violence, 2,* 46–56.

Davies, A. (1988). *Washington information directory.* Washington, DC: Congressional Quarterly.

Ehrhart, J. K., & Sandler, B. R. (1985). *Campus gang rape: Party games?* Washington, DC: Association of American Colleges.

Feild, H. S. (1978). Attitudes toward rape: A comparative analysis of police, rapists, crisis counselors, and citizens. *Journal of Personality and Social Psychology, 36,* 156–179.

Finkelhor, D. (1984). *Child sexual abuse: New theory and research.* New York: Free Press.

Finkelhor, D. (1986). *Sourcebook on child sexual abuse.* Beverly Hills, CA: Sage.

Finkelhor, D., & Browne, A. (1985). The traumatic impact of child sexual abuse: A conceptualization. *American Journal of Orthopsychiatry, 55,* 530–541.

Fox, M. F. (1989). Women and higher education: Gender differences in the status of students and scholars. In J. Freeman (Ed.), *Women: A feminist perspective* (pp. 217–235). Mountain View, CA: Mayfield.

George, W. H., & Marlatt, G. A. (1986). The effect of alcohol and anger on interest in violence, erotica, and deviance. *Journal of Abnormal Psychology, 95,* 150-158.

Glenn, E. N., & Feldberg, R. L. (1989). Clerical work: The female occupation. In J. Freeman (Ed.), *Women: A feminist perspective* (pp. 287–311). Mountain View, CA: Mayfield.

Green, R. (1987). Exposure to explicit sexual materials and sexual assault: A review of behavioral and social science research. In M. R. Walsh (Ed.), *The psychology of women: Ongoing debates* (pp. 430–440). New Haven: Yale University Press.

Henley, N., & Freeman, J. (1989). The sexual politics of interpersonal behavior. In J. Freeman (Ed.), *Women: A feminist perspective* (pp. 457–469). Mountain View, CA: Mayfield.

Hoffman, M. S. (1989). *The world almanac and book of facts.* New York: Scripps-Howard.

Kanin, E. J. (1957). Male aggression in dating–courtship relations. *American Journal of Sociology, 63,* 197–204.

Kanin, E. J. (1967). Reference groups and sex conduct norm violations. *Sociological Quarterly, 8,* 495–504.

Kanin, E. J., & Parcell, S. (1977). Sexual aggression: A second look at the offended female. *Archives of Sexual Behavior, 6,* 67–76.

Katz, S., & Mazur, M. (1979). *Understanding the rape victim: A synthesis of research findings.* New York: Wiley.

Korman, S. K., & Leslie, G. R. (1982). The relationship of feminist ideology and date expense sharing to perceptions of sexual aggression in dating. *Journal of Sex Research, 18,* 114–129.

Koss, M. P. (1985). The hidden rape victim: Personality, attitudinal, and situational characteristics. *Psychology of Women Quarterly, 9,* 193–212.

Koss, M. P., & Dinero, T. E. (1989). Discriminant analysis of risk factors for sexual victimization among a national sample of college women. *Journal of Consulting and Clinical Psychology, 57,* 242–250.

Koss, M. P., Dinero, T. E., Seibel, C. A., & Cox, S. L. (1988). Stranger and acquaintance rape: Are there differences in the victim's experience? *Psychology of Women Quarterly, 12,* 1-24.

Koss, M. P., Gidycz, C. A., & Wisniewski, N. (1987). The scope of rape: Incidence and prevalence of sexual aggression and victimization in a national sample of higher education students. *Journal of Consulting and Clinical Psychology, 55,* 162-170.

Linz, D., Donnerstein, E., & Penrod, S. (1987). Sexual violence in the mass media: Social psychological implications. In P. Shaver & C. Hendrick (Eds.), *Sex and gender* (pp. 95-123). Beverly Hills, CA: Sage.

Lips, H. M. (1989). Gender-role socialization: Lessons in femininity. In J. Freeman (Ed.), *Women: A feminist perspective* (pp. 197-216). Mountain View, CA: Mayfield.

Malamuth, N. M. (1981). Rape fantasies as a function of exposure to violent sexual stimuli. *Archives of Sexual Behavior, 10,* 33-47.

Malamuth, N. M., & Check, J. V. (1981). The effects of mass media exposure on acceptance of violence against women: A field experiment. *Journal of Research in Personality, 15,* 436-446.

Miller, J., Moeller, D., Kaufman, A., DiVasto, P., Pathak, D., & Christy, J. (1978). Recidivism among sex assault victims. *American Jounal of Psychiatry, 135,* 1103-1104.

Muehlenhard, C. L. (1988). Mininterpreted dating behaviors and the risk of date rape. *Journal of Social and Clinical Psychology, 6,* 20-37.

Muehlenhard, C. L., & Falcon, P. L. (in press). Men's heterosocial skill and attitudes toward women as predictors of verbal sexual coercion and forceful rape. *Sex Roles.*

Muehlenhard, C. L., & Linton, M. A. (1987). Date rape and sexual aggression in dating situations: Incidence and risk factors. *Journal of Counseling Psychology, 34,* 186-196.

Muehlenhard, C. L., & MacNaughton, J. S. (1988). Women's beliefs about women who "lead men on." *Journal of Social and Clinical Psychology, 7,* 65-79.

Murdock, G. P., & White, D. P. (1969). Standard cross-cultural sample. *Ethnology, 8,* 2.

Murphy, J. E. (1987). *Prevalence of child sexual abuse and consequent experience of date rape and marital rape in the general population.* Presented at the meeting of the National Council of Family Relations, Atlanta.

Pear, R. (1987, September 3). Women reduce lag in earnings but disparities with men remain. *The New York Times,* pp. 1, 7.

Peplau, L. A., & Campbell, S. M. (1989). The balance of power in dating and marriage. In J. Freeman (Ed.), *Women: A feminist perspective* (pp. 121-137). Mountain View, CA: Mayfield.

Rada, T. (1975). Alcohol and rape. *Medical Aspects of Human Sexuality, 9,* 48-65.

Rapaport, K., & Burkhart, B. R. (1984). Personality and attitudinal characteristics of sexually coercive college males. *Journal of Abnormal Psychology, 93,* 216-221.

Richardson, D., & Campbell, J. L. (1982). The effect of alcohol on attributions of blame for rape. *Personality and Social Psychology Bulletin, 8,* 468-476.

Russell, D. E. H. (1975). *The politics of rape: The victim's perspective.* New York: Stein & Day.

Russell, D. E. H. (1984). *Sexual exploitation: Rape, child sexual abuse, and workplace harrassment.* Beverly Hills, CA: Sage.

Russell, D. E. H. (1986). *The secret trauma: Incest in the lives of girls and women.* New York: Basic Books.

Russell, D. E. H. (1990). *Rape in marriage* (2d ed.), Bloomington: Indiana University Press.

Sanday, P. R. (1981). The socio-cultural context of rape: A cross-cultural study. *Journal of Social Issues, 37,* 5–27.

Selkin, J. (1978). Protecting personal space: Victim and resister reactions to assaultive rape. *Journal of Community Psychology, 6,* 263–268.

Sharp, J. A. (1987). *Date rape: Effects of victim/assailant intoxication, observer gender, and sex role stereotyping on attributions of responsibility.* Unpublished master's thesis, University of Kansas.

Shotland, R. L. (1989). A model of the causes of date rape in developing and close relationships. In C. Hendrick (Ed.), Close relationships (pp. 247–270). Newbury Park, CA: Sage.

Shotland, R. L., & Goodstein, L. (1983). Just because she doesn't want to doesn't mean it's rape: An experimentally based causal model of the perception of rape in a dating situation. *Social Psychology Quarterly, 46,* 220–232.

Spence, J. T., & Helmreich, R. (1972). The Attitudes Toward Women Scale: An objective instrument to measure attitudes toward the rights and roles of women in contemporary society. *JSAS Catalog of Selected Documents in Psychology, 2,* 1–48.

Stanko, E. A. (1988). Fear of crime and the myth of the safe home. In K. Yllo and M. Bograd (Eds.), *Feminist perspectives on wife abuse* (pp. 75–88). Newbury Park, CA: Sage.

Steil, J. M. (1989). Marital relationships and mental health: The psychic costs of inequality. In J. Freeman (Ed.), *Women: A feminist perspective* (pp. 138–148). Mountain View, CA: Mayfield.

Warshaw, R. (1988). *I never called it rape: The Ms. report on recognizing, fighting, and surviving date and acquaintance rape.* New York: Harper & Row.

Weis, K., & Borges, S. S. (1973). Victimology and rape: The case of the legitimate victim. *Issues in Criminology, 8,* 71–115.

Wilson, W., & Durrenberger, R. (1982). Comparison of rape and attempted rape

CHAPTER 12

Women as Victims: Antecedents and Consequences of Acquaintance Rape

CATALINA A. MANDOKI, PhD and BARRY R. BURKHART, PhD

CULTURAL ANTECEDENTS OF ACQUAINTANCE RAPE

To understand the nature of the sexual victimization of women, it is necessary to understand the social context undergirding the role functioning of men and women in our culture. This necessity is a consequent of two nonintuitive yet compelling conclusions emerging from basic epidemiological research about sexual victimization:

1. Sexual violence is extraordinarily common in the lives of women; and
2. By far the bulk of sexual victimization occurs in the context of the ordinary role functioning of women (Koss, Gidycz, & Wisniewski, 1987; Russell, 1984).

As reviewed elsewhere in this book, these two conclusions are clearly appropriate. For example, Russell (1984), in a large project assessing the lifetime incidence of sexual victimization at the level of rape and attempted rape, found that 44% of a randomly selected community sample had been victims of rape, attempted rape, or child sexual molestation. Koss et al. (1987), in a study based on a representative national sample of 3,187 college women, found that 27.5% had been raped or had experienced an attempted rape. Sexual violence is part of a larger pattern of victimization of women. For example, Kilpatrick, Saunders, Veronen, Best, and Von (1987) found that, in a random sample of women drawn from one community, 75% had been victims of a crime and 53% had experienced two or more crimes. Fifty-three percent of the women had been victims of at least one sexual assault, and sexual assaults represented 49% of the total cases.

The majority of victimization experiences, particularly sexual victimizations, occur in nonstranger contexts, with acquaintances, family, or friends; that is, these extraordinary events occur in the most ordinary social contexts.

In a fascinating review, Klein (1981) suggested that the manner of their occurrence is intrinsically characteristic of the victimization of women. Examining epidemiological and historical sources, Klein argued that women are most likely to be victimized in their fundamental social roles as childbearers, nurturers, and sexual partners. As childbearers, women have been victimized by legal and moral constraints on birth control and abortion or by coerced sterilization of those who are considered unfit. Women have been restricted in their ability to make decisions regarding when to have children and when not to have children. Victimization also has adhered to women's role as nurturers (wives and mothers). Wife battering may be present in as many as half of all intimate relationships (Gelles, 1972). Recent research has demonstrated that battering often precedes marriage and is a common feature of heterosexual relationships from high school dating (Roscoe & Callahan, 1985) through courtship dating (Cate, Henton, Koval, Christopher, & Lloyd, 1982; Comins, 1984; Makepeace, 1987) and between cohabiting partners (Lane & Gwartney-Gibbs, 1985).

However, women's role as victims has been most clear in their role as sexual beings. Contrary to popular thought, sexual violence is not separate from women's everyday life. The reality of sexual violence is that as children, as adolescents, and as adults, women are most likely to be victimized by their protectors, families, and intimate partners (Finkelhor, 1984; Burkhart & Stanton, 1988; Finklehor & Yllo, 1987). Thus, this introductory review leads to a macabre aphorism: By count and by context, victimization is women's lot in life. To the degree that women participate in culturally prescribed contexts, according to culturally prescribed gender roles and with those culturally prescribed as their most appropriate male partners, they are, to that degree, likely to be victimized.

Victimization, being so redefined, must therefore not be conceived as a "disease" separate from our ordinary life. The types and high rates of victimization cannot be explained solely by reference to individual psychological processes in either victims or offenders. Instead, we argue that this event, which is so frequent that it is common to a substantial proportion of the population and is embedded in ordinary roles of the participants, must be a function of social forces common to that population.

Thus, to understand the victimization of women, especially in acquaintance rape, social-psychological beliefs and attitudes reflective of the culture must be examined for their contributions because it is unlikely and illogical that anomalous psychological processes alone could produce prevalence rates of such magnitude.

SOCIAL-PSYCHOLOGICAL PROCESSES

What are the relevant antecedent social-psychological forces or processes? More specifically, what can we learn by examining social norms, shared beliefs and attitudes, and socialization practices for their role in predicting sexual violence?

These antecedents are most directly expressed by those attitudes in society which are specifically supportive of victimization of women. As Brownmiller (1975) noted, "These are the deadly male myths of rape, the distorted proverbs that govern female sexuality" (pp. 311–312). These are the beliefs that have the effect of disinhibiting male sexual violence ("All women want to be raped"), attributing responsibility to the victim ("No woman can be raped against her will"), and enhancing the status of the assailant ("Real men take what they want and they don't take no").

Burt (1980) found that rape myth acceptance is related to acceptance of interpersonal violence and the belief that relationships between men and women are adversarial. Similarly, Feild (1978) found that beliefs in traditional sex roles were associated with beliefs that rape is often a woman's fault and that rape serves as a release of sexual energy. Finally, Rapaport & Burkhart (1984) demonstrated a strong correlation between sexually aggressive conduct in acquaintance contexts and males' endorsements of attitudes supportive of male dominance and aggressiveness in heterosexual relationships.

Thus, according to this notion, rape, particularly acquaintance rape, is a "consequence of the firmly embedded cultural tradition of male dominance coupled with an acceptance of interpersonal violence toward women" (Burkhart & Stanton, 1988, p. 55). Weis and Borges (1973) suggested that the male-dominated society establishes and perpetuates the role of women as legitimate objects for victimization via gender-role socialization. Thus, gender-role socialization serves to promote the occurrence of sexual violence through the enculturalization and internalization of rape-supportive beliefs and attitudes and the encouragement of patterns of interaction between males and females that are conducive to sexual violence. To be consistent with the traditional male role—that is, to be "normal"—men must accept some forms of violence against women. It is not surprising that by early adolescence boys have incorporated values affirming a legitimate role for sexual violence in courtship (Giarrusso, Johnson, Goodchilds, & Zellman, 1979).

In an attempt to examine Brownmiller's thesis that acceptance of rape myths predicts, across cultures, a belief in the restriction of women's social roles and rights, Costin and Schwartz (1987) collected data about women's roles and rape myth acceptance in four countries (the United States, England, Israel, and West Germany). An example of a traditional sex-role belief was that "women should worry less about their rights and more about becoming good wives and mothers" (p. 50). Rape myth acceptance included such beliefs as "many women really want to be raped" (p. 49). In all four countries, women ascribed to these beliefs to a lesser degree than did men, thus implicating the impact of gender-role socialization in their transmission. Furthermore, rape myth acceptance was positively associated with belief in the restriction of women's social roles.

Attitudes about rape, by themselves, do not necessarily predict whether a person would actually engage in that behavior. Other components have to be activated, such as reliance on and acceptance of violence in one's own behavior.

Baron, Straus, and Jaffee (1988) developed and evaluated a "cultural spillover theory" based on these notions. Their study suggested that cultural support for rape may not be limited to attitudes and beliefs directly related to rape, but may also result from general cultural beliefs that indirectly legitimize interpersonal violence:

> The more a society tends to endorse the use of physical force to attain socially approved ends—order in the schools, crime control, and military dominance—the greater the likelihood that this legitimization of force will be generalized to other spheres of life, such as the family and relations between the sexes, where force is less approved socially.
>
> (p. 80)

To examine this theory, Baron et al. (1988) looked at the relationship between the incidence of rape in the United States (as reported in the annual FBI *Uniform Crime Reports*) and acceptance of noncriminal, socially approved violence and the attitudes supportive of violence. They found that the index of legitimate violence was positively correlated with the incidence of rape in each of the 50 states and the District of Columbia. Similarly, the approval of violence index had a strong positive relationship to the rate of reported rape. Baron et al. (1988) concluded that "legitimate violence tends to be diffused to relations between the sexes, resulting in an increased probability of women being raped (pp. 100–101)." They properly recognized that their analysis suggested that sexual violence and its antecedents are "woven into the fabric of American culture (p. 102)." Consequently, efforts to reduce the incidence of rape must contend with all the elements of the culture associated with the legitimization of violence. Their conclusions echo Burt's (1980) view that "the task of preventing rape is tantamount to revamping a significant proportion of our social values" (p. 229).

Sociological and cultural models clearly indicate that rape is a function of processes associated with a male-dominated society that supports the subordination of women and the use of violence. However, these theories merely suggest why all women are potential victims and may not be useful in the immediate sense for developing prevention programs and helping women who have already been victimized. A comprehensive model of sexual violence must integrate different levels of analysis. Macro-level cultural models must be articulated with micro-level descriptions of the actual behavior of the members of that culture. Thus, unless conceptual links clearly connect macro and micro levels of analysis, macro-level theoretical models will be difficult to evaluate and may have little practical utility. For example, little research has been directed toward examining the social-developmental processes by which cultural variables are transmitted to and incorporated into the beliefs or behavior of members of the culture. However, if the link between cultural variables and the development of individuals' attitudes and beliefs were specified, then prevention models could be focused on this link.

DIRECT ANTECEDENTS OF ACQUAINTANCE RAPE

In the context of this chapter, this notion implies a need to examine how and in what manner these cultural forces impact on the lives of women. However, prior to reviewing this research, a troublesome issue must be addressed. In the process of examining how individual factors interact with cultural forces in predicting victimization, it is easy to become involved in the process of "blaming the victim" (Ryan, 1971). Burkhart and Stanton (1988) described rape as "an event surrounded by myths . . . , most of which have pernicious attributions of responsibility for victims and exculpatory effects for offenders" (p. 47). Researchers (and reviewers) studying the behavior of victims must be clear about the distinction between analysis of and blaming for victimization. When examining victimization models that are predicated on micro-level analysis (Fattah, 1981), the link between the cultural level and the micro level must be preserved. Otherwise, the victim stands alone with her own victimization, and all variance not attributable to the offender becomes hers. Thus, when following Fattah's (1981) suggestions to examine victims' characteristics and responses to victimization as a way of predicting initial and repeated victimization, it is important not to allow the cultural myths about rape to intrude or become entangled with the empirical analysis. This task is difficult but critically necessary, to avoid the possibility of amplifying the cultural forces that initially produced the victimization.

Efforts to predict acquaintance rape based on the victim's characteristics have not been very effective, however. Kanin (1957), in the first study of this kind, examined demographic and social situational variables to determine whether women who had been "offended" sexually could be distinguished from nonoffended women. His findings, although mixed, suggested that relationship variables defining the offending pair were important, although individual characteristics of the female were not significant. Specifically, Kanin interpreted his data to suggest that socially inequitable pairings in which the woman was the partner at disadvantage were more likely to produce sexual offending. However, in later research, the findings could not be replicated (Kanin & Parcell, 1977) and few differences could be found between offended and nonoffended women, with the exception that women who were recently victimized had a more extensive history of victimization.

Koss (1985), based on her conceptual formulation, developed and examined three models of victimization: (a) social control—societal factors are responsible for sexual victimization; (b) victim precipitation—characteristics of the victim lead to victimization; and (c) situational blame—characteristics of the situation lead to sexual assault. She did not find a relationship between rape myth acceptance and attitudes toward women and sexual victimization. Likewise, personality characteristics of the victim were not predictive of sexual victimization. The only variables that discriminated victims from nonvictims were situational variables related to sexual behavior. Victims tended to have had more consensual sexual partners, were younger at the age of first intercourse, and had less conservative sexual values. Similarly, Mandoki and Burkhart (1989b) did not find differences between victims and nonvictims in assertiveness or dependence but found that number of dating partners and number of consensual sexual partners had a positive relationship to sexual victimization. Skelton (1984) found that, in addition to sexual and dating history, sexual victimization was associated with adversarial sexual beliefs, dating of stereotypical males, and reliance on nonverbal means of consent. However, these variables accounted for only a small portion of the variance, and the causal direction of the relationships could not be evaluated.

Koss (1985) found that victimization was primarily a result of exposure to sexually aggressive males and was not predictable based on victim characteristics. Apparently, variables such as dating frequency and number of sexual partners served to increase a woman's risk of exposure to sexually aggressive males. While this was found to be true in our work (Mandoki & Burkhart, 1989b), we also found that a group of women reported repeated victimization by acquaintances or dates. Thus, while all women are at risk for victimization, some women appear to become involved in a cycle where they are repeatedly victimized. Whether this increased vulnerability precedes their initial victimization or is a consequence of the initial victimization is not known. While research regarding victim vulnerability factors is criticized as victim-blaming (i.e., Klein, 1981), it may be useful in understanding patterns of repeated victimization. This research and other literature (Ellis, Atkeson, & Calhoun, 1982; Miller et al., 1978), suggests that there are groups of victims who are repeatedly victimized and there are also women who effectively resist victimization (Amick & Calhoun, 1987; Levine-MacCombie & Koss, 1986; Selkin, 1978). The ultimate responsibility for sexual aggression lies with the perpetrator, but it is important to understand the antecedents of victimization in order to prevent victimization and repeated victimization. No woman should be blamed for her victimization, but some women may be more vulnerable because of their behavior, personalities, and/or prior life experiences, many of which were beyond their control.

One possible vulnerability factor is a history of childhood sexual abuse. Fromuth (1986) found that, among college students, a history of childhood sexual abuse significantly correlated with a history of being raped. Mandoki and Burkhart (1989b), however, found that child victimization was not directly related to rate of adult victimization: 6% of the women they studied had experienced both child and adult sexual victimization, and this rate was consistent with estimations derived from base rates of victimization in the sample.

Koss and Dinero (1989), however, found that when childhood sexual abuse was considered as part of early traumatic experiences, it was predictive of sexual victimization. In researching the hypothesis that women who experienced childhood sexual violence may be at greater risk for repeated sexual victimization, these authors examined the roles of three sets of risk variables in predicting victimization: vulnerability-creating traumatic experiences, social-psychological characteristics, and vulnerability-enhancing situation variables. Vulnerability-creating traumatic experiences included family instability, family violence, treatment history, and childhood sexual abuse. Social-psychological characteristics included Burt's (1980) scales of Adversarial Sexual Beliefs, Acceptance of Interpersonal Violence, Sexual Conservatism, and Rape Myth Acceptance. Also included were indicators of negative femininity, androgyny, positive femininity (Spence, Helmreich, & Holahan, 1979), and an index of sexual attitudes based on questions developed by Koss and Dinero. The vulnerability-enhancing situations included alcohol use and exposure to sexual activity (prior to victimization). Koss and Dinero (1989) found that all of the risk variables received some support for predicting sexual victimization but the vulnerability-creating traumatic experiences were the only variables that improved prediction significantly above base rates for the group. A composite model based on a history of child sexual abuse, liberal sexual attitudes, higher-than-average alcohol use, and above-average sexual activity was the best predictor of victimization status.

They interpreted their findings based on Finkelhor and Browne's (1985) concept of traumatic sexualization, which suggested that components of sexual abuse may result in a process that shapes a child's sexual feelings and attitudes in a developmentally and interpersonally dysfunctional manner. These vulnerability factors were clearly present in only 10% of the women, however, and Koss and Dinero (1989) suggested that what may be most significant in discriminating victimized from nonvictimized women is their exposure to a sexually aggressive male.

Nevertheless, their results suggested that in some manner, and for a subset of women, childhood sexual abuse may lead to behaviors that are associated with increased risk of exposure to sexually aggressive males. In other words, adult victimization may be associated with child sexual victimization through association with a third, mutual correlate: To the degree that childhood sexual abuse is associated with a greater use of alcohol, greater sexual activity, and less conservative sexual attitudes, then the women will also be at a higher risk of acquaintance rape. Koss and Dinero (1989) found that 37% of the women with this profile had been raped, compared to 14% of the women who did not have these risk factors. A similar link was found in our research (Mandoki & Burkhart, 1989b). Both childhood sexual victimization and adult sexual victimization were significantly related to number of consensual sexual partners. Again, high rates of consensual sexual activity may be an effect of childhood sexual abuse which increases one's risk of exposure to sexually aggressive males.

In a methodologically powerful and in-depth study of the relationship between childhood sexual abuse and adolescent and adult sexual behavior, Wyatt (1988) found that childhood sexual abuse involving physical contact predicted an earlier onset of sexual behavior in adolescence, more sexual partners, and briefer sexual relationships than for nonabused women. This finding is consistent with the notion that child sexual abuse has significant impact on the sexual development of the child and results in an enhanced vulnerability to victimization.

Given that the majority of women who are victimized do not have a history of sexual abuse, it becomes important to examine the characteristics of the situations that predict sexual aggression. One approach, to identify characteristics of the victim and offender, has not been found to be very useful in predicting sexual victimization. Both attitudinal and personality factors, however, have been found to predict sexual aggression in males. In their review, Burkhart and Stanton (1985) reported that misogynistic and rape-supportive beliefs, as well as a tendency to see heterosexual relationships as sexual and adversarial, were associated with sexual aggression by males. Similarly, offenders tended to have deficits in basic socialization, were interpersonally irresponsible, and were hostile toward women.

A second approach has been to examine differences between women who have encountered an attempted rape versus women who have been victims of a completed rape. Selkin (1978), who compared "resisters" with victims of rape, found that women who had resisted rape were likely to have experienced anger and rage during the assault; victims were more likely to have experienced intense fear and panic. Interestingly, only 17% of the resisters were assaulted by acquaintances; 31% of the completed rape victims knew their assailant. Selkin suggested that the resisters' anger may have helped them to initiate an active response to the rape, while the victims' terror may have immobilized them. Resisters scored higher than victims on four scales of the California Personality Inventory (CPI): social presence, sociability, dominance, and communality. These results suggested that the resisters described themselves as more assertive, more confident, and more socially adept. Selkin interpreted his findings as supporting Brownmiller's (1975) assertion that "women are culturally conditioned to be victims of exploitation" (p. 268). Selkin (1978) recruited his subjects through newspaper advertisements, which may have limited the generalizability of his results.

Levine-MacCombie and Koss (1986) suggested that evidence regarding successful resistance based on self-identified victims might not generalize to "hidden" victims—women who do not define themselves as rape victims but have experienced an assault that meets the legal definition of rape. Consequently, Levine-MacCombie and Koss (1986) compared "avoiders" with acknowledged and unacknowledged victims of acquaintance rape.

Avoiders reported having experienced less fear, guilt, and helplessness during the assault but differed in their experience of more anger than victims. Avoiders perceived their assault as less violent and were more likely to run away or scream for help. While crying and reasoning were somewhat effective in resisting rape, active strategies were more successful. Quarreling, on the other hand, was associated with a completed rape and physical resistance was not found to differentiate victims from avoiders. Acknowledged and unacknowledged victims did not differ in their response strategies.

Amick and Calhoun (1987) tested the efficacy of three models (social control, victim precipitation, and situation blame) for predicting successful resistance to sexual aggression. Because the subjects were college students who had completed the Sexual Experiences Survey (Koss & Oros, 1982), they did not need to define themselves as rape victims to be included in the study. The victim precipitation model was tested using the Rosenberg Self-Esteem Scale, the Rathus Assertiveness Schedule, and four scales of the CPI: dominance, sociability, social presence, and communality. The social control model was measured using the Bem Sex Role Inventory, and Burt's scales of Sex Role Stereotyping, Sexual Conservatism, Acceptance of Interpersonal Violence, and Adversarial Sexual Beliefs. Situational blame was assessed using a situational questionnaire based on interview items by Koss and Oros (1982).

The social presence and dominance scales of the CPI were the only personality and attitudinal variables that differentiated successful resisters from unsuccessful resisters. The results suggested that successful resisters displayed more initiative, persistence, and leadership and were more socially poised and socially skilled than unsuccessful resisters.

The situational blame model was found to be the most useful for predicting successful versus unsuccessful resistance. Unsuccessful resisters reported higher rates of isolated victimization sites and were more likely to report a steady dating relationship with the offender and prior genital fondling and/or intercourse with the offender. In addition, unsuccessful resisters reported lower rates of clear consent. Victims' response strategies seemed to correspond to the offenders' method of coercion. For example, when an offender used physical threat and force, the victims tended to report higher use of physical tactics. When the offender's coercion involved verbal persuasion, the victims reported greater use of verbal self-protective strategies.

The findings suggested that successful resistance involved a nonisolated dating situation where the woman had had little previous experience with sexual victimization. Furthermore, the woman was likely to be socially poised and to display interpersonal dominance. In response to the male's undesired advances, the woman expressed clear nonconsent and was able to successfully resist the unwanted sexual activity.

The unsuccessful resisters, on the other hand, were more likely to be in an isolated dating situation with a steady dating partner with whom they had had prior intimacy. The woman was likely to be inexperienced with sexual victimization, less poised, and more compliant. The woman's response to the unwanted advances was not clear and resulted in unwanted sexual activity.

Amick and Calhoun's (1987) findings suggested differences in ambiguity between stranger and acquaintance rapes, necessitating different strategies for resistance. The ambiguity of the situation also differentiated victims of completed versus attempted sexual assaults in Mandoki's (1989) research. Women who successfully resisted an attempted rape (compared with women who were unsuccessful in resisting a molestation or unwanted intercourse) reported having been in a situation that was consistent with stereotypes regarding rape. These results suggest that the stereotypical qualities of the situation served as early cues for the successful resisters and prompted effective resistance.

The antecedents of acquaintance rape can thus be found at various levels. From the beliefs and attitudes of our culture, there is abundant evidence to suggest that attitudes supporting and legitimizing violence contribute to the victimization of women and that this cultural context encourages the victimization of women in a variety of roles, including their roles as dating and romantic partners. This same climate that supports interpersonal violence undoubtedly contributes to the high rates of emotional, physical, and sexual abuse of children. As demonstrated by Koss and Dinero (1989), childhood traumatic experiences such as these contribute to a woman's risk of sexual victimization by an acquaintance. Finally, research regarding successful versus unsuccessful resistance provides some support for the notion that women are socialized to be vulnerable to victimization: women who are passive and less clear in nonconsent are less effective in resisting sexual assaults. Amick and Calhoun's (1987) findings, as well as our own (Mandoki, 1989), suggested that if women are more aware of the possibility of an assault in a "benign" situation, such as a date with a steady dating partner, they may be more effective at resisting the assault. The ultimate responsibility, however, lies with the male aggressor. The women who reported successful resistance may well have encountered males who were more responsive to the women's resistance and less likely to follow through with unwanted sexual advances. Nevertheless, it is useful to know the characteristics of both the victim's aggressor and of situations that are associated with effective resistance.

CONSEQUENCES OF ACQUAINTANCE RAPE

There is a great deal of research regarding the effects of rape but most of it has focused on identified victims who report to agencies or respond to advertisements (see Ellis, 1983 for a review). Little research has specifically examined the consequences of acquaintance rape in unidentified populations, such as college students, who report a high rate of sexual aggression by dating partners. Kilpatrick et al. (1988), however, found that acknowledgment of rape and the relationship to the offender had little effect on mental health consequences. Using a community sample of women in which they compared unacknowledged and acknowledged victims of rape, they did not find any difference in the characteristics of the offense, including whether the assailant was a stranger or an acquaintance. Acknowledged victims were significantly more likely to have ever developed Post-Traumatic Stress Disorder than were unacknowledged victims. The presence of violence during the rape was associated with whether the victim acknowledged the experience as rape and with increased risk of development of Post-Traumatic Stress Disorder. All rape victims were significantly more likely than women who had not experienced a rape to have a current major depressive episode, current social phobia, and sexual problems. While the sample was based on a random community survey and did not rely on self-reporting to agencies, the generalizability of these results to college samples is not known. Nevertheless, these findings suggest that even among hidden victims there are significant mental health consequences following sexual assault and that there is little difference mediated by relationship status.

The effects of acquaintance rape among college students are just beginning to be researched. The research to date suggests that acquaintance rape has negative consequences for the victim. Rogers (1984) studied the effects of sexual assault on a sample of undergraduate women and found that exposure to a greater degree of sexual aggression was associated with significantly higher levels of anxiety, greater guilt associated with sexual behavior, and poorer overall social and family adjustment. Furthermore, the effects were not related to the length of time since the assault and did not appear to diminish over time.

These results are consistent with our findings (Mandoki, 1989; Mandoki & Burkhart, 1989a) when the effects of attributions and coping on post-assault adjustment among a sample of 813 female undergraduates were examined. These women completed anonymous questionnaires which asked about history of sexual victimization, attributions regarding these experiences, coping strategies used, and psychological effects of the experiences. Nineteen percent of the women reported having experienced forced intercourse; of these, approximately two-thirds reported victimization experiences involving an acquaintance or date. These women were compared to women who reported noncoital sexual aggression and to nonvictims. (Nonvictims responded to questions based on their adjustment following their most negative academic failure.) Rape victims were found to have significantly higher levels of distress (based on the global severity index of the *Symptom Checklist 90— Revised*) both during the time following the assault and currently. As with Rogers' (1984) findings, recency of assault was not related to level of distress. In fact, over 80% of the women had been assaulted over a year before, yet they still reported significantly higher levels of distress than did nonvictims. These findings highlight the significance of acquaintance rape as a traumatic, disruptive experience that is distinct from other common problems experienced during college (such as an academic failure) and that continues to have effects months and years following the assault. Attributions of blame were found to be the most important variable in predicting post-rape adjustment. Characterological self-blame was the only variable that was significantly associated with both initial levels of distress and current levels of distress among rape victims. Characterological self-blame was also associated with greater use of all coping strategies (active and passive); however, none of the coping strategies were associated with global levels of distress. Furthermore, blaming society or one's own behavior did not have a strong relationship to adjustment.

The distressing impact of acquaintance rape was highlighted by the victims' written descriptions of the effects of the assault. In a follow-up study (Sommerfeldt, Burkhart, & Mandoki, 1989), the written descriptions were categorized to describe attributions of causality and effects of victimization. Based on these descriptions, 46% of the women reported some form of self-blame and 40% blamed the aggressor. The most common effect was an increase in cautiousness and mistrust; victims also reported shame, anger, fear, depression, and diminished self-esteem. These effects are most evident from the victims' own words:

> Losing my virginity in that way gave me a feeling of guilt I never felt before. The feeling was so intense that suicide came in into my mind very often. Fear of pregnancy was also draining me emotionally and physically.

> I cried, felt violated, alone and unclean.

Most of the women blamed themselves for the assault:

> Because I was drunk and I didn't realize what was going on and there was no one around to help me. I shouldn't have let myself get into that situation.

> Because there was kissing and he got excited. Therefore, he was not thinking rationally. All he cared about was his sexual drive, not about me or my feelings. It was my fault for turning him on.

> It really hasn't affected me because I know it was my fault. I rarely dwell on it.

And the effects refuse to go away:

> This experience had a great impact on my life until about six months ago—because I called this guy and told him that because of what "happened" between us, I was now scared to trust other guys. Yes, it still affects my feelings towards guys. Several guys still kid me and say that I don't like to be touched, because almost every time a guy puts his hand on my leg, etc., I always tend to move away or grab his hand—just out of fear that something "might happen."

> Yes. It still affects me. It happened more than once. Because I was molested as a child, and he knew this. Yet, he continued to harass me. Both incidences, as a child and as a teenager, very much affect me now. I hate every one of them. It is

constantly on my mind. It seems I can't put it away and forget it. I probably never will.

These passages suggest that the consequences of acquaintance rape are both long-term and distressing. Victims of acquaintance rape feel guilty and blame themselves. These feelings of self-blame are associated with lasting distress and symptoms following the assault, even after years have passed. Furthermore, these self-deprecating feelings are not substantially altered by the coping strategies naturally employed by the victims. This may suggest that victims do not naturally employ effective coping strategies and/or these strategies are not sufficient to overcome societal beliefs that encourage self-blame and guilt.

CONCLUSION

The findings reviewed in this chapter have implications for prevention and treatment efforts. For example, data that suggest that women's vulnerability can be reduced through training for effective resistance would implicate the need for such programs. However, we would like to end this chapter with a caveat and a recommendation. In the process of writing about women as victims it is all too easy to focus on womens' victimization, its antecedents and consequences, without a full appreciation that victims can provide only one side of the story, their victimization. Therefore, the most critical components of the process of victimization are left out. Without attention to the sociocultural contexts of victimization and the dynamics of the perpetrators of victimization, the story is far less than even half-told. Further, without this effort, attempts at prevention are ultimately much less than half-done. Future research on prevention must be focused on impacting the values and behaviors of the potential perpetrators. It is discouraging to find so little empirical work that evaluates prevention programming.

Preventing sexual violence between acquaintances clearly entails addressing fundamental, deeply ingrained social and interpersonal processes; despite the difficulty inherent, this is a necessary task. Sexual violence is too pervasive and malignant to do otherwise.

REFERENCES

Amick, A. E., & Calhoun, K. S. (1987). Resistance to sexual aggression: Personality, attitudinal, and situational factors. *Archives of Sexual Behavior, 16,* 153–163.

Baron, L., Straus, M. A., & Jaffee, D. (1988). Legitimate violence, violent attitudes, and rape: A test of cultural spillover theory. In R. A. Prentky & V. L. Quinsey (Eds.), *Human sexual aggression: Current perspectives. Annals of the New York Academy of Sciences (Vol. 528,* pp. 79–110). New York: The New York Academy of Sciences.

Brownmiller, S. (1975). *Against our will: Men, women, and rape.* New York: Simon & Schuster.

Burkhart, B. R., & Stanton, A. L. (1988). Sexual aggression in acquaintance relationships. In G. Russell (Ed.), *Violence in intimate relationships* (pp. 43–65). Englewood Cliffs, NJ: PMA Press.

Burt, M. R. (1980). Cultural myths and supports for rape. *Journal of Personality and Social Psychology, 38,* 217–230.

Cate, R. M., Henton, J. M., Koval, J., Christopher, F. S., & Lloyd, S. (1982). Premarital abuse: A social psychological perspective. *Journal of Family Issues, 3,* 79–90.

Comins, C. A. (1984). *Violence between dating partners: Incidence and contributing factors.* Unpublished doctoral dissertation, Auburn University, Alabama.

Costin, F., & Schwarz, N. (1987). Beliefs about rape and women's social roles. *Journal of Interpersonal Violence, 2,* 46–56.

Ellis, E. M. (1983). A review of empirical rape research: Victim reactions and response to treatment. *Clinical Psychology Review, 3,* 473–490.

Ellis, E., Atkeson, B., & Calhoun, K. (1982). An examination of differences between multiple- and single-incident victims of sexual assault. *Journal of Abnormal Psychology, 91,* 221–224.

Fattah, E. A. (1981). Becoming a victim: The victimization experience and its aftermath. *Victimology: An International Journal, 6,* 29–47.

Feild, H. S. (1978). Attitudes toward rape: A comparative analysis of police, rapists, crisis counselors, and citizens. *Journal of Personality and Social Psychology, 36,* 166–179.

Finkelhor, D. (1984). *Child sexual abuse: New theory and research.* New York: Free Press.

Finkelhor, D., & Browne, A. (1985). The traumatic impact of child sexual abuse: A conceptualization. *American Journal of Orthopsychiatry, 55,* 530–541.

Finkelhor, D. & Yllo, K. (1987). *License to rape: Sexual abuse of wives.* New York: Free Press.

Fromuth, M. E. (1986). The relationship of childhood sexual abuse with later psychological and sexual adjustment in a sample of college women. *Child Abuse and Neglect, 10,* 5–15.

Gelles, R. J. (1972). *The violent home: A study of physical aggression between husband and wife.* Beverly Hills, CA: Sage.

Giarrusso, R., Johnson, P., Goodchilds, J., & Zellman, G. (1979, April). *Adolescents' cues & signals: Sex and assault.* Paper presented at the meeting of the Western Psychological Association, San Diego.

Kanin, E. J. (1957). Male aggression in dating–courtship relations. *American Journal of Sociology, 10,* 197–204.

Kanin, E. J., & Parcell, S. R. (1977). Sexual aggression: A second look at the offended female. *Archives of Sexual Behavior, 6,* 67–76.

Kilpatrick, D. G., Best, C. L., Saunders, B. E., Amick-McMullan, A. E., Lipovsky, J. A., & Haskett, M. (1988, August). *Does victim's acknowledgment of rape influence risk of mental health disorders?* Paper presented at the annual meeting of the American Psychological Association, Atlanta.

Kilpatrick, D. G., Saunders, B. E., Veronen, L. J., Best, C. L., & Von, J. M. (1987). Criminal victimization: Lifetime prevalence, Reporting to police, and psychological impact. *Crime & Delinquency, 33,* 479–489.

Klein, D. (1981). Violence against women: Some considerations regarding its causes and its elimination. *Crime & Delinquency, 27,* 64–81.

Koss, M. P. (1985). The hidden rape victim: Personality, attitudinal, and situational characteristics. *Psychology of Women Quarterly, 9,* 193–212.

Koss, M. P., & Dinero, T. E. (1989). Discriminant analysis of risk factors for sexual victimization among a national sample of college women. *Journal of Consulting and Clinical Psychology, 57,* 242–250.

Koss, M. P., Gidycz, C. A., & Wisniewski, N. (1987). The scope of rape: Incidence and prevalence of sexual aggression and victimization in a national sample of higher education students. *Journal of Consulting and Clinical Psychology, 55,* 162–170.

Koss, M. P., & Oros, C. J. (1982). Sexual experiences survey: A research instrument investigating sexual aggression and victimization. *Journal of Consulting and Clinical Psychology, 50,* 455–457.

Lane, K. E., & Gwartney-Gibbs, P. A. (1985). Violence in the context of dating and sex. *Journal of Family Issues, 6,* 45–59.

Levine-MacCombie, J., & Koss, M. P. (1986). Acquaintance rape: Effective avoidance strategies. *Psychology of Women Quarterly, 10,* 311–320.

Makepeace, J. M. (1987). Social factor and victim-offender differences in courtship violence. *Family Relations, 36,* 87–91.

Mandoki, C. A. (1989). *Coping with victimization: An analysis of the relationship between appraisals, coping strategies, and adjustment.* Unpublished doctoral dissertation, Auburn University, Alabama.

Mandoki, C. A., & Burkhart, B. R. (1989a, August). *Coping and adjustment to rape.* Paper presented at the annual meeting of the American Psychological Association, New Orleans.

Mandoki, C. A., & Burkhart, B. R. (1989b). Sexual victimization: Is there a vicious cycle? *Victims and Violence, 4,* 179–189.

Miller, J., Moeller, D., Kaufman, A., Divasto, P., Pathak, D., & Christy, J. (1978). Recidivism among sex assault victims. *American Journal of Psychiatry, 135,* 1103–1104.

Rapaport, K., & Burkhart, B. R. (1984). Personality and attitudinal characteristics of sexually coercive college males. *Journal of Abnormal Psychology, 93,* 216–221.

Rogers, L. C. (1984). *Sexual victimization: Social and psychological effects in college women.* Unpublished doctoral dissertation, Auburn University, Alabama.

Roscoe, B., & Callahan, J. E. (1985). Adolescents' self-reports of violence in family and dating relationships. *Adolescence, 20,* 545–553.

Russell, D. E. H. (1984). *Sexual exploitation.* Beverly Hills, CA: Sage.

Ryan, W. (1971). *Blaming the victim.* New York: Random House.

Selkin, J. (1978). Protecting personal space: Victim and resister reactions to assaultive rape. *Journal of Community Psychology, 6,* 269–274.

Skelton, C. A. (1984). *Correlates of sexual victimization among college women.* Unpublished doctoral dissertation, Auburn University, Alabama.

Sommerfeldt, T. G., Burkhart, B. R., & Mandoki, C. A. (1989, August). *In her own words: Victims' descriptions of hidden rape effects.* Paper presented at the annual convention of the American Psychological Association, New Orleans.

Spence, J. T., Helmreich, R. L., & Holahan, C. K. (1979). Negative and positive components of psychological masculinity and femininity and their relationships to self-reports of neurotic and acting out behaviors. *Journal of Personality and Social Psychology, 37,* 1673–1682.

Weis, K., & Borges, S. S. (1973). Victimology and rape: The case of the legitimate victim. *Issues in Criminology, 8,* 71–115.

Wyatt, G. A. (1988, August). The relationship between child sexual abuse and adolescent sexual functioning in Afro-American and white American women. In R. A. Prentky & V. L. Quinsey (Eds.), *Human sexual aggression: Current perspectives. Annals of the New York Academy of Sciences, (Vol. 528,* pp. 111–122). New York: The New York Academy of Sciences.

CHAPTER 13

Male Victims of Acquaintance Rape

CINDY STRUCKMAN-JOHNSON, PhD

In the past decade, the nation discovered that women are "hidden victims" of acquaintance rape. Recent surveys of college campuses and major metropolitan areas revealed that from 13% to 54% of women have had forced sexual contact and from 15% to 26% have been raped in their lifetime. The assailant in a majority of cases was not a stranger, but an acquaintance, friend, date, or lover of the victim (Koss, Gidycz, & Wisniewski, 1987; Russell, 1984; Sorenson, Stein, Siegel, Golding, & Burnam, 1987).

During the 1990s, we are finding that men, too, are hidden victims of acquaintance rape. Contrary to commonly held beliefs that men are "too big," "too strong," or "too much in control" to be sexually assaulted, a substantial number of men are victimized each year. This chapter discusses the prevalence of acquaintance rape and unwanted sexual experiences for men, the consequences of such experiences, and recommendations for addressing the problem. "Acquaintance rape" is defined here as an incident in which one uses physical force or threat of force or harm to obtain sexual intercourse from a nonfamily acquaintance. The terms "sexual assault" and "sexual abuse" refer to perpetration of any unwanted sexual contact—from fondling to sexual intercourse—through the use of verbal or physical pressure.

PREVALENCE RATES

The prevalence of sexual assault upon American men is difficult to determine because of a lack of research and official records. With the exception of studies on prison violence (Lockwood, 1980; Scacco, 1982), there are few articles in the sexual assault literature about adult male victims. One of the best sources for crime information—the Federal Bureau of Investigation's (FBI, 1988) annual *Uniform Crime Report*—does not include statistics for male rape victims because, by the Bureau's definition, the victims of forcible rape are always female. However, the U. S. Department of Justice (1988) publishes estimates of the number of men and women who are victimized by personal crime each year. Based on 1987 crime records, about one per 1,000 men, or approximately 9,400 men for the total U. S. male population, are victims of rape or attempted rape each year. This estimate, however, is based upon very small sample sizes and may be unreliable.

According to records from rape crisis centers, male rape victims account for a steady and possibly increasing percentage of patients. Kaufman, Divasto, Jackson, Voorhees, & Christy (1980) found that, between 1975 and 1978, the percentage of male victims treated at a rape crisis clinic in New Mexico increased from 0% to 10%. Forman (1982) determined that men accounted for 6% of the rape victims treated at a South Carolina clinic in 1978 and 1979. In an article for *Boston Magazine,* Krueger (1985) reported that almost 100 men raped by other men had received treatment at crisis centers in eastern Massachusetts in 1984.

Given that thousands of men are sexually assaulted every year, why is so little known about the problem? Nicholas Groth, one of the nation's foremost authorities on male rape, has suggested that our society has no place for the male victim of sexual assault. Because of our cultural beliefs that men initiate and control their sexual encounters, we assume they cannot be targets of a sexual attack (Groth & Burgess, 1980). In fact, many people believe that male rape happens only among homosexual men or imprisoned heterosexual men who have no sexual outlet (Miller, 1983). As a consequence, the public, social scientists, law enforcement personnel, and helping professionals have failed to identify and meet the needs of men who are sexually assaulted (Sarrel & Masters, 1982).

Our culture's ignorance of male rape is compounded by the fact that most male victims do not report their experience to the police, to health officials, or even to their friends and family (Calderwood, 1987; Kaufman et al., 1980; Krueger, 1985; Myers, 1989; Sarrel & Masters, 1982). Many men keep silent because of deeply entrenched attitudes about appropriate male social and sexual roles (Miller, 1983). Male victims are often too embarrassed and humiliated to admit that they were overpowered or made helpless by another person. They may blame themselves for not being strong enough or "man enough" to defend themselves (Groth & Burgess, 1980; Krueger, 1985). This embarrassment is especially acute if the assailant happens to be a woman or group of women (Rosenfeld, 1982). Reporting also violates another male norm of "toughing it out." Many victims feel that they should be able to cope on their own and do not want to ask for help (Miller, 1983).

Perhaps the major reason why heterosexual men do not report being raped by another man is that they are afraid of being labeled homosexual. Closeted gay men who are raped fear that an official investigation and trial will reveal their sexual identity to the public. In some communities, male rape victims may be classified by the police as "sodomized," not raped. In states where consensual sodomy is considered a crime, the victim potentially can be arrested for participating in "unnatural acts" (Groth & Burgess, 1980; Miller, 1983).

Some male victims do not know where to go to get treatment because they believe that rape crisis centers are places for women (Calderwood, 1987). Also, men expect and often receive unsympathetic and even hostile treatment from the police, medical personnel, and the court system. According to many experts, the current social climate for male rape victims is much like the atmosphere surrounding female rape victims 20 years ago—the authorities tend not to believe men's stories and/or blame them for getting into the predicament. The credibility problem is intensified for men who ejaculated during the attack because it erroneously implies that they enjoyed or consented to the encounter (Groth & Burgess, 1980; Krueger, 1985; Miller, 1983).

Most experts agree that because of the low report rate, the true prevalence of male sexual assault is much higher than percentages obtained from police or medical records (Calderwood, 1987; Groth & Burgess, 1980). More accurate estimates are available from research surveys in which men have been asked to report past experiences with sexual assault.

Community-Based Surveys

Some of the best evidence, to date, on the prevalence of male sexual assault has come from the Los Angeles Epidemiologic Catchment Area Project (Sorenson, personal communication, April 1989; Sorenson et al., 1987). This study was unique in that the authors conducted representative sampling of male and female whites and Hispanics living in a major population area. Of 1,480 male interviewees, 7.2% reported that, after the age of 16, they had been pressured or forced to have sexual contact (touching of sexual parts or sexual intercourse). Table 13.1 shows the percentages of assaulted men by age, race, and educational level.

The high-risk group were white, college-educated men between the ages of 18 and 39 years, with 16% reporting sexual assault. Nearly 80% of the assailants in the most recent assault were acquaintances or lovers (Table 13.2).* As shown in Table 13.3, about 62% of the victims reported that verbal pressure was used, 9% were physically harmed or threatened, and 29% endured a combination of harm, threats, and verbal pressure. Intercourse (oral, vaginal, or anal) occurred in 39% of the most recent episodes.

College Campus Surveys

Another important source of information about male victims is campus surveys on sexual assault. Although dozens of such prevalence surveys have been conducted over the past 30 years, most have focused on female, not

---

* I would like to thank Dr. Susan Sorenson for conducting additional analyses of her original data (Sorenson, Stein, Siegel, Golding, & Burnam, 1987) to provide distributions by sex of assailant for Tables 13.2 and 13.3.

TABLE 13.1. Prevalence of Adult Sexual Assault of Males, by Age and Education, Among Hispanics and Non-Hispanic Whites: The Los Angeles Epidemiologic Catchment Area Project, 1983–1984

	Age	
Ethnic Group and Education (years)	18–39 % Prevalence	40+ % Prevalence
Hispanics, by Education (years)		
0–10	4.1	2.5
11+	8.8	7.1
Non-Hispanic Whites, by Education (years)		
0–14	7.3	8.7
15+	16.3	7.3

Note: Contents of this table were originally published in Sorenson, S. B., Stein, J. A., Siegel, J. M., Golding, J. M., & Burnam, M. A. (1987). The prevalence of adult sexual assault: The Los Angeles Epidemiologic Catchment Area Project, *American Journal of Epidemiology, 126,* 1154–1164.

TABLE 13.2. Relation of Assailant to the Respondent in the Most Recent Adult Sexual Assault of Males, by Sex of Assailant: The Los Angeles Epidemiologic Catchment Area Project, 1983–1984

Relation of Assailant	% Total Men	Sex of Assailant*	
		% Male	% Female
Stranger	18.5	39.4 (11.5)**	6.7 (4.8)
Acquaintance	56.5	48.9 (14.3)	57.6 (41.7)
Acquaintance	28.4	29.1 (8.5)	27.3 (19.8)
Friend	28.1	19.8 (5.8)	30.2 (21.9)
Relative	1.2	2.7 (0.8)	0.7 (0.5)
Parent	0.0	0.0 (0.0)	0.0 (0.0)
Uncle/aunt	0.0	0.0 (0.0)	0.0 (0.0)
Other relative	1.2	2.7 (0.8)	0.7 (0.5)
Intimate	23.9	2.1 (0.6)	32.7 (23.7)
Spouse	5.9	0.0 (0.0)	8.3 (6.0)
Lover	18.0	2.1 (0.6)	24.4 (17.7)
Other	4.3	6.8 (2.0)	2.3 (1.7)
Unspecified	1.6	3.8 (1.1)	.7 (0.5)
Employer	1.5	3.1 (0.9)	.8 (0.6)
Teacher	1.2	0.0 (0.0)	.8 (0.6)
Date	0.0	0.0 (0.0)	0.0 (0.0)

Note: Respondents indicated all forms of assailants, therefore percentages may not total to 100.

* Percentages are not reported for 2.5% of the cases, which involved both male and female assailants.

**Numbers in parentheses are total percentages of all assailant categories combined.

(Sorenson, new data, 1989; see note, p. 194)

TABLE 13.3.   Pressure or Force Used and Outcome of Most Recent Adult Sexual Assault of Males, by Sex of Assailant: The Los Angeles Epidemiologic Catchment Area Project, 1983–1984

Category	% Total Men	Sex of Assailant*	
		% Male	% Female
Pressure or Force			
Verbal pressure only[a]	61.8	50.9 (13.9)**	67.1 (46.6)
Harm or threat of harm only[b]	9.0	15.1 (4.2)	5.9 (4.1)
Combination of pressure and harm or threat of harm[c]	29.2	34.9 (9.7)	26.9 (18.7)
Outcome			
Attempt at contact	32.2	42.2 (12.7)	27.0 (18.2)
Assailant touched respondent	26.9	31.6 (9.5)	25.2 (17.0)
Respondent touched assailant	2.0	6.6 (2.0)	0.0
Intercourse (oral, anal, vaginal)	28.4	15.9 (4.8)	35.0 (23.6)
Multiple, including intercourse	10.4	3.7 (1.1)	12.9 (8.7)

Note: Respondents indicated all forms of pressure or force and outcomes, therefore percentages may not total to 100.
* Percentages are not reported for 2.5% of the cases, which involved both male and female assailants.
**Numbers in parentheses are total percentages of all assailant categories combined.
[a] Persuasion, bribe, love withdrawal.
[b] Threatened harm, scared victim because they were bigger or stronger, physical restraint, weapon present, got victim drunk, physical harm.
[c] Combination of types listed under the two previous categories.
(Sorenson, new data, 1989; see note, p. 194)

male victims (Struckman-Johnson, 1988). Only in recent years have researchers begun to ask college men about victimization.

In one of the earliest studies, Schultz and DeSavage (1975) found that six of 20 (30%) college men had experienced a completed or attempted act of nonconsensual sodomy on or near their campus. Lott, Reilly, and Howard (1982) surveyed a stratified random sample of students, staff, and faculty in a large university community on their experiences with nonconsensual sexual contact through the use of force, threatened force, or a weapon. Combining university and lifetime incidents, 29 of 377 male respondents (8%) reported unwanted contact, and two men (.53%) reported an act of forced penetration. Over half of the assaults were perpetrated by an acquaintance, and nearly all assailants were male.

More recent surveys have established that male college students are also coerced into sexual activity by female acquaintances. Sandberg, Jackson, and Petretic-Jackson (1987) surveyed 408 psychology students at a small midwestern university and found that 48% of 141 male respondents had felt verbally pressured by a dating partner to have sex. When asked "Have you ever been physically forced by a dating partner to have sexual intercourse?," 6% said yes.

At another small midwestern university, Murphy (1984) determined that 12% of 230 male college students had had sexual intercourse with a date who had used psychological or physical force to gain their compliance. Nearly all the men said they were forced by psychological pressure; less than 1% reported that they were physically coerced.

In 1985, I administered my own "Sex on Campus" survey to 623 students at a small midwestern university (Struckman-Johnson, 1988). Students were asked: "In the course of your life, how many times have you been forced to have sexual intercourse while on a date?" Of 268 male respondents, 43 (16%) reported at least one past episode. In a follow-up survey, 21 of the male victims provided a written description of their most recent forced-sex episode. Classification of these descriptions revealed that a majority of the victims (52%) had sex due to verbal pressure such as pleading, demands, or blackmail. Several men (28%) were pressured by a combination of verbal pressure and some physical restraint, and a few (10%) were too intoxicated to consent. Only two (10%) of the victims were physically coerced into sex.

A more recent study (Struckman-Johnson & Struckman-Johnson, 1988) found that 83% of 72 male students had been pressured into "unwanted" sexual intercourse by female dates. Most of the men (52%) had yielded at least one time to verbal pressure, and a surprisingly high percentage (38%) had had unwanted sex when they were too intoxicated to consent. Over a fourth of the men (29%) had been "forcefully seduced" by a woman who used playful force or bondage. Only one man (1.4%) cited physical force.

Muehlenhard and her associates found that many college men engage in unwanted sexual activity on dates. Muehlenhard and Cook (1988) reported that 63% of 507 men had had unwanted sexual intercourse because of internal, situational, and partner-related pressures. Some of the most common pressures cited were sexual enticement (57%), altruism or a desire to help the woman (35%), and intoxication (31%). Some men were pressured by verbal coercion (13%) or were threatened with a breakup (7%). Only a few men (6.5%) said they had been physically forced to have sex.

In a similar study, Muehlenhard and Long (1988) found that 49% of 426 men had engaged in unwanted sex due to pressure from a partner or other persons. Reasons given included enticement (81%), altruism (58%), peer pressure (31%), intoxication (34%), and physical coercion (1.5%).

At least one study showed that coercive sex on dates is a problem for gay college students. Waterman, Dawson, and Bologna (1989) surveyed a very small sample of gay and lesbian students at several northeastern colleges and found that 12% of 36 gay men reported being victims of forced sex by their current or most recent partner.

Summary

Overall, the incidence/prevalence research shows that a substantial minority of adolescent and adult men have been sexually assaulted. According to

Sorenson et al.'s (1987) survey of a large community population, approximately 7% of men have experienced at least one episode of forced sexual contact. Estimates from the Sorenson et al. data indicate that from 2% to 3% of men have been pressured into sexual intercourse with an acquaintance. Although most of these men were verbally pressured, 38% (about .5% to 1% of men overall) were physically forced or threatened with harm.

Among college populations, the incidence of sexual assault of men by acquaintances is much higher. Surveys have found that from 12% to 16% of male students have been forced into sexual intercourse by dating partners, usually by verbal pressure (Murphy, 1984; Struckman-Johnson, 1988). From less than 1% to as many as 7% of men specifically reported being physically coerced into sex by dating partners (Muehlenhard & Cook, 1988; Murphy, 1984; Sandberg et al., 1987).

These estimates of male sexual assault, of course, are not nearly as high as comparable assault rates for women. For example, Sorenson et al. (1987) reported that 13.5% of adult women (compared to 7.2% of men) had experienced sexual assault, and Struckman-Johnson (1988) found that 22% of women (compared to 16% of men) had been forced into intercourse by a dating partner. However, the rates for men are sufficiently high to show that sexual assault is a real problem affecting the health and welfare of American males.

DYNAMICS AND CONSEQUENCES

Sexual Assault of Men by Men

According to research, the dynamics of male rape by men are surprisingly similar to female rape by men. Like female victims, men are typically assaulted by an acquaintance—a peer, workmate, authority figure, date, or lover—rather than by a total stranger (Myers, 1989; Sorenson et al., 1987). They are assaulted where they live, work, travel, and recreate (Groth & Burgess, 1980). Common acquaintance rape scenarios reported in the literature included assault by men who were encountered at parties or bars, gang rape by workmates in military settings, and seduction by trusted individuals such as physicians, priests, psychotherapists, and teachers. Most adult male victims were in their late teens and twenties when the assault occurred (Goyer & Eddleman, 1984; Groth & Burgess, 1980; Kaufman et al., 1980; Myers, 1989).

Men fall prey to the same assault tactics used against women: entrapment (e.g., being assaulted when one is too drunk to resist), intimidation by threats or weapons, use of brute strength, sudden attack, and use of authority or power (Groth & Burgess, 1980; Kaufman et al., 1980; Myers, 1989).

Contrary to common belief, men raped by men are not exclusively homosexual. Of 61 male victims cited in five studies of sexual assault, 36 (59%) were heterosexual and the rest were bisexual, asexual, or homosexual (Goyer & Eddleman, 1984; Groth & Burgess, 1980; Johnson & Shrier, 1987; Kaufman et al., 1980; Myers, 1989). Another myth is that assailants are always homosexuals. Groth and Burgess (1980) found that half of 16 offenders were heterosexuals who actively engaged in consenting sexual encounters with women.

Once under the control of a perpetrator, male victims are usually forced to engage in anal sex (sodomy) in which the perpetrator inserts his penis or an object into the victim's rectum. The second most common act is oral sex in which the perpetrator puts his penis in the mouth of the victim and/or fellates the victim's penis. Other reported acts include fondling or abuse of genitals, forced mutual masturbation, and ejaculation or urination of the perpetrator onto the victim. Several studies found that the perpetrator often attempts to make the victim ejaculate (Goyer & Eddleman, 1984; Groth & Burgess, 1980; Johnson & Shrier, 1987; Myers, 1989).

In answer to the question of how victims can have erections or ejaculate in a coercive situation, Sarrel and Masters (1982) offered several explanations. First, they cited Kinsey, Pomeroy, and Martin's (1948) finding that men can experience a generalized sexual response when put in situations that produce anxiety, fear, anger, or pain. Also, Sarrel and Masters stated that the male sexual response can be stimulated by spinal cord discharge without full cerebral control. Thus, the sexual response of a male victim can be explained as an involuntary reaction to the trauma of the assault.

Case Examples

Because many people do not understand how men can be sexually assaulted, I will summarize some actual incidents of acquaintance rape reported in the literature. Groth and Burgess (1980) described the case of a man who became intoxicated at an office party. The victim agreed to receive a ride home from his employer and then passed out in the car. He awoke to find himself in the back seat, stripped of clothing, being anally raped by his boss.

Myers (1989) cited the case of a homosexual male who, as a college student, was raped by an older man whom he met at a bar and took back to his apartment. Despite the inexperienced victim's protests, the man forced painful anal intercourse. The victim experienced anal and rectal pain and bleeding for several days, but told no one of the experience until interviewed by Myers nine years later.

Goyer and Eddleman (1984) described the case of a 20-year-old heterosexual male in the Navy who was assaulted by three shipmates. The victim was overpowered, beaten, and dragged to a secluded area of the ship but managed to escape as the men attempted anal intercourse. Three weeks later, the victim was overpowered by the same assailants, two of whom held him down while the third raped him anally. He was afraid to tell anyone of the assault for fear of being labeled homosexual and discharged from the Navy. When he eventually did inform superiors, no one believed him.

Goyer and Eddleman also described sexual assault practices among shipmates—"blanket parties," in which victims are forcibly wrapped in a blanket while others sexually abuse them, and "greasing," in which victims are stripped, covered with machinery oil, and have grease pumped forcefully into their rectum.

Impact of the Assault

Researchers have discovered that men who are sexually assaulted by other men undergo a trauma syndrome that is similar (but not identical) to the female postrape experience identified by Burgess and Holmstrom in 1974 (Forman, 1982; Groth & Burgess, 1980; Kaufman et al., 1980; Myers, 1989). Both male and female victims' initial reaction to the assault varies from "controlled" to "expressive." Males, however, seem more likely to exhibit the controlled response, exemplified by subdued acceptance, minimization, or denial of the trauma (Kaufman et al., 1980). For example, Kaufman et al. (1980) found that nearly all of 14 rape victims appearing for treatment at an emergency health service were "quiet, embarrassed, withdrawn, or unconcerned." Myers (1989) reported that most of his sample of 14 male victims of past sexual assault—typically by a male acquaintance—neglected to mention the incident until probed, and then minimized its significance. Kaufman et al. (1980) suggested that this controlled reaction reflects men's socialization to be inexpressive and stoic in the face of adversity.

However, many men do reveal an emotional reaction to the assault. In a study by Johnson and Shrier (1987), about two-thirds of 14 male-molested adolescents (most of whom were assailed by a known person) recalled the immediate impact of the assault as strong and devastating. Victims described in other studies displayed shock, confusion, flustered disbelief, severe self-blame, deep shame, anger, and a desire to kill the offender. Many victims have expressed a desire to kill themselves, and some have attempted suicide (Collins, 1982; Goyer & Eddleman, 1984; Groth & Burgess, 1980; Kaufman et al., 1980; Myers, 1989). In at least one documented case, a heterosexual male was so traumatized by a sexual assault from two men that he suffered from amnesia for five days (Kaszniak, Nussbaum, Berren, & Santiago, 1988).

In the weeks, months, and even years following the assault, most male victims—like female victims—report mood and life-style disturbances such as depression, inability to sleep, and loss of appetite (Goyer & Eddleman, 1984; Groth & Burgess, 1980). Some victims experience a type of Post-Traumatic Stress Disorder that involves nightmares, flashbacks, recurrent thoughts about the assault, panic attacks, psychic numbing, and exaggerated fears that another assault will occur (Myers, 1989).

Male victims' sexual behavior is often adversely affected by the assault. Victims have reported loss of sexual appetite, decreased enjoyment of sex, inability to have erections or to ejaculate, extreme passivity during sex, and difficulty in touching and embracing partners during consensual sex (Goyer & Eddleman, 1984; Johnson & Shrier, 1987; Myers, 1989).

The assault may affect victims' ability to maintain interpersonal relationships. Many male victims discussed in the literature had problems relating to their lovers and spouses following the assault. Some victims withdrew from friends and family and developed a mistrust of adult men, acquaintances, or strangers (Goyer & Eddleman, 1984; Groth & Burgess, 1980; Krueger, 1985; Myers, 1989.) Cotton (1980) suggested that this isolation behavior—perhaps reflecting the masculine norm of not asking for help—intensifies the stress suffered by the male victim.

One aspect of the rape trauma syndrome that is unique to men raped by men is a chronic "male gender identity" crisis related to a loss of masculinity and/or confusion about sexual orientation (Myers, 1989). Some men believe that the assault occurred because they were not "man enough" to avoid or escape the situation. They may keep reviewing the incident for years, trying to think of what they should have done to prevent it (Groth & Burgess, 1980).

Many heterosexual victims feel "emasculated" by the assault. A victim interviewed by Myers (1989, p. 210) said: "Hell, I've got no manhood left. . . . He's made me into a woman." They may become concerned about their sexual identity: Did something "homosexual" about themselves cause the assault? The reaction is intensified if the victim ejaculated during the assault. Groth & Burgess (1980) cited one victim's reaction:

> I always thought a guy couldn't get hard if he was scared, and when this guy took me off it really messed up my mind. I thought maybe something was wrong with me. I didn't know what it meant and this really bothered me.
>
> *(p. 109)*

Myers (1989) found that most of his heterosexual patients had guilty memories about having erections during the assault and felt ambiguous about their sexual orientation. Johnson and Shrier (1987) went so far as to suggest that the assault experience may cause very young, inexperienced males to mislabel themselves as homosexual.

Homophobia may be another consequence of the assault. Myers (1989) reported that many of his subjects—gays and straights alike—displayed an irrational fear and hatred of homosexuals because they assumed their assailant was gay.

Based on limited evidence, the prognosis of recovery for male victims assaulted by other men is good. Johnson and Shrier (1987, p. 652) concluded that "the vast majority of our study group are functioning well overall. . . ." Cotton (1980) and Kaufman et al. (1980) also reported that their subjects showed good progress in putting their lives together and getting on with normal activities. However, many researchers (Johnson & Shrier, 1987; Myers, 1989) believed that victims are likely to experience moderate long-term problems—particularly in the areas of gender identity, sexuality, and interpersonal relationships—unless effective treatment is received.

One limitation of this information is that researchers of the works cited did not distinguish between effects of stranger and acquaintance rape. Although acquaintance rape victims accounted for a majority of cases overall, the use of some stranger rape cases—which often involved use of weapons and physical injury—may have influenced the findings. In future research, it would be important to isolate and compare the dynamics and consequences of these two types of assault.

Motivation for the Assault

What motivates men to rape other men is not yet well understood. Groth (Groth & Burgess, 1982; cited in Miller, 1983) believed that same-sex male rape is a "sexual expression of aggression." He divided rapists into three types: power rapists who have a need to control and dominate their victim; anger rapists who rape for revenge and retaliation; and sadistic rapists who get pleasure out of degrading the victim. Groth speculated that the gender of the target may be irrelevant to these offenders.

Groth & Burgess (1980) suggested that some men may rape men because of unresolved and conflicting sexual identity. For example, a man who has a fear and loathing of his own homosexual impulses may rape another man as punishment for "tempting" him. These researchers also surmised that same-sex male rape can occur as a kind of group ritual. For example, a group of men may gang rape an outsider male in order to establish the group's dominance, strengthen membership bonds, or create status for participating members.

Groth's categories were based on a sample of offenders who in most cases had raped strangers. Additional research is needed to determine whether assailants in male acquaintance rape cases have similar motives. More recently, some authors (Anderson, 1988; Palmer, 1988; Shotland, 1985) suggested that sexual motives and relationship dynamics, as well as personality variables of the offender and victim, should be considered as causes of sexual assault.

Sexual Assault of Men by Women

As many as 16% of college men and 4% to 5% of adult men in a community setting have reported being pressured or forced to have unwanted sexual contact with a female acquaintance (Sorenson, personal communication, April 1989; Struckman-Johnson, 1988). Despite these findings, most people in our society view the assault of men by women as "inherently implausible" (Rosenfeld, 1982). Because we have been socialized to believe that women are always sexually passive (Cassell, 1984; Lott, 1987) and that men are ready and eager for sex at any opportunity (Zilbergeld, 1980; Franklin, 1988), it is hard to imagine a dominant female forcing a reluctant male to have sex.

It is also difficult to believe that a man can be overpowered or intimidated by a woman who is usually smaller and physically weaker (Anderson, 1988). Finally, many people doubt that a man can become sexually aroused and have intercourse with a woman if he is genuinely reluctant or afraid of her (Sarrel & Masters, 1982).

These beliefs were well illustrated in Lehfeldt's (1952) classic article "Unusual Sex Crime," perhaps the first case of male sexual assault by women to be discussed in a scientific journal. Lehfeldt described a newspaper account of how a "handsome youth of 21" picked up three young teenage girls hitchhiking on a New York highway. The girls allegedly used a knife to force the man into the back seat, drove him to a lonely side road, and coerced him to submit to "lovemaking and rape" with one of the girls. Lehfeldt's reaction to this report was:

> Our teen-age girls, then, did the paradoxical as well as the impossible. One may conceive of a strong young man being intimidated by two young girls fumbling around with a knife. But to assume that, being in a legitimate state of anxiety over his very life, the same young man should be capable of performing a sex act must be considered a product of phantasy, unbiassed (sic) by any knowledge about the simple facts of life.

> *(p. 177)*

This perspective on the "simple facts of life" was effectively challenged by Sarrel and Masters' groundbreaking article "The Sexual Molestation of Men by Women," published in 1982. In the process of treating sexual dysfunctions of adult men, the authors discovered 11 patients whose disorder was found to be related to past sexual abuse by women, who in most cases were known to the victim.

The women gained control over the men by forceful assault, use of authority and/or an age difference in the seduction of a younger male, and dominance—use of an aggressive but not forceful sexual approach. The female perpetrators pressured or forced the men to engage in a variety of activities including sexual intercourse, cunnilingus, and fellatio. The men's ability to achieve erection and ejaculate in these situations was, according to the researchers, an uncontrollable physiological response to an anxiety-filled situation.

Johnson and Shrier (1987) identified a sample of 11 adolescents who reported past molestation by a female who in most cases was an acquaintance. They found that female molesters engaged in the same types and variety of sexual activities as did male molesters in their study. In nearly all cases, the female molester used verbal persuasion, not physical force.

Sorenson's (personal communication, April 1989) analyses of data from the Los Angeles Epidemiologic Catchment Area Project provide a unique comparison of female- versus male-assaulted men. She determined that of 110 male victims of sexual assault, more men were assaulted by women (67%) than by men (32%) or by both men and women (2.5%). As shown in Tables 13.2 and 13.3, men assaulted by women were more likely to know their assailant (over 90%) than were men assaulted by other men (about 60%). A greater percentage of female-assaulted men were pressured by verbal tactics (about 70%) than were male-assaulted men (about 50%). Assaults by women, however, were more likely to involve some type of intercourse (48%) than were assaults by other men (20%).

Case Examples

Numerous accounts of acquaintance assault are reported in the literature, some of them involving violence. Sarrel and Masters (1982) and Murray (1982) provided details of a case in which a young medical student engaged in a playful game of sexual bondage with a woman, who tied him to a bed. The man suddenly had a panic reaction and tried to stop the game. The woman, however, became much more aggressive and threatened the man's genitals with a scalpel until he satisfied her sexually.

In another case described by Sarrel and Masters (1982), a man went to a motel with a female acquaintance after a night of drinking. He passed out and woke up to find himself stripped, tied, and blindfolded. Four women used him sexually for the next 24 hours, arousing him to erection and mounting him for intercourse. At times, they held a knife to his scrotum and threatened castration to force his cooperation.

A more typical scenario of acquaintance assault is seduction of a younger boy or man by an older girl or woman. Sarrel and Masters (1982) reported a case of "babysitter abuse" in which a 16-year-old girl sat on an 11-year-old boy and forced his penis into her vagina. (The babysitter syndrome is more common than one would believe. Risin and Koss (1988) found that 23% of male victims of child sexual abuse were molested by a female babysitter.)

Anderson (1988) described an "older woman" case study in which a 16-year-old boy was caught peeping into the window of a college-age female neighbor. She intimidated the boy by threatening to tell his parents about his behavior and then "punished" him by making him run errands and perform oral sex on demand for a three-week period. In a highly publicized case reported on an NBC-TV News documentary (1988), a 37-year-old librarian seduced a 14-year-old boy while they were hiking in the mountains. She eventually had sex with him over 10 times before the coercive relationship ended.

Most of the cases of forced sex on dates, documented by my own research, fall into the "dominant woman" category. In my 1985 survey (Struckman-Johnson, 1988), only two of 21 male victims described an episode involving clear physical force. One man wrote that on a first-time date, a woman "grabbed my dick and wouldn't let go of it" until they had sex. Another wrote that he was "thrown on a bed and attacked." Several victims were forced by a combination of verbal and physical pressure. One man wrote that an ex-girlfriend came to his fraternity room and "got fresh" with him. He tried to "push her off" several times but eventually gave in to intercourse. In another case, a man described being "set up" by a female:

> I was invited over for a party, unaware that it was a date. As the evening wore on, I got the message that the girl was my date. I didn't have to make a move on

her because she was all over me. She wouldn't take no for an answer. Usually I like to get to know the person. I felt I was forced into sex. After, I felt terrible and used.

Another man was riding in a car with a female acquaintance when they parked to drink beer. She "came on very heavily" and reached across and pushed his door lock down when he tried to get out. She insisted that they have sex before she would drive him home. A few men wrote that they passed out while intoxicated and woke up to find females having sex with them.

Two men were verbally blackmailed into sex by older women. One wrote:

I hate to admit it but I'm kind of a whimp (sic) when it comes to saying (sic) or yet disagreeing with an elder. She offered to take me to a concert. We went back to the apartment we were staying at. She changed into something very much more comfortable, laid beside me and told me she would get me fired (as she worked for my boss) if I didn't. I had no desire to.

In a more recent study (Struckman-Johnson & Struckman-Johnson, 1988), the only man who reported being physically forced into sex wrote that a female acquaintance tied him up while he was sleeping in bed. Several men described experiences with "forceful seduction" that had elements of physical coercion. One wrote:

She came into my room and wanted me to go to the liquer (sic) store. When I declined, she got on her knees and gave me a blow job. She came in later and I gave in. She later sat on me and tried to stick a finger in my behind. I had to forcibly wrestle her not to do it.

Another man said, "She really wanted to have sex, forcefully playing with me until I gave in." A third explained that the woman "through (sic) me on the bed and hopped on top and literally held me down."

Impact of the Assault

Anderson (1988) suggested that most people think that if a man is raped by a woman, it is somehow "not as bad" as when a female is assaulted. A study by Musialowski and Kelley (1987) found that subjects perceived a man raped by a woman as more likely to experience orgasm and enjoy the sexual activity, as less likely to feel frightened, and less in need of sympathy as compared to a woman raped by a man or a heterosexual man raped by another man.

Contrary to these beliefs, preliminary evidence indicates that men can be seriously harmed by assault perpetrated by females. Sarrel and Masters (1982) discovered that their patients exhibited a postassault trauma syndrome that had much in common with the syndromes of women and men assaulted by men. Except for a few victims who felt pleasure during the episode, most patients experienced a combination of fear, panic, and confusion during and immediately after it. Many felt guilt and loss of masculinity because they allowed the victimization to occur. In the days and months following the assault, most men exhibited sexual dysfunction—impotence, ejaculation problems, or loss of sexual desire. Many men felt that they were "abnormal" because they had responded to the situation with sexual arousal.

The patients had long-term problems with sexual dysfunction, feelings of isolation, mistrust of women, difficulties in establishing a sexual relationship with female partners, and unresolved issues relating to masculinity and self-confidence. According to Masters (1986) the "extreme inversion of stereotypic sex roles" seemed to create a deep sense of inadequacy in some men.

Sarrel and Masters (1982) stressed that, because their sample was drawn from the files of a sexual treatment clinic, their findings could not be generalized to all men who are sexually abused by women. Johnson and Shrier (1987), however, found similar postassault reactions among their community-based sample of 11 female-molested adolescents. About three-fourths of victims rated the immediate impact of the assault as strong or devastating, and one-fifth reported sexual dysfunction occurring up to several years after the event. Over half said there were long-lasting negative effects.

The prognosis for these two samples of victims was favorable. Sarrel and Masters (1982) and Masters (1986) reported that their patients responded satisfactorily to intense therapy for sexual dysfunction and relationship problems. As stated earlier, Johnson and Shrier's (1987) clients were judged as being reasonably well adjusted, despite some moderate problems with sexual relationships and identity.

Information about the effects of date rape among college men is quite limited. In my study (Struckman-Johnson, 1988), the 21 male victims reported mixed reactions to the forced-sex episode at the time it occurred: about one-fourth felt "good," another one-fourth felt "bad," and the remaining half felt "neutral." The overwhelming majority (69%) said they had not experienced any long-term effects, a minority (22%) said there were such effects, and the rest were unsure. The most commonly mentioned lasting effect was avoidance of aggressive women and pressured sex. One man wrote:

I will now say no to sex. I want to have feelings for a girl before intercourse. Just to have sex leaves me empty.

A few men said they had guilt feelings about the incident. The man who was blackmailed by the older woman wrote:

I had a girlfriend at the time and still do. I felt very guilty about what had happened. I needed the job for money to live with my girlfriend in ——————. It slowly died (the feeling) but hasn't gone away.

Perhaps men in these two studies were not more seriously traumatized because a majority were pressured by verbal persuasion and/or aggressive sexual stimulation, rather than physical force. It is also possible that, because of male sex-role norms, many of the men did not perceive themselves as being exploited in the situation. According to Muehlenhard and Cook (1988), men are so intensely socialized to behave sexually in dating situations that they may actually feel *obligated* to give in to a woman's sexual demands. In other words, to use Muehlenhard and Cook's (1986) phrase, "Real men don't say no." As a consequence, male victims of date rape may feel that even though they were coerced into intercourse, they still behaved appropriately "as men" by performing sexually. This may explain the paradox of why a portion of male victims in my study reported that they were forced into sex but they felt good about it afterward.

Another possibility is that some of these men were denying or not expressing their bad feelings about being coerced into sex. As the research has suggested, the masculine norms of self-reliance and inexpressiveness preclude men from reporting, discussing, and complaining about sexual victimization.

As with same-sex male rape, much more research is needed to document the short- and long-term consequences of sexual assault of men by women. It would be important to determine how the impact of the assault is affected by variables such as age of the victim (child, adolescent, or adult), relationship with the assailant (stranger versus acquaintance), type of pressure used (verbal versus physical force), status of the relationship (first date versus steady relationship), and victim's adherence to traditional masculine values.

Motivation for the Assault

Very little is known about the motivation of the sexually coercive female. Masters (1986) proposed that women sexually assault men for the same reason that men rape women: the desire to control. Citing Rada's rape motivation model (1978), Masters suggested that women vary in how they accomplish the control during the assault: Many seek sexual control, some are aggressive, and others humiliate the victim.

Some support for the "power" motivation came from a study by Craig (1988) on the attitudes and affective characteristics of sexually coercive college women. Craig determined that 19% of her sample of 191 female undergraduates admitted to having sexually coerced their dating partners. Compared to the other women, coercive women had less traditional sexual beliefs and reported being aroused by and attaining feelings of power and control in their sexual relationships.

Anderson (1989) also found that women's sex-role attitudes are related to their sexual aggressiveness with men. He discovered that of a sample of 212 women in an eastern college campus, over 50% had used sexually coercive behavior (from kissing to intercourse) and 10% had used physical force or weapons to obtain sexual intercourse. Sexually coercive women were more likely to believe that male–female sexual relationships are basically adversarial. In addition, coercive women were more likely to have had a history of past sexual abuse.

Shotland (1985) suggested that the high frequency of acquaintance rape (female victim, male perpetrator) can best be understood by a simple model that combines personality traits of the participants, stage of the relationship, and misperception of sexual intent between males and females. He proposed that men with sexually aggressive personality traits (e.g., a strong desire for sexual contact; rape-supportive attitudes; a belief that women disguise sexual interest) are likely to misread women's verbal and nonverbal cues and coerce them into unwanted sexual activity. I propose that this causal model can also help explain coercive sex by female perpetrators.

Due in part to the women's movement, availability of birth control, and new norms of sexual equality, young women in our society are now socialized, like men, to view themselves as "sexually interested" (Levine & Kanin, 1987). I suggest a pool of women now exists with personality traits and attitudes that predispose them to be sexually coercive: they have a high need for sexual contact; enjoy the feelings of power and control; view men as sexual adversaries; or assume men are "ever ready" and mutually interested in sex. These women are likely to misread or ignore men's signals of sexual intent in dating encounters and consequently coerce them into unwanted sexual activity.

RECOMMENDATIONS FOR PREVENTION, TREATMENT, AND FUTURE RESEARCH

The first step toward prevention and treatment of sexual assault of men is education. Our cultural ignorance of male rape must be countered by awareness campaigns and programs directed at the general public, students, educators, and professionals in medicine, law, and the human services.

Many current models of rape prevention programs (Parrot, 1988; Sandberg et al., 1987) could easily be expanded to provide more information on male victims. Specifically, men should be informed of the prevalence, dynamics, and impact of assault and should be instructed in conventional strategies for avoiding high-risk situations such as being alone with people recently encountered at bars or parties. It is essential to encourage men to report to the authorities future assaults that may occur, to obtain medical evidence, and to seek appropriate medical treatment and counseling.

Because of the high frequency of coercive sexuality that occurs in dating relationships, high school and college students should have access to programs that (a) discuss current male and female sexual scripts, (b) identify gender-related differences in interpreting sexual intent, and (c) teach effective communication strategies for sexual decision making. Given that a high percentage of unwanted sex is associated with intoxication (Muehlenhard & Long, 1988; Struckman-Johnson & Struckman-Johnson, 1988), programs should address the role of alcohol and drugs in coercive sexual interaction. A special effort should be made to teach boys and young men that it is acceptable to say "no" to sexual opportunities and that no one has the right to demand sex from them. As Astrachan wrote (1986, p. 262):

> Women are taught they can say no from an early age and used to be taught that they *should* say no. Most American men don't know that we too are entitled to say no. We are learning now that we can and sometimes should, that like women we are entitled to choose. . . .

Along with education, it is essential to improve treatment for male victims of sexual assault. A crucial step is to alert helping professionals to the possibility that male victims may require help. For example, physicians and medical personnel should be able to recognize the physical symptoms of men who have been raped anally or orally and to question patients about the cause of this trauma. (See Braen, 1980; Calderwood, 1987; and Schiff, 1980 for guidelines for examining the male rape victim.) Medical history questionnaires administered in emergency rooms, medical and crisis centers, and social welfare agencies should routinely include gender-neutral questions about sexual assault.

Personnel in these professions should be prepared to interview male clients about possible sexual assault, to react in a sensitive and compassionate manner, and to recommend appropriate treatment and counseling. Dimock (1986) prepared the following list of guidelines for interviewing male victims of sexual abuse. The advice can be applied to assault situations.

1. When you ask about the possibility of various abuse/assault experiences, be as specific as possible. If you are uncomfortable, he will be more so.
2. If he acknowledges one experience, don't assume that is all there is.
3. If he cannot recall specific details or denies anything happened, don't push. Ask him to think about it, and move to other questions.
4. If he does begin to talk about it, let him give it to you however he can. Don't push for feelings, but affirm feelings that are expressed. Affirm his masculinity by telling him how much courage it takes to be vulnerable.
5. Reassure him that what happened was not his fault and there was nothing he could do to protect himself at the time. He did the best he could under the circumstances. The sexual experience is not a failure on his part.
6. Give him any information you know on the effects of sexual abuse/assault. Tell him these effects don't usually go away by themselves and he needs to consider getting professional help. Volunteer to assist him and follow through.
7. Affirm to him that he is doing a very self-caring step by talking about what has happened and agreeing to seek help. (p. 2)

Rape crisis and emergency care centers should advertise that their services are available to both female and male victims of assault. Support services for crisis counseling and referrals for male victims should be developed or expanded (Donaldson, 1986).

It is also important for police officials to inquire about sexual assault when men report crimes and to establish policies for appropriate and sensitive treatment of homosexual and heterosexual male rape victims. Courtroom trial procedures should be modified to afford male victims the same protections that are provided for female victims (Groth & Burgess, 1980).

In conjunction with treatment modifications, legislative changes are needed to create laws that do not discriminate against male victims. As of 1987, 13 states still defined rape as an act that occurs to female victims by male perpetrators; 17 states limited their definition of rape to vaginal penetration (Searles & Berger, 1987). Some states have statutory rape laws in which a man, but not a woman, can be charged with sexually assaulting a minor (Masters, 1986). In others (e.g., New York) women can be charged with statutory rape, but not with first-degree or forcible rape (NBC-TV News, 1988). In particular, "sodomy statutes," which cause many male rape victims technically to be defined as criminals, should be eliminated.

My final suggestion is to increase the data base on sexual assault of boys and men. In the past, most researchers—like helping professionals—have failed to ask male subjects about sexual victimization (Struckman-Johnson, 1988). I recommend that sexual assault prevalence surveys include male subjects and allow both men and women to report their experiences with victimization as well as perpetration.

As public awareness of male sexual assault increases, research interest in all dimensions of the topic should follow. As more studies accumulate, we will be able to determine accurate incidence rates, fully describe the characteristics of offenders and victims, and firmly establish the short- and long-term consequences. Ultimately, future research may uncover the predictors of male sexual assault which will, in turn, help society to address this hidden problem.

REFERENCES

Anderson, P. B. (1988, November). *Female heterosexual assault.* Paper presented at the annual meeting of the Society for the Scientific Study of Sex, San Francisco.

Anderson, P. B. (1989). *Adversarial sexual beliefs and past experience of sexual abuse of college females as predictors of their sexual aggression toward adolescent and adult males.* Unpublished doctoral dissertation, New York University.

Astrachan, A. (1986). *How men feel.* New York: Anchor Press.

Braen, R. (1980). The male rape victim: Examination and management. In C. Warner (Ed.), *Rape and sexual assault: Management and intervention* (pp. 67–71). Germantown, MD: Aspen Systems Corporation.

Burgess, A. W., & Holmstrom, L. L. (1974). Rape trauma syndrome. *American Journal of Psychiatry, 131,* 981–986.

Calderwood, D. (1987, May). The male rape victim. *Medical Aspects of Human Sexuality,* 53–55.

Cassell, C. (1984). *Swept away: Why women fear their own sexuality.* New York: Simon & Shuster.

Collins, G. (1982, January 18). Counseling male rape victims. *The New York Times,* p. 15A.

Cotton, D. J. (1980). The male victim of sexual assault: Patterns of occurrence, trauma reactions and adaptive responses. *Dissertation Abstracts International, 41,* 3568-3569-B.

Craig, M. E. (1988, November). *The sexually coercive college female: An investigation of attitudinal and affective characteristics.* Paper presented at the annual meeting of the Society for the Scientific Study of Sex, San Francisco.

Dimock, P. (1986). *Guidelines for interviewing male victims of sexual abuse.* Unpublished material available from author, 1656 Laurel Ave., St. Paul, MN, 55104.

Donaldson, S. (1986, April). Sexual assault of men: A hidden crime. *Newsline: The Newsletter of the New York City Gay and Lesbian Anti-Violence Project,* New York, p. 5.

FBI (Federal Bureau of Investigation). (1988). *Uniform Crime Reports—1987* (p. 14). Washington DC: U. S. Government Printing Office.

Forman, B. D. (1982). Reported male rape. *Victimology: An International Journal, 7,* 235–236.

Franklin, C. W. (1988). *Men and society,* Chicago: Nelson-Hall.

Goyer, P. F., & Eddleman, H. C. (1984). Same-sex rape of nonincarcerated men. *American Journal of Psychiatry, 141,* 576–579.

Groth, A. N., & Burgess, A. W. (1980). Male rape: Offenders and victims. *American Journal of Psychiatry, 137,* 806–810.

Groth, A. N., & Burgess, A. W. (1982). Rape: A sexual deviation. In A. M. Scacco, Jr. (Ed.) *Male rape: A casebook of sexual aggressions* (pp. 231–240). New York: AMS Press.

Johnson, R. L., & Shrier, D. (1987). Past sexual victimization by females of male patients in an adolescent medicine clinic population. *American Journal of Psychiatry, 144,* 650–652.

Kaszniak, A. W., Nussbaum, P. D., Berren, M. R., & Santiago, J. (1988). Amnesia as a consequence of male rape: A case report. *Journal of Abnormal Psychology, 97,* 100–104.

Kaufman, A., Divasto, P., Jackson, R., Voorhees, D., & Christy, J. (1980). Male rape victims: Noninstitutionalized assault. *American Journal of Psychiatry, 137,* 221–223.

Kinsey, A. C., Pomeroy, W. P., & Martin, C. E. (1948). *Sexual behavior in the human male.* Philadelphia: Saunders.

Koss, M. P., Gidycz, C. A., & Wisniewski, N. (1987). The scope of rape: Incidence and prevalence of sexual aggression and victimization in a national sample of students in higher education. *Journal of Consulting and Clinical Psychology, 55,* 162–170.

Krueger, F. (1985, May). Violated. *Boston Magazine,* pp. 138, 140–142.

Lehfeldt, H. (1952). Unusual "sex crime." *Journal of Sex Education, 4,* 176–177.

Levine, E. M., & Kanin, E. J. (1987). Sexual violence among dates and acquaintances: Trends and their implications for marriage and the family. *Journal of Family Violence, 2,* 55–65.

Lockwood, D. (1980). *Prison sexual violence.* New York: Elsevier.

Lott, B. (1987). *Women's lives: Themes and variations in gender learning.* Monterey, CA: Brooks-Cole.

Lott, B., Reilly, M. E., & Howard, D. R. (1982). Sexual assault and harassment: A campus community case study. *Signs: Journal of Women in Culture and Society, 8,* 296–319.

Masters, W. H. (1986). Sexual dysfunction as an aftermath of sexual assault of men by women. *Journal of Sex and Marital Therapy, 12,* 35–45.

Miller, N. (1983, November 22). Male rape: When men are victims. *Boston Phoenix,* pp. 1, 12–14.

Muehlenhard, C. L., & Cook, S. W. (1986, June) *"'Real men' don't say no": Do men have sex when they don't want to?* Paper presented at the annual Midcontinent meeting of the Society for the Scientific Study of Sex, Madison, WI.

Muehlenhard, C. L., & Cook, S. W. (1988). Men's self-reports of unwanted sexual activity. *Journal of Sex Research, 24,* 58–72.

Muehlenhard, C. L., & Long, P. L. (1988, November). *Men's and women's experiences of coercive sexual intercourse: How are they pressured and how do they react?* Paper presented at the annual meeting of the Society for the Scientific Study of Sex, San Francisco.

Murphy, J. E. (1984, August). *Date abuse and forced intercourse among college students.* Paper presented at the Second National Conference for Family Violence Research, Durham, NH.

Murray, L. (1982, July). When men are raped by women. *Sexual Medicine Today.* pp. 14–16, 20.

Musialowski, D. M., & Kelley, K. (1987, April). *Male rape: Perception of the act and the victim.* Paper presented at the Eastern Regional Meeting of the Society for the Scientific Study of Sex, Philadelphia.

Myers, M. F. (1989). Men sexually assaulted as adults and sexually abused as boys. *Archives of Sexual Behavior, 18,* 203–215.

NBC-TV News. (1988, June). *Summer showcase: Of macho and men.* Transcript available from Radio TV Reports, Inc., New York.

Palmer, C. T. (1988). Twelve reasons why rape is not sexually motivated: A skeptical examination. *Journal of Sex Research, 25,* 512–530.

Parrot, A. (1988, November). *Evaluating the effectiveness of an interdisciplinary model for acquaintance rape prevention for high school students.* Paper presented at the annual meeting of the Society for the Scientific Study of Sex, San Francisco.

Rada, R. T. (1978). Psychological factors in rapist behavior. In R. T. Rada (Ed.), *Clinical aspects of the rapist.* New York: Grune & Stratton.

Risin, L. I., & Koss, M. P. (1988). The sexual abuse of boys: Childhood victimizations reported by a national sample. In A. W. Burgess (Ed.), *Rape and sexual assault (Vol. II,* pp. 91–104). New York: Garland.

Rosenfeld, A. (1982, September). When women rape men. *Omni Magazine*, pp. 28, 194.

Russell, D. E. (1984). *Sexual exploitation: Rape, child sexual abuse, and workplace harassment.* Beverly Hills, CA: Sage.

Sandberg, G. G., Jackson, T. L., & Petretic-Jackson, P. (1987). College dating attitudes regarding sexual coercion and sexual aggression: Developing education and prevention strategies. *Journal of College Student Personnel, 28,* 302–310.

Sarrel, P. M., & Masters, W. H. (1982). Sexual molestation of men by women. *Archives of Sexual Behavior, 11,* 117–131.

Scacco, A. M., Jr. (1982). *Male rape: A casebook of sexual aggressions.* New York: AMS Press.

Schiff, A. F. (1980). Examination and treatment of the male rape victim. *Southern Medical Journal, 73,* 1498–1502.

Schultz, L. G., & DeSavage, J. (1975). Rape and rape attitudes on a college campus. In L. G. Schultz (Ed.), *Rape victimology* (77–90). Springfield, IL: Thomas.

Searles, P., & Berger, R. J. (1987). The current status of rape reform legislation: An examination of state statutes. *Women's Rights Law Reporter, 10,* 25–43.

Shotland, L. (1985). A preliminary model of some causes of date rape. *Academic Psychology Bulletin, 7,* 187–200.

Sorenson, S. B., Stein, J. A., Siegel, J. M., Golding, J. M., & Burnam, M. A. (1987). The prevalence of adult sexual assault: The Los Angeles Epidemiologic Catchment Area Project. *American Journal of Epidemiology, 126,* 1154–1164.

Struckman-Johnson, C. (1988). Forced sex on dates: It happens to men, too. *Journal of Sex Research, 24,* 234–241.

Struckman-Johnson, C., & Struckman-Johnson, D. (1988, November). *Strategies to obtain sex from unwilling dating partners: Incidence and acceptability.* Paper presented at the annual meeting of the Society for the Scientific Study of Sex, San Francisco.

U. S. Department of Justice, Bureau of Justice Statistics, (1988). *Sourcebook of Criminal Justice Statistics—1987* (p. 221). Washington, DC: U. S. Government Printing Office.

Waterman, C. K., Dawson, L. J., & Bologna, M. J. (1989). Sexual coercion in gay male and lesbian relationships: Predictors and implications for support services. *Journal of Sex Research, 26,* 118–124.

Zilbergeld, B. (1980). *Male sexuality.* New York: Bantam.

PART 6

Assailants

CHAPTER 14

Sexually Coercive College Males

KAREN R. RAPAPORT, PhD and C. DALE POSEY, PhD

SELF-REPORTED SEXUALLY COERCIVE MALES

The majority of research on rapists has focused on characteristics of adjudicated perpetrators. A review of this literature lends credence to an individual pathology model of rape behavior, wherein rapists are found to be characterologically different from other types of offenders. Rapists have been found to have a need to intimidate, dominate, and control their victims in order to achieve personal mastery through sexual coercion (Groth, 1979; Groth, Burgess, & Holmstrom, 1977). They have been found to be psychopathic, hostile, resentful, and alienated, in comparison to child molesters (Armentrout & Hauer, 1978).

Adjudicated rapists have also been found to have different patterns of sexual arousal. Abel, Barlow, Blanchard, and Guild (1977) found that rapists became more sexually aroused relative to controls when hearing audiotaped presentations of rape.

The studies on the characteristics of rapists support the notion that rapists exhibit personality abnormalities that distinguish them from other types of offenders and, presumably, from the population at large. Support for this individual pathology model of rape is found in research aimed at the identification of a group of behaviors or personality traits underlying and/or associated with rape. However, a focus on criminal rapists does not provide an empirical basis for the prediction of sexually coercive behavior among males whose rape behavior does not conform to traditional depictions of rape and who are not likely to ever be adjudicated.

By turning their attention to sexually coercive behavior in the population at large, investigators have been forced to develop alternative means for identifying perpetrators, since by definition this target group has not been detected by authorities. Reliance must be placed on self-report methods under conditions of anonymity to isolate this group, composed primarily of acquaintance rapists, from their sexually noncoercive counterparts.

SELF-REPORT METHODS

It is difficult to measure behaviors such as sexual coercion and rape. Since the behaviors cannot be directly observed in a systematic way, estimates must come from some method of self-report—either self-identification as engaging in rape behavior or being identified as such.

Abel and associates (1977) suggested that sexual responsiveness to rape depictions indicated a proclivity to rape. In theory, this measure could be used to identify men who were highly likely to rape, even if they do not recognize these tendencies. Another method to measure the propensity to rape was developed by Malamuth (1981) and his colleagues. Malamuth, Haber, and Feshbach (1980) investigated the issue of the potential for college males to engage in rape. The sample was composed of male and female undergraduate students. These subjects believed that close to half of the male population would rape if assured of not being caught and punished and, in addition, *over half* of the male subjects stated that they might be likely to rape if given the same assurance. Malamuth (1981) reported that a consistent proportion of males indicated that they would be likely to rape if assured of not being caught. Across a series of studies noted by Malamuth, an average of 35% of males indicated some likelihood of raping and an average of about 20% indicated a *high* likelihood of raping.

Briere and Malamuth (1983) found that subjects who were classified as being likely to use sexual force, regardless of whether they were likely to actually rape, shared attitudes that were not found in the majority of males who were unlikely to be sexually coercive. Students who were likely to use force generally considered rape reports to be manipulative gestures. They believed that victims are actually responsible for rape, that males should be sexually dominant, and that domestic violence is acceptable. The potentially coercive subjects endorsed the beliefs that women enjoy sexual violence and that relationships between men and women are necessarily adversarial. These beliefs indicate a view of heterosexual relationships wherein there are few inhibitions against rape. In fact, sexual coerciveness, violence, and rape would seem to be inevitable consequences of this view of women and sexual relationships.

Tieger (1981), who also investigated the attitudes of men judged as being likely to rape, found that they believed that women enjoy being raped and that other men would be likely to rape if assured of not being caught. Tieger's subjects generally minimized the trauma of rape. These disinhibitory beliefs, so named because they imply less inhibition to rape, were found by Tieger to correctly differentiate with 83% success those likely to rape from those unlikely to rape.

Malamuth (1983) tested the relationship between laboratory aggression toward women and Likelihood of Raping (LR) reports, as well as other factors hypothetically related to rape behavior. Subjects who were mildly rejected and insulted by women confederates were allowed to aggress via the application of aversive noise, although the aversive stimulus was not actually presented to the women. Subjects who had earlier, in an unrelated experimental phase, reported that they would be likely to rape if assured of not being caught were also high in anger toward the women and more likely to demonstrate behavioral aggression, and reported a desire to hurt the women. Thus, reports of likelihood to rape were related to laboratory measures of aggression against women.

Another method of identifying sexually coercive males is a self-report on a variety of coercive behaviors. Recent theoretical and experimental literature suggests that a spectrum of sexually coercive behavior should be investigated within the population at large. It is also reasonable, though, to question the veracity of self-reports. Because most adjudicated rapists do not acknowledge the crimes (Wolfe & Baker, 1980), other men would not be expected to identify themselves as having committed rape. This is particularly true of acquaintance rapists. But if sexually coercive behavior is assessed on a continuum, without using the word *rape,* then men might be expected to acknowledge some of this behavior. Research (Koss & Gidycz, 1985; Risin & Koss, 1986) has indicated that there is a consistency in self-reported sexual experience across time. However, frequencies of self-reports of sexually coercive behavior indicate that males do not report committing the acts enough to match female reports of victimization (Koss & Oros, 1982). Thus, it is likely that males underreport having date-raped because of social desirability factors, or they may not consider their actions as rape. Some may also overreport, perhaps out of a desire to appear more "manly" and sexually active, and thus the veracity of self-reports can always be questioned.

Given the imperfection of a self-report sampling method, what can such statistics offer to further the knowledge of rape and sexually coercive behavior? The information gained from self-reports can expand our knowledge of the realities of rape and can be employed in rape education and prevention programs (Parrot, 1983).

SELF-REPORTED RAPISTS

In an effort to understand the dynamics and characteristics of rape behavior in college males, Rapaport and Burkhart (1984) investigated personality and attitudinal characteristics of sexually coercive college males. Based in part on studies of adjudicated rapists, the investigation focused on personality characteristics associated with a reckless, antisocial mode of behavior. Attitude assessment was centered on beliefs that were felt to be associated with a callous and exploitative attitude toward sexual interactions. General attitudes toward women in traditional and more contemporary roles were also assessed. In the initial phase of the study, men were asked if they had ever engaged in any of 19 sexually coercive behaviors.

These ranged from unwanted touching to forced intercourse, threats, and physical aggression. Forty-three percent of the sample reported engaging in behaviors that were considered to be coercive, including use of coercive sexual methods ranging from ignoring a woman's protests to using physical aggression and finally forcing sexual intercourse. Approximately 15% of the men acknowledged acquaintance rape and 11% employed physical restraint. None of the subjects reported using a weapon to coerce a woman into sexual activities. The subjects were classified into the mutually exclusive categories of forced sexual intercourse, sexually coercive, and noncoercive males, based on survey responses. All of the incidences of force or coercion took place between acquaintances.

In general, sexually coercive behavior was found to be associated with personality test scores (the California Psychological Inventory) indicating immaturity, irresponsibility, and a lack of social conscience. Attitude characteristics found to be highly correlated with sexually coercive behavior were those referring specifically to the use of force against women and to beliefs that heterosexual relationships are characterized by manipulation and mistrust. An example of this type of item was, "In a dating relationship, a woman is largely out to take advantage of a man." These attitude scales were Burt's (1980) Acceptance of Interpersonal Violence and Adversarial Sexual Beliefs scales. In her study of the correlates of rape myth acceptance, Burt (1980) found that endorsement of these scale items was highly associated with reports of rape myth acceptance. Rapaport and Burkhart (1984) found that attitudes related to dynamics between dating individuals were highly related to self-reports of sexually coercive behavior. However, attitudes related to sex-role stereotyping not necessarily within a dating context were not found to be highly related to sexual coerciveness.

Other incidence reports of sexually coercive behavior have consistently found high self-reports of these activities among college students (Kanin, 1969; Koss & Oros, 1982). Kanin found that 25% of his sample of college males reported that they had been involved in some sexually coercive behavior since they had entered college. Similarly, 23% of the males in Koss and Oros's (1982) college sample reported having forced a woman to have intercourse because they felt that their sexual arousal was so great that it would have been useless to stop.

In a further investigation of the characteristics of sexually coercive college males, Rapaport and Burkhart (1987) again assessed the incidence of sexually coercive behavior and personality and attitudinal characteristics of acquaintance rapists but added an assessment of the subjects' responsiveness to rape pornography. Hypotheses concerning the value of debriefing in rape research were also addressed. Subjects (N = 166) completed a questionnaire booklet that included personality and attitudinal measures and coercive sexuality measures. Measures selected on the basis of previous studies included a nonconformity index (Gynther, Burkhart, & Hovanitz, 1979), Burt's (1980) attitudinal scales, the Sexual Experiences Survey (Koss & Oros, 1982) the Coercive Sexuality Scale (Rapaport & Burkhart, 1984), and Likelihood of Raping items (Malamuth, 1981).

INCIDENCE OF COERCIVE SEXUALITY

Consistent with previous findings (Rapaport & Burkhart, 1984), Coercive Sexuality Scale (CSS) items involving a greater degree of physical intrusiveness or coercion received less endorsement. Least endorsed items on the Coercive Sexuality Scale referred to removal of one's own (male's) clothing and forced oral, anal, and genital intercourse. Of those subjects who reported having forced a woman to have intercourse, 76% reported engaging in this behavior once and 24% reported engaging in the behavior more often.

The Sexually Coercive Methods (SCM) scale, an adjunct to the Coercive Sexuality Scale (CSS), assessed the methods that the subjects reported they had employed when engaging in sexually coercive behavior, for example, ignoring the woman's protests, employing verbal threats, and using physical restraint. Methods receiving the highest endorsements were "never engaged in the behavior" and ". . . did what I wanted, even though I knew she didn't want me to." Methods involving verbal and physical threats and use of physical force were the least endorsed items. Thus, the subjects' self-reports were that they did not rely on the use of force in dyadic sexual encounters.

Across the coercive sexuality measures, the majority of college males (64%) reported involvement in some sexually coercive behavior in the past. Regarding specific types of coercive sexual behavior, 46% of the respondents admitted touching a woman's crotch area against her wishes, and 75% stated that they had touched a woman's crotch, breast, or thigh against her wishes. Thirteen percent had forced a woman to participate in oral sex and 4% had forcibly performed anal sex. Finally, a total of 10% of the respondents admitted having sexual intercourse with a woman against her wishes.

Regarding sexual coercion methods, 1% of the sample reported using physical aggression to force a woman to have intercourse. Physical aggression or threats of aggression were denied as methods for all other sexually coercive acts. Across all sexually coercive behaviors, the most frequent methods involved either ignoring the woman's protests or engaging in the behavior when they knew that the woman did not want to have sexual contact.

CHARACTERISTICS OF SEXUALLY COERCIVE MALES

The nonconformity, attitude, and likelihood of raping scales were combined to predict the total CSS score. These variables accounted for 40% of the variance in the CSS scores, which indicated that the variables were strong predictors of self-reported sexually coercive behavior. Nonconformity (NC) and two attitude measures were the most powerful predictors of CSS scores. Of the attitude measures, Burt's (1980) Adversarial Sexual Beliefs and Acceptance of Interpersonal Violence were most productive; the acceptance of rape myths had relatively less prediction value, as did three Likelihood of Raping measures. The most significant prediction factors suggested that sexually coercive males tend to act impulsively, irresponsibly, and, at times, aggressively. An adversarial stance toward women also suggests that these men channel this aggressiveness toward women in particular.

RESPONSES TO RAPE DEPICTIONS

To determine the distinctiveness of sexually coercive and noncoercive males, the subjects were initially divided into groups based on their responses to criterion instruments. The groups were formed in the following way: In Group 1, the acquaintance rape group, were placed subjects who endorsed items referring to forced sexual intercourse; in Group 2, the sexually coercive group; subjects not endorsing forced intercourse items but endorsing other intrusive sexually coercive items (such as touching a woman's genital area against her wishes); in Group 3, the non-coercive group, the remaining subjects.

A comparison of the three groups on the Sexually Coercive Methods (SCM) scale revealed that Group 1 reported employing the greatest number of sexually coercive methods, followed by Group 2 and Group 3. The most coercive method reported by Group 1 was the use of physical aggression. Group 2 reported physical restraint as the most coercive method employed, and Group 3 reported ignoring a woman's protests as the most coercive method employed.

Groups were formed, in part, to assess the sexual responses of sexually coercive males to written descriptions of rape. Feminists have contended that the aggressive and misogynous themes of rape pornography disinhibit males to act out in a sexually aggressive manner, by reinforcing rape myths and providing justification for sexually coercive behavior (Brownmiller, 1975; Dworkin, 1981; Gager & Schurr, 1976; Griffin, 1981). However, research has indicated that, under normal conditions, nondeviate males were not sexually aroused to violent rape themes (Barbaree, Marshall, & Lanthier, 1979). Barbaree et al. argue that it is conceivable that rapists were not necessarily aroused by rape but the violent components of rape failed to inhibit their arousal.

In a series of studies, Malamuth and his colleagues (Donnerstein & Malamuth, in press; Malamuth, 1981; Malamuth & Check, 1980a, b, 1981; Malamuth & Donnerstein, 1982; Malamuth, Haber, & Feshbach, 1980; Malamuth, Heim, & Feshbach, 1980) investigated the association between disinhibiting cues and sexual arousal to pornographic stimuli in nondeviate subjects. They questioned whether nondeviates would exhibit sexual arousal to rape themes with disinhibiting cues, and which of these cues would be the most highly correlated with disinhibition, or arousal to rape. Across studies, the rape victim's lack of arousal has been the central, or most effective, disinhibiting factor in sexual arousal to rape depictions (Malamuth & Check, 1980a, b; Malamuth, Heim, & Feshbach,

1980). Malamuth and Check (1980b) found that, when the female was depicted as experiencing involuntary physiological sexual arousal during a rape, college males tended to become aroused following exposure to the scenario. They did not become aroused as a function of the victim's experiencing pain or whether she consented or not. Sexual arousal by a woman being raped is a fairly common theme in pornography; its frequent depiction might lead one to believe that rape can be sexually exciting for a woman. Given that normal men find this sexually arousing, it is possible that some could commit rape under the assumption that women find it stimulating.

Extending Malamuth's research, Rapaport (1984) found that both acquaintance rapists and sexually coercive males were significantly more sexually responsive to rape *and* consenting depictions, when compared with noncoercive males. The results are presented in Figure 14.1. Comparisons between responses to the rape stories revealed striking differences in the attributions made for the woman's motivation. In response to "I think that the woman in the story wanted to have sex with the man," 92% of the subjects indicated that they did not agree, following the presentation of a story depicting a woman being raped and feeling disgust afterward (The Rape–Disgust story). However, only 42% of these subjects indicated disagreement with the same attribution statement following the presentation of a story wherein a woman was raped and experienced an involuntary orgasm (Rape–Involuntary Orgasm story). Similar results were obtained on the attribution statements, "I think that the woman in the story enjoyed having sex with the man" and "I think that the woman in the story encouraged the man to act as he did." Thus, when rape was paired with female sexual responsiveness (involuntary orgasm), male subjects made assumptions that the woman was provocative and that her motive was to have sex.

Both the acquaintance rapists and sexually coercive males reported that the woman in the Rape–Disgust story wanted to have sex with the man, that she enjoyed it, that the man was provoked, and that they would likely behave the same way. Interestingly, all three groups, including the noncoercive subjects, tended to endorse that the woman encouraged the rape and that most men would do the same thing.

A similar pattern was found for the Rape–Involuntary Orgasm story, with sexually coercive groups having the highest percentages of response. However, *all three groups* gave higher endorsements to *all* attribution items, as compared with responses to the previous rape depiction. A large majority of all the groups felt that the woman had enjoyed the experience. The forced intercourse group were notably higher on "I think that the man in the story had good reason to act as he did" and both coercive groups responded that they would be likely to act as the man in the story did. Thus, when the woman was depicted as experiencing an involuntary orgasm, all groups, and sexually coercive groups in particular, saw her as encouraging the rape and saw the man as having more valid reasons for acting as he did than when the

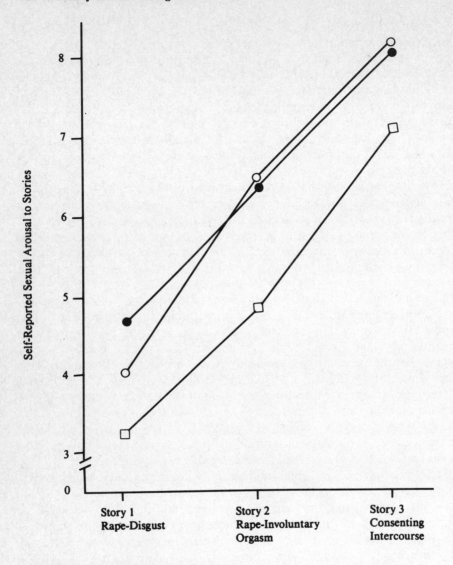

Figure 14.1.   Self-reported sexual arousal to rape and consenting depictions by college male groups.

woman reacted to the experience with only disgust. They also saw themselves as more likely to behave as the man in the story did than in the case of Rape–Disgust. These findings suggest that sexually coercive males are particularly reactive to the woman's lack of arousal as a disinhibiting cue for rape. Acquaintance rapists most consistently reported the highest likelihood of sexual acting out across Rape–Disgust, Rape–Involuntary Orgasm, and Consenting Intercourse stories.

The self-reported acquaintance rapists and sexually coercive group were strikingly similar in their self-reported sexual arousal to both rape stories and a third story depicting consenting sex. Both of these groups had a higher level of arousal following all three stories than did the noncoercive group. It appears that sexually coercive males, including acquaintance rapists, are generally more sexually arousable, whether to consenting or rape stimuli.

Groups were compared on their endorsement of the statement, "How likely would you be to rape a woman if you were guaranteed that you would not be caught and punished?" (Malamuth, 1981). Twenty nine percent and 14% of Groups 2 and 3, respectively, endorsed this item to some degree. The extreme groups were significantly different in response to this item. Thus, the forced intercourse group were more impulsive when aroused and they seemed to rationalize their behavior on the basis of their arousal. They also held more callous and adversarial attitudes toward women.

CONCLUSIONS

These findings support a model of rape in which both enculturation and individual pathology play a part in sexually coercive behavior. First, the data provided strong support for the "normality of rapists" (Malamuth, Haber, & Feshbach, 1980), with the majority of these ostensibly normal college students reporting some past involvement in sexually coercive behavior. In addition, sexual responsiveness of *all* groups was disinhibited by the presentation of the female rape victim as experiencing an involuntary orgasm. It is not a giant conceptual leap to suppose that our culture instills the attitudes that men should take advantage of women and that women may actually enjoy being violated.

However, there were also differences between the groups on such variables as likelihood of raping and disinhibition to rape. Therefore, among college males, a select proportion have a relatively greater propensity to rape when compared with their cohorts. Thus, a model of their behavior should include both exposure to a pro-rape culture and differences in relative proclivity to rape.

Enculturation models, such as Brownmiller's (1975) and Burt's (1980), emphasized rape as an outgrowth of a culture that creates and propagates rape myths, which target the female as the culprit of the crime and exonerate the rapist. Brownmiller stated that myths such as "All women want to be raped" (1975, p. 346) are distortions employed by males as rationalizations for their own behavior. She also stated that the media, and pornography in particular, actually glorify the rapist, thus providing a sanctioned model of rape behavior. The discovery that normal college males find it arousing when a man rapes a woman and she eventually receives sexual pleasure tends to support Brownmiller's view. It is possible that a woman's physiological response causes some men to infer that forcing sex is acceptable.

While it is certainly true that these arguments are well-grounded theoretically and empirically, there is still the question of the particular characteristics that make some men more likely to act out these distorted cultural values. It is a reasonable assumption that individual differences exist, within the structure of a pro-rape culture. Those who support adversarial sexual beliefs, are hostile toward women, and have a propensity to act out impulsively are likely to act out sexually, based on the studies by Rapaport (1984) and Rapaport and Burkhart (1984).

Recent rape research challenges traditional definitions and explanations of rape. Sexual coercion, when conceptualized as a spectrum of behaviors, suggests that rape concepts and rape research should focus on a complex model wherein personality characteristics, situational factors, and socialization all play a role in the development of sexual coerciveness in general, and rape in particular.

REFERENCES

Abel, G. G., Barlow, D. H., Blanchard, E., & Guild, D. (1977). The components of rapists' sexual arousal. *Archives of General Psychiatry, 34,* 895–903.

Armentrout, J., & Hauer, A. (1978). MMPI's of rapists of adults, rapists of children, and non-rapist sex offenders. *Journal of Clinical Psychology, 34,* 330–332.

Barbaree, H., Marshall, W., & Lanthier, R. (1979). Deviant sexual arousal in rapists. *Behavior Research and Therapy, 17,* 215–222.

Briere, J., & Malamuth, N. (1983). Self-reported likelihood of sexually aggressive behavior: Attitudinal versus sexual explanations. *Journal of Research in Personality, 17,* 315–323.

Brownmiller, S. (1975). *Against our will: Men, women, and rape.* New York: Simon & Schuster.

Burt, M. (1980). Cultural myths and supports for rape. *Journal of Personality and Social Psychology, 38,* 217–230.

Donnerstein, E., & Malamuth, N. (in press). Pornography: Its consequences on the observer. In L. Schlesinger (Ed.), *Sexual dynamics of anti-social behavior.* Springfield, IL: Thomas.

Dworkin, A. (1981). *Pornography: Men possessing women.* London: Women's Press.

Gager, N., & Schurr, C. (1976). *Sexual assault: Confronting rape in America.* New York: Grosset & Dunlap.

Griffin, S. (1981). *Pornography and silence: Culture's revolt against nature.* New York: Harper & Row.

Groth, A. N. (1979). *Men who rape: The psychology of the offender.* New York: Plenum.

Groth, A., & Burgess, A. (1977). Rape: A sexual deviation. *American Journal of Orthopsychiatry, 47,* 400–406.

Groth, A., Burgess, A., & Holmstrom, L. (1977). Rape: Power, anger, and sexuality. *American Journal of Psychiatry, 134,* 1239–1243.

Gynther, M., Burkhart, B., & Hovanitz, C. (1979). Do face valid items have more predictive validity than subtle items? The case of the MMPI *Pd* scale. *Journal of Consulting and Clinical Psychology, 47,* 295–300.

Kanin, E. (1969). Selected dyadic aspects of male sex aggression. *Journal of Sex Research, 5,* 12–28.

Koss, M. P., & Gidycz, C. A. (1985). Sexual experiences survey: Reliability and validity. *Journal of Consulting and Clinical Psychology, 53,* 422–423.

Koss, M. P., & Oros, C. J. (1982). Sexual experiences survey: A research instrument investigating sexual aggression and victimization. *Journal of Consulting and Clinical Psychology, 50,* 455–457.

Malamuth, N. M. (1981). Rape proclivity among males. *Journal of Social Issues, 37,* 138–157.

Malamuth, N. (1983). Factors associated with rape as predictors of laboratory aggression against women. *Journal of Personality and Social Psychology, 45,* 432–442.

Malamuth, N., & Check, J. (1980a). Penile tumescence and perceptual responses to rape as a function of victim's perceived reactions. *Journal of Applied Social Psychology, 10,* 528–547.

Malamuth, N., & Check, J. (1980b). Sexual arousal to rape and consenting depictions: The importance of women's arousal. *Journal of Abnormal Psychology, 89,* 763–766.

Malamuth, N., & Check, J. (1981, August). *The effects of exposure to aggressive pornography: Rape proclivity, sexual arousal, and beliefs in rape myths.* Paper presented at the annual meeting of the American Psychological Association, Los Angeles.

Malamuth, N., & Donnerstein, E. (1982). The effects of aggressive-pornographic mass media stimuli. In L. Berkowitz (Ed.), *Advances in experimental social psychology (Vol. 15).* New York: Academic Press.

Malamuth, N., Haber, S., & Feshbach, S. (1980). Testing hypotheses regarding rape: Exposure to sexual violence, sex differences, and the "normality" of rapists. *Journal of Research in Personality, 14,* 121–137.

Malamuth, N., Heim, M., & Feshbach, S. (1980). Sexual responsiveness of college students to rape depictions: Inhibitory and disinhibitory effects. *Journal of Personality and Social Psychology, 38,* 399–408.

Parrot, A. (1983). *Strategies parents may employ to help their children avoid involvement in acquaintance rape situations.* Paper presented at convention of the New York State Federation of Professional Health Educators, Binghamton, NY.

Rapaport, K. (1984). *Sexually aggressive males: Characterological features and sexual responsiveness to rape depictions.* Unpublished doctoral dissertation, Auburn University, (1–135).

Rapaport, K., & Burkhart, B. R. (1984). Personality and attitudinal characteristics of sexually coercive college males. *Journal of Abnormal Psychology, 93,* 216–221.

Rapaport, K. R., & Burkhart, B. R. (1987). Male aggression symposium: Responsiveness to rape depictions. Paper presented at the Society for the Scientific Study of Sex, Atlanta, GA.

Risin, L. I., & Koss, M. P. (1986). The sexual abuse of boys: Prevalence and descriptive characteristics of the childhood victimizations. *Journal of Interpersonal Violence, 3,* 309–323.

Tieger, T. (1981). Self-rated likelihood of raping and the social perception of rape. *Journal of Research in Personality, 15,* 147–158.

Wolfe, J., & Baker, V. (1980). Characteristics of imprisoned rapists and circumstances of the rape. In C. Warner (Ed.), *Rape and sexual assault.* London: Aspen.

CHAPTER 15

Attraction to Sexual Aggression

NEIL M. MALAMUTH, PhD and KAROL E. DEAN

Recent social psychological research regarding the causes of sexual aggression has focused on both the values and messages of the culture, on individual differences among men within that culture, and on the interaction between culture and individual differences. Each of these lines of research has considered factors that may be conducive to various expressions of violence and antisocial behavior against women.

This chapter describes some developments within the individual differences approach. Such work has long recognized the inadequacy of relying exclusively on samples of rapists identified by the judicial system (Koss & Leonard, 1984; Weis & Borges, 1973). Not only is it well known that only a small percentage of rapes are reported to the police (Law Enforcement Assistance Administration, 1975; Russell, 1984), but there are various sexually aggressive acts that do not necessarily meet the legal definition of rape or sexual assault. Researchers have, therefore, often studied men from the general population who in confidence report having committed various degrees of sexual aggression, as well as studying incarcerated individuals.

For some time, we have contended that it is important to go beyond studying actual sexual aggressors in nonincarcerated populations and to also study men who have some attraction to sexual aggression but who may or may not admit to having committed such aggression (Malamuth, 1981, 1984). The construct of attraction has been defined as the belief that aggressing sexually is likely to be a sexually arousing experience, both to aggressors and victims, so that the man believes that he might aggress were it not for fear of punishment or other inhibitory factors (Malamuth, 1989a). This definition suggests that sexual aggression may have differing degrees of positive valence to men who have not necessarily actually aggressed. We contend that men from the general population may be described along a dimension that varies in the degree of attraction to such aggression.*

This chapter first examines the relevance of attraction research to theoretical models of sexual aggression. We then summarize recent developments

---

* The terms *rape, forced sex,* and *coercive sex* are used interchangeably here to refer to sexual aggression.

in which a multi-item attraction to sexual aggression (ASA) scale was used. We also discuss the relationship between attraction and actual aggression and review recent work (primarily studies not as yet reviewed elsewhere) that has used measures of attraction to sexual aggression. Finally, several areas that merit additional research are considered.

THEORETICAL MODELS OF THE CAUSES OF SEXUAL AGGRESSION

There exist a wide variety of theoretical models designed to explain sexual aggression, although no model to date has been shown to be very satisfactory. We suggest that the concept of a dimension of attraction to sexual aggression is not antithetical to any of the current theoretical approaches, although it is considerably more embedded in some models than in others. This can be illustrated by discussing three of the leading approaches to the study of sexual aggression—the psychodynamic, sociobiological, and feminist perspectives.

Psychodynamic Theories

Researchers who have applied psychodynamic concepts to sexual aggression have typically emphasized the pathology of aggressors and their distinctiveness from "normal" men. In general, psychodynamic theorists have attributed the motivation to aggress sexually as rooted in intrapsychic conflicts stemming from relationships with parents, particularly with a demanding, dominating, and often rejecting mother (Cohen, Garofalo, Boucher, & Seghorn, 1971; Groth, Burgess, & Holmstrom, 1977). Growing up with such a parent is hypothesized to sometimes create fixation at early stages of development, symbolic power and hostility conflicts, an inability to sublimate sexual and aggressive impulses adequately, and a desire to control and perhaps humiliate women. In some cases, this may result in a need for aggression to attain sexual excitement and hostility toward those who are sexually desired, as well as a fear of sexual inadequacy. The rapist's motivation may involve displacement of his hostility onto the victim, defensiveness against dependency needs, and/or homosexual wishes. Although most psychodynamic approaches have placed emphasis on the relationship with the mother, a recent study using this approach reported that the conflict in sexually aggressive men may be more related to the father (Lisak & Roth, 1989). It should also be noted that psychodynamic theories emphasize the existence of differing types of rapists with varied developmental histories (Knight, Rosenberg, & Schneider, 1985).

Even though psychodynamic theories have generally been associated with a pathology, or a "sick man" approach to sexual aggression, such models suggest that many men who do not actually rape may experience varying intensities of the emotional and power conflicts and, more generally, the neuroses reported in rapists. These men may therefore be expected to be attracted, in varying degrees, to sexual aggression. For many men, other means of expressing and/or resolving their psychological conflicts may prevent the occurrence of actual aggression. It appears, then, that the construct of attraction to sexual aggression is not inconsistent with psychodynamic approaches, and to some degree is implicit in them, although it is not as germane to them as to the next two models to be discussed, the sociobiological and the feminist approaches.

Sociobiological Adaptation

Shields and Shields (1983) described a model of behavioral control that they used to explain how sexually aggressive behavior is related to the reproductive drive in men. For both men and women, sexuality has been shaped by evolutionary forces of natural selection to maximize the arousal patterns and associated behavioral strategies that would be most likely to lead to reproductive success. Because of the differing ways by which men and women can most effectively transmit their genes to offspring (i.e., for men by impregnating as many women as possible and for women by becoming pregnant by men who will "invest" in the rearing of their children), the most "selected for" strategies have been disparate for men and women. Men are more inclined to be easily aroused and to desire intercourse with as many females as possible, with or without their consent, whereas females are more likely to be selective and cautious in sexual relations. According to this theory, sexual aggression is but one of several strategies that men may use to get women to have sexual relations, although in most societies it would not be likely to be the first strategy used, but rather one employed by those men who do not have other means of persuading women to have sex with them.

Although the approach outlined above already conceptualizes sexual aggression as a "normal" male strategy, a recent sociobiological model described by Thornhill and Thornhill (1990) went further in suggesting what could be interpreted as an evolutionary adaptation favoring sexual aggression. They argued that male sexual needs involve a desire to control female sexuality since that would increase the probability of paternity by that male. Men are therefore predisposed, according to this model, to want to dominate and control women sexually. Such a need would theoretically be favored by evolution since men who possess it would be more likely to be the sole beneficiary of a particular female's reproductive ability and to therefore transmit that need genetically to their offspring. The need to dominate and control women sexually might be quite easily translated into an attraction to sexual aggression, wherein control and power over the woman are clearly evident. The idea of a continuum of attraction to sexual aggression among men is therefore fully consistent with earlier sociobiological models (Shields & Shields, 1983) but may be particularly easily embraced by the more recent version suggested by Thornhill and Thornhill (1990). (Also see Ellis, 1989).

The Feminist Approach

Although the sociobiological and feminist approaches differ in many respects, they surprisingly share a rather close affinity with the idea that there is a continuum of attraction to sexual aggression among men generally. However, the feminist model perceives the basis for such attraction in patriarchal culture and the values it encourages, rather than in evolutionary development. According to feminists, this type of culture teaches men that sexual aggression is an acceptable way to demonstrate power, anger, and male "supremacy." They learn that they are ". . . entitled to goods and services, including sex, from women as a class" (Bart & O'Brien, 1985, p. 103) and that women enjoy sexual aggression (Burt, 1980). These messages are embedded within men's socialization processes by sources such as peers, family, and the media. The pervasiveness of misogynistic messages in these socializing institutions led Bart and O'Brien (1985) to assert: "The question we should ask then, is not why men rape, but why don't *all* men rape?" (p. 102). It is apparent that the notion of a dimension of attraction to sexual aggression is fully in keeping with such feminist approaches.*

THE RELATIONSHIP BETWEEN ATTRACTION AND ACTUAL AGGRESSION

Theoretically, it is expected that different information would be derived from assessing attraction to forced sex as compared to measures of self-reported past sexual aggression (Koss & Oros, 1982; Malamuth, 1986). For the purposes of explication, consider crossing these two variables, with each having two levels, a low versus a high score, thereby yielding the following four cells:

1. Some men may not have engaged in any sexual aggression and may have no desire or attraction to do so.

2. Some men may not have committed any sexual aggression, but may have some desire to do so if they could avoid punishment. Such desire may not have been expressed in actual behavior for various reasons. These could include fear of the consequences, the lack of opportunity to aggress, or having certain attributes or emotions (e.g., empathy) that are incompatible with acting out aggressively.

3. Some men have been sexually aggressive in the past but may now report relatively little desire for forcing sex. Some may regret their previous aggression or have changed their attitudes, emotions, or other characteristics. Others may not recognize or admit to themselves that their past behavior constitutes coercive sex or, in certain instances, rape.

---

* We wish to acknowledge that our motivation to assess attraction to sexual aggression was initially based on feminist literature.

4. Some men who have been sexually aggressive may still have considerable attraction and desire to engage in such behavior.

ASSESSING SEXUAL AGGRESSION

Reported Likelihood of Forced Sex

Most of the research that has attempted to assess attraction to sexual aggression has relied on two items. On these, respondents indicate the likelihood they would engage in forced sex if they could be assured of not being identified or punished. One of these items asks subjects to report their Likelihood to Rape (LR) and the other, their Likelihood of Forcing (LF) sex against a woman's wishes (Briere & Malamuth, 1983; Malamuth, 1981; Malamuth, Haber, & Feshbach, 1980). Although quite highly correlated, these two phrasings generally result in quite different responses, as exemplified in the data described below. This work has shown some similarities between men with attraction to sexual aggression and actual offenders. Other investigators have generally found the same relationships we have described, both with college students and men from the general population (Murphy, Coleman & Haynes, 1986; see Malamuth, 1988a, c, and 1989a for more details).

Embedding Within Other Likelihood Items

The early research using reported likelihood of coercive sex either (a) presented men with a scenario depicting forced sex and asked them how likely they were to behave as the depicted man did, if they could avoid negative consequences, or (b) asked about the likelihood they would rape or force sex, without referring to any scenario. In both cases, however, no questions were asked about the likelihood they might engage in other antisocial behaviors (Malamuth et al., 1980; Tieger, 1981). It is possible that a person indicating some likelihood of sexual aggression may be equally likely to indicate likelihood of engaging in any antisocial or "deviant" act. To address this possibility, more recent research has frequently embedded questions about coercive sex within other items asking about a variety of socially acceptable and antisocial behaviors that the person might engage in if he were assured of avoiding negative consequences (e.g., anal sex, armed robbery, and so on).

The pattern of data obtained in such research can be illustrated by the findings reported by Malamuth (1989a, b), who compared frequencies obtained of subjects' reported likelihood to force sex or to rape versus the other reported likelihoods. Earlier work showed the utility of dividing the subjects into those who indicated no likelihood of committing the act versus those indicating any likelihood (Malamuth, 1984). It may be that the strongest difference occurs at the level of those who totally rule out the possibility of engaging in the behavior as compared to those who conceive of some possibility of participating in it. Consequently, each of the variables was dichotomized to those indicating a 1 (not at all likely) versus those indicating a 2 or above.

Using the percentages of subjects who indicated any likelihood of engaging in the acts, Malamuth (1989a, b) found that between 16% to 20% indicated some likelihood of raping. The percentages that indicated some likelihood of "forcing sex" ranged from 36% to 44%. Tests for statistical significance showed that when the term *forced sex* was used, a significantly larger number of men indicated some likelihood of committing it than other nonnormative behaviors (such as pedophilia, murder, rape, transvestism, homosexuality, and armed robbery). When the term *rape* was used, fewer men indicated any likelihood of such an act than several other behaviors. (The issue of a general tendency to respond in a more deviant way is discussed more fully below.)

The pattern of the intercorrelations among the reported likelihoods indicated that, although some of the variance may be explained by the degree to which a behavior may be considered "deviant" (e.g., a person who indicates some likelihood of committing an extreme act such as murder shows a general tendency to report some likelihood of committing other extreme acts), the magnitude of the correlations also revealed that people generally did not indiscriminately indicate there was some likelihood they would commit any act if assured of avoiding negative consequences. The pattern of the correlations suggested that factors such as whether the act involved violence and/or sex, in addition to its perceived social deviance, may have affected subjects' reported likelihoods. It appears that such self-reports may indeed be indicative of the extent to which respondents consider various acts attractive, if assured of avoiding the negative consequences.

Multi-Item Scale

In recognition of the possibility that there may be components to men's reactions to sexual aggression that are not being adequately tapped with the likelihood to rape or force sex items, Malamuth (1989a, b) recently devised a multi-item attraction to sexual aggression (ASA) scale. We describe this work in considerable detail here in view of its potential importance to future work in this area.

The ASA scale retained the use of the LR and LF items in addition to a variety of other items. The 14 items retained for the ASA scale are presented in Table 15.1, embedded within similar items used to assess attraction to other acts (e.g., oral sex, transvestism, pedophilia, and so on). The items comprising the ASA scale consisted of those referring to "rape" and to "forcing a female to do something sexual she didn't want to." The combined classification using LF and LR (Briere & Malamuth, 1983) has been found to correlate highly (e.g., .69 by Malamuth, 1989a) with the 14-item ASA scale.

As indicated in Table 15.1, two items (one referring to rape and one to forced sex) asked whether the person had ever thought of trying the activities, and two items asked about the extent to which he found the idea of engaging in these activities sexually arousing. Similarly, two items asked about the respondent's beliefs about the percentage of females who would find the activities sexually arousing (i.e., raping and forcing a male), but a third item was added in this set asking about the subjects' beliefs about the percentage of females who would be sexually aroused by being forced to do something sexual that they did not want to do. In addition, three items inquired about the extent to which the subject himself believed that he would be sexually aroused by engaging in rape, forcing a female to do something sexual she did not want to do, and being forced to do something sexual he did not want to do. Finally, two items inquired about the likelihood that the respondent would engage in the behavior if he ". . . could be assured that no one would know and that you could in no way be punished." These 14 items were first standardized and then added together to create a total ASA score.

On the basis of *a priori* classification confirmed by factor analyses, the other items described in Table 15.1 were used to create five additional scales: (a) *Attraction to Bondage* (12 items) encompassed both the "bondage" and "whipping, spanking" items; (b) *Attraction to Conventional Sex* (18 items) included the items referring to necking, petting, oral sex, and heterosexual intercourse; (c) *Attraction to Homosexuality* (5 items) consisted of the items inquiring about homosexual sex; (d) *Attraction to Unconventional Sex* (11 items) consisted of items concerning anal intercourse and group sex; (e) *Attraction to Deviant Sex* (12 items) encompassed the items referring to pedophilia and transvestism.

Data concerning the validity of the ASA scale were gathered in several similar studies involving male students and nonstudents. In all of these, subjects responded to a variety of questions on a "paper and pencil" questionnaire. The survey consisted of the ASA items and those of the other attraction scales (see Table 15.1). Also included were: Burt's (1980) Acceptance of Interpersonal Violence (AIV), measuring subjects' perceptions of how much violence is acceptable; Rape Myth Acceptance (RMA), indicating the degree to which subjects endorse various rape myths; and Adversarial Sexual Beliefs (ASB), measuring the extent to which subjects believe that the two genders are necessarily at odds in sexual interactions; a Dominance Scale, measuring the motivation to control another person as an incentive for engaging in sexual acts (Nelson, 1979); Check and Malamuth's (1983) Hostility Toward Women Scale (HTW), measuring subjects' antagonism toward women; the Psychoticism Scale from Eysenck's Personality Questionnaire, measuring antisocial traits (Eysenck, 1978); the Sexual Behavior Inventory, assessing subjects' experience in several heterosexual acts (Bentler, 1968); and an assessment of subjects' affective response to media depictions of sexual activities. In addition, the research included a self-report of sexual aggression that requested subjects to indicate how many times they had engaged in sexual encounters in which they had used some form of force or coercion (Koss & Oros, 1982), and the Marlowe-Crowne Social Desirability Scale, assessing the extent to which

TABLE 15.1. Items Used to Create the Attraction to Sexual Aggression (ASA) Scale and the Other Scales

ASA Scale Items

1 & 2.   People frequently think about different activities even if they never do them. For each kind of activity listed please indicate whether or not you have ever though of trying that activity.

	Have Never Thought of It	Have Thought of It

     a. Necking (deep kissing)
     b. Petting
     c. Oral sex
     d. Heterosexual intercourse
     e. Anal intercourse
     f. Male homosexual acts
     g. Group sex
     h. Bondage (e.g., tying up self or sex partner)
     i. Whipping, spanking
     j. Rape
     k. Forcing a female to do something sexual she didn't want to
     l. Transvestism (wearing clothes of opposite sex)
     m. Pedophilia (sex with a child)

3 & 4.   Whether or not you had ever thought of it, do you find the idea:

Very Attractive	Somewhat Attractive	Somewhat Unattractive	Very Unattractive

     [Same behaviors as in item 1 were listed here.]

5 & 6.   What percentage of *males* do you think would find the following activities sexually arousing?

     [The same behaviors as in item 1 were listed, followed by 11-point scales, ranging from 0% to 100% in increments of 10%.]

7, 8, & 9.   What percentage of *females* do you think would find the following activities sexually arousing?

     [The same behaviors as in item 1 were listed with the addition of the following item: "Forcing a male to do something sexual he didn't want to." Also, subjects were asked about females being forced into sexual acts rather than about forcing other females. The scales that followed these items were the same as for item 5.]

10, 11, & 12.   How sexually arousing do you think *you would find* the following sexual activities if you engaged in them (even if you have never engaged in them)?

     [Same behaviors as in item 1 were listed with the addition of the following item: "Being forced to do something sexual you didn't want to." The scales that followed were the same as in item 5.]

13 & 14.   If you could be assured that no one would know and that you could in no way be punished for engaging in the following acts, how likely, if at all, would you be to commit such acts?

     [Same behaviors were listed as in item 1, but only including "e" (anal intercourse) through "m" (pedophilia). In some of the studies, items referring to murder and armed robbery were also included. Scales that followed ranged from (1) "not at all likely" to (5) "very likely."]

Reprinted by permission from Malamuth, 1989a.

subjects responded in line with what is considered socially acceptable (Crowne & Marlowe, 1960).

In two of the studies, subjects also participated in a separate phase in which they were presented with depictions portraying consenting sex and rape. Their reactions to these portrayals were assessed by self-reported sexual arousal and by penile tumescence. Previous research (Abel, Barlow, Blanchard, & Guild, 1977) had suggested that the degree to which a man is sexually aroused by rape depictions relative to his arousal to consenting sex is an indictor of a "proclivity" to aggress sexually.

The series of predictions and associated data described below (selected from Malamuth, 1989a, b) supported the construct validity of ASA and demonstrated the utility of the concept of attraction to sexual aggression.

Relationship with Characteristics Linked to Aggressors

Men who are higher on attraction to sexual aggression, even if they have never actually aggressed, should be more similar on relevant dimensions to actual sexual aggressors than their counterparts who are lower on attraction to sexual aggression. The differences between men who are highly attracted to sexual aggression but have not aggressed as compared to those who have actually aggressed may be (a) in the extent to which they possess certain characteristics (e.g., those who have aggressed may be very high in hostility toward women, while those attracted to aggression who have not actually aggressed may also be quite high in hostility but not high enough to overcome inhibitions to actually aggress), and (b) those not aggressing may not have had many "opportunities" to aggress due to youth and/or inexperience. As indicated in Table 15.2, generally strong support was found by Malamuth (1989b) for the prediction that higher ASA scores would be associated with a variety of characteristics previously found to be associated with actual aggressors. These included attitudes supportive of violence against women, hostility toward women, antisocial personality characteristics, dominance motives, sexual arousal in response to aggression, perceptions of rape victims, and affective reactions to portrayals of forced sex in the mass media.

Overall, these analyses clearly demonstrated the usefulness of ASA as a measure for discriminating within men who are low in sexual aggression. For all the measures except for sexual experience, the pattern suggests that when low-aggression men score higher on ASA, they are more similar to men who are high in sexual aggression. Interestingly, low-sexual-aggression men who are high on attraction to sexual aggression report what appears to be a rather low level of sex experience (11.63), although statistically this differs significantly only from the high-sexual-aggression men. Based on their scores on the other measures, it appears that these low-sexual-aggression, high-ASA men may have some relatively higher "risk" for committing sexual aggression, but that inhibitory or other factors have prevented them from engaging in much sexual activity, including sexual aggression. However, these men are

TABLE 15.2.   Criterion Measures as a Function of Sexual Aggression and Attraction to Sexual Aggression (ASA)

	Low Sexual Aggression			High Sexual Aggression		
	Low ASA	Med ASA	High ASA		$F(3,150)$	Trend
	(n=71)	(n=28)	(n=42)	(n=19)		
*Criterion Measures:**						
Attitude Composite	$-.82_a$	$.45_b$	$.42_b$	1.62_b	6.63**	Linear
Hostility	6.78_a	8.70_a	9.49_b	13.36_c	6.54**	Linear
Psychoticism	1.65_a	2.30_a	2.41_b	3.58_c	6.73**	Linear
Dominance	15.91_a	16.26_a	17.17_a	20.53_b	6.00**	Linear
Sex Experience	13.86_a	14.04_{ab}	11.63_a	18.37_b	$3.57^†$	Quadratic
	(n=42)	(n=14)	(n=27)	(n=12)	$F(3,94)$	
Sexual Arousal Measures:						
Tumescence index	-32.76_a	-25.71_a	-12.78_a	2.04_b	$2.79^†$	Linear
Self-report index	-30.95	-31.43	-24.82	-15.83	1.07	—

* Variables not sharing a common subscript differ significantly by the Duncan procedure, which is used to make comparisons among any two groups.
**$p < .0005$
† $p < .05$

Note: Attitude Composite = attitudes supporting violence against women computed by combining scores on the Acceptance of Interpersonal Violence, Rape Myth Acceptance, and Adversarial Sexual Beliefs scales; Hostility = Hostility Toward Women scale; Psychoticism = Psychoticism scale; Dominance = Dominance as a motive scale; Sex Experience = Sex Experience scale. Tumescence index = physiological sexual arousal to rape depiction minus arousal to consenting depiction; self-report index = self-reported sexual arousal to rape depiction minus reported arousal to consenting depiction. Reprinted by permission from Malamuth, 1989b.

also significantly lower than high sexual aggressors on most of the criterion measures (i.e., hostility, psychoticism, and dominance). It may be that some "threshold" exists on these dimensions that distinguishes those who actually engage in relatively high levels of sexual aggression.

Projected Relationship to Future Aggressive Behavior

ASA should relate to the subjects' reports of their behavioral potential and possibly, under some circumstances, to actual aggression. Significant relationships were found between ASA and subjects' reports that they had forced sex in the past and that they might possibly rape or force sex in the future. However, as expected, the correlation between ASA and actual past sexual aggression was significant but not strong (although some studies, e.g., Petty & Dawson, 1989, do report relatively high associations). The correlations between ASA and the possibility that the subject might rape and force sex in the future were strong. In particular, a high correlation measured in this research between ASA and the possibility of forcing sex seems to indicate that people who are attracted to it believe that they might actually behave aggressively in the future.

Deviancy Motive for Attraction to Aggression

Why do men differ in their ASA scores? Could it be due to a general tendency to be more deviant? Might differences in the desire to be socially appropriate or desirable be crucial? Perhaps men with higher ASA scores are simply more sexually "liberal" than others and may report more attraction to any behavior. That is, they may find a variety of sexual behaviors arousing or interesting even though they do not personally engage in them. These possibilities were assessed by comparisons using ASA and the other attraction scales (measuring "deviant," conventional, and unconventional sex) as well as by using the social desirability scale assessing a subject's desire to appear socially desirable or appropriate.

On the whole, the findings did not support a "deviancy" or a "liberal" explanation. Instead, the data suggested that ASA is primarily measuring an attraction specifically linked to sexual aggression. Further, although responses on ASA were weakly correlated with social desirability, controlling for social desirability tendencies did not significantly change the findings.

RECENT DEVELOPMENTS IN ATTRACTION RESEARCH

Over the past few years, there has been considerable research using measures of attraction to sexual aggression. Since some of this literature has been summarized elsewhere (Malamuth, 1981, 1988a, 1989a) we will focus here on examples of recent developments not included in previous reviews. These include research (a) examining the general cognitive, affective, and personality variables discriminating among men with differing levels of attraction to sexual aggression, (b) assessing the influence of various types of exposures designed to increase or decrease such attraction, and (c) extending this type of research to related areas.

Discriminating Variables

Weir and Branscombe (1989) noted that attraction to coercive sex as measured by LR and LF items are often studied in relation to rape-related concepts only. These authors suggested that such attraction may also relate to more general cognitive, affective, and personality tendencies. To examine this possibility, they conducted a discriminant analysis of subjects based on their response to LR and LF items. In support of earlier research (Malamuth, 1981), they concluded that it is clear that certain characteristics previously shown to be associated with rapists are important in the prediction of attraction to sexual aggression. However, they also concluded that differences in attraction to coercive sex may be further enhanced on the basis of more general cognitive measures, such as Machiavellianism and customary anger expression patterns. Further, their data suggested that the tendency to support exploitation as an appropriate means to deal with others may have an important role in the belief system of men who are sexually aggressive.

In related research, Ceniti and Malamuth (1989) found that the MMPI scales that best discriminated among different levels of attraction to sexual aggression were those assessing suspiciousness, hypersensitivity, and unconventional thinking. Taken together, the findings of both of these studies may prove helpful in the development of more elaborate theoretical models in which general factors are integrated with more specific variables to explain a range of sexually aggressive inclinations and acts (see Malamuth, 1988b for a more detailed discussion of this issue).

Increasing Attraction

There has been some research examining whether exposure to certain types of media messages (e.g., sexual violence) increases the levels of attraction to sexual aggression. Although some studies have reported increases in attraction to coercive sex following exposure to such media (Check & Gulolan, 1989; Donnerstein, 1984), others have not (Malamuth & Ceniti, 1986). There are considerable methodological and other differences in these studies that could account for the discrepant findings. A full discussion of these is beyond the scope of this chapter. At this point, it may be more appropriate to accept the "null" hypothesis rather than conclude that there is sufficient evidence that exposure to sexually violent or similar media increases attraction to sexual aggression.

A recent study by Demare, Briere, and Lips (1988) provided some interesting correlational data on the relationship between certain types of media and attraction to sexual aggression. The authors surveyed the type of pornography male subjects had used in the past, categorizing these materials as nonviolent pornography (consenting sex), violent pornography (e.g., mutilation of women), and sexually violent pornography (coercive sex). They also assessed attraction to sexual aggression and subjects' attitudes. Although all three types of pornography correlated with greater attraction to sexual aggression, only sexually violent pornography made a unique contribution to a discriminant analysis. Attitudes accepting of violence against women also contributed uniquely to the discriminant analysis.

Decreasing Attraction

There have been attempts to both directly and indirectly change attraction to coercive sex. An example of a relatively direct intervention was reported by Stille (1984), who exposed subjects to (a) a documentary film that portrayed the horrible, long-term consequences of rape for the victim or (b) a control condition. Subjects' attraction to sexual aggression was measured some days later in a context ostensibly unrelated to the earlier exposure. The investigator reported that the documentary was effective in reducing attraction to aggression.

An example of a more indirect intervention was recently reported by Johnson and Russ (1989). They manipulated the salience of consciousness-raising information and analyzed the effect of this information on subjects' reactions to acquaintance and stranger rape scenarios. When information about the "historical and contemporary mistreatment of women in American society" (p. 1186) was made cognitively available to subjects through a speech administered during the experiment, male subjects' assessment of their own likelihood to rape was significantly lower than subjects in the condition that did not receive this salient information. Also, in the manipulation of the type of rape (acquaintance versus stranger), men who read an acquaintance rape vignette reported a higher likelihood to rape than those who read a stranger rape story. The authors suggested that the salience manipulation affected the male subjects' attraction items by activating a cognitive construct about the negative aspects of such aggression. In the acquaintance/stranger rape manipulation, they indicated that the ambiguity in the situation and the less serious perception of acquaintance rape that most people have (i.e., acquaintance rape is not "real" rape) may have affected the subjects' report of their likelihood to behave in the same way as the aggressor in the story. If the often used dependent measure of likelihood to rape can be affected by salience manipulations, the authors suggested that this may be a way to devise effective interventions and educational programs without exposing audiences to actual rape depictions, which may be either arousing or disturbing to the general public.

Extensions to Other Areas

Two researchers extended the work on men's self-reported likelihood of aggressing sexually to develop similar measures of attraction in related areas of inquiry. Pryor (1987) studied likelihood of sexually harassing. He developed 10 hypothetical scenarios portraying a male who could sexually exploit a woman by virtue of his social role (e.g., professor–student, executive–secretary). Male undergraduates were asked to imagine themselves in each of these roles and to consider what they would do if they could avoid any negative consequences to themselves from sexually harassing the woman. Respondents indicated the likelihood that they would choose such behavior on a scale ranging from 1 (*not at all likely*) to 5 (*very likely*). Pryor found that men's reported likelihood of exploitative behavior was similar in the 10 situations, enabling the computation of an overall likelihood of sexual harassment (LSH) score for each subject. Pryor obtained data supporting the predictive validity of the LSH reports in an ostensibly unrelated laboratory task where subjects were asked to teach a woman how to putt in a golf game. It was found that those with higher LSH scores more frequently used the golf task to sexually touch the woman. Interestingly, LSH ratings correlated strongly with subjects' reported likelihood of raping as well as with measures of their beliefs and attitudes regarding violence against women. These data are consistent with the view that diverse violent and nonviolent antisocial acts against women (e.g., rape and sexual harassment) relate to and are possibly caused by similar factors (Malamuth & Briere, 1986).

Using a variation of the likelihood to rape measure, Briere (1987) assessed males' self-reported likelihood to "wife-batter" and related it to measures of attitudes toward women, acceptance of interpersonal violence, and attitudes toward wife abuse. The likelihood to batter (LB) scale questions: If the respondent were married and were in an argument with his wife about a number of specified topics (i.e., she had had sex with another man), how likely would the respondent be to hit his wife? Results indicated that 79% of the men reported at least some likelihood of hitting their wife. The measured attitudes (e.g., attitudes toward women, acceptance of interpersonal violence, and attitudes toward wife abuse) were associated with LB. While the author cautioned that this type of measure cannot be used to predict specific behaviors for any individual, the widespread proclivity to engage in this behavior as measured in a university population is significant.

FUTURE RESEARCH

There is clearly a need for more systematic research on attraction to sexual aggression. We suggest here some potentially fruitful areas—expectancies, cross-cultural comparisons, contributing factors and underlying processes, self-awareness and expressions of attraction in nonviolent acts, and decisions to desist from antisocial behavior.

Outcome Expectancies

Attraction research may benefit from a relatively large body of research on alcohol-related expectancies and motivations for drug use. The term *expectancy* has been used in that literature to refer to the anticipated consequences of alcohol use. Brown, Goldman, Inn, and Anderson (1980) described six independent expectancies about alcohol (e.g., transforming experiences in a positive way, enhancing sexual performance and experience, and so on). This research found that even prior to any direct experience with alcohol, relatively well-developed expectancies exist about its consequences. These expectancies are probably based primarily on indirect experiences mediated by parents, peers, and the media. Expectations of effects were shown to contribute to alcohol use, over and above pharmacological effects or demographic or background variables.

The connection with the present line of research is that the concept of attraction as defined and operationalized by Malamuth (1989a) included both an "expectancy" component (that aggressing is likely to be sexually arousing to aggressors and to victims), and a "lure" component (the respondent believes that he might aggress were it not for fear of punishment or other inhibitory factors). The sources of information about outcome expectancies concerning sexual aggression may also be indirect experiences provided, in particular, by mainstream and pornographic media and by peers. A question that arises in comparing the present research to that of alcohol expectancy and drug motivations concerns the relatively weaker relationship found here with actual behavior. Since alcohol consumption is clearly a far more frequently occurring behavior than sexual aggression, it provides more opportunity for a strong relationship to be found between attraction and behavior because of the much greater range of the distribution of behavior for alcohol drinking. In the area of sexual aggression, fear of punishment and other inhibitory factors may be more likely to exert a strong influence on behavior than in the alcohol area.

Cross-Cultural Comparisons

It would be of considerable interest to assess the level of attraction to coercive sex in differing nations and to examine the extent to which any systematic differences correlate with differences in actual violence against women in those societies. This type of research may help clarify the causes of such attraction. For example, the sociobiological and the feminist theories described earlier make contrasting predictions regarding the cross-cultural consistency of such attraction across societies, since the former emphasizes evolutionary causes while the latter emphasizes cultural factors.

Contributing Factors

Research is also needed on the factors contributing to the development of attraction to sexual aggression and the processes underlying it, including cognitive and affective factors. One potential approach was suggested by the recent work of Pryor and Stoller (1989). These investigators explored the cognitive processes underlying likelihood to sexually harass ratings and hypothesized that social dominance and male sexuality form a schematic construct in the minds of high LSH men (i.e., these men view an inherent connection between dominance and sexuality). To test this notion, the researchers first selected words that were connected with either sexuality or dominance, but not both. Then they presented subjects with a series of word pairs. Different combinations of paired words were used, using *sexual, dominance,* and other words. They found that high-LSH men overestimated the co-occurrence of sexuality and dominance words, supporting the hypothesis that they have a sexuality/dominance schema.

Self-Awareness

Future research should investigate subjects' reactions to the awareness that they are attracted to sexual aggression. Many subjects are quite aware of such attraction of arousal to thoughts of such aggression (Malamuth, Check, & Briere, 1986). The consequences of such awareness may be very diverse. One person may be quite upset by such realization and become more inhibited in varied sexual encounters for fear of the "hidden forces" that he believes lurk within him. Another individual may actually seek out situations where there may be opportunities to aggress in order to find out whether the actual behavior would be as arousing as the fantasy.

Attraction, Behavior, and Desistance

Although attraction to sexual aggression may be manifested for some men in actual physical aggression, it is possible that for others such attraction and/or the factors causing this attraction will be expressed in nonviolent behaviors only, such as unjustifiably blaming the victim in a rape trial, supporting another man's aggression in a "locker room" conversation, or sexually harassing and discriminating against women (Malamuth & Briere, 1986). Of course, some men who report attraction to sexual aggression may, due to internal prohibitions or morals, not show any behavioral expressions. It may be particularly useful to study men with similar levels of attraction but with different behavioral expressions, to assist in the prevention of sexual aggression and other antisocial acts. Determining the differences among such groups of men may be beneficial in changing the behavior of aggressors and in guiding interventions designed to prevent the development of such aggression. Such work may benefit from research in other areas on the cessation of undesirable behaviors. For example, Paternoster (1989) analyzed the effect of affective ties, material considerations, informal and formal sanctions, and moral considerations on the decision to desist from offending by juvenile delinquents. Similarly, Fagan (1989) examined desistance from violence by wife batterers and concluded that common processes can be identified in the cessation of disparate behaviors by diverse populations in various settings. While such work analyzes the reasons that people who have already aggressed or committed another antisocial act desist from repeating it, the present suggestion is to study those who have not yet committed such acts, despite their attraction to such behaviors.

Finally, it is important to investigate under what conditions, if any, attraction to aggression is a precursor to actual violent behavior. A great deal of caution must be exercised to avoid labeling certain individuals in a manner that could affect others' reactions to them, as well as their reactions to themselves. With such caution in mind, we are currently conducting longitudinal research that will determine whether ASA scores predict later behaviors.

REFERENCES

Abel, G. G., Barlow, D. H., Blanchard, E., & Guild, D. (1977). The components of rapists' sexual arousal. *Archives of General Psychiatry, 34,* 895–903.

Bart, P. B., & O'Brien, P. (1985). *Stopping rape: Successful survival strategies.* Elmsford, NY: Pergamon.

Bentler, P. M. (1968). Heterosexual behavior assessment—1: Males. *Behavior Research and Therapy, 6,* 21–25.

Briere, J. (1987). Predicting self-reported likelihood of battering: Attitudes and childhood experiences. *Journal of Research in Personality, 21,* 61–69.

Briere, J., & Malamuth, N. M. (1983). Self-reported likelihood of sexually aggressive behavior: Attitudinal versus sexual explanation. *Journal of Research in Personality, 17,* 315–323.

Brown, A. A., Goldman, M. S., Inn, A., & Anderson, L. R. (1980). Expectations of reinforcement from alcohol: Their domain and relation to drinking patterns. *Journal of Consulting and Clinical Psychology, 48,* 419–426.

Burt, M. R. (1980). Cultural myths and supports for rape. *Journal of Personality and Social Psychology, 38,* 217–230.

Ceniti, J., & Malamuth, N. M. (1989). *MMPI scales and attraction to sexual aggression.* Manuscript in preparation.

Check, J. V. P., & Gulolen, T. H. (1989). Reported proclivity for coercive sex following repeated exposure to sexually violent pornography, nonviolent dehumanizing pornography, and erotica. In D. Zillmann and J. Bryant (Eds.), *Pornography: Research advances and policy considerations* (pp. 159–184). Hillsdale, NJ: Erlbaum.

Check, J. V. P., & Malamuth, N. M. (1983). *The Hostility Toward Women scale.* Paper presented at the Western meeting of the International Society for Research on Aggression, Victoria, Canada.

Cohen, M. L., Garofalo, R., Boucher, R., & Seghorn, T. (1971). The psychology of rapists. *Seminars in Psychiatry, 3,* 307–327.

Crowne, D. P., & Marlowe, D. (1960). A new scale of social desirability independent of psychopathology. *Journal of Consulting Psychology, 24,* 349–354.

Demare, D., Briere, J., & Lips, H. M. (1988). Violent pornography and self-reported likelihood of sexual aggression. *Journal of Research in Personality, 22,* 140–153.

Donnerstein, E. (1984). Pornography: Its effects on violence against women. In N. M. Malamuth & E. Donnerstein (Eds.), *Pornography and sexual aggression* (pp. 53–81). Orlando, FL: Academic Press.

Ellis, L. (1989). *Theories of rape.* iv Hemisphere.

Eysenck, H. J. (1978). *Sex and personality.* London: Open Books.

Fagan, J. (1989). Cessation of family violence: Deterrence and dissuasion. In L. Ohlin & M. Tonry (Eds.) *Family violence.* (pp. 377–425). Chicago: The University of Chicago Press.

Groth, N., Burgess, A. W., & Holmstrom, L. L. (1977). Rape: Power, anger, and sexuality. *American Journal of Psychiatry, 134,* 1239–1243.

Johnson, J. D., & Russ, I. (1989). Effects of salience of consciousness raising information on perceptions of acquaintance versus stranger rape. *Journal of Applied Social Psychology, 19,* 1182–1197.

Knight, R. A., Rosenberg, R., & Schneider, B. A. (1985). Classification of sexual offenders: Perspectives, methods, and evaluation. In A. W. Burgess (Ed.), *Rape and sexual assault: A research handbook* (pp. 222–293). New York: Garland.

Koss, M. P., & Leonard, K. E. (1984). Sexually aggressive men: Empirical findings and theoretical implications. In N. M. Malamuth & E. Donnerstein (Eds.), *Pornography and sexual aggression* (pp. 211–232). Orlando, FL: Academic Press.

Koss, M. P., & Oros, C. (1982). Sexual Experiences Survey: A research instrument investigating aggression and victimization. *Journal of Consulting and Clinical Psychology, 50,* 445–457.

Law Enforcement Assistance Administration, United States National Criminal Justice Information and Statistics Service. (1975). *Criminal victimization surveys in 13 American cities.* Washington, DC: U.S. Government Printing Office.

Lisak, D., & Roth, S. (1989). *Motives and psychodynamics of self-reported, nonincarcerated rapists.* Unpublished manuscript.

Malamuth, N. M. (1981). Rape proclivity among males. *Journal of Social Issues, 37,* 138–157.

Malamuth, N. M. (1984). Aggression against women: Cultural and individual causes. In N. M. Malamuth & E. Donnerstein (Eds.), *Pornography and sexual aggression,* (pp. 19–52). Orlando, FL: Academic Press.

Malamuth, N. M. (1986). Predictors of naturalistic sexual aggression. *Journal of Personality and Social Psychology, 50,* 953–962.

Malamuth, N. M. (1988a). A multidimensional approach to sexual aggression: Combining measures of past behavior and present likelihood. In R. A. Prentky & V. L. Quinsey (Eds.), *Human sexual aggression: Current perspectives. Annals of the New York Academy of Sciences (Vol. 528),* pp.(123–132). New York: The New York Academy of Sciences.

Malamuth, N. M. (1988b). Predicting laboratory aggression against female and male targets: Implications for sexual aggression. *Journal of Research in Personality, 22,* 474–495.

Malamuth, N. M. (1988c). Research on "Violent Erotica": A reply. *Journal of Sex Research, 24,* 340–348.

Malamuth, N. M. (1989a). The attraction to sexual aggression scale: Part one. *Journal of Sex Research, 26,* 26–49.

Malamuth, N. M. (1989b). The attraction to sexual aggression scale: Part two. *Journal of Sex Research, 26,* 324–354.

Malamuth, N. M., & Briere, J. (1986). Sexual violence in the media: Indirect effects on aggression against women. *Journal of Social Issues, 42,* 75–92.

Malamuth, N. M., & Ceniti, J. (1986). Repeated exposure to violent and nonviolent pornography: Likelihood of raping ratings and laboratory aggression against women. *Aggressive Behavior, 12,* 129–137.

Malamuth, N. M., Check, J. V. P., & Briere, J. (1986). Sexual arousal in response to aggression: Ideological, aggressive and sexual correlates. *Journal of Personality and Social Psychology, 50,* 330–340.

Malamuth, N. M., Haber, S., & Feshbach, S. (1980). Testing hypotheses regarding rape: Exposure to sexual violence, sex differences, and the "normality" of rapists. *Journal of Research in Personality, 14,* 121–137.

Murphy, W. P., Coleman, E. M., & Haynes, M. R. (1986). Factors related to coercive sexual behavior in a nonclinical sample of males. *Violence and Victims, 1,* 255–278.

Nelson, P. A. (1979). *Personality, sexual function, and sexual behavior: An experiment in methodology.* Unpublished doctoral dissertation, University of Florida.

Paternoster, R. (1989). Decisions to participate in and desist from four types of common delinquency: Deterrence and the rational choice perspective. *Law and Society Review, 23,* 7–40.

Petty, G. M., & Dawson, B. (1989). Sexual aggression in normal men: Incidence, beliefs, and personality characteristics. *Personality and Individual Differences, 10,* 355–362.

Pryor, P. S. (1987). Sexual harassment proclivities in men. *Sex Roles, 17,* 269–289.

Pryor, J. B., & Stoller, L. M. (1989). *Evidence for a sexuality/dominance schema in men who are high in the likelihood to sexually harass.* Unpublished manuscript.

Russell, D. E. H. (1984). *Sexual exploitation: Rape, child sexual abuse and workplace harassment.* Beverly Hills, CA: Sage.

Shields, W. M., & Shields, L. M. (1983). Forcible rape: An evolutionary perspective. *Ethology and Sociobiology, 4,* 115–136.

Stille, R. G. (1984). *Rape myth acceptance and hostility toward women: Antecedents, prediction of rape proclivity, and effects on perception of a realistic rape portrayal.* Unpublished doctoral dissertation, University of Manitoba, Canada.

Thornhill, R., & Thornhill, N. W. (1990). *The evolutionary psychology of human rape.* Unpublished manuscript.

Tieger, T. (1981). Self-rated likelihood of raping and the social perception of rape. *Journal of Research in Personality, 15,* 147–158.

Weir, J. A., & Branscombe, N. R. (1989). *Discriminating between males who do and do not possess a proclivity for sexual aggression.* Unpublished manuscript.

Weis, K., & Borges, S. S. (1973). Victimology and rape: The case of the legitimate victim. *Issues in Criminology, 8,* 71–115.

PART 7

Effects of
Acquaintance Rape

CHAPTER 16

The Psychological Impact of Stranger versus Nonstranger Rape on Victims' Recovery*

BONNIE L. KATZ, PhD

Despite the increasing focus on acquaintance rape in the past decade, little progress has been made in actually demonstrating the effects of prerape familiarity on the victim. A review of the literature (Burt & Katz, 1985; Katz, 1987) revealed almost no agreement on this issue. Several studies used this variable to describe the sample but did not report its effects on the outcomes measured (Resick, Calhoun, Atkeson, & Ellis, 1981). Some authors argued strongly that the overall trauma is greater for victims of stranger rapes (Queens Bench, 1975; Ruch & Chandler, 1983); others argued the same for victims of non-stranger rapes (Katz & Mazur, 1979; Shore, Baum, & Sales, 1980). At the same time, other researchers found no significant stranger-nonstranger differences on their measures of psychiatric symptomatology (Veronen & Kilpatrick, 1983). Some findings that have not been directly contradicted by other studies are that stranger rapes yield more fear, more depression, and more fatigue (Ellis, Atkeson, & Calhoun, 1981), less anger (Hassell, 1981), less impaired social functioning (Queens Bench, 1975), and greater impairment of hetero-sexual relationships (McCahill, Meyer, & Fischman, 1979). The expectation has been stated that nonstranger rapes would yield more difficulties with trust (Burgess & Holmstrom, 1979b), although no actual data were reported to support this.

The absence of research findings of consistent differences due to familiarity is itself at odds both with the prevalent clinical impression of important stranger–nonstranger differences and with theoretical arguments that such a difference should exist. The very nature of rape leads the victim's prerape

* The data in this study were collected as part of a larger research project on the effects of counseling interventions and patterns of recovery from rape (supported by National Institutes of Mental Health grant #1 RO1 MH38337 to Martha R. Burt, and conducted at The Urban Institute, Washington, DC).

familiarity with the rapist to play an integral role in determining rape's psychological consequences. Rape is an act of power and control, intended by the rapist to humiliate the victim. Rape does, however, get acted out via sexual intercourse, which in different circumstances is the epitome of inter-personal intimacy. It seems only reasonable to expect that the subjective experience of undergoing a violent and shocking attack which uses sexual means for an aggressive end would be affected by different degrees of famil-iarity of the victim with the perpetrator. Specifically, it could be argued that rape by someone familiar is a more personal and less random event than rape by a stranger. Also, unlike rape by a stranger, it involves a betrayal of trust. The victim–offender relationship also has important implications for the victim's experience because of its effects on others' responses to her. Social psychologists' research in this area confirms the importance of the victim–rapist relationship for subsequent perceptions of the victim's credibility and legitimacy as a victim (Burt & Albin, 1981).

Another important factor to consider in the recovery process is the effect of the passage of time. During the past 10 years, a few studies have collected and published data that clearly showed that for a sizable minority of women, "recovery" is not complete even after as many as six years have elapsed (Burgess & Holmstrom, 1979a, b; Ellis et al., 1981). Still, most of the data collected in rape studies focus primarily on functioning in the first year postrape (Kilpatrick & Veronen, 1983). This relatively short-term focus is at odds with the author's understanding of rape and its impact. Rape is seen by the author as being tremendously disruptive for the victim for at least several months, during which time she must focus all of her psychological and physi-cal energy on simply surviving emotionally. Only at the point where she is functioning more normally (for her) and regaining minimal equilibrium would the victim be able to consciously experience and actively deal with the feelings and thoughts she has about the rape. Differences in the recovery process for women raped by men with varying degrees of familiarity would be likely to become apparent only once the initial, overwhelming distress had begun to abate. This chapter outlines a model of recovery from rape and then describes in detail one research project that studied recovery. In this study, the effects of prerape familiarity were examined, alone and in conjunction with the effects of time elapsed postrape. The results of the study and their implications are discussed.

CONCEPTUALIZING RECOVERY AND THE EFFECTS OF FAMILIARITY

The theoretical understanding of rape in which this study is grounded grows out of the feminist analyses developed in the mid-1970s (Brownmiller, 1975; Clark & Lewis, 1977; Medea & Thompson, 1974; Russell, 1974). Rape is a phenomenon of violence that is only partially the result of individual men aggressing against individual women for reasons specific to the particular circumstances. It is also an extreme exaggeration of the prescribed and accepted sexual and social roles played by women and men (see Malamuth, Haber, & Feshbach, 1980, for empirical support for this statement). Its prevalence is a reflection of the extent to which rape is tolerated by society.

The rape experience has been described as involving a total loss of control over one's life, one's body, and the course of events. Most women experience a rape as a violation and as being hostile and violent even when it is not described by the victim as brutal. Rape is a degrading and humiliating experience. It also comes as a shock, destroying an individual's ability to maintain the important illusion of personal safety or invulnerability, and threatening many assumptions and beliefs which the individual may have had about herself and the world around her. It may be similar to other life crises in terms of loss of control, loss of invulnerability, and loss of self-worth (Taylor, 1983, discussed these three phenomena as responses to a variety of threatening life events). These losses and the process of dealing with them seem to be similar to the grieving process involved in mourning the loss of a loved one.

According to the model presented by Stewart (1982), recovery from a traumatic event involves several phases. Initial helplessness and dependence give way to attempts to control the situation. Mastering or understanding the event forms the basis for integrating the event and its effects into the fabric of one's personality and life experience. The self-evaluation required for this mastery and integration is the domain in which recovery from the two types of rape probably differs the most. Rape by someone familiar is an even more personal attack than is rape by a stranger. It is a traumatic victimization, but in a context that is otherwise associated with safety and privacy and in which the woman specifically chose to be with the rapist. Rape by a total stranger is also traumatic and certainly a violation of personal safety and body integrity. However, by definition it involves no prior interaction with the rapist, and therefore does not necessarily call into question the woman's own behavior, judgment, and social competence.

Women may already struggle with conflicts surrounding their roles in social relationships. Object relations theorists (Eichenbaum & Orbach, 1983) have posited that women learn that they are expected to be trusting and caretaking in relation to men, and at the same time to be dependent on men. Social and psychological forces push a woman to be attached to a man as a source of identity and also for protection against the outside world. Equally powerful, however, are the clear societal messages to women about the potential danger that men present. Women learn that it is their responsibility to avoid rape, presumably by staying away from strangers, dark alleys, and unfamiliar settings, and by relying on the men (or man) they trust (or feel close to) for protection.

A woman raped by a man she knows may have to contend with a sense of not being able to trust herself and her own judgment. She is likely to feel that she was following, as well as she knew how, the unwritten rules of safety, which are supposed to work; her conclusion will probably be that there was something wrong with how she followed them. Only a short step further is the inference that there was/is something wrong with her. If her own internal "security check" of the man who raped her had categorized him as "okay," trustworthy, and safe to be with, then she could easily conclude that her skills for perception and evaluation are lacking. In addition, the rape could be expected to activate whatever conflicts the woman already experiences regarding herself in social relationships.

Perceiving a man as being familiar, regardless of the actual relationship, places a woman in a vulnerable position in that the perception brings into effect powerful social scripts for relationships, as opposed to norms for interacting with strangers. For a woman, relationship scripts include being nice. She might ignore her own suspicions in deference to such a script, thinking: "I don't want to make him feel bad by letting him know I have doubts or am wary of him, even though I'm feeling uncomfortable or that something is not quite right." Another example of such thoughts is: "He seems like a nice guy, and maybe it would be safer to let him take me home than to take the bus at this hour of night (after all, the streets are dangerous)."

A woman raped by a stranger experiences the violence and humiliation of the attack, but other elements of the rape experience are different from those of a nonstranger rape. It is probably easier for her to see her own victimization as a more random and less personal event. She may blame herself for having been in a vulnerable situation (for example, on a street that she normally avoided, or in her home but without locks on the windows, or alone at her office), but there are fewer characteristics of the assault that bring her identity as a social being into question. She certainly may feel that the rape fuels psychological conflict, but the stranger rapist's selection of her as a victim generally does not raise doubts (either her own or others') about her competence to function in relationships. She is likely to find herself doubting that there is a just order in the world and feeling afraid of places and situations that are reminiscent of the attack.

Psychological Conflict in Recovery from Rape

Given that both rape and personality construction are rooted in a social context and in socially prescribed sex roles, the impact of and recovery from rape can be expected to involve a reshuffling of personality dimensions as they relate to the social context (Burt & Katz, 1988). This creates many conflicts, because recovering may require shifts that run counter to the very things by which women have learned to define themselves. For example, women's performance of a caretaking/nurturing role is a primary source of approval from self and others. Women also commonly have trouble feeling that their own needs are legitimate or that they deserve attention. It could be quite overwhelming to be confronted suddenly with one's own intense neediness and wish for nurturance from others after a rape when one's role in life is to take care of others and to satisfy others' needs before one's own. The conflict is compounded for many women when they find themselves surrounded after a rape by loved ones who "fall apart" and expect to be reassured by the victim herself. These issues comprise just a few of the important dimensions of a woman's self-concept. Resolving and mastering these conflicts are critical to the recovery process and may set the stage for changes in self-concept as well.

Although this theoretical formulation points to the existence of differences in the experiences of women raped by strangers versus by men they knew, the research literature has not successfully tapped these differences in rape impact and recovery. The study described below was designed to try to remedy this disparity, primarily by basing the choice of variables on this analysis of recovery. (See Burt & Katz, 1987, for a more extensive discussion of recovery.)

THE CURRENT STUDY

The study was designed to address the specific question of whether differences do, in fact, exist between the impact of, and the course of recovery following, rape by a stranger versus rape by someone familiar. The type of relationship, prerape trust levels, and prerape closeness levels were each considered as indicators of familiarity. Based on information provided by study participants, prerape relationships were categorized by the researchers along the following continuum: Stranger, Acquaintance, Close Friend, and Intimate. Levels of prerape trust and closeness were based on participants' own ratings of how close they were with the rapist, and of how much they trusted him, before the rape. Time elapsed since the rape was also selected as an independent variable.

Outcome Measures

Outcomes chosen to represent rape impact and recovery were self-concept, completeness of recovery, self-blame, and psychiatric symptoms.

Self-Concept

A victim may, out of the necessity of coping with the crisis of the rape, focus on issues central to her self-concept and to her feminine identity. In reevaluating herself and her situation in life as part of the process of understanding her own experience, she might have an opportunity to begin to see herself in a different light than she did before the rape. The self-concept score was based on scores on three measures tapping different aspects of self-concept: the Rosenberg Self-Esteem Scale (Rosenberg, 1965), the Romantic Self-Image Scale (Estep, Burt, & Milligan, 1977), and the How I See Myself Now Scale (Burt & Katz, 1987) developed for this study.

Recovery Ratings

Previous researchers typically measured extent of recovery by assessing the relative presence or absence of distressing symptoms, based on their assumption that the disappearance of symptoms is indicative of recovery. However, recovery from rape is actually a complex process that goes beyond symptomatology. Victims' self-assessments of their own recovery were seen as an important source of information about the subjective experience of rape and the process of recovery from it. Accordingly, extent of recovery from the rape was measured with the question: "Given your conception of recovery, how completely would you say you had recovered?" Responses were ratings on a seven-point scale, from "Not at all recovered" to "Completely recovered."

Self-Blame

The phenomenon of self-blame following rape has been reported frequently in both clinical and research contexts. Janoff-Bulman (1979, 1982) argued that certain types of self-blame are actually beneficial in recovering from a rape, but a few recent papers presented contradictory results (Meyer & Taylor, 1986; Katz & Burt, 1988). Self-blame of all types has been shown to be associated with relatively high distress levels and has emerged as one of the clear themes of the postrape experience. Self-blame was measured in this study using the participant's response to an interview question asking her to divide 100% of the blame for the rape among the rapist, society, herself, and elsewhere, based on her feelings right after the rape.

Symptoms

Past rape recovery research measured functioning largely in terms of psychiatric symptomatology, with a focus on the affects of fear, anxiety, and depression. We included these widely used symptom outcomes in the current study to facilitate comparison of the results with those obtained in other studies. Level of psychological distress and the nature of affective responses ("Symptoms") were measured using the Profile of Mood States (McNair, Lorr, & Droppelman, 1971), the Impact of Events Scale (Horowitz, Wilner, & Alvarez, 1979), the Modified Fear Survey (Resick, Veronen, Kilpatrick, Calhoun, & Atkeson, 1984), and the Brief Symptom Inventory (Derogatis & Spencer, 1982). Scores on these measures were statistically combined into a single score representing the underlying dimension of psychological distress. (For a more detailed discussion of the methods used to derive this and other outcome scores, see Katz & Burt, 1988.)

Research Hypotheses

The major hypothesis of the study posited that increasing rapist–victim familiarity would be associated with higher levels of self-blame and with slower recovery and less positive self-concept. In addition, it was hypothesized that increased time elapsed since the rape would be associated with lower self-blame, more complete recovery, fewer symptoms, and more positive self-concept. Furthermore, an interaction between time and familiarity was expected: victims of nonstrangers were expected to initially report less positive self-concept and less complete recovery than victims of strangers, but, over time, the victims of nonstrangers were expected to feel more positively about themselves and more completely recovered than the strangers' victims.

METHODS

Sample Characteristics and Participant Referral

Participants for this study were referred by five Washington (DC) area rape crisis centers and were also recruited using media advertisements. Women were included in the study if they had been raped, if they were over the age of 17 at the time of the rape for which they came to the crisis center, if they had no known history of father–daughter or repeated incest, if the rape had occurred at least six months prior to the interview, and if they had no physical handicap that would prevent them from being interviewed with the standard protocol. Marital rapes were excluded.

The final sample consisted of 87 women with a broad range of demographic characteristics, though by no means in an even distribution (see Table 16.1 for sample characteristics for the 87 participants). Women were ages 18 to 55 when raped, but 55% were ages 18 to 25. Although anywhere from six months to 15 years had elapsed since the rape, 56% of the women had been assaulted 6 months to 3 years prior to the interview. Other characteristics of the sample were as follows: race (77% were white); prerape psychological functioning (68% had no previous history of severe disturbance); socioeconomic status (on a six-point scale, 40% identified themselves as middle class); police report of rape (76% had reported); number of assailants (89% had only one); number of sexual assault experiences (80% had only one); and relationship with the rapist (55% were total strangers).

Data were collected from January through June, 1985, using both written, self-report questionnaires and in-person, semistructured interviews. All participants were paid $20.00. At the end of the interview, participants always had a chance to ask the interviewer questions.

RESULTS AND DISCUSSION*

First we addressed the question of whether "Strangers" (women raped by total strangers) would have different postrape experiences than

---

* For a more complete and technical description of the data reduction and analysis, see Katz (1987).

TABLE 16.1.   Selected Characteristics of Study Sample

Characteristic		Number of Participants	Percent of Participants
Relationship type	Total stranger	48	55%
	Just met	9	10
	Known	7	8
	Solid acquaintance	13	15
	Close friend	5	6
	Ex-boyfriend	4	5
	Current boyfriend	1	1
Time since rape	6–18 months	28	32%
	1½ to 3 years	21	24
	3½ to 5 years	21	24
	5½ to 9 years	10	12
	9½ to 15½ years	7	8
Socioeconomic status	Lower class	4	5%
	Working class	11	13
	Lower middle class	23	26
	Middle class	35	40
	Upper middle class	13	15
	Upper class	1	1
Prerape psychiatric distress	No suicide attempt, no hospitalization	59	68%
	Suicidal, ideation alone	14	16
	Suicide attempt, no hospitalization	7	8
	Psychiatric hospitalization	7	8
Age at time of assault	18–20	15	17%
	21–25	33	38
	26–30	13	15
	31–35	7	8
	36–40	11	13
	41–50	7	8
	over 50	1	1
Race	Black	18	21%
	White	67	77
	Asian	2	2
Social support	No one told	5	6%
	All responses negative	5	6
	Some negative, some positive	48	55
	All responses positive	29	33
Hours of counseling	None	12	14%
	1–5 hours	23	26
	6–20 hours	33	38
	21–50 hours	15	22
	over 90 hours	4	5
Police report	No	21	24%
	Yes	66	76
Number of rapes	One	70	80%
	Two	14	16
	Three or four	3	4
Number of assailants in indexed rape	One	77	89%
	Two	9	10
	Three	1	1

"Nonstrangers" (women raped by nonstrangers). We found that these two groups of women differed significantly in their responses to three of the four measures of rape effects. The Strangers blamed themselves less for the rape, saw themselves in a more positive light, and felt more completely recovered from the rape than did the Nonstrangers. In contrast, these two groups did not display markedly different levels of psychological distress.

Next we compared responses of victims who had varying levels of prerape familiarity with their rapists: Total Strangers, Acquaintances, Friends, and Intimate Others. Women raped by total strangers had the most positive self-concept; women raped by acquaintances had the least positive self-concept. The group of women raped by strangers blamed themselves less for the rape than did the women in the other groups; the women raped by friends blamed themselves more for the rape than did the other women. No significant differences were found among these groups for Recovery or Symptoms.

Women who were raped by a known man were grouped according to how much they had trusted the rapist and how close they had felt to him prior to the rape. These groups were found to differ in the extent to which they blamed themselves for the rape. Women who knew their rapists but had placed little trust in them blamed themselves most for the rape; women raped by strangers blamed themselves least. Different levels of prerape trust were also found to affect Self-concept: women who had had substantial trust in their rapists exhibited the least positive self-concepts; women who were raped by strangers showed the most positive self-concepts. Increasing levels of prerape closeness with the rapist were associated with increasing self-blame: the group of women raped by strangers blamed themselves the least for the rape and the group of women who had felt closest to the rapist blamed themselves the most.

To explore the effects of the passage of time on recovery from rape, the women were divided into four groups: those who were ½ to 1½ years postrape, 1½ to 3 years postrape, 3 to 5 years postrape, and more than 5 years postrape, respectively. Women who were 1½ to 3 years postrape assigned significantly less blame (about 9%) to themselves right after the rape than did any of the other groups. It is interesting to note that the other groups of women reported self-blame levels that were very close to one another (between 32% and 36%), even with widely disparate amounts of time since the rape (the range was from ½ year to 14 years). Despite the initial expectation that all four outcomes would show differences as a function of time postrape, such differences were not found for Self-concept, Recovery, or Symptoms.

The differences between women in the Stranger and Nonstranger groups were also examined as a function of how long ago the rape had occurred (see Figures 16.1–16.3). This analysis revealed that Self-blame levels of Nonstrangers were much more affected by the passage of time than were those of Strangers. Among Nonstrangers, the group of women raped most recently (6 to 18 months prior to the study) reported the most postrape self-blame;

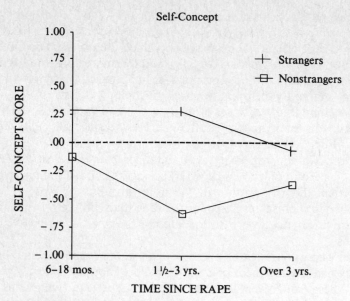

Figure 16.1.   Time by relationship.

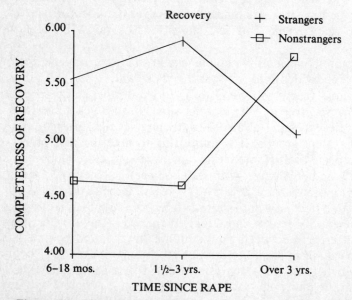

Figure 16.2.   Time by relationship.

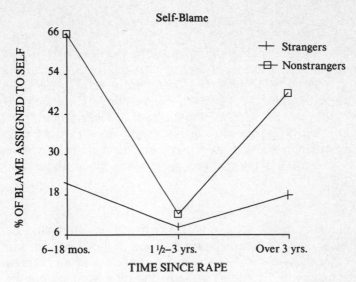

Figure 16.3. Time by relationship.

women raped 18 months to 3 years prior to the study reported the least postrape self-blame. In contrast, the reported self-blame of the Strangers did not change dramatically as a function of time postrape.

The pattern of Stranger versus Nonstranger differences on Recovery ratings was also found to be affected by the amount of time passed since the rape. Among the women 3 years or less postrape, the Nonstrangers rated themselves as less recovered than did the Strangers. In contrast, among women who were more than 3 years postrape, the Nonstrangers rated themselves as *more* recovered than did the Strangers. Similarly, among Nonstrangers, the recovery ratings of the group of women more than 3 years postrape were significantly higher than those of the groups of women 3 years or less postrape. At the same time, the Strangers' recovery ratings were significantly *lower* for the group of women more than 3 years postrape than they were for the group of women 18 months to 3 years postrape.

Further analysis was done to explore the extent to which the obtained results were affected by factors not already considered. Specifically, it was suspected that prerape mental health and current socioeconomic status might have had systematic effects on the measured outcomes. The presence of more severe prerape psychiatric difficulties was found to be associated with less positive self-concept and with less complete recovery from the rape. Higher socioeconomic status (SES) was correlated with more positive self-concept and with less complete postrape recovery. However, this analysis revealed that, in general, the relationship, time, trust, and closeness effects went beyond the effects that they shared with these other determinants.

UNDERSTANDING THE RESULTS

The results of this study are striking for their clear demonstration of systematic differences in the course of postrape psychological recovery following stranger versus nonstranger rape. The findings are consistent with the theoretical formulation of recovery presented above. Contrasting courses of recovery were understood as stemming from differences in the experience of the rape itself. The question arises as to why clear and theoretically consistent Stranger/Nonstranger differences *did* emerge in this particular study. There are several points to consider in explaining these results.

Time

Perhaps the most important distinction between this study and most previous ones was the theoretically based decision to focus only on women who had been raped *at least six months* prior to the interview. It seemed clear that a rape experience would so globally disrupt a woman's life that regardless of the identity of her rapist, her life would be in an uproar for the first several weeks and even months. Again, the theoretical assumption made here was that the real work of recovery begins only when the symptoms begin to subside and the woman can resume a more normal level of psychological functioning. The real differences that exist emerge later in the course of the recovery; the first several months following a rape are more similar than different for these two types of victims.

Relationship, Trust, and Closeness

Although these three variables representing prerape familiarity were highly related to one another, the pattern of their statistical effects on the outcome measures confirmed that they tapped somewhat distinct aspects of prerape familiarity. Closeness had the smallest effect of the three variables on Self-concept, and Trust was the only one of the familiarity variables to have a significant effect on Symptoms.

For Self-blame and Self-concept, at least, the type of prerape relationship may be less important in determining rape impact than the extent to which feelings of trust and closeness were a part of that relationship. As the trust and closeness ratings in this study showed, a woman might trust a man and even feel somewhat close to him without knowing him very well or for very long. Even barely known men might be perceived as familiar and be trusted because of some common link or shared experience. Conversely, a woman may know a man well, or even intimately, and not trust him. How a woman *feels* about a relationship, how much her own identity is tied to the relationship, and how vulnerable she has chosen to be in it, may all be more important elements than *type* of relationship per se in determining how she experiences the rape and its aftermath. This distinction may explain why, on some of the outcomes measured here, women raped by intimates tended to score more like women raped by strangers than they did like women raped by acquaintances or friends. It is certainly feasible that in many intimate relationships (particularly those that end in a rape), there is actually very little trust.

While the high correlation of Relationship with Trust and with Closeness makes it, more generally, a reasonably good estimate of familiarity, it is clear that adding these components as additional variables made important contributions to understanding the effects of familiarity on recovery. It will be critical for future researchers to continue to explore the interwoven roles of these dimensions and to identify others that might have an impact on the process of recovery from rape.

Measuring Recovery from Rape

In previous studies, the choice of symptom-focused measures also contributed to the failure to find Stranger/Nonstranger differences in rape impact. In going beyond the standard symptom measures, this study asked questions that reflected current theoretical formulations of the impact of rape and of the process of recovery. Here, the reliance on women's own evaluations of their recovery progress and extent of self-blame, and the construction of a self-concept measure specifically designed to assess adult women, both proved to be effective strategies for studying the role of pre-rape relationship in the recovery process. The use of a general recovery rating together with more specific measures was also important, in that it allowed for the emergence of new patterns of rape impact and for victim-generated assessments of recovery. It is critical for future researchers in this area to consider carefully what outcome measures can most successfully tap the full range of issues involved in the process of recovery.

Alternative Explanations

Although the findings of this study strongly suggested that prerape familiarity affects rape recovery, the possibility exists that some of the results obtained were due to extraneous sources. Sampling biases, differences in self-selection criteria for women in the different familiarity or time categories, or interviewer expectations could all have had systematic effects on the measured outcomes. It is important also to consider the possibility that inherent personality differences existed between the Strangers versus the Nonstrangers, which would have led the Nonstrangers to look more distressed on the measured outcomes even without having been raped. Although it is unfortunate that individual women are put in the position of protecting themselves from potential sexual assault, the need for competence in this area is a reality. There are many psychological strengths upon which emotional and physical self-protection depends. When interacting with a man who is willing to rape, these same self-protection skills may allow a woman to prevent herself from being raped. There is reason to believe that some women are more able than others to escape being raped by a known man because of their skills for accurately perceiving threatening situations and for taking effective action to end such situations.

This is not to imply that nonstranger rapes are in any way the victim's fault, or that she is any more responsible for having caused the rape than is a woman who is randomly attacked by a total stranger. Personality structure and functioning could, however, make some women more vulnerable than others to this type of rape. Women who lack clear psychological boundaries, who have difficulty in accurately reading social messages from others because of distortions introduced by their own psyches, who feel that they do not deserve to be treated with respect and autonomy, who are unassertive and poor at setting limits, or who see themselves in a negative light, may be more vulnerable to sexual victimization.

These personality characteristics are also likely to be associated with relatively negative self-concepts, high levels of self-blame, slower recovery from the rape, and high levels of psychiatric symptomatology. It is evident that these are indeed the same characteristics found in the Nonstrangers in this study; thus, the inherent personality characteristics of the two groups of women might account for some portion of the differences that were attributed to the contrasting types of rape experiences. However, it is interesting to note that in this study one of the outcomes, Self-blame, was unrelated to a prerape estimate of psychological distress. The strong statistical effects on Self-blame, found for Relationship, Trust, Closeness, and Time even after prerape psychological distress was accounted for, suggest that preexisting personality traits do not explain all of the observed Stranger–Nonstranger differences.

The results of this study also lend empirical support to the theoretical argument that self-blame is a key issue for rape victims, and that it is central particularly to the differences between Nonstrangers and Strangers. The weak associations found between the Self-blame measure and indicators of prerape psychosocial adaptation also make Self-blame a relatively reliable outcome to be used in future studies of rape impact where prerape factors cannot be controlled for statistically.

Implications of the Study

The results of the study will provide clinicians working with women recovering from rape with more understanding of the likely course of recovery and with better insight into the differences between stranger and nonstranger victims. By providing documentation of the long-term and real effects of rape by someone known, the findings of this study have important implications for the criminal justice system and its bias against women raped by men known to them. It will be important to make information such as this available to judges and juries who base criminal sentencing, victim compensation, and civil lawsuit awards on the crime's impact on the victim. The findings that women raped by nonstrangers are often *more* distressed, and that they take longer to feel recovered, go a long way toward establishing acquaintance rape as a crime with serious consequences for its victims.

Another important implication of this study's findings lies in the question of whether a woman can ever really recover from a rape. About half of the women in this sample felt completely or nearly completely recovered at the time they participated in the study. Feeling recovered did not necessarily preclude feeling that the rape still affected one's life, whether in terms of lasting elevated levels of fear or suspiciousness (possibly a realistic and pragmatic world view that the rape forced them to confront), or in terms of life changes (e.g., moves, job changes) or personal changes (e.g., learning self-defense and feeling more self-confident) that grew out of efforts to recover from the rape. The experiences and responses of women in this sample, then, clearly suggest that although rape may have lifelong effects, it is also possible to feel recovered from it.

Growth Outcomes of Recovery

One of the key findings of this study was the fact that patterns of recovery over time differed for Strangers versus Nonstrangers. The assertion that the tasks of recovery following these two types of rape differ gained support from the observed increases in Nonstrangers' positive self-concepts and recovery ratings for the group of women longest postrape, with no parallel increase for Strangers. The devastatingly personal nature of rape by a nonstranger may lead to more initial distress (here, as reflected in relatively less positive self-concept), but the process of self-evaluation that follows also could allow for a conscious reorganization that includes elements of psychological growth. Although this potential for rebuilding seems likely for both types of rape, the results of this study show evidence of it only in the group of women raped by nonstrangers. It is probable that women raped by strangers would focus their recovery work more on concerns regarding the unpredictability and danger in the world around them—still allowing for change and growth, but in somewhat different areas than were measured here.

Caution must be taken not to begin describing rape as a beneficial experience, or as being "good for women," but at the same time, the potentially productive and growth-promoting aspects of the recovery process should not be overlooked. Several researchers have commented on this aspect of recovery from rape, with observations of some "positive" outcomes (Burgess & Holmstrom, 1979b). Moreover, some investigators have reported being impressed with the ability of so many women to cope with the rape experience and of some women to manage to effect positive, growth-producing changes as a result of this coping effort (Nadelson & Nortman, 1984; Williams & Holmes, 1981). The first presentation in the scholarly literature of possible models for how a rape experience may lead to positive life change was in a 1983 chapter by Veronen and Kilpatrick. Still, such changes have not been the focus of subsequent research on rape recovery, though they have certainly been addressed in research on other populations.

Although it may be possible for such research to be misused and misinterpreted to argue that rape is a good experience for women, it would be a disservice to rape victims to avoid further study of growth outcomes following rape. Research on the factors associated with such outcomes and increased understanding of how they come about would be extremely valuable contributions to clinical knowledge about treatment following rape. If the nature of the positive changes that grow out of coping with rape—and their relationship to negative effects of rape—were better understood, then clinical approaches for facilitating growth and minimizing debilitating effects could be developed.

DIRECTIONS FOR FUTURE RESEARCH

Research on rape impact and recovery poses many challenges, one of which lies in the domain of sample recruitment and retention. This study operated within the same constraints as previous studies have, and its results led to several specific suggestions for future studies.

The existence of differences between women raped by strangers versus nonstrangers has been fairly well established, as has the fact that differences among types of nonstranger rapes also exist. To gain a clearer picture of the variations among the groups of women who knew their rapists but with differing levels of familiarity, a study might focus only on women who are victims of known rapists. A control group of women raped by strangers could be used for comparison, but the need is for larger numbers of victims who had each of the types and components of prerape relationship with their rapists.

One of the challenges in doing research on rape recovery is the difficulty of obtaining large participant samples. It is critical for researchers to continue to find ways to recruit larger samples so that more statistical methods can be used—with greater confidence. At the same time, it will be important not to lose sight of the value of qualitative data. Women who have been raped, speaking in their own words, still hold answers to many questions. Examining themes in women's descriptions of their recovery, in their feelings about themselves or about the rape, could shed light, for example, on the unanswered question from this study of why women who were raped by an intimate other responded more like victims of stranger rape than they did like women raped by friends.

While this study found strong differences between groups of women who were different lengths of time postrape, its design allowed only for inference regarding the differences that might be found in any individual woman as she recovers over time after a rape. Here, retrospective data were used to gather prerape information about women's lives and personalities, and also to reconstruct how they had felt at given points in time postrape. It is important for many of the questions asked here to be examined again using prospective data collection, following participants as they traverse the recovery process. The information such a study would provide could serve to validate (or invalidate) the use of the much more common (and more easily obtainable) retrospective data that comprise the bulk of research in this area.

The problem of assessing the role of prerape personality or other prerape factors in eventual rape impact would be solved only through a massive effort to follow a large population of women over several years and then to compare the women who eventually become rape victims with those who do not. Although such a study would be difficult and costly to implement, this methodology could provide definitive answers to many of the questions only partially addressed in any study that begins at the time of the rape. Furthermore, such an investigation would yield rich data on the psychology of adult women that could provide a much needed empirical context for the growing understanding of rape and its impact.

CONCLUSIONS

The major conclusion of this study is that women raped by nonstrangers follow a different path toward recovery than do women raped by strangers. Women raped by men they knew attribute more blame for the rape to themselves, see themselves in a less positive light, and tend to have higher levels of psychological distress. Women raped by strangers also appear to feel recovered sooner than women raped by nonstrangers. The results of this study also underline the central role of the relationship components of trust and closeness as determinants of rape impact and recovery.

It is unclear to what extent preexisting personality characteristics rather than some element of the rapes per se account for these differences. Regardless of the source of the differences, however, it is clear that women in these two groups do not have identical tasks to accomplish in their efforts to recover. Clinicians, researchers, and criminal justice system personnel could all benefit from making this distinction among victims of different types of rape. While taking care to avoid stereotyping victims, this information could enhance their ability to focus on the particular set of issues most likely to be of concern to the individual victims with whom they are working. More research is needed to elaborate fully the differences and the similarities among women raped by men with varying degrees of prerape familiarity, but this study has taken an important first step in establishing that some such differences do exist.

REFERENCES

Brownmiller, S. (1975). *Against our will: Men, women, and rape.* New York: Simon & Schuster.

Burgess, A. W., & Holmstrom, L. L. (1979a). Adaptive strategies and recovery from rape. *American Journal of Psychiatry, 136,* 1278–1282.

Burgess, A. W., & Holmstrom, L. L. (1979b). *Rape: Crisis and recovery.* Englewood Cliffs, NJ: Prentice-Hall.

Burt, M. R., & Albin, R. (1981). Rape myths, rape definitions, and probability of conviction. *Journal of Applied Social Psychology, 11,* 212–230.

Burt, M. R., & Katz, B. L. (1985). Rape, robbery, and burglary: Responses to actual and feared criminal victimization, with special emphasis on women and the elderly. *Victimology, 10,* 325–358.

Burt, M. R., & Katz, B. L. (1987). Dimensions of recovery from rape: Focus on growth outcomes. *Journal of Interpersonal Violence, 2,* 57–81.

Burt, M. R., & Katz, B. L. (1988). Coping strategies and recovery from rape. In R. A. Prentky & V. L. Quinsey (Eds.), *Human sexual aggression: Current perspectives,* New York: The New York Academy of Sciences.

Clark, L. M. G., & Lewis, D. J. (1977). *Rape: The price of coercive sexuality.* Toronto: Canadian Women's Educational Press.

Derogatis, L. R., & Spencer, P. M. (1982). *The brief symptom inventory administration, scoring, and procedures manual—I.* Baltimore: Clinical Psychometric Research.

Eichenbaum, L., & Orbach, S. (1983). *Understanding women: A feminist psychoanalytic approach.* New York: Basic Books.

Ellis, E. M., Atkeson, B. M., & Calhoun, K. S. (1981). An assessment of long-term reaction to rape. *Journal of Abnormal Psychology, 90,* 263–266.

Estep, R., Burt, M. R., & Milligan, H. (1977). The socialization of sexual identity. *Journal of Marriage and the Family, 2,* 99–112.

Hassell, R. (1981, March). *The effects of victim–rapist relationship on recovery from rape.* Paper presented at national conference of Association for Women in Psychology, Boston.

Horowitz, M. J., Wilner, N., & Alvarez, W. (1979). Impact of event scale: A measure of subjective stress. *Psychosomatic Medicine, 41,* 209–218.

Janoff-Bulman, R. (1979). Characterological versus behavioral self-blame: Inquiries into depression and blame. *Journal of Personality and Social Psychology, 37,* 1798–1809.

Janoff-Bulman, R. (1982). Esteem and control bases of blame: "Adaptive" strategies for victims versus observers. *Journal of Personality, 50,* 180–192.

Katz, B. L. (1987). *Prerape victim–rapist familiarity and recovery from rape: Psychological consequences.* Unpublished doctoral dissertation, Boston University.

Katz, B. L., & Burt, M. R. (1988). Self-blame in recovery from rape: Help or hindrance? In A. W. Burgess (Ed.), *Rape and sexual assault* (Vol. II, pp. 191–212). New York: Garland.

Katz, S., & Mazur, M. A. (1979). *Understanding the rape victim: A synthesis of research findings.* New York: Wiley.

Kilpatrick, D. G., & Veronen, L. J. (1983). Treatment for rape-related problems: Crisis intervention is not enough. In L. Cohen, W. Claiborn, & G. Specter (Eds.), *Crisis intervention.* New York: Human Services Press.

Malamuth, N. M., Haber, S., & Feshbach, S. (1980). Testing hypotheses regarding rape: Exposure to sexual violence, sex differences, and the "normality" of rapists. *Journal of Research in Personality, 14,* 121–137.

McCahill, T. W., Meyer, L. C., & Fischman, A. M. (1979). *The aftermath of rape.* Lexington, MA: Lexington Books.

McNair, D., Lorr, M., & Droppleman, L. (1971). *Manual, profile of mood states.* San Diego: Educational & Industrial Testing Service.

Medea, A., & Thompson, K. (1974). *Against rape.* New York: Farrar, Straus & Giroux.

Meyer, C. B. & Taylor, S. E. (1986). Adjustment to rape. *Journal of Personality and Social Psychology, 50,* 1226–1234.

Nadelson, C. C., & Nortman, M. T. (1984). Psychodynamics of sexual assault experiences. In I. R. Stuart & J. G. Greer (Eds.), *Victims of sexual aggression: Treatment of children, women, and men,* pp. 3–17. New York: Van Nostrand Reinhold.

Queens Beach Foundation. (1975). *Rape victimization study: Final report.* San Francisco: Author.

Resick, P. A., Calhoun, K. S., Atkeson, B. M., & Ellis, E. M. (1981). Social adjustment in victims of sexual assault. *Journal of Consulting and Clinical Psychology, 49,* 705–712.

Resick, P. A., Veronen, L. J., Kilpatrick, D. G., Calhoun, K. S., & Atkeson, B. M. (1984). *Assessment of fear reactions in sexual assault victims: A factor-analytic study of the Veronen–Kilpatrick Modified Fear Survey.* Unpublished manuscript, University of Missouri, St. Louis.

Rosenberg, M. (1965). *Society and the adolescent self-image.* Princeton: Princeton University Press.

Ruch, L. O., & Chandler, S. M. (1983). Sexual assault trauma during the acute phase: An exploratory model and multivariate analysis. *Journal of Health and Social Behavior, 24,* 174–185.

Russell, D. E. H. (1974). *The politics of rape.* New York: Stein & Day.

Shore, B., Baum, M., & Sales, E. (1980). *Examination of critical process and outcome factors in rape.* Washington, DC: NIMH Center for Prevention and Control of Rape.

Stewart, A. J. (1982). The course of individual adaptation to life changes. *Journal of Personality and Social Psychology, 42,* 1100–1113.

Taylor, S. E. (1983). Adjustment to threatening events: A theory of cognitive adaptation. *American Psychologist, 38,* 1161–1173.

Veronen, L. J., & Kilpatrick, D. G. (1983). Rape: A precursor of change. In E. Callahan & K. McCluskey (Eds.), *Life-span development psychology: Nonnormative life events.* New York: Academic Press.

Williams, J. E., & Holmes, K. A. (1981). *The second assault: Rape and public attitudes.* Westport, CT: Greenwood Press.

CHAPTER 17

The Effects of Acquaintance
Rape on the Female Victim

CHRISTINE A. GIDYCZ, PhD and MARY P. KOSS, PhD

Victimization experiences, whether they are rapes, other crimes such as burglaries, natural disasters, or illnesses, are undeniably traumatic. They are personally aversive because they involve a loss of resources or status, which leads to feelings of loss of control and contributes to lowered self-esteem (Hobfoll, 1989; Taylor, Wood, & Lichtman, 1983). Victims of all types experience common emotional reactions, including confusion, shock, helplessness, fear, anxiety, and depression. It has been theorized that these postvictimization symptoms occur as a result of a failure to adequately process a traumatic event. Cognitive theorists believe that much of the trauma associated with victimizing events is the result of the shattering of basic assumptions that victims hold about themselves and their world (Janoff-Bulman, 1985a; Taylor, 1983).

Although theorists have focused on the common thread among victimizations, this review illustrates that acquaintance rape victims' experience differs in important respects from that of victims of other crimes and disasters and even from stranger rape victims. Because of the pervasive, malevolent social context of acquaintance rape (Burt & Katz, 1987), acquaintance rape victims, relative to other types of victims, appear to be at a greater risk for experiencing behavioral, emotional, and cognitive consequences. The following themes are discussed here:

1. Acquaintance rape is a pervasive and widespread problem.
2. Although the symptomatic pattern of acquaintance rape is similar to stranger rape, acquaintance rapes involve unique situational factors that place the victims at risk for more long-standing difficulties.
3. Acquaintance rape is different from stranger rapes and other types of victimizations in that it presents a unique challenge to a woman's belief system.
4. The process of resolution of the rape trauma involves reworking one's beliefs about oneself so that they "fit" with the new personal data of having been victimized (Janoff-Bulman, 1985a).

THE SCOPE OF ACQUAINTANCE RAPE

Over the past several years, evidence has been accumulated which suggests that a sizable number of rapes involve people who are acquainted with each other (Koss, 1988). For example, The National Crime Survey (NCS) reported that 52% of completed rapes in 1982 were perpetrated by someone who was known to the victim (U.S. Department of Justice, 1984). However, official surveys such as the NCS are likely to underestimate the actual proportion of acquaintance rapes, because research has indicated that the majority of acquaintance rape victims do not conceptualize their experience as such (Koss, 1985, 1988). If a victim does not conceptualize her experience as rape, it is unlikely that she will be counted in these official estimates.

To understand the true magnitude of the problem, it is necessary to survey large samples of women who do not come to the attention of authorities. Two studies, conducted with adult women, assessed the frequency of sexual assault among a probability sample of San Francisco women (Russell, 1984) and two community samples of women in Los Angeles (Sorenson, Stein, Siegel, Golding, & Burnam, 1987). The rates of sexual assault varied somewhat across these two studies. Russell (1984) found that 44% of the women had experienced an attempted rape or a rape at some time in their lives; Sorenson et al. (1987) reported that 16.7% of the women had experienced some form of sexual assault during their lifetimes. Twenty four percent of Russell's (1984) sample and approximately 6% of Sorenson et al.'s (1987) sample were victims of rape. Koss and her colleagues (Koss, Gidycz, & Wisniewski, 1987; Koss, Woodruff, & Koss, 1989) surveyed two additional groups of women: a national sample of college students and a group of primary care patients in Cleveland, Ohio. In the national study with college women they found that over half of the women (54%) had had some form of forced sexual contact, with 15% of them reporting that they had had an experience that met the legal definition of rape. Comparable rates of rape (14%) were found for the primary care patients. It is significant that although the rates of sexual assault and rape varied somewhat across these studies, the percentages of assaults perpetrated by acquaintances were consistent and high. Between 78% and 89% of the assaults reported in these studies were perpetrated by acquaintances (Koss et al., 1987; Koss et al., 1989; Russell, 1984; Sorenson et al., 1987).

Although research has indicated that women between the ages of 17 and 25 are at the greatest risk for a sexual assault (Koss & Burkhart, 1989), recent studies conducted with adolescents revealed that acquaintance rape among younger populations is of growing concern. For example, Ageton (1983) interviewed a probability sample of adolescent girls, aged 11 to 17, yearly for several years. The rate at which female teenagers reported a sexual assault by peers was 5% to 11% per year. Hall and Flannery (1984) conducted a random-digit-dial telephone survey of 508 adolescents and found comparable results: 12% of the girls had experienced "rape or sexual assault." Gidycz & Koss

(1989a) surveyed a small convenience sample of adolescent girls, and their results were consistent with existing literature. Fifty five percent of the girls surveyed had experienced at least one sexual victimization, and 7.5% (of the total sample) had been raped. The girls' average age was 13 years, and 97% of them were assaulted by acquaintances. Most of the acquaintances were reported to be either "friends or boyfriends."

Given the alarming rate of sexual assaults by acquaintances, it is not surprising that researchers have concluded that "sexual abuse may be frequent, if not inevitable life experiences for many people" (Carmen, Rieker, & Mills, 1984, p. 378). These statistics have also provided an impetus for studying the impact of acquaintance rape on its victims.

SYMPTOMATIC IMPACT OF ACQUAINTANCE RAPE

The typical way to assess symptomatic responses to a sexual assault has been to take a group of adult sexual assault victims who have reported to a rape crisis center and compare their responses, on standardized measures of adjustment, to those of comparison groups of nonvictims. Research studies that assessed victims' reactions at one point in time postassault and longitudinally over the course of years will be reviewed only briefly because extensive reviews are available elsewhere (Ellis, 1983; Resick, 1987).

Immediately after an assault, victims are more anxious (Kilpatrick, Veronen, & Resick, 1979) and depressed (Atkeson, Calhoun, Resick, & Ellis, 1982), exhibit more social maladjustment (Calhoun, Atkeson, & Ellis, 1981), and experience greater disturbances in sexual functioning (Ellis, Atkeson, & Calhoun, 1981) than comparison groups of nonvictims. Unfortunately, for a number of women, these symptoms seem to persist for a substantial period of time. Long-term follow-up studies with sexual assault victims suggest that many of them experience long-standing difficulties. For example, Kilpatrick, Resick, and Veronen (1981) reported that at one year postassault, victims still scored higher than nonvictims on standardized anxiety measures. Santiago, McCall-Perez, Gorcey, and Biegel (1985) found that victims who had been raped at least two years prior to the assessment were more anxious than a group of nonvictims. Becker, Skinner, Abel, Axelrod, and Treacy (1984) noted that depressive symptoms were still present in a substantial number of women who were assaulted on the average almost 12 years earlier. Problems with sexual functioning are also long-standing for some victims (Ellis, Calhoun, & Atkeson, 1980). Kilpatrick et al. (1981) suggested that only 20–25% of victims who do not seek assistance are relatively symptom-free a year after the assault.

Although these studies highlight the severity of a victimization experience, they are limited in terms of generalizability because research has suggested that only 5% of acquaintance rape victims actually report to a crisis center (Koss, 1988). These samples, therefore, contain a disproportionate number of stranger rape victims. Given this limitation, researchers have recently begun to investigate the impact of a sexual assault among victims who do not seek crisis services. Although these studies typically contain a small percentage (less than 20%) of stranger rape victims, it is believed that they more adequately represent the experience of acquaintance rape victims. Following are a case description of an acquaintance rape victim and an overview of the major symptoms exhibited by acquaintance rape victims.

An Acquaintance Rape Victim

Georgette was a first-year university student who was raped by the resident advisor in her dormitory. Georgette was standing outside of her apartment after coming home from a party. Mel, the resident advisor, started to make advances at her. Georgette repeatedly told Mel "no" and attempted to fight. He, however, dragged her into her room and raped her. When Georgette was interviewed (Warshaw, 1988), she described her experience as follows:

> I didn't tell anyone. In fact, I wouldn't even admit it to myself until about four months later when the guilt and fear that had been eating at me became too much to hide and I came very close to a complete breakdown. I tried to kill myself, but fortunately I chickened out at the last minute.
>
> There's no way to describe what was going on inside of me. I was losing control and I'd never been so terrified and helpless in my life. I felt as if my whole world had been kicked out from under me and I had been left to drift all alone in the darkness. I had horrible nightmares in which I relived the rape and others which were even worse. I was terrified of being with people and terrified of being alone. I couldn't concentrate on anything and began falling asleep in several classes. Deciding what to wear in the morning was enough to make me panic and cry uncontrollably. I was convinced I was going crazy, and I'm still convinced I almost did.
>
> *(Warshaw, 1988, p. 67–68).*

Common Symptoms of Acquaintance Rape Victims

Anxiety

As Georgette's case illustrates, fearfulness and anxiety are often the initial reactions to an acquaintance rape. As with stranger rapes, feelings of shock, anger, and confusion are often reported to occur both during and immediately after the assault. For example, in a national study of sexual victimization among college students, Koss (1988) found that the rape victims reported feeling "quite a bit" frightened and angry during the assault. This pattern of physical, cognitive, and behavioral responses, characteristic of Georgette and acquaintance rape victims (as well as of victims of other types), is consistent with the *Diagnostic and Statistical Manual of Mental Disorders* (DSM III-R; American Psychiatric Association, 1987) criteria for Post-Traumatic Stress Disorder (PTSD). Victims who suffer from PTSD persistently reexperience the event in the form of dreams or flashbacks, attempt to avoid the stimuli associated with the trauma, and experience symptoms of increased arousal such as difficulty in concentrating or sleeping (American Psychiatric Association, 1987). Georgette experienced these symptoms immediately after the assault; however, some victims do not develop PTSD until months or years after the assault (Koss & Harvey, 1987).

Unfortunately, for some victims, this immediate post-rape distress response fails to resolve. Kilpatrick, Saunders, Veronen, Best, and Von (1987), who assessed the psychological impact of a variety of victimization experiences (including sexual assault) among a community sample of adult women, found that the lifetime and current crime-related PTSD rates were highest for completed rape victims. Despite the fact that the rape victims were assaulted on the average of 17 years earlier, approximately 17% of them still were experiencing PTSD. Other anxiety disorders found to be more prevalent in adult women who have been sexually assaulted, relative to nonvictims, include phobic, obsessive compulsive, and panic disorders (Burnam et al., 1988). In fact, Burnam et al. (1988) concluded that victims have a two- to fourfold increased risk for developing phobic, obsessive compulsive, and panic disorders after an assault. These high rates of anxiety disorders are understandable, given that for acquaintance rape victims, "both the woman's personal world and the world at large are now seen as threatening. There's nowhere that is safe, no one who may be trusted" (Warshaw, 1988, p. 70).

Depression

In addition to feeling anxiety and fear, acquaintance rape victims, like stranger rape victims, often initially experience feelings of depression. Koss (1988) found that the rape victims in her national study of college students felt "quite a bit" depressed after the assault. For some victims, these feelings of depression seem to be long-lasting.

Gidycz and Koss (1989a) utilized the Beck Depression Inventory (Beck, Ward, Mendelson, Mock, & Erbaugh, 1961), a standardized measure of depression, to compare adolescents who had been victimized to nonvictimized adolescents. Despite the fact that half of the victims were assaulted a year or more before the time of assessment, the victims' scores were twice as high and significantly different from the nonvictims' scores. The Beck Depression Inventory was also used in this investigation to classify participants as "not depressed," "mildly depressed," "moderately depressed," or "severely depressed." Gidycz and Koss (1989a) found that while 7% of the nonvictims were moderately depressed and none were severely depressed, 27% of the victims were moderately depressed and 11% of them were severely depressed. Studies with other groups of adolescents (Ageton, 1983) and college students (Koss, Dinero, Siebel, & Cox, 1988) corroborated these findings that victims typically report more depression than nonvictims. Additional research has indicated that the depression may often be severe enough to warrant the diagnosis of Major Depression (Burnam et al., 1988).

These elevated levels of depression are of particular concern because of the link between depression and suicidal ideation (thinking about suicide). In the case study, Georgette wanted to commit suicide but "chickened out" at the last minute. Research findings suggest that suicidal ideation, as well as actual suicidal attempts, are all too common in victims of sexual assault. For example, in a community study of adult women, Kilpatrick et al. (1985) found that nearly half of the victims (44%) experienced suicidal thoughts and 20% of them attempted suicide. Comparatively, only 7% of the nonvictims experienced suicidal ideation and 2% of them attempted suicide. This link between suicidal ideation and a sexual assault experience was corroborated in samples of college women (Koss, 1988) and high school students (Gidycz & Koss, 1989a). This finding that a substantial number of acquaintance rape victims consider or attempt suicide underscores the importance of victims' seeking assistance services. However, research has shown that acquaintance rape victims often feel that something is wrong with them or that they have used poor judgment in trusting the offender. These feelings, unfortunately, seem to prevent acquaintance rape victims from seeking immediate assistance (Stewart et al., 1987).

Relationship and Sexual Difficulties

It is common for victims of acquaintance rapes to experience sexual difficulties after the assault. Warshaw (1988) interviewed a number of acquaintance rape victims and reported that some women chose not to have sex for a while and others, especially those who felt devalued after the assault, had sex more often than before. The results of a national study of sexual victimization were consistent with Warshaw's interviews. Victims in this study exhibited wide variability in the number of sex partners that they had after the assault. In addition to changes in the frequency of sexual encounters, victims reported less sexual satisfaction with a variety of sexual behaviors such as intercourse and oral genital contact after an assault (Orlando & Koss, 1983). As with anxiety and depression, these sexual difficulties can be long-standing for some victims (Orlando & Koss, 1983). For example, Leona, a woman interviewed by Warshaw (1988), remained celibate for three years after the assault. Another woman, Patty, experienced a delayed reaction: she repressed the memory of her sexual assault for four years. When Patty began processing the assault, four years after its occurrence, she was unable to have sex with her husband. She reported that every time she tried to make love with her husband, she saw the offender's face (Warshaw, 1988).

In relation to these sexual difficulties, it has been argued that acquaintance rape victims' feelings of trust are uniquely violated. Unlike the stranger rape victim, who is harmed by someone unknown to her, the acquaintance rape victim is often assaulted by someone she knows and implicitly trusts. Research with college students showed that a substantial number of acquaintance rape victims had prior sexual intimacy with the offender (Koss, 1988). Given that acquaintance rape often takes place in the context of an ongoing mutual relationship, it is not surprising that the breakdown in feelings of trust and interpersonal safety may be particularly acute (Janoff-Bulman, 1985b); it is as if there is no one who can be trusted after an assault. Alice, a woman interviewed by Warshaw (1988), stated:

"One thing I'll never get over is my distrust of men" (p. 75). Because of the intense feelings of vulnerability experienced by acquaintance rape victims, it is important that professionals of all kinds (police, mental health workers, physicians, and others) as well as family members and friends react with the utmost sensitivity when working with these women.

Physical Symptoms

Although stranger rapes, on the average, are more violent than acquaintance rapes (Koss et al., 1988), acquaintance rapes can at times be physically violent. For example, while Koss et al. (1988) found that stranger rapes were more likely to involve threats of bodily harm, hitting and slapping, and a weapon, stranger and acquaintance rapes were equally as likely to involve the offender's twisting the victim's arm or holding her down, choking, and beating. For example, in 60% of the acquaintance rapes the offenders tried to restrain the victim by twisting her arm or holding her down, and 7% of the offenders tried to choke or beat the victim. Actual tissue damage may result, especially where force is excessive. Some victims may attempt to escape by jumping out of cars or windows. These types of resistance strategies can, of course, lead to injuries (Burt & Katz, 1985). Some victims experience vaginal bleeding after a rape because of the man's roughness, their attempts at resistance, and/or a lack of lubrication (Warshaw, 1988).

Perhaps more common than actual physical injury, however, are the fear of pregnancy, fear of sexually transmitted diseases (STDs), and, more recently, fear of acquiring AIDS (Burt & Katz, 1985; Warshaw, 1988). Because of the possibility of pregnancy or STDs, it is imperative that acquaintance rape victims seek medical assistance after an assault. However, fewer than 5% of acquaintance rape victims actually seek immediate medical assistance (Koss, 1988).

Some recent evidence suggests that while acquaintance rape victims may not seek immediate medical assistance, they are more likely than nonvictims to seek medical assistance in the years following the assault. In addition, victims (compared to nonvictims) have been found to report that they are in poor health and that they experience limitations in functioning (Golding, Stein, Siegel, Burnam, & Sorenson, 1988; Koss et al., 1989). While the specific medical complaints that acquaintance rape victims experience over the long term remain to be empirically demonstrated, these findings suggest that sexual assault may have serious long-term physical consequences that require medical assistance (Golding et al., 1988).

Other Symptoms

Some victims of acquaintance rape report changes in their behaviors or life-style after the assault. In a national study of sexual victimization, Koss (1988) found, for example, that approximately 80% of the victims felt that the assault led them to change their behaviors or feelings. Sexually assaulted women may restrict their activities, change jobs, or even change their appearance after an assault (Warshaw, 1988). While excessive drinking appears to be a risk factor for a sexual assault (Koss & Dinero, 1989; Burnam et al., 1988), there is evidence that some victims may increase their use of alcohol after an assault (Burnam et al., 1988).

These are the *typical* symptomatic responses of acquaintance rape victims; not all victims experience identical symptom patterns. A number of factors may modify the intensity of a victim's reaction to an acquaintance rape. Research with acquaintance rape victims has shown, for example, that variables such as the age of the victim at the time of the assault (Burnam et al., 1988), a victim's coping skills (Mandoki & Burkhart, 1989), the level of force involved in the assault, and a victim's preassault psychological functioning (Gidycz & Koss, 1989b) may all influence a victim's response to an assault. Most current research that has investigated how situational and victim personality variables interact with rape trauma has utilized stranger rape victims (Atkeson et al., 1982; Burgess & Holmstrom, 1979; Frank & Stewart, 1983). Research with acquaintance rape victims is needed to better understand why some victims develop more chronic symptom patterns.

However, this summary of the common symptom pattern of acquaintance rape victims warrants some important conclusions. First, acquaintance rape victims experience many of the same symptoms as stranger rape victims. Empirical evidence suggests, for example, that when stranger and acquaintance rape victims were compared on standardized symptom measures, minimal differences were found between victims on measures of depression (Atkeson et al., 1982; Becker et al., 1984; Frank, Turner, & Stewart, 1980; Koss et al., 1988), anxiety (Koss et al., 1988; Santiago et al., 1985), social adjustment (Frank et al., 1980), and sexual adjustment (Becker et al., 1984; Norris & Feldman-Summers, 1981). While clinical evidence suggests that acquaintance rape victims may exhibit more difficulties related to trust, this still remains to be assessed empirically. These findings are particularly alarming because acquaintance rape victims are less likely to seek crisis services, to discuss the experience with someone, to report to the police, and to believe that they should have sought therapy despite the fact that they seem to experience symptoms similar to those of stranger rape victims (Koss et al., 1988). Given that Davis and Friedman (1985) suggested that talking about a crime experience is the single most therapeutic behavior engaged in by victims, it is quite possible that acquaintance rape victims may take longer to resolve the trauma than stranger rape victims.

In addition, acquaintance rape victims are less likely than stranger rape victims to conceptualize their experience as rape. For example, the national study of sexual victimization of college students found that approximately 60% of acquaintance rape victims, as compared to 20% of stranger rape victims, did not conceptualize their assault as rape (Koss et al., 1988). This failure to conceptualize the experience as rape can have deleterious consequences for the victim. As stated by Warshaw (1988), "because the rape victim doesn't believe that what happened to her is rape, she sometimes decides to give her attacker another chance" (p. 63). Research has shown, for example, that acquaintance rape victims were twice as likely as stranger rape victims to be assaulted multiple times by the same man (Koss et al., 1988). These findings seem to be consistent with the conclusion that "it is abundantly clear that a history of victimization is a strong risk factor for the development of . . . lifetime mental health problems" (Kilpatrick, Veronen, et al., 1987, p. 65).

COGNITIVE IMPACT OF SEXUAL ASSAULT

Presently, most of the work on the cognitive disruptions in rape victims has been theoretical in nature. For example, it has been theorized that acquaintance rape, like other types of victimization, contradicts beliefs that have been confirmed over many years. Janoff-Bulman (1985a) described three types of assumptions that are shattered by any victimization experience. The first is a belief in invulnerability. According to Janoff-Bulman, people acknowledge that disasters and victimization experiences strike others, but they believe that they can't happen to them. Similarly, Taylor and Brown (1988) contended that people tend to believe that they are less likely than their peers to encounter negative events such as criminal victimizations.

A second belief that is shattered is that the world is meaningful. People try to make sense of their world by regarding events as being controllable (Janoff-Bulman, 1985a). For example, they believe that they can be protected from misfortunes if they are good and worthy people and if they engage in precautionary behaviors.

Finally, people tend to believe that they are worthy and decent people (Janoff-Bulman, 1985a). They tend, for example, to indicate that positive traits are more characteristic of themselves than are negative traits (Taylor and Brown, 1988).

Cognitive theorists imply that acquaintance rape victims' beliefs about themselves and their world are uniquely challenged by their victimization experience. Victims of all types feel an overwhelming sense of vulnerability; however, for a woman who has been assaulted by someone she knows, this breakdown in feelings of safety and security seems to be particularly acute (Janoff-Bulman, 1985b). Warshaw (1988), for example, stated that, in any rape, a woman feels violated because she has been unable to control her own safety. Stranger rape victims, however, can hold on to a sense (however fragile) that friends and family will provide a zone of protection and support. This is usually not the case for the acquaintance rape victim. A rape victim can no longer say that "it can't happen to me" (Janoff-Bulman, 1985a).

In addition to experiencing intense feelings of vulnerability, acquaintance rape victims find that their beliefs in the predictability and orderliness of their world and in their own self-worth are likely to be challenged. As a group, acquaintance rape victims seem to be undeniably stigmatized by others. Warshaw (1988) stated that society does not blame the victims of most crimes but it blames acquaintance rape victims. For example, Warshaw contended that society does not blame a mugging victim for carrying a pocketbook or a store owner for handing over the money when threatened. However, acquaintance rape victims are often blamed for the assault because they were drinking, because they ignored a "bad feeling" that they might have had about the offender, or because they had some prior involvement with the offender. Furthermore, acquaintance rapes, compared to stranger rapes, are less likely to be perceived as "real rapes" (Check & Malamuth, 1983). Given that acquaintance rape victims are embedded in a culture that reacts negatively toward them, it is not surprising that theorists have suggested that these victims are particularly vulnerable to feelings of self-blame, powerlessness, and lack of control over their lives.

Clinical evidence focusing on feelings of self-blame and powerlessness in acquaintance rape victims has tended to substantiate these theoretical propositions. Ruth, an acquaintance rape victim interviewed by Warshaw (1988), married the man who raped her. Ruth reported that she "felt like a tramp" and believed that the rape was her fault (p. 64). Sadly, research findings seem to substantiate that many acquaintance rape victims are like Ruth in that they blame themselves for the assault and believe that the rapist really cares about them. Katz and Burt (1988) assessed self-blame in 80 rape victims, of whom 62% were raped by strangers and 38% were raped by acquaintances. Consistent with Janoff-Bulman's conceptualization, they found that women raped by acquaintances felt significantly more self-blame than victims raped by strangers. Further, the victims who blamed themselves for the assault were more likely to have needed psychiatric hospitalization, to have been suicidal, and to have experienced low self-esteem postassault than women who did not blame themselves. A recent study illustrated that the deleterious effects of self-blame appear to be a long-standing problem for victims of acquaintance rape (Mandoki & Burkhart, 1989). Finally, most likely reflecting victims' feelings of powerlessness (Warshaw, 1988), Koss (1988) found that 41% of college student acquaintance rape victims believed that they would be assaulted again.

These results warrant two important conclusions. First, much more research is needed to further test cognitive theories of impact among acquaintance rape victims. An emphasis should be placed on the coping strategies or appraisals that mediate, and perhaps moderate, the relationship between a traumatic experience and the symptomatic outcome (Koss, 1990). Second, treatment programs for acquaintance rape victims need to focus on a victim's appraisal or interpretation of the event, to help decrease a victim's feelings of self-blame and restore her feelings of power.

CONCLUSION: A RESOLUTION OF THE TRAUMA

The majority of published treatment studies for rape victims have focused on target symptoms such as anxiety and depression (e.g., Frank et al., 1988).

While these treatments may be appropriate for stranger rape victims, who seek assistance soon after the assault, they are inadequate for acquaintance rape victims, who often delay seeking treatment (Stewart et al., 1987). This review suggests that it is crucial for professionals working with acquaintance rape victims to help them to make cognitive reappraisals or to rework their beliefs about themselves and their world so that they fit with the new data of having been victimized (Janoff-Bulman, 1985a).

Specifically, therapists working with victims of acquaintance rape have a number of important tasks. First, professionals need to help victims redefine the event (Janoff-Bulman, 1985a; Taylor, 1983). One way to accomplish this is to discourage victims from conceptualizing the rape as an event that they precipitated or something that was their fault. Research on self-blame has shown that any type of self-blame seems to impede recovery (Katz & Burt, 1988; Mandoki & Burkhart, 1989; Meyer & Taylor, 1986). Thus, it should be communicated to victims that even if they utilized poor judgment, that does not make them responsible for the assault (Warshaw, 1988). Second, professionals need to help victims find meaning in their lives once again (Janoff-Bulman, 1985a; Taylor, 1983). To facilitate the search for meaning, victims should be helped to answer questions such as "What caused the event to happen?" and "What does my life mean now?" (Taylor, 1983). Finally, to promote resolution and feelings of empowerment, the victim should be helped with strategies that may prevent further victimizations and encouraged to seek social support (Janoff-Bulman, 1985a; Taylor, 1983). Since family and friends are often misinformed about acquaintance rape, it may be appropriate to educate victims' significant others about the dynamics of acquaintance rape. "Without the opportunity to develop a positive or, at least, strengthening reinterpretation of her experience, the rape victim may assimilate degradation and helplessness into her beliefs and behavior" (Koss & Burkhart, 1989, p. 35).

This review has focused on the severity of the impact of acquaintance rape experiences. It is important to conclude, however, by emphasizing that when victims are able to make the necessary reappraisals, they can and often do recover. Some victims have reported that they experienced positive changes or "growth outcomes" (Burt & Katz, 1987). By facilitating the victim's search for meaning and helping her to regain her feelings of empowerment, we will ultimately be able to help victims become true survivors.

REFERENCES

Ageton, S. (1983). *Sexual assault among adolescents.* Lexington, MA: Heath.

American Psychiatric Association. (1987). *Diagnostic and statistical manual of mental disorders* (3rd ed. rev.). Washington, DC: Author.

Atkeson, B., Calhoun, K. S., Resick, P. A., & Ellis, E. (1982). Victims of rape: Repeated assessment of depressive symptoms. *Journal of Consulting and Clinical Psychology, 50,* 96–102.

Beck, A. T., Ward, C. H., Mendelson, M., Mock, J., & Erbaugh, J. (1961). An inventory for measuring depression. *Archives of General Psychiatry, 4*, 561–571.

Becker, J. V., Skinner, L. J., Abel, G. G., Axelrod, R., & Treacy, E. C. (1984). Depressive symptoms associated with sexual assault. *Journal of Sex and Marital Therapy, 10*, 185–192.

Burgess, A. W., & Holmstrom, L. L. (1979). Rape: Sexual disruption and recovery. *American Journal of Orthopsychiatry, 49*, 648–657.

Burnam, M. A., Stein, J. A., Golding, J. M., Siegel, J. M., Sorenson, S. B., Forsythe, A. B., & Telles, C. A. (1988). Sexual assault and mental disorders in a community population. *Journal of Consulting and Clinical Psychology, 56*, 843–850.

Burt, M., & Katz, B. (1985). Rape, robbery, and burglary: Responses to actual and feared criminal victimization with special focus on women and the elderly. *Victimology: An International Journal, 10*, 325–358.

Burt, M., & Katz, B. (1987). Dimensions of recovery from rape: Focus on growth outcomes. *Journal of Interpersonal Violence, 2*, 57–82.

Calhoun, K. S., Atkeson, B. M., & Ellis, E. M. (1981). Social adjustment in victims of sexual assault. *Journal of Consulting and Clinical Psychology, 49*, 705–712.

Carmen, E. H., Rieker, P. P., & Mills, T. (1984). Victims of violence and psychiatric illness. *American Journal of Psychiatry, 141*, 378–383.

Check, J. V. P., & Malamuth, N. M. (1983). Sex role stereotyping and reactions to depictions of stranger versus acquaintance rape. *Journal of Personality and Social Psychology, 45*, 344–356.

Davis, R. C., & Friedman, L. N. (1985). The emotional aftermath of crime and violence. In C. R. Figley (Ed.), *Trauma and its wake: The study and treatment of post-traumatic stress disorder* (pp. 90–111). New York: Brunner/Mazel.

Ellis, E. M. (1983). A review of empirical rape research: Victim reactions and response to treatment. *Clinical Psychology Review, 3*, 473–490.

Ellis, E. M., Atkeson, B. M., & Calhoun, K. S. (1981). An assessment of long-term reaction to rape. *Journal of Abnormal Psychology, 90*, 263–266.

Ellis, E. M., Calhoun, K. S., & Atkeson, B. M. (1980). Sexual dysfunction in victims of rape: Victims may experience a loss of sexual arousal and frightening flashbacks even one year after the assault. *Women and Health, 5*, 39–47.

Frank, E., Anderson, B., Stewart, B. D., Dancu, C., Hughes, C., & West, D. (1988). Efficacy of cognitive behavior therapy and systematic desensitization in the treatment of rape trauma. *Behavior Therapy, 19*, 403–420.

Frank, E., & Stewart, B. D. (1983). Treating depression in victims of rape. *Clinical Psychologist, 36*, 95–98.

Frank, E., Turner, S. M., & Stewart, B. D. (1980). Initial response to rape: The impact of factors within the rape situation. *Journal of Behavioral Assessment, 2*, 39–53.

Gidycz, C. A., & Koss, M. P. (1989a). The impact of adolescent sexual victimization: Standardized measures of anxiety, depression, and behavioral deviancy. *Violence and Victims, 4*, 139–149.

Gidycz, C. A., & Koss, M. P. (1989b). *The prediction of trauma among a national sample of sexually victimized women.* Manuscript submitted for publication.

Golding, J. M., Stein, J. A., Siegel, J. M., Burnam, M. A., & Sorenson, S. B. (1988). Sexual assault history and use of health and mental health services. *American Journal of Community Psychology, 16*, 625–644.

Hall, E. R., & Flannery, P. J. (1984). Prevalence and correlates of sexual assault experiences in adolescents. *Victimology: An International Journal, 9*, 398–406.

Hobfoll, S. E. (1989). Conservation of resources: A new attempt at conceptualizing stress. *American Psychologist, 44*, 513–524.

Janoff-Bulman, R. (1985a). The aftermath of victimization: Rebuilding shattered assumptions. In C. R. Figley (Ed.), *Trauma and its wake: The study and treatment of post-traumatic stress disorder* (pp. 15–35). New York: Brunner/Mazel.

Janoff-Bulman, R. (1985b). Criminal vs. non-criminal victimization: Victims' reactions. *Victimology: An International Journal, 10*, 498–511.

Katz, B., & Burt, M. (1988). Self blame in recovery from rape: Help or hindrance. In A. W. Burgess (Ed.), *Sexual assault (Vol. II)*. New York: Garland.

Kilpatrick, D. G., Best, C. L., Veronen, L. J., Amick, A. E., Villeponteaux, L. A., & Ruff, G. A. (1985). Mental health correlates of criminal victimization: A random community survey. *Journal of Consulting and Clinical Psychology, 53*, 866–873.

Kilpatrick, D. G., Resick, P. A., & Veronen, L. J. (1981). Effects of a rape experience: A longitudinal study. *Journal of Social Issues, 37*, 105–121.

Kilpatrick, D. G., Saunders, B. E., Veronen, L. J., Best, C. L., & Von, J. M. (1987). Criminal victimization: Lifetime prevalence, reporting to police, and psychological impact. *Crime & Delinquency, 33*, 479–489.

Kilpatrick, D. G., Veronen, L. J., & Resick, P. A. (1979). The aftermath of rape: Recent empirical findings. *American Journal of Orthopsychiatry, 49*, 658–669.

Kilpatrick, D. G., Veronen, L. J., Saunders, B. E., Best, C. L., Amick-McMullan, A., & Paduhovich, J. (1987). *The psychological impact of crime: A study of randomly surveyed crime victims*. Final report on grant no. 84-IJ-CX-0039, submitted to the National Institute of Justice.

Koss, M. P. (1985). The hidden rape victim: Personality, attitudinal, and situational characteristics. *Psychology of Women Quarterly, 9*, 193–212.

Koss, M. P. (1990). The women's mental health research agenda: Violence against women. *American Psychologist, 45*, 374–380.

Koss, M. P. (1988). Hidden rape: Incidence, prevalence, and descriptive characteristics of sexual aggression and victimization in a national sample of college students. In A. W. Burgess (Ed.), *Sexual assault (Vol. II)* (pp. 3–25). New York: Garland.

Koss, M. P., & Burkhart, B. R. (1989). A conceptual analysis of rape victimization: Long-term effects and implications for treatment. *Psychology of Women Quarterly, 13*, 27–40.

Koss, M. P., & Dinero, T. E. (1989). Discriminant analysis of risk factors for sexual victimization among a national sample of college women. *Journal of Consulting and Clinical Psychology, 57*, 242–250.

Koss, M. P., Dinero, T. E., Seibel, C. A., & Cox, S. L. (1988). Stranger and acquaintance rape: Are there differences in the victim's experience? *Psychology of Women Quarterly, 12*, 1–24.

Koss, M. P., Gidycz, C. A., & Wisniewski, N. (1987). The scope of rape: Incidence and prevalence of sexual aggression and victimization in a national sample of higher education students. *Journal of Consulting and Clinical Psychology, 55,* 162–170.

Koss, M. P., & Harvey, M. (1987). *The rape victim: Clinical and community approaches to treatment.* Lexington, MA: Stephen Greene Press.

Koss, M. P., Woodruff, W. J., & Koss, P. G. (1989). *Criminal victimization among women primary care patients: Incidence, prevalence, and role in the prediction of health perceptions.* Manuscript submitted for review.

Mandoki, C. A., & Burkhart, B. R. (1989, August). *Coping and adjustment to rape.* Paper presented at the annual meeting of the American Psychological Association, New Orleans.

Meyer, C. B., & Taylor, S. E. (1986). Adjustment to rape. *Journal of Personality and Social Psychology, 50,* 1226–1234.

Norris, J., & Feldman-Summers, S. (1981). Factors related to the psychological impact of rape on the victim. *Journal of Abnormal Psychology, 90,* 562–567.

Orlando, J. A., & Koss, M. P. (1983). The effect of sexual victimization on sexual satisfaction: A study of the negative-association hypothesis. *Journal of Abnormal Psychology, 92,* 104–106.

Resick, P. A. (1987, September). *The impact of rape on psychological functioning.* Paper presented at Conference on State of the Art in Sexual Assault, Charleston, SC.

Russell, D. E. H. (1984). *Sexual exploitation.* Beverly Hills: Sage.

Santiago, J. M., McCall-Perez, F., Gorcey, M., & Beigel, A. (1985). Long-term psychological effects of rape in 35 rape victims. *American Journal of Psychiatry, 142,* 1338–1340.

Sorenson, S. B., Stein, J. A., Siegel, J. M., Golding, J. M., & Burnam, M. A. (1987). Prevalence of adult sexual assault: The Los Angeles epidemiologic catchment area study. *American Journal of Epidemiology, 126,* 1141–1164.

Stewart, B. D., Hughes, C., Frank, E., Anderson, B., Kendall, K., & West, D. (1987). The aftermath of rape: Profiles of immediate and delayed treatment seekers. *Journal of Nervous and Mental Disease, 175,* 90–94.

Taylor, S. (1983). Adjustment to threatening events: A theory of cognitive adaptation. *American Psychologist, 38,* 1161–1173.

Taylor, S., & Brown, J. D. (1988). Illusion and well-being: A social psychological perspective on mental health. *Psychological Bulletin, 103,* 193–210.

Taylor, W., Wood, J. V., & Lichtman, R. R. (1983). It could be worse: Selective evaluation as a response to victimization. *Journal of Social Issues, 39,* 19–40.

U.S. Department of Justice, Bureau of Justice Statistics. (1984). *Criminal victimization in the United States, 1982.* (Publication No. NCJ-92820) Washington, DC: U.S. Government Printing Office.

Warshaw, R. (1988). *I never called it rape: The Ms. report on recognizing, fighting, and surviving date and acquaintance rape.* New York: Harper & Row.

PART 8

Societal Response

CHAPTER 18

Conceptual and Practical Analysis of Therapy for Acquaintance Rape Victims

BARRY R. BURKHART, PhD

"This experience lowered my self-esteem. I turned to drugs just after it happened. I would not talk to any males on a personal, one-on-one level. I felt used, worthless, and abused. I had a bad attitude, didn't want anyone (including my friends and family) to care about me. *They were too good* for me. I was filled with hate and anger."

"I kinda felt like I had been raped because he would not leave me alone and he was too big to fight off. All I could do was lie there. I wondered if he thought I was slutty or had come on to him. I was very upset."

"I cried, felt violated, alone and unclean."

These are the words of three women who participated in a research project examining coping processes in victims of acquaintance rape (Mandoki & Burkhart, 1989a). As a component of the study, victims were asked (Sommerfeldt, Burkhart, & Mandoki, 1989) to describe, in their own words, the effects of their victimization. I begin with their words for two reasons:

1. Denial has been the fundamental process compromising the development of an adequate conceptual and practical analysis of treatment models for acquaintance rape victims. In their directness and passion, the words of victims have the power to transcend the processes of denial, to illuminate in a compelling manner the reality of acquaintance rape. Thus, these words serve as a crucible for the analysis offered in this chapter: Does it do justice to the experience—does it articulate with the words—of these and all other victims?

2. These victims' words brightly illuminate the conceptual domain that must be involved in this analysis. Guilt, self-esteem damage, trust, shame, violation, alienation: these form the pain, and these are what must be understood if therapeutic efforts are to be effective.

This illumination is all the more necessary because therapists treating victims of acquaintance rape will find very little light and direction from the scholarly or empirical literature. At the time this chapter was being written, there was but one conceptual paper (Koss & Burkhart, 1989) written about treatment specific to the acquaintance rape victim/survivor. Further, there have been no controlled clinical trials or comparative treatment studies with this population. Thus, there is little empirical referent for the therapist of the victim of an acquaintance rape.

The purposes of this chapter are to redress this conceptual deficit in the literature and, insofar as is possible, use this conceptual analysis to develop a heuristic treatment protocol for victims of acquaintance rape. Because of the dearth of conceptual and empirical work in the area of treatment of the acquaintance rape victim, this analysis, in part, will be derived from adjacent areas that have been more adequately researched. The basic domains upon which this chapter is based are:

1. Current available literature on acquaintance rape, with particular focus on the sociopsychological contexts and effects of victimization; and
2. Literature drawn from work with other forms of sexual exploitation, in particular "traditional" stranger rape and child sexual abuse.

In part, this chapter is predicated on the assumption that the development of a treatment model for acquaintance rape victims can be well informed by generalizing from the conceptual and empirical work in the stranger rape and child sexual abuse areas. Simply stated, the dynamics of acquaintance rape and treatment models appropriate to these dynamics appear to share common conceptual groups from these two bodies of literature. Thus, drawing upon the rich conceptual and empirical work in the stranger rape and child sexual abuse literature allows for the development of a treatment model even in the relative absence of an immediately and directly relevant literature. To help ensure this value, the chapter is also richly informed by the voices of the acquaintance rape victims/survivors who shared their experiences and understandings in our program of research and our clinical work (Burkhart & Stanton, 1989; Koss & Burkhart, 1989).

This chapter is dedicated to these women; may they fully be heard.

SOCIAL PSYCHOLOGICAL CONTEXTS OF VICTIMIZATION

Excepting the absolute magnitude of the prevalence data for acquaintance rape (Burkhart & Stanton, 1988; Koss, Gidycz, & Wisniewski, 1987), perhaps the most striking aspect of the phenomenon of acquaintance rape, particularly in concert with the high prevalence rates, is how hidden it has been from awareness. This process of denial is the first and central issue with which therapeutic interventions have to contend. There is, finally, a reasonable level of awareness about the reality of rape as a pathogen if the rape involves strangers; however, for those coercive sexual events not involving strangers, it is very different (Weis & Borges, 1973). Instead of the event being defined by a clear set of legal criteria with clear attributions of responsibility, it is defined by reference to a peculiar and distinct set of social criteria. As Burkhart and Stanton (1988) stated previously about this process of denial:

> . . . it is evident that the social definition of rape is quite incongruous with the legal definition and displays a characteristic set of biases primarily reflecting what Burt (1980) has labeled a rape supportive belief system. Thus the question "What is a rape?" is not answered by a powerful legal litmus test but through a system of beliefs that derive from a misogynistic social context, the "rape culture" (Brownmiller, 1975). Pertinent to this chapter is the consistent finding that relationship status is a very powerful component of the social definition of rape (Burt, 1980; Klemmack & Klemmack, 1976; Koss, 1985; Skelton & Burkhart, 1980) with the degree of acquaintance being negatively correlated with an attribution of rape by victims, offenders, and other citizens.
>
> *(pp. 43–44)*

Such denial has profound and far-reaching implications for the analysis and development of a therapeutic model for victims of acquaintance rape. In particular, this process denies to victims the most fundamental need of any human being: the need to have reality as a referent, to have what is experienced affirmed as real. In the case of acquaintance rape, the victim's reality is denied. Instead of receiving comfort from others through the affirmation of her victimization, she is denied even affirmation in her own phenomenology. "I kinda felt like I had been raped . . . ." "I wondered if he thought I was slutty." Koss (1985) described acquaintance rapes as hidden rapes. This is an accurate term because what defines the psychological consequences is not simply the acquaintance status of the perpetrator. More fundamentally, the denial of the event as a function of this relationship status accounts for much of the harm. The rape *is* hidden, from perpetrators, who assert not only their innocence but their entitlement to a legitimate and even praiseworthy goal; from society, writ large, which defines the term *acquaintance rape* as an oxymoron; and even from those who are designated as society's caregivers— police, physicians, counselors, and so on—who often draw a clear distinction between "real" rapes and date rapes. This distinction implies that there is a fundamental difference between acquaintance/date rape and stranger rape, a difference that reflects a fundamental distinction of reality: one is real and one isn't (Klemmack & Klemmack, 1976; L'Armand & Pepitone, 1982).

The consequences of this definition of denial are pervasive and malevolent. If someone is raped by a stranger then that person has been *raped.* If someone is raped by an acquaintance, then that person has "let things go too far" or "let things get out of hand," and "should have known better" and should "be more careful the *next time*" (Sommerfeldt et al., 1989). What does it mean that one has "let things get out of hand" or has to be "more careful the next time"? It means that the event (a) is the victim's responsibility, (b) is common enough to be predictable, and thus (c) should be without "real" consequences. The only consequence logically flowing from this meaning context is self-blame. The reality is, however, that to be raped, to have someone invade one's body, is traumatic—devastatingly so. Moreover, the trauma, rather than being attenuated, is amplified by the relational status between victim and perpetrator. "If I couldn't trust him, whom could I trust?" Thus, the victim of an acquaintance rape is faced with an apparently irreconcilable dilemma. On the one hand, she must deal with the trauma of her violation, the effects of which are exacerbated by the often trusting relationship that frames the context of her victimization. On the other hand, her culture and her own personal sense of responsibility for her choices deny her the reality of these feelings. It is a classic double bind.

The literature on reactions and attributions to acquaintance versus stranger rape reflects the themes defining this double bind. Victims of acquaintance rape are seen as more responsible for and less harmed by their victimization than victims of stranger rape (Skelton & Burkhart, 1980). However, the reality is that victims of acquaintance rape are, by objective measure, traumatized at levels equal to or exceeding the effects of victimization by strangers (Koss, Dinero, Seibel, & Cox, 1988).

In an important study directly focused on the relative impact of acquaintance versus stranger rape, Kilpatrick, Best, Saunders, and Veronen (1988) found:

> . . . no evidence to support the assumption that rape by a husband or a boyfriend had less severe long-term psychological consequences than rape by a stranger. Multivariate analysis revealed that women assaulted by spouses or dates were just as likely as those assaulted by strangers to be depressed, fearful, obsessive-compulsive, and sexually dysfunctional years after the assault. Common assumptions about women assaulted by strangers having a more difficult time adjusting to the event than women raped by husbands and boyfriends appear to be incorrect.

> The best conclusion at this time is that the impact of rape is severe whether the assailant is a stranger, husband, or boyfriend. There are no differences in either the immediate or long-term effect of rape based upon the role of the perpetrator.

(p. 343)

Although the ultimate effects of the victimization are similar, victims cope with stranger versus acquaintance victimization in very different ways. For victims of acquaintance rape there is no affirming context; it is as if their victimization did not happen. As a consequence, victims do not define their rape as real (Kibler, 1986; Koss, 1985); they do not report it to authorities, nor do they seek treatment from socially sanctioned healers (Koss et al., 1988). In effect, every opportunity for external support and affirmation is denied and they must cope on their own. Thus, victims of acquaintance rape have to cope with the victimization itself and with the pervasive, malignant denial of the victimization. The consequence of this irresolvable double bind to victims is "a sort of cognitive-emotional paralysis wherein their only recourse is to simply deny that the experience really happened" (Koss & Burkhart, 1989, p. 32). "Led to believe she is responsible for any sexual experience and faced with an unsupportive social environment . . . the woman experiences herself as having only the choice of responsibility and self-blame, or denial" (p. 35).

This process is much like that described by Summit (1983) in his classic paper on the accommodation syndrome in child sexual abuse victims. The victim of child sexual abuse, faced by the denial of her victimization or by victim-blaming processes operating in the family or social context, is forced to accommodate to rather than assimilate her victimization. Instead of the experience being assimilated into the victim's development processes, the victim's development becomes organized around the victimization and its sequallae. Thus, normal developmental processes are thwarted and, instead, traumagenic factors such as traumatic sexualization, stigmatization, betrayal, and powerlessness (Browne & Finkelhor, 1986) drive the child's development.

Parallel developmental processes can be seen in acquaintance rape victims. The highest rates of acquaintance rape are in the courtship age (17 to 25 years old), a time when a young woman is without the perspective of multiple experiences and full maturation of her cognitive development (Koss et al., 1987). Thus, "rape during adolescence may be particularly shattering because it is during this period that girls formulate their generalized views of the world as well as their specific views of men, authority figures, and themselves" (Silver, Boon, & Stone, 1983). ". . . In this context the adolescent victim may be, therefore, even more likely to rely on the malevolent social myths about rape as the source of her cognitive appraisals for her victimization thus increasing her vulnerability to guilt, self-blame, and a sense of helplessness, and unworthiness" (Koss & Burkhart, 1989, p. 35).

It is not difficult to understand how these traumagenic factors (Browne & Finkelhor, 1986) which define the coping processes of the child sexual assault victim have parallels with the victim of an acquaintance rape. Traumatic sexualization is clearly involved when 59% of women report their acquaintance rape as their first experience with sexual intercourse (Mandoki & Burkhart, 1989b). Stigmatization, betrayal, and powerlessness, likewise, become the psychological contexts for the acquaintance rape victim. To be raped is to be exposed to the ultimate assault on one's dignity, value, and power of self-determination. To be raped by someone you trusted and often selected to date is to be betrayed, not just by the perpetrator, but by your own judgment.

In larger part, the parallel processes of victimization in child sexual abuse and acquaintance rape have to do with how these experiences define and direct the victims' coping strategies. Several researchers have noted that with the child sexual abuse victim the trauma is to the child's world view, the way in which meaning is assigned to self, others, and relational processes (Conte, 1988; Jehu, Klassan, & Gazan, 1985–1986; Silver et al., 1983). Likewise, these effects become the center of the rape victim's process of resolution. Moreover, because of the malevolent social context of acquaintance rape, resolution becomes accommodation. In a previous work, Sommerfeldt, et al. (1989) found that the most common consequence of acquaintance rape was self-blame.

Burt and Katz (1988), in their excellent work on coping processes in rape victims, identified several coping styles associated with rape recovery. Relevant to this analysis are their findings that self-destructive and avoidant behaviors showed significant positive relationships with levels of guilt and self-blame. Furthermore, the amount of self-blame for the rape correlated positively with negative coping styles (avoidance, nervous/anxious, and self-destructive) and negatively with positive coping patterns.

Thus, what comes to define the victim's coping processes is not only the victimization per se. Instead, it is the meaning assigned to this event, a meaning forged from the essence of rape culture: If you are raped it is your own fault and it means you are an unworthy and a blameworthy human being. This meaning set tends to establish two complementary negative coping processes:

1. Enhancement of denial-mediated avoidant, and self-destructive coping behaviors such as drinking, drug taking, suicidal ideation, self-blame, and continued involvement with callous men; and
2. Paralysis of expressive, support-seeking, self-affirming coping behaviors such as disclosing the victimization and giving self-permission to experience feelings and to express these feelings.

IMPLICATIONS FOR TREATMENT

In the process of reviewing for and writing this chapter, it became evident that the literature on treatment of rape victims was of only limited utility in dealing with the victim of an acquaintance rape. In a previous work (Koss & Burkhart, 1989), these limitations were detailed. The most fundamental limitation is that the empirical treatment literature is almost entirely focused on the symptoms that result from the immediate impact of rape. Very little of this work deals with the delayed treatment seeker who is most likely to have been victimized by an acquaintance, and none of this work is founded on a comprehensive conceptual account of the traumagenic effects of victimization, particularly rape by an acquaintance.

Again, however, the literature on treatment of the child sexual abuse victim/survivor can serve as a salient resource for the development of treatment strategies for the acquaintance rape victim/survivor. The parallels noted in the processes of accommodation, coping, and resolution of victimization provide the conceptual foundation from which treatment interventions can be generalized from the child sexual abuse context to the acquaintance rape context. In the remainder of this chapter, treatment recommendations for the acquaintance rape victim will be provided which have been framed by this conceptual generalization and have been forged in the clinical process of our psychotherapeutic work with victims. As such, a caveat is in order. At this point, direct empirical foundations for these recommendations are simply not available. Thus, these guidelines should be seen as treatment recommendations and as hypotheses for empirical work in the field's next phase of development. Conceptual coherence and clinical utility, however necessary for the early development of a field and for clinical functioning in the absence of data-based protocols, are not sufficient grounds for the establishment of clinical methods.

THERAPEUTIC PHILOSOPHY AND CONCEPTUAL FRAMEWORK

The centrality of values to the psychotherapeutic enterprise is conceded by most knowledgeable observers of this process (Bergin, 1985; Lakin, 1988; Tjeltneit, 1986). It has become axiomatic to note that therapists have values and beliefs and that these values and beliefs play a central role in their provision of psychotherapy. Thus, as part of a conceptual analysis those values anathema and those facilitative to positive therapeutic processes should be articulated. Further, beyond the core values of respect for and commitment to the client, those values specifically salient to the treatment of victims of sexual aggression should be integrated with the technical aspects of the therapeutic model.

What values, then, have empirical relevance to this task? A starting point is to examine pathogenic values; those values, beliefs, and/or attitudes which potentiate the process of victimization. By defining these pathogenic values, the process of identifying therapeutically benevolent values can begin. Briefly stated, these critical pathogenic value sets are:

1. Those that have been eloquently identified in the pioneering work of Brownmiller (1975) as defining the rape culture and compellingly operationalized in the work of Burt (1978, 1980) to describe rape myths and their power in disinhibiting sexual aggression against women; and

2. Those supportive of developmental processes encouraging the social construction of complementary gender roles, particularly in the encouragement of hypermasculinity, aggressiveness, and misogyny in men and the encouragement of passivity and dependence in women at the expense of self-determination and autonomy.

The conceptual position that both provides a conceptually compelling account of pro-victimization values and points the way toward a framework for prevention of victimization is a feminist analysis of sexual exploitation (Russell, 1984). Feminist theories, by recognizing the social context of misogyny and the hierarchal distribution of power, provide an accounting of the victimization process (Russell, 1984) and the most powerful conceptual model for therapy models (Walker, 1985). The values contained in a feminist analysis provide a nonblaming conceptual framework and encourage development of those psychological dimensions empirically related to prevention of victimization at a cultural level (Sanday, 1981) and at the personal level (Koss & Burkhart, 1989).

To be an effective therapist, therefore, one must understand the pathogenic forces and values that undergird sexual exploitation. This is necessary because a critical component of therapy involves conveying to the victim/client that distinctions must be drawn between her own psychological issues and those embedded in culture. Therapy inevitably involves the dawning of a new gestalt wherein clients exchange self-blame for the right of self-determination.

In the treatment model presented below, this process is operationalized. In the remainder of the chapter, 10 treatment processes are presented and discussed. The foundation in feminist values and the conceptual foundation outlined above usually are self-evident. Where they are not clear, connections between treatment recommendations and the contexts of values and theory will be drawn.

COMPONENT PROCESSES OF TREATMENT

In essence, the psychotherapeutic process is a seamless web of intertwined components; however, for ease of communication it will be described herein as being organized by 10 component processes. Although these will be described as separate, they are interlocked and organized in mutual dependency.

The 10 component processes are:

1. Clinical case finding
2. Creating a therapeutic alliance
3. Managing symptomatic presentations
4. Identifying metacausal connections
5. Integrating affective understanding
6. Reframing cognitive appraisals
7. Encouraging expressiveness
8. Supporting autonomy
9. Assimilation of therapeutic tasks
10. Resolution and termination

Clinical Case Finding

Perhaps the issue with the strongest empirical support and therefore the clearest consensus for a recommended treatment protocol is to neutralize the hidden nature of the victimization. Acquaintance rape victims, like child sexual abuse survivors, often do not disclose their victimization experience and rarely seek immediate treatment. Thus, the first task of the clinician is to establish the victimization. Koss and Harvey (1987) recommended several methods of clinical case finding, including:

1. Examining presenting problems to determine correspondence between client's presenting concerns and symptoms known to be consequences of rape;
2. A comprehensive assault history component as part of the pretherapy information gathering; and
3. Examining the client's presentation and symptom picture for evidence of vulnerability factors.

In effect, these procedures, by amplifying signals of victimization vulnerabilities and effects, bias therapists toward the perception of victimization. The question becomes: Does turning up the gain, by amplifying the victimization signals and by lowering the threshold for signal detection, result in more noise (incorrect identification of victimization) or signal (correct identification of victimization)? There are compelling data suggesting that this process will result in more correct identification of previously unacknowledged victims. Several factors suggest that this assumption is correct: (a) the failure of victims to spontaneously self-identify, either because of the stigmatization of acknowledgment or because of not having conceptualized themselves as victims; (b) the high base rates of victimization in the population, particularly if a comprehensive and sensitive victimization assessment is completed (Russell, 1984); and (c) the clinical consequences of a false negative relative to a false positive identification.

Thus, the clinician must always inquire about victimization and must ask in a way that provides the client the maximum latitude to affirm a victim status. As Courtois and Spier (1988) wrote so eloquently in the context of child sexual abuse:

> It may be necessary for the therapist to continuously ask and indicate a willingness to hear about the abuse. In many ways, the therapist will function as a witness to the past who attests to and validates it with the survivor.

> *(p. 284)*

Creating a Therapeutic Alliance

The next task in the treatment of the acquaintance rape victim is the establishment of a working alliance between therapist and client. Much recent general psychotherapy literature has highlighted the critical and central nature of the therapeutic alliance to the psychotherapy process. If anything, the significance of a benevolent therapeutic alliance is amplified in working with rape victims. The development of a "holding" environment that is safe, secure, nonblaming, and nurturing is the sine qua non for treating victims who are easily threatened, ashamed, and experiencing little security in their engagement with others.

An organizing concept of considerable value in operationalizing a therapeutic alliance is provided by the notion of the accommodation syndrome. To understand that the client's coping is driven by her needs to accommodate to her victimization allows the therapist room to accept, empathize with, and support the client's struggles while not falling into the trap of either participating in a process of blame or providing bland reassurances to the effect that the client is "really a good person." Clients know that something is wrong, but misidentify the wrongness as inherent in themselves. Therapists, therefore, must be able to acknowledge the client's sense of wrongness while using the therapeutic process to broaden the client's perspective and so begin to neutralize the shame-mediated self-blame that is the core of the client's pathology and forms a negative, closed, causal attribution loop. It should be obvious, moreover, that therapists must genuinely respect and care for their clients.

Managing Symptoms

The initial symptom presentation of victims is often characterized by an acute symptom constellation consisting of anxiety, phobic reactions, and/or depressive symptoms. Frank et al. (1988) suggested this admixture of symptoms indicates "the existence of a distinct symptom complex (consistent with current diagnostic thinking as represented by DSM-III and DSM-III-R) specific to traumatic reactions, that includes features of depression, phobia, and anxiety." These authors indicated that there are different variations in the symptom picture but did not connect these differences to any particular presenting context. However, clinical experience suggests that the recently victimized or those whose earlier but unresolved victimization reemerged suddenly in the context of symbolic or actual cues tend to have symptom pictures characteristic of the first phase of the rape-trauma syndrome (Burgess & Holmstrom, 1974), with anxiety and the distress of disorganization predominating. The second major style of presentation is found in nonrecent victims whose accommodation process has led them into a developmental cul-de-sac. As they find themselves stuck in negative, repetitive patterns, these women become depressed and demoralized as a consequence of their unsuccessful, denial-mediated struggle to accommodate to their victimization. These are victims for whom the recommendations about clinical case findings are particularly salient in that they rarely directly connect their emotional difficulties to their earlier victimization. Acquaintance rape victims are very likely to be delayed treatment seekers of this sort.

The majority of literature has focused on the treatment of the recently victimized client and there are several reviews of this area (Ellis, 1983; Holmes & St. Lawrence, 1983; Kilpatrick & Veronen, 1983). In general, the findings are mixed. Of those clients who stay in immediate post-rape treatment, "a comparison of the results from the assessment-only studies with the assessment and treatment studies would suggest that active treatment does not have a powerful effect on the rate or extent of recovery" (Frank et al., 1988). Furthermore, a very high percentage of clients are unwilling to enter treatment or drop out of treatment (Koss & Burkhart, 1989).

These findings suggest that while behaviorally focused treatment programs may be helpful, particularly in addressing some of the immediate behavioral inhibitions, they are clearly not sufficient. Part of the early task of symptom management, therefore, must be oriented around laying track to deal with delayed emotional sequallae emerging from the victim's accommodation to her victimization.

Identifying Links Between Symptoms and Victimization

This process merges into the fourth component of this treatment protocol, identifying metacausal connections. In effect, this involves helping the victim begin the process of identifying the connections between her often delayed emotional responses and her victimization. This can be as simple and direct as helping a victim see that her withdrawal from heterosexual relations is "logical," given the history of her victimization, to an analysis of complex and convoluted patterns of accommodation. For example, one woman whose initial presentation was depression with intense suicidal ideation and hopelessness attributed her problems to her belief that she was worthless. She held to this belief because she had developed a pattern of promiscuous sexual involvement that usually resulted in rejection by the men with whom she was involved. Only when she could understand and experience her intense, overwhelming anxiety in relationships with men, which she controlled by sexualizing relationships, could she begin to connect her behaviors to the context of her earlier victimization.

Integrating Affective Responses

This process of "making human" a victim's reactions and accommodation has powerful therapeutic effects and is central to the fifth treatment component, integrating affective understanding. When the victims' reactions are defined as expected, human behavior begins to neutralize the burden of shame experienced by victims. By providing an affective antagonist to the shame and guilt, this therapeutic engagement allows for the emergence of alternative attributions which begin to free the client from their closed-loop thinking. A useful technique is to have clients see their symptoms through an "as-if" perspective. In the previous example, the client was asked to examine her behavior "as if" it meant or described something about herself. She was able to see that her pattern was just "as if" she did not believe in her own right to her dignity. It was as we pondered how it could be that she would not grant herself that right that she disclosed an earlier instance of repetitive victimization. She had not been able to resolve this event because her only way of emotionally processing this victimization was to experience herself as shameful and valueless. Her lack of value thereafter was continually proved by her as though she had no worth or dignity.

An additional value of identifying affective responding as misunderstood rather than alien is that this neutralizes the estrangement from the self often experienced by victims. As they learn that their feelings and emotional responses are not senseless but instead are grounded in the meaning provided by an understanding of their victimization, victims are able to weld together often dissociated affective and cognitive systems. Thus, rather than be in conflict with their emotional sense of themselves and the world, they are able to begin to use their feelings as the critical source of information about the inter- and intrapersonal world that the affect system should be.

Reframing and New Understanding

This capacity, in interaction with the next treatment component, reframing cognitive appraisals, becomes the heart of the intrapersonal change of the victim. She begins to reframe her experience and develop cognitive appraisals (Koss & Burkhart, 1989) with growth-enhancing (Burt & Katz, 1988) rather than inhibiting coping effects. In this transformation, she becomes victim/survivor instead of victim.

This process of developing new, benign, cognitive appraisals in place of the malevolent attributions of self-blame is the mechanism through which therapeutic generalization is developed. As the transformation of appraisals occurs, the client becomes more able to really look at what happened to her, to learn how she was victimized and, by way of bearing witness to her own memories, free herself from the entanglements of guilt, shame, and self-blame. The therapist's task is to encourage this reappraisal of the past and to support the current implications of such reappraisal. If she was not blameworthy—if her only crime was her innocence—then she is empowered now to stand with herself in pride and strength. This is the miracle of successful therapy.

Expressiveness and Recovery

Burt and Katz (1988) presented an eloquent analysis of the different patterns of coping spontaneously arising in rape victims. Their work clearly signaled the importance of both emotion-focused and problem-focused coping strategies and identified the potential therapeutic value of the encouragement of affective expression. "We believe, from our counseling experience with rape victims, that the ability to express feelings about the rape is *necessary* for most women if they are to achieve full-integrated recovery" (p. 246). This human need for expression and validation was demonstrated by the findings of Davis and Friedman (1985) that almost all crime victims talk about their victimization for a long time after their experience. The unique difficulty for the acquaintance rape victim is that she must contend with responses which, unlike the sympathetic responses provided to the victim of nonsexual criminal conduct, are filtered through the socially transmitted myths about rape and, thus, often attribute responsibility and blame to her.

However, as the victim, secured by her reappraisals of what happened and what this has done to her, begins to express herself first in therapy and then in life, she begins to live the changes accomplished in therapy. Clients who have become free to tell their stories and own their feelings become free from them and are no longer trapped in the denial–shame feedback loop.

Supporting Autonomy

If a victim yields to the pressure of the malevolent rape myths, then the cost is her autonomy. She is no longer free to determine her worth or her way; instead she becomes entangled in the web of social expectations and beliefs. The task for the therapist is to help the victim disengage from these and seek, instead, to lean into her innermost sense of herself. At the beginning of this process, the client often can feel only the pain of her victimization. The therapeutic response is to acknowledge the pain: it is real and it is a measure of the reality of her victimization. This is her starting point in the process of developing autonomy through her affective experience of herself. Her pain is real, thus her victimization is real. As she begins to affirm her victimization, her anger begins to be revealed. Anger provides energy to the work of coping and drives her toward new ways of being in the world.

In a paradoxical fashion, the autonomy of self-expression often serves to break down her sense of estrangement and feelings of isolation. Sharing her experiences, she tries new ways of being with others. Thus, she discovers that she is not alone, not doomed to be separated, in shame, from others. Most often, the first interpersonal context characterized by nonsecrecy and expressive contact is the therapeutic relationship. This is why the therapeutic alliance must be predicated on the therapist's knowledge of the myths about rape and the therapist's ability to provide alternative cognitive appraisals.

Assimilation of Therapy

As the client and therapist work on these tasks, the client is able to assimilate her victimization. Burt and Katz (1987, 1988) identified the process and outcomes of growth oriented assimilation. Positive outcomes included improved self-concept and self-directed activities as well as reduced passivity and stereotyped attitudes. Likewise, Veronen and Kilpatrick (1982) suggested ways in which rape can be assimilated as a positive event. Specifically they identified consciousness raising, renewed appreciation of life, and enhanced self-efficacy or mastery of challenge as three of the ways in which victims could positively assimilate their experiences. Such trauma-forged beliefs may, in fact, better prepare women to live in a victimizing culture.

Clinical contact with victims appears to support the thesis advanced by Burt and Katz (1988) that rape resolution is powerfully mediated by the victim's ability to restore and enhance previous meaning, mastery, and self-esteem. Thus, therapeutic intervention should seek as its goal, not just acceptance, but the transcendence of victimization through an establishment of a new gestalt organizing the relationship between the victim, now a survivor, and her world.

Resolution and Termination

Such transcendent resolution is the foundation for therapy termination. As the client senses her new compact with her culture and her self and is willing to confront trespasses against her dignity and worth, preparing for termination is advisable.

It is clear from the preceding treatment analysis that the work involved in treating victimization is not simple and, as a consequence, is not particularly well suited to very brief interventions. This is especially true of delayed treatment seekers who have wrapped their identities around the experience of themselves as unworthy and powerless.

In fact, it may well be, even for immediate treatment seekers, that the relatively brief crisis stabilization treatment should be followed by a second treatment phase organized about the themes and processes developed in the present chapter. In any event, it is clear that more work is needed in resolving this issue (Koss & Burkhart, 1989).

Termination of treatment for the victim/survivor often includes one issue specific to the acquaintance rape situation. As a victim experiences her anger and autonomy, she may seek to confront her assailant. Because he is known to her and often, in fact, continues to intrude in her life, there is ample opportunity for this to occur. Although the opportunity to confront her assailant and define her responsibility has considerable power in resolution of the rape trauma, there are also some risks attendant to this process of which therapists should be aware. The first is, of course, the obvious risk of retaliation by the assailant; even if assailants do not physically retaliate, they almost always continue to deny responsibility, shift blame to their victims, or attempt to revictimize them psychologically. Thus, the therapist must work with the client to be prepared to prevent the possibility of physical revictimization and to help the woman be immune to any psychological retribution. It is important, moreover, that the therapist and client explore, in detail, the rationale for the confrontation because it may have some "magic" meaning for the client which renders her vulnerable to the assailant. Alternatives to face-to-face intervention, such as letter writing or therapy-situated symbolic confrontations, should be explored.

CONCLUSION

The superordinate treatment goal in acquaintance rape is for the victim to be enabled to live without the past persisting into and thereby distorting the present. Becoming a survivor involves this ability to transcend the victimization and its damaging consequences. To be a survivor is, in the words of one of our clients, "to live well in spite of my rape . . . to be able to see who I am and what my friends see in me . . . and not what he saw in me."

REFERENCES

Bergin, A. E. (1985). Proposed values for guiding and evaluating counseling and psychotherapy. *Counseling and Values, 29,* 99–116.

Browne, A., & Finkelhor, D. (1986). The traumatic impact of child sexual abuse: A conceptualization. *American Journal of Orthopsychiatry, 55,* 530–541.

Brownmiller, S. (1975). *Against our will: Men, women, and rape.* New York: Simon & Schuster.

Burgess, A. W., & Holmstrom, L. L. (1974). Rape trauma syndrome. *American Journal of Psychiatry, 131,* 981–986.

Burkhart, B. R., & Stanton, A. L. (1988). Acquaintance rape. In Gordon W. Russell (Ed.), *Violence in intimate relationships* (pp. 43–65). New York: PMA Press.

Burt, M. R. (1978). Attitudes supportive of rape in the American culture. In House Committee on Science and Technology, Subcommittee on Domestic and International Scientific Planning, Analysis, and Corporation (Ed.), *Research into violent behavior: Sexual assault* (Hearing, 95th Congress, Second Session, January 10–12, 1978, pp. 277–322). Washington, DC: Government Printing Office.

Burt, M. R. (1980). Cultural myths and supports for rape. *Journal of Personality and Social Psychology, 38,* 217–230.

Burt, M. R., & Katz, B. L. (1987). Dimensions of recovery from rape: Focus on growth outcomes. *Journal of Interpersonal Violence, 2,* 57–82.

Burt, M. R., & Katz, B. L. (1988). Coping strategies and recovery from rape. In R. A. Prentky & V. L. Quinsey (Eds.), *Human sexual aggression: Current Perspectives. Annals of the New York Academy of Sciences (Vol. 528,* pp. 345–358). New York: The New York Academy of Sciences.

Conte, J. R. (1988). The effects of sexual abuse on children: Results of a research project. In R. A. Prentky & V. L. Quinsey (Eds.), *Human sexual aggression: Current perspectives. Annals of the New York Academy of Sciences (Vol. 528,* pp. 310–326). New York: The New York Academy of Science.

Courtois, C. A., & Spier, J. E. (1988). Retrospective incest therapy for women. In L. E. A. Walker (Ed.), *Handbook of sexual abuse of children* (pp. 270–308). New York: Springer.

Davis, R. C., & Friedman, L. N. (1985). The emotional aftermath of crime and violence. In C. R. Figley (Ed.), *Trauma and its wake: The study and treatment of post-traumatic stress disorder,* (pp. 90–111). New York: Brunner/Mazel.

Ellis, E. M. (1983). A review of empirical rape research: Victim reactions and response to treatment. *Clinical Psychology Review, 3,* 473–490.

Frank, E., Anderson, B., Stewart, B. D., Dancu, C., Hughes, C., & West, D. (1988). Immediate and delayed treatment of rape victims. In R. A. Prentky & V. L. Quinsey (Eds.), *Human sexual aggression: Current perspectives. Annals of the New York Academy of Sciences (Vol. 528,* pp. 296–309). New York: The New York Academy of Sciences.

Holmes, M. R., & St. Lawrence, J. S. (1983). Treatment of rape induced trauma: Proposed behavioral conceptualization and review of the literature. *Clinical Psychology Review, 3,* 417–433.

Jehu, D. C., Klassan, D., & Gazan, D. (1985–1986). Cognitive restructuring of distorted beliefs associated with childhood sexual abuse. *Journal of Social Work and Human Sexuality, 4,* 46–69.

Kibler, K. J. (1986). *Differential labeling of acquaintance rape.* Unpublished master's thesis. Auburn University, Auburn, Alabama.

Kilpatrick, D. G., Best, C. L., Saunders, B. E., & Veronen, L. J. (1988). Rape in marriage and dating relationships: How bad is it for mental health? In R. A. Prentky & V. L. Quinsey (Eds.), *Human sexual aggression: Current perspectives. Annals of the New York Academy of Sciences (Vol. 528,* pp. 335–344). New York: The New York Academy of Science.

Kilpatrick, D. G., & Veronen, L. J. (1983). Treatment for rape-related problems: Crisis intervention is not enough. In L. H. Cohen, W. Clairborn, & G. Specter (Eds.), *Crisis intervention* (pp. 165–185). New York: Human Sciences Press.

Klemmack, S. H., & Klemmack, D. L. (1976). The social definition of rape. In M. J. Walker & S. L. Brodsky (Eds.), *Sexual assault* (pp. 135–147). Lexington, MA: Heath.

Koss, M. P. (1985). The hidden rape victim: Personality, attitudinal, and situational characteristics. *Psychology of Women Quarterly, 9,* 193–212.

Koss, M., & Burkhart, B. R. (1989). A conceptual analysis of rape victimization: Long-term effects and implications for treatment. *Psychology of Women Quarterly, 13,* 27–40.

Koss, M. P., Dinero, T. E., Seibel, C. A., & Cox, S. (1988). Stranger and acquaintance rape: Are there differences in the victim's experience? *Psychology of Women Quarterly, 12,* 1–24.

Koss, M. P., Gidycz, C. A., & Wisniewski, N. (1987). The scope of rape: Incidence and prevalence of sexual aggression and victimization in a national sample of higher education students. *Journal of Consulting and Clinical Psychology, 55,* 162–170.

Koss, M. P., & Harvey, M. R. (1987). *The rape victim: Clinical and community approaches to treatment.* Lexington, MA: Stephen Greene Press.

Lakin, M. (1988). *Ethical issues in the psychotherapies.* New York: Oxford University Press.

L'Armand, K., & Pepitone, A. (1982). Judgments of rape: A study of victim–rapist relationship and victim sexual history. *Personality and Social Psychology Bulletin, 8,* 134–139.

Mandoki, C. A., & Burkhart, B. R. (1989a, August). *Coping and adjustment to rape.* Paper presented at the annual meeting of the American Psychological Association, New Orleans.

Mandoki, C. A. & Burkhart, B. R. (1989b). Sexual victimization: Is there a vicious cycle? *Violence and Victims, 4,* 179–190.

Russell, D. E. H. (1984). *Sexual exploitation.* Beverly Hills: Sage.

Sanday, P. R. (1981). The socio-cultural context of rape: A cross-cultural study. *Journal of Social Issues, 37,* 15–27.

Silver, R. L., Boon, C., & Stone, M. H. (1983). Searching for meaning in misfortune: Making sense of incest. *Journal of Issues, 39,* 81–102.

Skelton, C. A., & Burkhart, B. R. (1980). Sexual assault: Determinants of victim disclosure. *Criminal Justice and Behavior, 7,* 229–236.

Sommerfeldt, T., Burkhart, B. R., & Mandoki, C. A. (1989, August). *In her own words: Victims' descriptions of hidden rape effects.* Paper presented at the annual meeting of the American Psychological Association, New Orleans.

Summit, R. L. (1983). The child sexual abuse accommodation syndrome. *Child Abuse and Neglect, 7,* 177–193.

Tjeltneit, A. C. (1986). The ethics of value conversion in psychotherapy: Appropriate and inappropriate therapist influence of client values. *Clinical Psychology Review, 6,* 515–537.

Veronen, L. J., & Kilpatrick, D. G. (1982, November). *Stress inoculation training for victims of rape: Efficacy and differential findings.* Paper presented at the meeting of the Association for Advancement of Behavior Therapy, Los Angeles.

Walker, L. E. A. (1985). Feminist therapy with victims of violence. In L. B. Rosewater & L. E. A. Walker (Eds.), *Handbook on feminist therapy: Psychotherapy issues with women* (pp. 203–214). New York: Springer.

Weis, K., & Borges, S. (1973). Victimology and rape: The case of the legitimate victim. *Issues in Criminology, 8,* 71–115.

CHAPTER 19

Medical Community Response to Acquaintance Rape—Recommendations

ANDREA PARROT, PhD

"Rape is the ultimate invasion of privacy. The rapist murders the ego even when he allows the body to survive" (Hicks, 1988, p. 108). Although one in four women are sexually abused, fewer than 10% of victims seek medical help or discuss the sexual assault with anyone (Beckmann & Groetzinger, 1989). If primary care practitioners recognize the signs of sexual assault, know how to care for victims, and understand victims' forensic care requirements, they may be able to minimize the serious physical and emotional risks that are associated with lack of care following a sexual assault (Beckmann & Groetzinger, 1989). Rape (by an acquaintance or a stranger) may lead to psychological trauma as evidenced by depression, eating disorders, or sexually inappropriate behaviors that may require medical and/or psychological intervention. This discussion focuses on the psychological and medical needs of *acquaintance* rape victims.

Assailants *and* victims of acquaintance rape are usually between the ages of 15 and 25. Therefore, in primary care, a discussion of acquaintance rape should be included in the history and physical, starting in the early teen years. Both male and female patients should receive information about acquaintance rape because members of either sex can be victims or assailants. (Because females are usually the victims in acquaintance rape, the feminine pronoun is used to refer to victims in this chapter, and because most acquaintance rapes are committed by men, the masculine pronoun is used to refer to assailants.)

Male assailants, surprisingly, may commit acquaintance rape without thinking they are doing anything wrong. Many males grow up with the messages that females never mean no when they say no and if the male is persistent, both people on a date will get what they want. Consequently, a man may push a woman to have intercourse, believing that although she may have protested, she really wanted sex but was trying to protect her reputation. The victim and the law may agree that rape occurred but the assailant may think that the sex was consensual.

Although incidence statistics vary by jurisdiction, approximately one in four women and one in eight men are victimized sexually (Rosenberg, 1986). Yet, according to the Federal Bureau of Investigation *Uniform Crime Reports* (FBI, 1982), only about one in 10 rapes is reported to police. Most of the unreported rapes are committed by acquaintances (Koss, 1988).

Rape victims who seek medical attention for rape most often go to a hospital emergency room (D'Epiro, 1986). Of those who go to private practitioners, more seek help from general or family practitioners than from obstetrician-gynecologists, and only occasionally are psychiatrists consulted (McGuire & Stern, 1976). Victims seek medical help from pediatricians, surgeons, or internists less often following a rape.

The needs of rape victims who seek medical attention immediately following the assault are slightly different from those of victims who wait. Victims who seek immediate attention will require both physical and psychological crisis intervention; those who wait will require emotional help but will need little, if any, medical help for physical problems directly related to the rape. They may, however, have indirectly related physical symptoms such as sleep disturbances, problems with memory, eating disorders, and nausea.

Most victims do not call what happened to them "rape" and few report the crime immediately after it happens. Medical practitioners will therefore probably not need to collect evidence for a rape kit or to attend to a victim's medical needs, such as pregnancy prevention and treatment of lacerations, as they would immediately following the rape. Health care practitioners who see acquaintance rape victims long after the rape occurred will need to attend primarily to their psychological needs, which may be related to their psychosomatic physical symptoms. Rarely are health care practitioners called upon to provide emergency medical evaluation and treatment, including evidence collection, following an acquaintance rape.

Acquaintance rape victims are not likely to present the practitioner with any evidence of physical trauma although they are likely to have suffered emotional trauma. Although acquaintance rapes are much more common than stranger rapes, acquaintance rape victims are not as easily identified because they rarely fight with their attackers and thus rarely sustain bruises or physical injury. Hence, health care practitioners will probably see victims of acquaintance rape, but the rape victimization will not be obvious and the victims will probably not identify themselves as such. Most acquaintance rape victims do not label what has happened to them "rape," but they almost always experience emotional trauma as a result of the event (Koss, 1988). If an acquaintance rape victim does identify her experience as rape, the identification will probably not happen for weeks, months, or even years after the rape has occurred. She usually identifies the experience as rape after she has read of or heard an expert describe acquaintance rape and realizes that her experience fits that category.

WHY VICTIMS DON'T CALL IT RAPE

The degree of force used in the rape seems to be the most powerful determinant in the victim's decision to call an experience a rape. Having no prior acquaintance with the assailant is associated with greater willingness to report the rape to police (Skelton & Burkhart, 1980). Because most acquaintance rapes occur without associated violence and the victim knows the assailant, the report rate is much lower for acquaintance rapes than for stranger rapes. Researchers estimate that as few as one in 100 acquaintance rapes are reported to law enforcement or school authorities (Burkhart, 1983).

At least four reasons account for victims' not identifying acquaintance rape as rape: concern for the rapist, self-blame, the social stereotype of "real" rape, and the victim's attempt to repress the rape memory (Parrot, 1986). The victim may blame herself because she feels that she contributed to the rape in a number of ways. Common examples include: agreeing to go out with her attacker, dressing in a "seductive" manner, inviting the rapist to her apartment (for something other than sex), or even having had sex with him in the past. In many instances, the threat of violence to the victim or to family members or friends is sufficient for the rapist to have controlled the victim (Beckmann & Groetzinger, 1989). It is sometimes difficult for an acquaintance rape victim to believe that legally rape occurs *any* time a woman is forced to have intercourse, even with her husband, against her will, unless the wife lives in one of the few states where husbands can rape their wives without prosecution. As of January 1990, the following states still legally allowed husbands to rape their wives: Kentucky, Missouri, New Mexico, North Carolina, Oklahoma, South Carolina, and Utah. (See Chapter 9 for a more complete discussion of this issue.)

The woman is often "excused" from responsibility for a sexual encounter when violence is used to force her to comply with the man's sexual desires (Skelton & Burkhart, 1980). The rape stereotype develops from the notion that women are responsible for the outcome of sexual interactions unless their responsibility has been usurped (Klemmack & Klemmack, 1976; Weis & Borges, 1975). The greater the degree of force used in an acquaintance rape, the less embarrassed the victim is about the experience. And, the more liberal the victim's attitudes toward women's roles, the more likely she is to report a rape. If the woman chooses not to report the event to the police, she faces greater skepticism from legal and medical professionals and from her friends (Bohmer, 1973; Feild, 1978; Schwendinger & Schwendinger, 1974).

Most victims believe the rape stereotype. They do not call what has happened to them rape because they believe that rape is committed only by a stranger, with violence, upon a "blameless" victim. If the victim did something she views as having "caused" the rape, she may assume the guilt and responsibility for the rape and will probably not report the rape to the police or to health care providers.

HISTORY TAKING

A diagnosis of pregnancy may precipitate the first report of a rape. However, a report of a rape months or years after the fact may be precipitated by depression, anxiety, and emotional disturbance regarding the victim's sexuality or self-confidence (Beckmann & Groetzinger, 1989). If victims do not seek help soon after a rape, they may suffer in silence or present to a physician with vague complaints of chronic epigastric or pelvic pains, constant fatigue, or headaches. If no organic cause is found, these patients may be sent away with the assurance that nothing is wrong and that "it is all in your head" (Beckmann & Groetzinger, 1989).

The health care practitioner may have to apply investigative skills when taking the medical history, to determine whether the patient has been raped. In a complete history and physical, these questions may elicit information about acquaintance rape victimization:

Have you ever had sex when you didn't want to?

Have you ever been forced to have sex?

Do you have difficulty saying "no" when you don't want to have sex?

When a patient responds affirmatively to any of these questions, many practitioners will ask the following questions to discredit the individual. These questions may be a form of victim blaming, especially if they are asked in a judgmental way:

Have you had sex with this person before?

Are you married to this person?

Did you sustain any injuries during the unwanted sexual encounter?

Were you drunk at the time?

Did you report the crime to the police? (Parrot, 1990).

According to the law, none of those factors excuses rape; they are not even relevant. The victim may feel devastated and traumatized by the rape regardless of her relationship with the assailant, the degree of injury she sustained, or her degree of intoxication at the time. She may be suffering from chronic depression induced by her feelings of hopelessness, helplessness, guilt, and shame.

Cognitive dysfunction (an inability to think clearly) is common in the rape trauma syndrome (described in a later section of this chapter). As a consequence, the victim may have difficulty remembering her medical history and her remarks may be inconsistent (Beckmann & Groetzinger, 1989). These inconsistencies should not be viewed as proof that she was not raped.

"When the patient seeks medical care more than 72 hours following the assault, most jurisdictions no longer accept the evidence collected"

(Beckmann & Groetzinger, 1989, p. 81). However, a delay in seeking care should never be interpreted as an indication that the report is false or that the patient is not emotionally or physically traumatized (Beckmann & Groetzinger, 1989).

CLINICAL MANIFESTATIONS

Generally, there are differences in clinical manifestations and emotional responses for victims of stranger and acquaintance rape. Generally, if acquaintance rape victims seek medical care, there will not be any bruises or signs of a struggle apparent, even if the victim did struggle, because weeks or months will probably have passed since the rape. It may be past the time when discussion of pregnancy is relevant. For a victim who seeks medical care after weeks or months have passed, the routine physical examination and sexually transmitted disease (STD) evaluation are still indicated, with special focus on any symptomatic complaints.

Rape victims may respond to questioning during a history and physical with relief at being able to recount the details of the event, or they may feel degraded, embarrassed, and frightened. Some women, especially if they have never had an internal exam before, may feel raped again by the gynecologic exam (Nadelson & Nortman, 1985), and because they may be tender in places, the bimanual exam should be performed gently. A tranquilizer *offered* prior to the pelvic exam may be helpful to calm an agitated rape victim (Rosenberg, 1986). During a rape, victims feel that they have lost control of their lives; after a rape, victims need to regain that control. Consequently, if a victim does not want a tranquilizer, even if the tranquilizer would make the exam easier, her wishes should be respected.

Most rape victims do not express a preference regarding the gender of the examiner. A nonthreatening, supportive, and empathetic male physician, however, may help a victim reestablish healthy relationships with men (Beckmann & Groetzinger, 1989). Regardless of the gender of the practitioner, it is important that the exam be performed with sensitivity (Riesenberg, 1987). Rape victims have reported that they feel comfortable with a physician who expresses personal concern and professional objectivity (Martin, Warfield, & Braen, 1983). The presence of a female nurse may help to calm a distraught patient. Police representatives are *not* required in the exam room when medical evidence is collected as long as the evidence passes directly from the practitioner to police immediately following the exam (D'Epiro, 1986).

The history following a rape should include a discussion of sodomy, fellatio, manual invasion of the vagina, ejaculation and urination on her body, and other sexual acts that may have been performed (Hicks, 1988). Patients may be too embarrassed to bring some of these things up unless they are asked about them in a nonjudgmental way. All questions should be asked in a nonmoralistic and nonjudgmental manner and tone. For example, it would be better to ask "Did he put his penis in your mouth?" rather than to ask "You didn't perform oral sex on him, did you?" The wording of the first question does not imply that the woman was a willing participant in sex, but that of the second question might.

The victim may be more likely to provide complete information if she is told that these acts are not uncommon in rape situations. Since the medical record may become part of a court proceeding, the health care practitioner should make all entries legible, detailed, and to the point. The practitioner should try to use lay terminology whenever possible. For example, it would be better to report that "Semen was present in the vagina" than to write that "Acid phosphatase was found in the vaginal asperate." A summary of the victim's statements and a medical record of her status provide sufficient information to be fully defensible legally, because the medical record is considered a professional evaluation (Beckmann & Groetzinger, 1989). Practitioners should refrain from drawing conclusions about the rape. If the victim had contusions on her throat and semen was present in her vagina and mouth, it would be better to write that "Semen was found in the vagina and mouth, and her throat was bruised" than " She appears to have been raped and sodomized." Notations that preempt the responsibility of a jury to draw conclusions may prejudice the jury and consequently may be thrown out of court.

The practitioner should look for abrasions, swelling, lacerations, contusions, and scratches on the victim's body. The rapist may have grabbed her, leaving marks on her neck, upper arms, breasts, or thighs. The internal exam should be done with a water-moistened speculum, since lubricants may alter forensic test results (Hicks, 1988). A Wood's ultraviolet-light lamp should be used to search for semen, which fluoresces; and vaginal asperate should be checked for acid phosphatase, which is present in seminal fluid (Riesenberg, 1987). If the rapist has had a vasectomy, the presence of acid phosphatase rather than sperm would indicate that ejaculation occurred during the rape. However, ejaculation is not necessary for an incident to be legally considered rape.

Summary for Conducting and Documenting the Rape Exam (Burgess & Holmstrom, 1988)

In the information compiled from the findings of the physical exam and the victim's brief description of the rape, the following elements should be present:

Length of time between rape and exam;

Presence of pain, dysuria (painful urination), or tenesmus (a feeling of urinary urgency);

Type of sexual penetrations (anal, vaginal, oral);

A culture of any areas that were penetrated;

Evidence of stains on clothing that fluoresce using ultraviolet light;

Victim's activities following the assault (such as bathing, douching, urinating);

Photos and a description of the precise location and extent of the injuries;

Results of the pelvic examination.

PSYCHOLOGICAL AND EMOTIONAL RESPONSES OF THE VICTIM

The health care practitioner must attend to the psychological and emotional as well as the physical needs of the patient. Acquaintance rape victims are likely to experience the *rape trauma syndrome*.

Burgess and Holmstrom (1974, 1979, 1988) identified the rape trauma syndrome as the victim's emotional response to rape—a cluster of somatic, cognitive, psychological, and behavioral symptoms exhibited in varying degrees by most rape victims (Burgess & Holmstrom, 1988). The rape trauma syndrome which occurs in stranger and acquaintance rape victims, has two stages: the acute or disorganization phase and the reorganization phase.

In the *acute* or *disorganization phase* the victim experiences guilt and shame. She may have difficulty sleeping and may report digestive system disorders, fatigue, headache, vaginal discharge, and an exaggerated startle response. During this phase some victims exhibit an "expressive" reaction in which anger, fear, anxiety, tension, and crying are common. Other victims exhibit a "controlled" reaction during which the victim may appear controlled, calm, and subdued. This initial phase may last for weeks.

In the *reorganization phase,* the victim may become depressed, show anger toward men, avoid others in social situations, and experience impaired memory or concentration and/or rapid mood swings. This phase may last months or years. With therapy or the counsel of an understanding and informed support person, the victim may be able to put the rape in perspective and get on with her life. However, it is unlikely that she will be able to forget the rape or regain the level of trust she had before the rape.

Burkhart (1983) identified three of the most typical behavior patterns an acquaintance rape victim may exhibit, following her initial emotional reaction; she may (a) withdraw from social interactions, (b) attempt to repress memory of the rape, or (c) exhibit nondiscriminating sexual behavior patterns. These patterns may be exhibited immediately after the rape or up to many years later.

The acquaintance rape victim may *withdraw from social interactions* because she no longer feels she can trust her judgment. When she did trust her judgment, she chose to interact with a rapist; her judgment was faulty. Consequently, she stops making decisions that rely on her judgment.

She may *repress the rape memory* in the hope that she will be able to forget it and return to "normal." In this pattern she may exhibit occasional emotional explosions when she is under stress or is reminded of the rape.

Her reaction may be triggered by something as innocuous as a man's touching her shoulder or a physician's examining her thyroid in the same place or manner in which the rapist touched her. Later recollections of the rape often precipitate recurring crises in other relationships.

The victim may *exhibit nondiscriminating sexual behavior patterns* (sex with more people than usual). If she was a virgin prior to the assault and believed that "virginity is good" and "nonvirginity is bad," she may think that she is bad and has no legitimate reason to refuse requests for sex by any man in the future. Consequently, she may adopt a sexually promiscuous behavior pattern after the rape.

One possible way to approach this type of patient is to attempt to "give her back her virginity" by helping her understand that one loses virginity only by having consensual sex. Contrary to popular belief, virginity is not determined by the presence or absence of a hymen, since many women no longer have intact hymens by the time they are teenagers. Acquaintance rape does not involve consensual sex and is a crime. A robbery victim who freely gives up his or her money during the robbery cannot be called a philanthropist. In the same way, we cannot call what happened to a rape victim consensual sex. If the victim has not yet had consensual sex, she is still a virgin because consensual sex is the only way to lose virginity. It may help to think of virginity as a state of mind and not a physical condition.

If the victim displays any of these three behavior patterns, she will need counseling to help her get over her feelings of self-blame and guilt, which often interfere with present and future interpersonal relationships and with feelings of positive self-esteem.

COUNSELING ISSUES

It is not the role of the health care practitioner to determine whether rape occurred. Rather, the role should be to provide whatever medical care is necessary and to refer the victim to a counselor trained in working with victims of acquaintance rape.

Although many primary care physicians enjoy counseling, and are good at it, few have the time necessary to deal comprehensively with the psychological aftermath of sexual assault. A counselor should be available to talk to the woman whenever she needs it, because inaccessibility can be misinterpreted as rejection, reinforcing the patient's sense of worthlessness.

(Hicks, 1988, p. 120)

The rape victim needs assistance in reducing her inevitable fears, stresses, and anxieties and in restoring her self-esteem and self-confidence (Burgess & Holmstrom, 1988). The victim usually needs to recall the details of the rape, with the support of friends, family, or a counselor. This will allow her to regain control over the memory of the rape, which should eliminate some of the power it holds to distress her. This method gradually desensitizes the victim and allows her to remember the assault without being terrified (Burgess & Holmstrom, 1988).

Few individual health care professionals possess the skills and knowledge needed to meet all the physical and emotional needs of rape victims. Physicians, nurses, and counselors are most effective working collaboratively (Beckmann & Groetzinger, 1989).

ROLE OF THE HEALTH CARE PRACTITIONER

No two rape victims react exactly the same way. Some may respond with overt emotion; others may appear quiet, exhausted, or withdrawn (Hicks, 1988). A health care practitioner may not appreciate the extent of the trauma the victim is experiencing, especially if she is not hysterical and has few serious physical injuries. Rape should be treated as a medical emergency because "how the victim is treated from the moment she walks into the office or emergency department has a tremendous impact on her ability to recover." (Hicks, 1988, p. 108.)

One of the most important things the health care practitioner can do is help a victim regain her sense of control. This should be started in the examination, in decisions about her treatment. At each stage of the examination the practitioner should explain what is about to happen and ask for the victim's permission to proceed, especially during the pelvic exam (Hicks, 1988). Rules about having a support person in the exam room with the victim should be flexible enough to allow her to have whatever level of support she wants. Even bringing her a cup of coffee without her requesting it may be seen by her as part of her inability to control her environment, especially if she has refused a cup of coffee earlier.

The practitioner can help the victim to regain a sense of control over her life and improve her self-esteem, and can empower her to be able to avoid future acquaintance rapes. Many counselors in a community may be trained in helping victims of stranger rape, but they may do more harm than good unless they also know how to help acquaintance rape victims. Those who do not understand acquaintance rape are likely to blame the victim for having "caused" or "contributed to" the rape. They may say or imply something like "You were asking for it by going to his room and getting drunk." In fact, a victim is never responsible for a rape. The victim may have done some things to increase her vulnerability, such as going to the apartment of a man whom she did not know well, but that does not mean that she deserved to be raped. Reminding the victim, and those around her, that "poor judgment is not a rapable offense" should help to place the blame where it belongs—with the assailant (Beckmann & Groetzinger, 1989).

The same standards should apply to acquaintance rape victims as to victims of other crimes. For example, if a man who is wearing an expensive suit and a Rolex watch is mugged while walking down a street in New York City, he is not held responsible for the mugging. He increased his vulnerability by dressing in expensive clothing but did not want to be mugged and does not have to show bruises to prove that he fought back hard enough and did not enjoy the mugging. Yet victims of acquaintance rape frequently hear comments implying that they "asked to be raped."

Health care practitioners who want to counsel acquaintance rape victims should make the assumption that the victim is telling the truth. Victims stand to lose more than they would ever gain by reporting an acquaintance rape to police or school authorities. They risk losing the support and friendship of family and friends, who may be forced to choose between loyalty to the victim or the the assailant. The false report rate of acquaintance rape is very low (New York City Police Department, 1972; Warshaw, 1988). A woman who reports a rape that did not happen needs psychological help, because emotionally healthy people do not falsely accuse others of crimes. In any event, if a woman tells a health care practitioner that she is a victim of acquaintance rape, it is best for the practitioner to believe her (or act as if he or she does) and refer her to a trained therapist or counselor. The health care practitioner may help the victim to consider the options available to her.

OPTIONS FOR THE VICTIM

The family or significant other of the victim may become emotionally upset and require counseling. The health care provider may want to offer a supportive role to them as well as to the victim (Nadelson & Nortman, 1985). Family and friends may be secondary victims and may feel as if they have been raped too. These people often have traumatic reactions similar to those of the primary victim and may need counseling referral (Burgess & Holmstrom, 1988).

The victim and the family may need information about available options. An acquaintance rape victim may want to *tell her family* about the rape, but that may not be wise if her family will blame her and be unsupportive. She may want to *tell friends,* but again, she should look for those who will support her and will not insist on any course of action to which she is opposed (such as reporting the rape to the police). Another option available to her is to *seek therapy* with a counselor or therapist who understands acquaintance rape. She may want to *confront the assailant* after she is emotionally healed, to tell him how she perceived what he did to her. If the rape happened on school grounds or between two people who attend the same school, she can *report it to school authorities.* The assailant may be transferred, suspended, or expelled so she will not have to see him every day in her classes.

She can report to the police to *give information only;* she is not obligated to give her name or press charges. She may choose to *press charges for criminal prosecution.* Victims may have good reasons for deciding not to report the rape, but they never should refrain from doing so because of shame. Health care practitioners should attempt to help patients understand that being the victim of a rape should be no more shameful than being the victim of any other tragedy, such as an automobile accident or a robbery (Hicks, 1988).

She may also *sue the assailant in civil court* for pain and suffering and for therapy and medical costs. She will probably have a better chance of winning in civil court because, unlike criminal court, she will not need the entire jury's belief that the alleged assailant is guilty beyond a reasonable doubt. In addition, she may *sue a third party* who "contributed" to the rape (Parrot, 1989).

Regardless of what she decides to do about reporting and seeking help, she needs to learn how to decrease her vulnerability, to help her avoid acquaintance rape situations in the future. She can use her mind as a weapon by learning to assess situations to determine whether they are potentially dangerous and by exercising assertive behavior to get out of those situations or avoid them completely. She can learn to use her voice as a weapon, for example, by yelling for help or by yelling at her attacker to leave her alone. By learning self-defense techniques, practicing them to gain expertise, and being willing to execute them forcefully, she can use her body as a weapon to defend herself if she is being exploited by another person. She must feel good enough about herself to know that she has the right to defend herself against someone she knows and likes who is forcing her to do something against her will. She will need information and positive self-esteem to accomplish these goals.

CONCLUSION

The most important thing victims can do to regain control over their lives is to place blame and responsibility for the rape where it belongs—with the rapist. Acquaintance rape victims may need help finding a good support system and may benefit from short- or long-term counseling. If the victim is in a relationship, it may be wise for both the victim and her partner to enter into counseling together.

Health care practitioners should ask themselves: Under what circumstances do I believe a victim's accusation of rape? Do I believe a rape victim more if she has bruises? Am I relieved if a victim is calm? Do I believe a rape victim when she is calm? How do I feel if a rape victim is hysterical? The answers to these questions may help practitioners determine whether they should be treating rape victims or referring them to others. Dr. Dorothy Hicks (1988), Director of the Rape Treatment Center at James M. Jackson Memorial Hospital in Miami believes that no individual who harbors any feelings that a rape victim in some way brought the experience on herself, or secretly enjoyed it, should come in contact with rape victims.

Health care practitioners should offer medical services, referrals, and counseling services (when appropriate) for victims of rape. Rape victims need special care to minimize the fear, shame, guilt, pain, and embarrassment they may already be experiencing. The following summary list of suggestions for health care practitioners will help to minimize some of the trauma that a rape victim may be experiencing:

Express regret that the victim has been assaulted.

Reassure the patient that she is safe with you.

Even if you do not believe her, act as if you do.

Do not blame her.

Help to give her back control by doing as she asks.

Let her have someone she trusts to comfort her during the exam.

Ask her questions she will understand.

Explain procedures to the victim before and during the exam.

Use her language and make sure you know what she means.

Refer her to a trained counselor for emotional help.

Help arrange for an appointment with the counselor, and follow up to make sure she went.

Advise the victim's friends and family of her needs.

Explain the rape trauma syndrome to her and assure her that her feelings are normal.

Do not assume that you know how she feels.

Don't use the term "rape" to describe the incident unless she has already done so. It might frighten her.

Learn more about rape.

Explain to other medical practitioners the importance of the behaviors listed above.

The primary health practitioner's role is to identify victims, treat their physical symptoms, help them determine a course of action, and refer them to a trained counselor.

REFERENCES

Beckmann, C. R. B., & Groetzinger, L. L. (1989). Treating sexual assault victims: A protocol for health professionals. *The Female Patient, 14,* 78–83.

Bohmer, C. (1973). Judicial attitudes toward rape victims. *Judicature, 57,* 303–307.

Burgess, A. W., & Holmstrom, L. L. (1974). Rape trauma syndrome. *American Journal of Psychiatry, 131,* 981–986.

Burgess, A. W., & Holmstrom, L. L. (1979). *Rape crisis and recovery.* Bowie, MD: Robert J. Brady Co.

Burgess, A. W., & Holmstrom, L. L. (1988). Treating the adult rape victim. *Medical Aspects of Human Sexuality, 22,* 36–43.

Burkhart, B. (1983, December). *Acquaintance rape statistics and prevention.* Paper presented at the Acquaintance Rape and Rape Prevention on Campus Conference, Louisville, KY.

D'Epiro, D. (1986). Examining the rape victim. *Patient Care,* 98–123.

FBI (Federal Bureau of Investigation). (1982). *Uniform crime reports,* Washington, DC: U.S. Department of Justice.

Feild, H. S. (1978). Attitudes toward rape: A comparative analysis of police, rapists, crisis counselors, and citizens. *Journal of Personality and Social Psychology, 36,* 156–179.

Hicks, D. (1988, November). The patient who's been raped. *Emergency Medicine,* pp. 106–122.

Klemmack, S. H., & Klemmack, D. L. (1976). The social definition of rape. In M. J. Walker & S. L. Brodsky (Eds.), *Sexual assault* (pp. 135–147). Lexington, MA: Heath.

Koss, M. P. (1988). Hidden rape: Incidence, prevalence, and descriptive characteristics of sexual aggression and victimization in a national sample of college students. In A. W. Burgess (Ed.), *Sexual assault Vol. II.* pp. 1–25. New York: Garland.

Martin, C. A., Warfield, M. C., & Braen, G. R. (1983). Physician's management of the psychological aspects of rape. *Journal of the American Medical Association, 249,* 501.

McGuire, L. S., & Stern, M. (1976). Survey of incidence of and physicians' attitudes towards sexual assault. *Public Health Reports, 91,* 103–109.

Nadelson, C. C., & Nortman, M. T. (1985). Caring for the rape victim. *The Female Patient, 10,* 84–91.

New York City Police Department. (1972). *Special rape analysis squad report.* New York: Author.

Parrot, A. (1989). Acquaintance rape among adolescents: Identifying risk groups and intervention strategies. *Social Work and Human Sexuality, 8,* 47–61.

Parrot, A. (1990, April). Date rape. *Medical Aspects of Human Sexuality,* pp. 28–31.

Parrot, A. (1986, June). *The emotional impact of acquaintance rape on college women.* Paper presented at the Midcontinent Region Convention of the Society for the Scientific Study of Sex, Madison, WI.

Riesenberg, D. (1987). Treating a social malignancy—rape. *The Journal of the American Medical Association, 257,* 726–727.

Rosenberg, M. (1986). Rape crisis syndrome. *Medical Aspects of Human Sexuality, 20,* Vol. 3, 67–71. Schwendinger, J., & Schwendinger, H. (1974). Rape myths: In legal, theoretical, and everyday practice. *Crime and Social Issues, 4,* 18–26.

Skelton, C. A., & Burkhart, B. R. (1980). Sexual assault: Determinants of victim disclosure. *Criminal Justice and Behavior, 7,* 229–236.

Warshaw, R. (1988). *I never called it rape: The MS. report on recognizing, fighting, and surviving date and acquaintance rape.* New York: Harper & Row.

Weis, K. & Borges, S. (1975). Victimology and rape: The case of the legitimate victim. In L. Schultz (Ed.), *Rape victimology.* Springfield, IL: Thomas.

CHAPTER 20

Acquaintance Rape and the Law

CAROL BOHMER, PhD

The standard starting point for a discussion of proof of consent in rape law is the resounding pronouncement of Matthew Hale, the British jurist whose description of the common law of England formed the foundation of some of our laws. His statement on rape is the quintessential embodiment of Western society's ambivalence toward rape. "It is true, rape is a most detestable crime, and therefore ought severely and impartially to be punished with death; but it must be remembered that it is an accusation easily to be made and hard to be proved; and harder to be defended by the party accused, though ever so innocent" (Hale, 1680, p. 635).

This ambivalence in the attitudes of the law and those who implement it is nowhere more apparent than in the case of acquaintance rape. The law and those who implement it are extremely punitive toward those cases which they consider "real," but the situation is far different in less clear-cut situations (Estrich, 1987). "Real" rape cases are those perpetrated by a stranger, in circumstances in which no one would consent to sexual intercourse. As a friend who was raped once said, "Who would consent to being raped in a dark alley in January?" It is partly because rape is such a "detestable crime" that it is very difficult for the traditional legal system to put its weight behind what are viewed as questionable charges. One of the situations in which the charges are most likely to be questioned is when the victim and the alleged perpetrator know one another. This is not because of the way the law itself is written but rather how it is interpreted. Rape laws are framed in such a way as to cover *all* rapes, whether perpetrated by strangers or by acquaintances. For this reason, most of the legal writing on rape law treats acquaintance and stranger rape together.

The laws themselves are thus only part of the story. The rest of the story, that part which is most important to a discussion of acquaintance rape, is how the courts interpret those laws in order to apply them to a particular set of facts. Predictions about how a court will apply the law are also central to the decision-making process of the actors in the court scene: the police, the prosecution, and the defense attorneys.

This chapter briefly examines the law concerning rape, with special reference to acquaintance rape; the changes that have taken place in the laws of rape in recent years and how those changes have affected cases of acquaintance rape; and how the participants involved in the process of bringing a case to trial function within the legal system.

WHAT IS RAPE?

Under traditional law, rape was defined as an act of sexual intercourse undertaken by a man with a woman, not his wife, by force and against her will (Harris, 1976). It included only penile-vaginal intercourse, and required penetration, "be it ever so slight," as the phrase I learned in law school went. Rape was also limited to acts performed by a man on a woman, although a woman could be charged with the crime if she were involved in it, as, for example, holding down another woman while she was raped by a man. This technical exception notwithstanding, neither male on male nor female on female forced sex was included in the definition. Nor were sexual acts other than intercourse covered in the definition, though they might have been covered under other statutes, such as assault or "deviant sex." As we will see, all these aspects of traditional rape law have been subject to criticism by feminists, and all have been changed in one way or another as a result of recent rape reform laws. Nevertheless, most people still think of rape as an offense committed by a man against a woman, which remains statistically true today. For this reason, unless there is a special point to be made, this chapter will refer to the rapist as "he" and the victim as "she."

Susan Brownmiller, whose extensive treatise on rape galvanized feminists when it was published, discussed in detail the history of rape (Brownmiller, 1975). The crime of rape had its origins in property rights, and essentially involved a claim by one man against another for damage to property owned by the claimant. A father whose daughter was raped would have less chance of marrying her off successfully, and a husband's property interest in his wife would be diminished by her having been sullied by another man. The word *rape* comes from the Latin *rapere,* meaning to steal. Rape was originally viewed as an insult to family honor rather than an act that caused trauma to the woman. Despite the fact that rape is now an offense against the woman herself (or against a man, in states that have made their laws applicable to acts against both sexes) rather than against her "owner," vestiges of this old view remain in our current attitudes toward the law of rape.

Traditional attitudes are central in a rape case when the question is whether the event that is the subject of the charge was one to which the victim consented or whether it was forced. As mentioned above, this is particularly true in cases that are not, as Estrich (1987) put it, "real" rape.

CONSENT

There are four legal defenses to a charge of rape (Lafree, 1989). The first defense a defendant can offer is: "It wasn't me." In this situation, he is not disputing that the events alleged by the prosecution took place, but he is disputing the claim that it was he who perpetrated them. The second defense is that no sex took place, a defense that is relevant under those laws which define rape as intercourse only. A third defense, which is not particularly significant here, is that the defendant is not responsible for his behavior.

The fourth defense is the most significant in acquaintance rape cases. It acknowledges that the sexual encounter took place between the defendant and the victim but argues that it was consensual. In cases of acquaintance rape, the first three defenses are not as central to the rape charge as they can be in stranger rape. The victim is claiming that she was raped by a particular person, and therefore the question of identity has already been decided. The second and third defenses, while possible in acquaintance rape, are dealt with by a law that includes lesser offenses; the third defense is extremely rare. By contrast, the defense of consent is more likely to succeed in acquaintance rape than in stranger rape. For, while we find it hard to believe that someone would consent to sex with a person she has never seen before in her life, the same is not true for someone she knows, however slightly. The better the two people know one another, the easier it is to believe that the encounter was consensual. The only exception to this is in cases where someone is raped by a member of her family. This is usually dealt with under incest statutes but may be charged as rape in some states (Lafree, 1989). The heart of the legal issue in cases of acquaintance rape is consent and its proof. Recognizing this, the recent rape law reform movement has concentrated part of its effort on changes designed to make consent less central in a rape trial.

Lack of consent has been defined in the law by phrases such as "by force" and "against her will," sometimes used synonymously and sometimes as separate elements of consent (Harris, 1976, p. 613). However they are used, these definitions have not proven particularly helpful in aiding judges and juries to decide whether rape or consensual sexual intercourse has taken place.

Sexual encounters, like all social events, have different shades of meaning to each person involved. These social psychological "definitions of reality" make the proof of consent or lack thereof an especially difficult legal issue. To illustrate this, let us look at a hypothetical example. If one is told that a person had intercourse with someone who tied her down, that information would not be enough to decide whether the intercourse was forced. One first needs to know the details of the circumstances whereby the woman was tied down. Did she want to be tied down? Or did she attempt to resist the force used to tie her down against her will? Even asking the participants themselves will not necessarily provide the answer. The woman might say that she did not want to be tied down and the man might say that she did. What she intended as resistance, he interpreted as part of the game he thought they were playing to heighten their sexual pleasure. Both interpretations are plausible; people do engage in the activities described above as part of consensual sexual intercourse. If interpretation of the meaning of behavior is so difficult in this rather extreme example, imagine how difficult it is in more ordinary situations.

On an even broader level, sex in our society is not viewed as a straightforward transaction in which one person asks another whether he or she wants to engage in sexual intercourse and the other agrees without further ado. Many people would be rather shocked by such directness—but not in all societies. I was at a party in Iceland a number of years ago with a male friend who was approached by a woman who spoke to him in Icelandic. He explained that he did not speak Icelandic, so she translated. She had said, "Do you want to screw?" This was apparently a perfectly ordinary way for her to approach a man. It would hardly be viewed as ordinary were it to happen in the United States!

The way in which we view sex has a significant impact on the way the courts interpret testimony in rape cases. The law therefore cannot be viewed in the absence of an understanding of these attitudes. For example, American societal norms hold that men should be the initiators in sex and women the responders. A woman who initiates a sexual encounter like the Icelandic woman described above is seen as "unfeminine," aggressive, and even immoral. By the same token, a woman should not appear too eager in her response to a man who initiates sex. To take this one step further, some people consider it appropriate for a woman to pretend not to be interested and to have to be persuaded to engage in sexual intercourse.

Certain kinds of behavior are considered evidence of sexual provocation and a woman is expected to take the consequences for those actions. This may be particularly true in acquaintance rape situations where the woman is defined as having "asked for it" by showing her availability in a number of ways. A woman who goes to a man's apartment, who dresses too provocatively, who allows herself to get drunk, or who hitchhikes may often find her behavior being interpreted as evidence of her willingness to engage in sex.

In addition, a woman whose life-style is deviant—for example, one who drinks a lot, who uses drugs, or who has intercourse outside marriage—may also find that she is unprotected by the law when she is raped. Feminists have argued that these attitudes are a punishment for women who violate appropriate gender-role expectations. Empirical research on this subject supports their view. In acquaintance rape cases, jurors were more influenced by their assessment of the victim's life-style than by physical evidence or the seriousness of the event as measured by several variables.

Using opinions about the victim's life-style or behavior as a way of deciding whether a rape has taken place is one of several circumstances in which rape cases are evaluated differently than other crimes. A man who gets drunk and flashes his money around in a sleazy neighborhood may be considered to have been stupid when he is mugged. The evidence of his behavior would not, however, be relevant to the proof of the crime at the robbery trial of the mugger.

Just as women risk a charge that they "got what they deserved" by engaging in socially inappropriate behavior, so too are they considered responsible for calling a halt to any foreplay that could result in sexual intercourse. If they wait too long before asking the man to stop, they are expected to take the consequences because men are not supposed to be able to control their raging sexual urges. In such cases the court system is incorporating the legal doctrines of contributory negligence and assumption of risk from the civil law into the criminal law, where they do not belong (Berger, 1979). The criminal law is not supposed to take into account whether the victim was partially responsible for the crime. A theft is a theft regardless of whether the person contributed to it by leaving property in a place that made it available to the thief. In the civil law, on the other hand, the doctrine of contributory negligence is relevant to the assessment of damages. It has nothing to do with deciding whether the event was a crime.

These traditional views about appropriate behavior are clearly not the sexual attitudes of all members of our society. Quite the contrary: the sexual revolution has gone a long way toward making attitudes toward sex more egalitarian, especially among the younger members of our society. The difficulty is that those who administer our criminal justice system are more likely to adhere to traditional attitudes. For this reason, the laws themselves and their interpretation are more likely to embody traditional rather than modern attitudes.

It is easy to see how traditional cultural attitudes feed into misunderstanding of a woman's response to her date's overtures. What she may see as a refusal, he may see as socially appropriate coyness. In such a situation, he may go ahead and press her further. The outcome, sexual intercourse, which she considers forced, may be viewed by him—and by the participants in the courtroom who share his cultural attitudes—as consensual intercourse. Rape laws themselves are not sensitive enough to take into account such variation in interpretation of a single event. As Catherine MacKinnon pointed out, rape laws have assumed that a single objective state of affairs existed (MacKinnon, 1983). A rape occurred or it did not; consent was given or it was not. In fact the reality is often split: "A woman is raped but not by a rapist" (MacKinnon, 1983, p. 654). In focusing on the accused's state of mind, the law concludes that the rape did not happen. In the mind of a woman in an acquaintance rape case, however, rape *did* happen.

The legal definition of consent is usually not very helpful, because it is spare enough to require fleshing out in each individual case. That fleshing out is done in terms of the social attitudes discussed above. The defendant's assertions that he did not mean to force the woman into sexual intercourse focus attention on the woman's behavior. He is arguing that he thought she consented, so the prosecutor then has to refute that argument. This can only be done by convincing the judge or jury that she really did not consent. In the absence of circumstantial evidence or of very convincing testimony on the part of the victim, it is an uphill battle for the prosecution to obtain a conviction in the typical acquaintance rape case.

The victim's own definition of the event is problematic in acquaintance rape cases because the issue of consent is so central. Because of the cultural attitudes discussed above, a victim may not have given a clear signal about whether she wanted to engage in sexual intercourse. Her ambivalent message may have been defined as consent by her date, if not by her. The opposite may also be true. What may in fact have been forced sex is sometimes not defined as such by the victim, who may consider it just an unpleasant encounter.

Closely related to the centrality of traditional attitudes toward sex in determining whether there has been consent, are attitudes toward rape itself. A profusion of myths and incorrect stereotypes about rape exists in our society (Brownmiller, 1975; Feild, 1978). These range from the idea that a woman cannot be raped against her will to the beliefs that all women secretly want to be raped and that most rape complaints are faked. The myths also present rapists as sex-starved men who simply cannot resist following their sexual impulses. All these myths combine to create a climate hostile to rape victims, a climate in which the victim is blamed for the rape. A woman's behavior may be used to reinforce the myth. For example, a woman who goes to a man's apartment or who accepts a ride in a car from him is asking for trouble, since all women secretly want to be raped. In one survey of a cross-section of American adults, 50% agreed with the statement: "A woman who goes to the home or apartment of a man on the first date implies she is willing to have sex" (Wrightsman, 1986).

The definition of whether an event is a rape or consensual intercourse has been shown to be affected by the extent to which a person accepts commonly held rape myths (Burt & Albin, 1981). Although there is no direct research of the extent to which attitudes about sex and rape affect the decisions of judges and juries, it is likely that they have a significant influence. Since juries are composed of the same people on whom the research about rape attitudes and acceptance of rape myths has been conducted, it can safely be assumed that those people will take their attitudes and beliefs into the courtroom when they act as jurors.

RAPE LAW REFORM—NONCONSENT

The heavy emphasis on nonconsent and the need to substantiate it with some objective evidence have made conviction extremely difficult in cases that do not fall within the "classic" image of rape: in a dark alley, by a stranger who uses a weapon or inflicts significant injury. Acquaintance rape cases are less likely to have such objective evidence. This leaves little else but the victim's testimony about her behavior and her description of the defendant's actions on which to base a prosecution. Because of these difficulties, many jurisdictions have reformed their law with the intention of moving the attention away from the victim's behavior. These reforms, unfortunately, do not do much in acquaintance rape cases both because of how they have been interpreted and because some of the circumstances are relevant only to cases in which a weapon or physical injury is a factor. These are usually not the ambiguous cases. In the absence of other evidence, the court is likely to fall back on traditional attitudes to judge the appropriateness of both the victim's and the defendant's behavior.

Many states have replaced the rule that a woman had to show nonconsent by resisting "to the utmost" with a rule based on an examination of the acts of the defendant to determine whether force was used. This should be a promising reform for cases like acquaintance rapes in which objective measures of nonconsent are often unavailable. The problem, however, is that force ends up being defined by courts in terms of a woman's resistance, the same old standard that the reforms were designed to avoid (Estrich, 1987). It is also defined in male terms, with the model being that of a fight, in which one is expected to fight back in some way, using one's fists, knees, or elbows. Thus, what is considered "reasonable" in a situation where a woman is about to be raped is in fact not the behavior of a reasonable *woman* at all. As Estrich put it, "their [the judges'] version of a reasonable person is one who does not scare easily, one who is not passive, one who fights back, not cries. The reasonable woman, it seems, is not a schoolboy 'sissy'; she is a real man" (Estrich, 1987, p. 65). The difficulty is that many women do not fight back in the way expected of a reasonable man and in fact are discouraged by our social mores from doing so. Using a male standard in this way, courts may conclude that no force was used because the victim did not fight back.

The issue of consent, always a difficult one in rape cases, is thus doubly difficult in cases of acquaintance rape despite recent reform. As long as society's ambivalent attitudes toward sex and rape are mirrored in our legislatures and courtrooms, and as long as women have difficulty in communicating their wishes and men in honoring those wishes, consent will remain a central issue in the prosecution and trial of such cases.

OTHER RECENT CHANGES IN RAPE LAW

Over the past 15 years, the women's movement has made rape law reform one of its central goals. The grass roots movement of the early 1970s led to the establishment of rape crisis centers, the existence of which we almost take for granted now. Part of the purpose of the rape crisis centers was to make the process of reporting a rape and testifying in the subsequent trial less traumatic.

It was clear to women involved in the movement to set up rape crisis centers that they could not effectively minimize the trauma of the rape trial unless the law was changed. As long as attorneys were permitted to engage in what feminists saw as legal character assassination in an attempt to exonerate their clients in court, many would continue to find the trial as much a violation in its own way as the rape itself (Bohmer & Blumberg, 1975). Feminists also believed that the structure of the law reinforced sexist cultural stereotypes of women. Without changes in these laws, they argued, women could never reach equality in other spheres.

Ironically, the impetus for change in rape laws coincided in many states with a movement for general reform in the criminal law. Some changes reflected a need to accommodate changing social attitudes, for example, changes in the age of consent in statutory rape; others reflected a need to strengthen the criminal law in the face of a growing crime rate. Feminist rape law reformers and law and order legislators made strange bedfellows. In part, because of this odd alliance, the rape law reform movement has been only partially successful in achieving the goal of a fairer, less sexist trial experience for rape victims. It also appears that the movement for change in rape laws has now given way to other concerns. Thus, most of the changes took place in the late 1970s and early 1980s.

The legal change in which consent terminology was replaced by a definition based on force has already been discussed above. The other reform of major significance to acquaintance rape cases is that which covers what have come to be known as rape shield laws. These laws deal with the admissibility of testimony concerning the prior sexual behavior of the victim. Traditional rape law allowed evidence to be admitted on this issue, on the grounds that past sexual history was relevant to whether the victim was likely to have consented to the alleged rape. According to this logic, a virgin was less likely to consent to sex than one who had previously engaged in sex, especially if that person were shown to be "promiscuous." As Rosemarie Tong pointed out (1984), the likelihood that a woman who has consented to sex before is more likely to consent again can be either specific or general. In the first situation, the defense produces evidence that on some previous occasion or occasions the victim had sexual intercourse with some person who is named. As to the second situation, Tong said: "(W)here the defense is unable to come up with a list of past indiscretions, it can instead show that the alleged victim of rape has a *general* reputation in the community for promiscuity" (Tong, 1984, p. 106). Such a woman would not be so concerned about one more act of intercourse with the defendant.

What this argument actually means is that once a woman has had sex, she has thereby reduced, or even (e.g., in the cases of prostitutes) eliminated, any legal protection she might get for future situations in which she does not consent. As in so many other situations, it is the woman who is punished for *her* sexual behavior, rather than the man for *his*.

Prior sexual history is considered relevant not only to the issue of consent, but also to the issue of credibility. Courts continue to believe that a "virtuous" woman is more likely to tell the truth than one who is not "chaste." They believe that the latter is more likely to lie in general because her sexual conduct has shown that she is of low moral character. More specifically, they believe, she might claim that the encounter was a rape as a way of protecting herself from being punished for some inappropriate behavior. For example, a wife who did not want her husband to know that she was having an affair, or a young woman whose parents found out about her sexual activities, would claim that she had been raped, to avoid the ire of husband or father.

Feminists find these arguments not only offensive but also unconvincing. The idea of classifying a woman as chaste or virtuous seems as dated as the bustle. Sex outside marriage is now the norm rather than the exception, so a division of women into good women and bad women is irrelevant. There is also no foundation for the belief that women who are sexually active are more likely to be liars. In addition, given the well-known difficulties in making a rape charge and carrying it through the court process, it is hardly likely that a woman would be more willing to undergo the trauma of a rape trial than be shown to have committed adultery. The empirical evidence is actually quite the opposite. Vast numbers of women who are raped, especially by people they know, choose not to make a complaint to the police, and many who do complain subsequently drop the charges because they decide they cannot bear to go through a trial (Lafree, 1989).

Rape reform statutes have abolished several evidentiary rules that previously singled out rape as a crime to be tried differently from other crimes. Rules that were abolished included the requirement that there be special corroboration in rape cases, proof of resistance, and special instructions to the jury about the need for caution in assessing the testimony of the victim (Berger, Searles, & Neuman, 1988). As discussed above, there have also been changes in the rules about the admissibility of testimony of the prior sexual history of the victim (known as rape shield laws), though they have been much less extensive than feminist reformers would wish. As of 1980, by which time most of this legislative change had taken place, more than 40 states had passed statutes that limit in some way the freedom of the defense to introduce evidence about the victim's past (Feild & Bienen, 1980). The most extreme of these statutes totally exclude evidence of the victim's past sexual history with anyone except the defendant. Most states have not gone so far and merely require a hearing to determine whether the judge considers the evidence to be relevant. Defense attorneys have questioned the constitutionality of these new rules, arguing that they violate the defendant's Sixth Amendment right to confront his accuser. Perhaps as a response to this pressure, some states (e.g., Hawaii, Iowa, and North Carolina) have already repealed their rape shield laws (Berger et al., 1988).

Rape shield statutes can operate to the benefit of a victim in an acquaintance rape case if the victim has not had a prior sexual relationship with the defendant. If she has, the evidence will continue to be admissible. In addition, a judge may still decide to admit evidence of the victim's sexual past in those states where the discretion to do so remains.

Another area in which there has been much legislative activity has been that of redefining rape. Some states no longer have a crime of rape but rather a series of graded offenses with penalties depending on such variables as the amount of coercion, the infliction of injury, and the age of the victim (Feild & Bienen, 1980). The purpose of this change was to try to increase the conviction rate, on the assumption that injuries might convict more defendants on a wider range of offenses if the definitions and the penalties were more closely tailored to fit the circumstances. The replacement of the term *rape* with *sexual assault* or, in some cases, *assault* alone, was also designed to emphasize that rape was a violent rather than a sexual crime. Some feminists do not agree with this goal, while others doubt whether the change has had the intended effect (MacKinnon, 1987; Tong, 1984).

The definition of rape has also been extended by making the laws gender-neutral and by expanding the acts that constitute the crime of rape. Sexual assault between people of the same sex, either by males or females, is now covered in some of the new statutes; in others it is dealt with under statutes that cover deviant sexual behavior. The acts covered under the new laws include oral and anal penetration, sexual penetration with objects, and, in some cases, touching of intimate body parts (Berger et al., 1988).

THE IMPACT OF RAPE REFORM LAWS

Preliminary studies of the impact of changes in rape laws indicate that many of these reforms have had limited effect on the experience of the victim or the likelihood that there will be a conviction. Court personnel seem still to be wedded to traditional assumptions regarding sexual behavior and the conduct of a rape trial and apparently do not always comply with the spirit of the new statute (Berger et al., 1988; Feild & Bienen, 1980). For example, in those states with discretionary rape shield laws, a trial judge may continue to believe that the victim's past sexual behavior is relevant both to consent and credibility. In this situation, he or she will exercise discretion and admit that evidence.

To date, those few studies that have been undertaken on the impact of the rape reform laws have found that there has been no significant increase in the percentage of rape complaints that have resulted in conviction, nor in the reporting or arrest rates (Loh, 1980, 1981; Polk, 1985). The only significant change has been an increased likelihood that a defendant, once convicted of rape, would receive an institutional sentence (Polk, 1985). This difference is probably one example of more punitive sentencing in general, rather than for rapists in particular, since felons other than rapists are also receiving tougher sentences.

The lack of change in the conviction rate comes as a setback especially for those reformers who believed that a redefinition of the crime of rape as one of varying degrees of criminal sexual assault would result in more convictions. This redefinition has been adopted in a number of states, the most important of which is Michigan, which has been used by other states as a model (Feild & Bienen, 1980). In addition to its anticipated benefits in conviction rates, the reform was seen by its exponents as a way of downplaying the issues of consent which have been so troublesome. By making changes in the definition and description of rape, it was hoped that the focus in a trial would be less influenced by the traditional notions of acceptable female behavior discussed above (Tong, 1984). In a trial to prove that the defendant had committed a kind of assault, the victim's prior sexual history becomes as irrelevant as any other aspect of her life or as irrelevant as it would be in any other kind of assault. These benefits are particularly significant in the case of acquaintance rape, in which traditional attitudes toward sexual behavior frequently make a conviction all but impossible. Empirical research has not yet revealed whether incorporating rape law into that of criminal assault has indeed had any effect on the conviction rate of acquaintance rape per se.

MARITAL RAPE

The decision to include discussion of the laws about marital rape requires explanation to readers who may find it odd to lump together rape between a married couple with the rape of a woman out on a date. Such a discussion is appropriate here for several reasons. First, there is a significant difference in legal and social attitudes toward a woman who knows her assailant, regardless of how well she knows him, as opposed to a victim of a stranger rape (Lafree, 1989). Second, the law that exempts from prosecution the husband of a woman who alleges that she has been raped by him has in some states been extended to cover couples who are living together or, more rarely, couples who are "voluntary social companions"—dates (Finkelhor & Yllo, 1987). Third, the elimination of what is known as the spousal exemption (which precludes prosecution of husbands for raping their wives) was one of the goals of the rape law reformers. How they have fared with this reform tells us much about the state of the law as well as about current social attitudes.

Like the other reform efforts, the attempt to abolish the spousal exemption has been only partly successful. Despite a plethora of law review articles over the past 15 years and at least two books based on empirical research about women who are raped by their partners, seven states retain some form of the marital rape exemption.

Matthew Hale, whose commentary on the law of England was cited above, was apparently the first to argue in favor of the existence of the exemption. Departing from his normal practice, he does not seem to have offered judicial support for the pronouncement, but rather to have developed it from his negative views of women and his understanding of social attitudes of the early 17th century. He may have taken it from the doctrine that a man has a duty to support his wife and in return she has a duty to provide "services." The definition of these services is an elastic one and can include sexual services. If a husband fails to support his wife, however, the law limits her remedies to separation or divorce. It also provides no remedies for enforcement of other kinds of services owed by the wife. It seems strange, therefore, that he is permitted in this one situation to resort to force to enforce his wife's duty to provide sex. At the time of Hale's commentary, a husband and wife become one legal unit at the time of their marriage. Under this doctrine of marital unity, a husband raping his wife was legally raping himself. This doctrine has, however, been long dead in the law. Hale also believed that the exemption came from the marital contract, in which the wife permanently gave up the right to refuse her husband sexual access. Since the marital contract in the common law system is unwritten, it is hard to see how such an allegation could be either proved or disproved.

Despite the possibility that the doctrine of spousal exemption was invented out of whole cloth, it seems to have struck a responsive chord among the legal community both in Britain and in the United States, where it has since been considered a principle of the common law.

Other rationales have been offered in support of the marital rape exemption. If wives are permitted to bring charges against their husbands, the argument goes, the chance that the couple will reconcile is minimized. This concern is part of a larger concern about the sanctity and privacy of the marital relationship, in which the courts are very reluctant to interfere. The area of family law is replete with such concern. In this situation, it seems to stem from a legal misunderstanding or perhaps an unwillingness to recognize the nature of the typical marital rape case. The stereotype of the marital rape case is a woman who pleads that she "has a headache" and the man who "persuades" her to indulge him anyway. This kind of thinking is very like the misapprehension about the nature of acquaintance rape generally, in which the woman is simply being coy and needs to be "persuaded" into a sexual encounter. The reality, made clear from Russell's work and that of Finkelhor and Yllo, is that marital rape is much more likely to be part of a package of domestic violence (Finkelhor & Yllo, 1987; Russell, 1990).

Given the fact that many marital rape cases take place in a situation of domestic violence, it seems odd for the law to be more concerned about holding together the marriage than protecting the woman from this type of violence. If a woman is desperate enough to bring charges against her husband for rape, the marriage is probably not worth saving. In an age of no-fault divorce, the concern for holding together such a marriage seems particularly out of place. So, too, is the concern that the violence be kept "private." Refusing to allow a woman to press charges under such circumstances can hardly be seen as appropriate noninterference in the smooth running of a harmonious marriage.

The final rationale offered for the existence of a spousal rape exemption is also consistent with attitudes about rape in general. Allowing women to charge their spouses with rape supposedly would open the floodgates and inundate the courts with complaints filed as a way of resolving a marital spat. This has been shown not to be true in states such as California, which have abolished the exemption (Finkelhor & Yllo, 1987). The reporting rate is very low, especially when compared to the incidence rates found by Russell (1990) and Finkelhor and Yllo (1987). Cases that do get reported are on the whole the most violent and often take place between couples recently separated (Finkelhor & Yllo, 1987).

Many articles have argued against the exemption for a variety of reasons, ranging from its questionable status as a principle of common law to its inequity from a feminist point of view, but very few states have completely abolished it. A number of states have limited the exemption to married couples living together; others, to couples not legally separated. Other states, however, as mentioned above, have not only not abolished the exemption but have extended it to couples living together whether they are legally married or not. Thus, women in nonmarital living arrangements are protected neither by the laws of marriage nor by the laws for unmarried couples.

It is hard to understand the logic behind the extension of the exemption to couples not married. Hale's justification based on the marriage contract is obviously irrelevant, as are the arguments about the sanctity and privacy of marriage as a social institution. It may be a way of punishing a woman for her immoral life-style. It may also be yet another example of the view that a woman in a relationship "owes" her partner her sexual favors especially if she has had a prior sexual relationship with him. This is not unlike the belief that a woman on a date "owes" her date sex. Indeed, states that have extended the exemption to "voluntary social companions" (who need not be living together but only to have had a previous sexual relationship) seem to have enshrined this belief in the law.

The law relating to marital rape has changed as a result of the rape reform movement, but many legislators have been as resistant to this reform as to the other reforms. The title of one of the articles on the marital rape exemption is telling. It is a quote from a California state legislator who apparently said, "But if you can't rape your wife, who can you rape?" (Freeman, 1981).

THE USE OF DISCRETION AND THE LIMITS OF THE LAW

As discussed above, the law reforms that have been initiated have to some extent been limited in their usefulness by the reluctance of the courts to exercise discretion in such a way as to benefit the victim in the courtroom. Indeed, the negative effect of discretion exercised by various actors in the legal system actually begins long before the case gets to court, if it ever does. After a rape victim files a complaint, the police may decide that the case is not worth pursuing and the case will go no further. In police terminology the decision is made to "unfound" the case, a graphic if ungrammatical term.

Police officers believe that rape complaints are generally less valid than other complaints (Lafree, 1989). Rape is the only serious crime for which the FBI calculates an unfounding rate (Hilberman, 1976). The police argue that the rate of "unfounded" rape cases is an indication that women press charges in circumstances that are not really rape or women are using the process for inappropriate reasons (Estrich, 1987). But that very exercise of discretion is based on traditional attitudes, which define as rape only those events that fit the (male) police officer's perception of a rape case (Lafree, 1989). Evidence in support of this interpretation of the exercise of discretion comes from the New York and Philadelphia police departments. When they added a woman to the investigative team, the rate of cases considered suitable for unfounding was reduced (Brownmiller, 1975).

Some cases of acquaintance rape will not even get as far as a prosecutor who could exercise his (or her) discretion as to whether to proceed; the cases will have already been unfounded by the police. A higher proportion of acquaintance rape cases meet this fate than do cases of stranger rape (Chappell & Singer, 1977, p. 260).

Prosecutors are involved in exercising their discretion in much the same way as the police and are strongly influenced by the police (Lafree, 1989). They will decide, based on various factors, including whether the victim and assailant knew one another, whether it is worth expending scarce resources to try to get a conviction (Estrich, 1987). Another way in which the prosecutor exercises discretion (using the same variables) is in the process of plea bargaining. Most studies show that approximately 90% of all cases are dealt with by plea bargaining and do not therefore result in a trial. The figures for rape are likely to be similar.

The legal process in rape cases, even more than in other crimes, is a vast funnel that gets narrower as fewer and fewer cases are retained. This exercise of discretion at every stage in the process puts into perspective the limits of law reform in another way. Most of the reforms are involved with the conduct of the trial. Since most cases are either dropped or plea bargained to a guilty plea, these reforms have a tiny impact on the role of the law in any rape case, especially an acquaintance rape case.

ACQUAINTANCE RAPE AND THE CIVIL LAW

A central tenet of our legal system (often missed by those concerned about the treatment of victims in court) is that, in a criminal case, the victim's status is that of the prosecuting witness for the state's case against the defendant. She is not a party to the suit and thus her only legal rights are as a witness. The only way in which a victim can become a plaintiff in a suit against her assailant is if she herself initiates a civil lawsuit against him. Since an acquaintance rape victim by definition knows her assailant, she has no difficulty naming her defendant. She must still prove that the rape was without her consent and that she suffered damage as a result of it. She risks suffering the same kind of humiliation at the hands of the defense attorney as she might experience in a criminal case. Since rape shield laws apply only to criminal cases, the defense attorney can introduce any kind of evidence she or he can prove is relevant to the plaintiff's claim, which could include evidence of her past sexual history.

The standard of proof required in a civil case ("preponderance of probability") is a lower one than in a criminal case (proof beyond a reasonable doubt). This lower standard might make it possible for an acquaintance rape victim to win in civil litigation, even when the defendant has not been convicted in a criminal court.

For many if not most victims, this is not a very attractive option. The problems of negative treatment in court still exist whether the victim is the state's witness or a plaintiff in her own right, and the chance that she can extract monetary damages from her attacker may be slight even if she wins. But apart from any psychological satisfaction a victim might get from winning a civil judgment in court, this option may offer her the opportunity to sue someone in addition to her assailant. If the victim can prove that a third party can be held responsible for the rapist's behavior (as, for example, the college attended by both parties), that party can be named as a defendant. In one recently filed case, a student has sued Colgate University and a fraternity there, claiming that they were responsible for a sexual attack on her which took place at a party in a fraternity house. Her argument is that the university should have prohibited the fraternity from holding the party because the fraternity had already been found guilty of violating the school's alcohol policies. She is also arguing that the guards at the party should have stopped fraternity members from serving alcohol to underage members ("Colgate student sues university," 1989). The case has not yet been heard.

It is fairly difficult to prove such third-party responsibility, especially in a campus dating situation that turns into an acquaintance rape. The case law on this subject is sketchy, partly because of the dearth of suits and also because when a lawsuit is filed, the college or other third party has a great interest in minimizing the negative publicity and in settling without a court case that might provide a legal precedent. Although such settlements may extract silence from the victim as a price, they are likely to serve at least one very useful function: sensitizing institutions to their responsibility to educate their students about appropriate sexual behavior.

CONCLUSION

This chapter has discussed the law as it relates to acquaintance rape and the changes that have taken place in the law since the early 1970s. As we have seen, these legal changes have not had a great deal of impact on the way rape is treated by the law. Clearly, there is little interest in making further legal changes, both because they do not seem to have much effect and because our society is now involved in other issues which are seen as more urgent. Even the field of rape research and scholarship provides evidence of this. There is still a great deal we do not know about how rape cases in general and acquaintance rape cases in particular fare in our legal system. However, the scholarly research peaked in the late 1970s and early 1980s, when public interest was at its height and there was more funding available. Since then, many of the gaps in knowledge remain unfilled. Thus, it has not been possible to provide empirical data about many aspects of acquaintance rape. The FBI and other agencies that keep crime statistics do not distinguish between cases of stranger rape and those of acquaintance rape. Research is needed to provide this information. So far, very little of this kind of research has been undertaken. What we do know is that our legal system remains an inhospitable environment for the trial and prosecution of rape.

The law that applies to acquaintance rape, like rape in general, is closely related to social attitudes about appropriate sexual behavior. As long as sex and rape are seen in traditional ways, the likelihood is that a woman (or a man) who is raped by an acquaintance is at the mercy of the whole legal system's interpretation as to whether a crime was committed. There is much less need to change the law in the area of rape, and especially acquaintance rape, than there is to change the way we view sexual behavior.

REFERENCES

Berger, R. J., Searles, P., & Neuman, W. L. (1988). The dimensions of rape reform legislation. *Law and Society Review, 22,* 329–357.

Berger, V. (1979). Man's trial, woman's tribulation: Rape cases in the courtroom. *Columbia University Law Review, 77,* 1–103.

Bohmer, C., & Blumberg, A. (1975). Twice traumatized: The rape victim and the legal process. *Judicature, 58,* 390–399.

Brownmiller, S. (1975). *Against our will: Men, women, and rape.* New York: Simon & Schuster.

Burt, M. R., & Albin, R. S. (1981). Rape myths, rape definitions, and probability of conviction. *Journal of Applied Social Psychology, 11,* 212–230.

Chappell, D., & Singer, S. (1977). Rape in New York City: A study of material in the police files and its meaning. In D. Chappell, R. Geis, & G. Geis (Eds.), *Forcible rape* (pp. 245–271). New York: Columbia University Press.

Colgate student sues university and fraternity. (1989, June 12). *Ithaca Journal,* p. 7A.

Estrich, S. (1987). *Real rape.* Cambridge, MA: Harvard University Press.

Feild, H. S. (1978). Attitudes toward rape: A comparative analysis of police, rapists, crisis counselors, and citizens. *Journal of Personality and Social Psychology, 36,* 166–179.

Feild, H. S., & Bienen, L. B. (1980). *Jurors and rape.* Lexington, MA: Lexington Books.

Finkelhor, D., & Yllo, K. (1987). *License to rape: Sexual abuse of wives.* New York: Free Press.

Freeman, M. D. A. (1981). But if you can't rape your wife, who(m) can you rape?: The marital rape exemption reexamined. *Family Law Quarterly, 15,* 1–29.

Hale, M. (1680). *History of the pleas of the crown* (Vol. 1). (Emlyn ed. 1847).

Harris, L. R. (1976). Towards a consent standard in the law of rape. *University of Chicago Law Review, 43,* 613–645.

Hilberman, E. (1976). *The rape victim.* New York: Basic Books.

Lafree, G. D. (1989). *Rape and criminal justice.* Belmont, CA: Wadsworth.

Loh, W. D. (1980). The impact of common law and reform rape statutes on prosecution: An empirical study. *Washington Law Review, 55,* 543–652.

Loh, W. D. (1981). Q: What has reform of rape legislation wrought? A: Truth in criminal labelling. *Journal of Social Issues, 37,* 28–52.

MacKinnon, C. (1983). Feminism, marxism, method and the state: Toward feminist jurisprudence. *Signs: Journal of Women in Culture and Society, 8,* 635–658.

MacKinnon, C. (1987). *Feminism unmodified.* Cambridge, MA: Harvard University Press.

Polk, K. (1985). Rape reform and criminal justice processing. *Crime and Delinquency, 31,* 191–205.

Russell, D. E. H. (1990). *Rape in marriage* (2nd ed.). New York: Macmillan.

Tong, R. (1984). *Women, sex, and the law.* Totowa, NJ: Rowman & Allanheld.

Wrightsman, L. S. (1986). *Psychology and the legal system.* Monterey, CA: Brooks/ Cole.

PART 9

Avoidance and Prevention

CHAPTER 21

The Personal Perspective of Acquaintance Rape Prevention: A Three-Tier Approach

PATRICIA D. ROZÉE, PhD, PY BATEMAN, MS, and THERESA GILMORE, MA

Sexual assault has multiple overlapping causes and any effective prevention strategy must provide multiple approaches to the problem. The solutions must relate to the prevention of sexual assault in a way that satisfies both the needs of a society in which sexual assault has become an intolerable endemic problem, and the immediate needs of a woman faced with an assailant or a woman trying to avoid sexual assault. Sole emphasis in rape prevention on what women can do to prevent rape supports the attitude that they are responsible for its occurrence (Gordon & Riger, 1989). To produce social change in the incidence and consequences of acquaintance rape will require the involvement of individual males, families, social and religious groups, and legal, educational, economic, and political institutions.

In dealing with sexual assault prevention, this chapter uses a three-tier approach developed by Bateman in her community-based prevention education work (Bateman, 1984). Tier one, the more global issues in the world in which we live, is the level that has the most far-reaching effects on the lives of all women (societal responsibility). Tier two addresses the demands of everyday life (individual awareness). Tier three focuses on the immediate concerns of potential victims and the actual confrontation between victim and rapist (self-protection).

TIER I: THE WORLD IN WHICH WE LIVE

The world in which we live contributes much to the occurrence of rape (Rozée-Koker, 1987; Rozée-Koker & Polk, 1986). We live in a patriarchal culture that has at its roots a nonconscious ideology of male supremacy (Bem & Bem, 1976). Our culture values males and maleness and devalues females and femaleness. Such ideology is reflected in media portrayals of the objectification of women, the presentation of women as victims, and the sexualizing of violence against women. The ideology of male supremacy is

337

supported by systematic discrimination against women in the legal and judicial handling of complaints of male violence. It is perpetuated in child-rearing and socialization practices that provide succeeding new generations of boys and men with the message that aggressive, sexually coercive behavior is acceptable and even desirable.

Child-Rearing and Socialization Practices

U.S. socialization practices produce aggressive males (Lott, 1987). Aggressive, sexually coercive behaviors among adolescent and adult males are common (Kanin, 1967; Koss, 1985) as are attitudes that indicate a proclivity to rape (Malamuth, 1981). So acceptable are these sexually aggressive behaviors that Warshaw (1988) reported, of those males who committed acquaintance rape, 84% believed that what they had done was definitely not rape.

Men, in general, tend to view the world more sexually than women (Abbey, 1982; Bart & O'Brien, 1985), and date rapists appear to do so in the extreme. Kanin's (1984) report indicated there are socialization differences between self-identified date rapists and other males. Date rapists come from a much more erotically oriented peer group. This differential socialization starts in junior high or high school. Sexual activity becomes closely tied to feelings of self-worth. As sexual desire escalates, date rapists become more indiscriminate in the tactics they employ to obtain sexual goals. In comparison to other males, these men pursue a more active interest in dating, women, and sex. Sexually coercive and assaultive males report a much greater number of sexual intercourse partners (Koss, Leonard, Beezley, & Oros, 1985). However, in contrast to others, these men are more apt to evaluate their sexual achievements as unsatisfactory (Kanin, 1984).

In addition to more sexually oriented peer group socialization, four other characteristics may distinguish date rapists: sexual entitlement, power and control, hostility and anger, and acceptance of interpersonal violence (Bateman, 1987; Groth, 1979; Mahoney, 1983; Malamuth, 1986; Smithyman, 1978).

Sexual Entitlement

Males, especially those who hold traditional attitudes, believe rape is more justifiable than do women (Muehlenhard, 1988). Sexually aggressive males and males who believe rape myths are less likely to perceive forced sexual intercourse as rape and more likely to believe the woman truly desires sex (Jenkins & Dambrot, 1987). Date rapists also believe that women who say no to sexual intercourse really mean yes (Koss et al., 1985) and are offering only token resistance (Check & Malamuth, 1983; Kanin, 1984).

Regardless of the dating situation, men more often interpret women's behavior as indicative of wanting sexual intercourse (Muehlenhard, 1988). Muehlenhard examined several variables in dating situations that may lead to these conclusions. She found the most indicative situations were when the woman initiated the date, went to the man's apartment or let him pay all the expenses (Muehlenhard, 1988; Muehlenhard, Friedman, & Thomas, 1985). In these situations, males saw rape as more justifiable.

Date rapists also feel that blame for the incident belongs with the victim (Jenkins & Dambrot, 1987; Kanin, 1984). One-third of Kanin's sample of date rapists absolved themselves of guilt, blaming the female's sexual conduct. The remainder shared the blame with the victim. The men in this study saw their rape offenses as equivalent to drunk driving or disorderly conduct, but certainly not as major offenses.

Power and Control

Besides sexual entitlement, sexual aggression among acquaintances is related to power and control. American dating customs legitimize the use of force, power, and control by males in sexual advances toward females (Burt, 1980; Check & Malamuth, 1983; Lewin, 1985). This is exacerbated by females' subordinate position as well as their being socialized to put men's needs ahead of their own (Lewin, 1985). Traditionality enhances this power differential (Koss et al., 1985; Russell, 1984). However, date rape is not simply due to overbearing males preying on passive females or to problems in communication. In situations where date rape occurs, many women are assertive and do emphatically state their limits but are not taken seriously (Kanin, 1984). A frequently used strategy by date rapists is to simply ignore the woman's protests (Rapaport & Burkhart, 1984).

Hostility and Anger

Clark and Lewis (1977) have suggested that hostility toward women originates in social customs in which women are seen "as the hoarders and miserly dispensers of a much desired commodity (sex). . . . Men naturally come to resent and dislike women because they see them as having something they want and have a perfect right to, but which women are unwilling to give them freely" (pp. 128–129). Date rapists see relationships as a form of game-playing (Muehlenhard, 1988). They are more likely to attribute adversarial qualities to interpersonal relationships (Koss et al., 1985; Muehlenhard & Linton, 1987) and to see women as sly and manipulative (Koss et al., 1985). Malamuth (1986) found a predictive relationship between attitudes of hostility toward women, among other factors, and self-reported experiences of sexual aggression.

Acceptance of Interpersonal Violence

As Bart and O'Brien indicated, violence is the basis of social control of women (1985). While men in general are more accepting of rape myths (Feild, 1978; Jenkins & Dambrot, 1987), those men who are most accepting of rape myths also accept interpersonal violence against women and show a greater tolerance of rape (Burt, 1980; Muehlenhard & Linton, 1987; Rozée-Koker & Polk,

1986). These researchers have also found that the more a male agrees with these myths the more he blames the victim, believing she wants to have sexual intercourse. Malamuth (1989) found that males attracted to conventional heterosexual sex are less likely to hold attitudes supporting violence against women, while men attracted to sexual aggression hold attitudes supportive of violence against women.

Date rapists believe the intermingling of sex and aggression is normal (Koss et al., 1985). The more sexually aggressive the man is, the more likely he is to believe this. Sexually aggressive males and males who accept rape myths also see the assailant's behavior in an acquaintance rape encounter as less violent. Rape proclivity in men is associated with greater acceptance of rape myths and higher arousal to rape depictions (Check & Malamuth, 1983). Sexual arousal in response to portrayals of sexual aggression has been shown to predict both laboratory aggression against women (Malamuth, 1983) and self-reported sexual aggression (Malamuth, 1986). Such males also see rape prevention as entirely the female's responsibility.

These factors in male gender-role socialization may be translated directly into the behavioral danger signals of acquaintance rape. Women who become aware of the signals may be in a better position to avoid further contact with such acquaintances. Some of these behavioral danger signals are discussed later in this chapter.

Rape Awareness Education

Socialized attitudes can be changed through a variety of educational methods. One of these is rape awareness education (Gordon & Riger, 1989). Promotion of rape awareness programs on college campuses appears to be one solution (Gordon & Riger, 1989; Lee, 1987; Roark, 1987; Warshaw, 1988). However, such programs vary in effectiveness, depending on the way material is presented and by whom (Warshaw, 1988).

Borden, Karr, and Caldwell-Colbert (1988) examined one university's rape prevention program for effectiveness in changing attitudes toward rape. A pretest showed males were less empathic and sensitive in their attitudes toward rape than were females. Students listened to a 45-minute lecture covering rape prevention, rape trauma, legal issues, and support services. Although a significant difference in attitudes was noted for females when students completed a one-month follow-up questionnaire, there were no significant changes in attitudes for males.

The experiential, rather than didactic, approach has been much more successful in changing male attitudes (Lee, 1987). The goal of Lee's program was to educate males about rape and increase their empathic understanding. In three separate sessions, the male participants engaged in discussion about rape myths, listened to a first-person account of a rape, and participated in a guided fantasy. Program results indicated that it was effective in changing men's attitudes about rape.

Whether groups are conducted by individuals or by female/male teams, the key to lasting attitude change seems to be the active participation of males both as presenters and recipients of rape awareness information. Experiential exercises requiring males to draw upon their own life-style, experiences, and knowledge are particularly effective in eliciting attitude change.

Social Institutions

Because changes in attitudes do not necessarily result in changes in behavior, interventions aimed specifically at behavior change must concurrently be enacted. California has passed legislation regarding date rape on college campuses. It requires colleges and universities to provide rape awareness workshops as well as crisis and counseling centers on campus (Warshaw, 1988). More reform and monitoring of laws and the legal system is needed (Gordon & Riger, 1989), as well as better enforcement of current laws.

The use of public media, such as television, to present facts about acquaintance rape and to dispel myths may also be effective; television not only informs the public, but conveys the importance of issues (Youn, 1987). In recent years, popular television dramas have portrayed victimization by date rape, but prevention techniques and strategies have yet to be dramatized. Of particular concern are media images that pair sex and violence in an erotic context (Furby, Fischhoff, & Morgan, 1989; Gordon & Riger, 1989). Such portrayals may encourage both males and females to see rape as a less serious crime than had they not watched the media presentation (Gordon & Riger, 1989).

Media rape depictions and news reports of actual rapes have a direct effect on women's levels of fear of rape (Gordon & Riger, 1989). This is important because lower levels of fear are associated with rape avoidance (Levine-MacCombie & Koss, 1986; Warshaw, 1988). Gordon and Riger (1989) noted that the newspaper policy of reporting only completed rapes gives women the impression that they cannot escape rape. The authors compared the ratio of attempted to completed rapes according to police reports (1:4), victimization studies (4:1) and media reports (1:13). Completed rapes are more likely to be reported to police and reported by the media, even though attempted rapes are four times more likely to occur. Thus, contrary to actual fact, women are likely to think that most rapes are completed and that women have little chance of fighting off a rapist. This, coupled with disproportionate reporting of the most grisly rapes may instill in women exaggerated fears and a conviction that resistance is futile.

TIER II: EVERYDAY LIFE

Fear of rape is quite prevalent among women, as are self-imposed restrictive behaviors in everyday life (like not walking alone at night), intended primarily to avoid rape (Riger & Gordon, 1981; Rozée-Koker, 1988; Warr, 1985). Among women under 35, rape is feared more than any other offense including murder, assault, and robbery (Warr, 1985). Rozée-Koker (1988) found that on the single item, "I am scared of rape," 55% of the women in her study marked the highest possible scores of 6 or 7 on a 7-point scale. When asked to what extent they thought getting raped would be devastating to their lives, nearly two-thirds of the women marked the highest possible agreement. Women who are the most fearful are likely to feel that fear of rape is "the hum that's always there." However, after taking self-defense lessons, women reported feeling stronger, more in control, and less fearful (Gordon & Riger, 1989).

Women's fear of crime, especially rape, results in their use of more precautionary behaviors than do men (Riger & Gordon, 1981; Rozée-Koker, 1988) and is the best predictor of the use of both isolation behaviors (Riger, Gordon, & LeBailly, 1982) and assertive behaviors (Rozée-Koker, 1988). Indeed, most women perform dozens of rape preventive behaviors daily (Rozée-Koker, Wynne, & Mizrahi, 1989).

Women have adopted many habits of everyday life that they hope will make them less vulnerable to sexual assault. But women tend to be torn between what they must do for their safety and what they want to do in order to enjoy a certain quality of life. Nowhere is this tension between safety and quality of life more intense than in the area of acquaintance rape. While most women do not see keeping their doors locked and avoiding contact with strangers on the street as a very significant loss in the quality of their lives, many balk, understandably, at treating friends as potential threats. Women must therefore find ways of protecting themselves without having to isolate themselves.

In our community rape prevention programs, we encourage women to examine the life habits they have adopted for safety and to weigh the safety gained against the quality of life. Safety practices or avoidance strategies serve best when they are consistent with one's personality, values, and lifestyle.

That women may sometimes choose quality of life over safety does not cast blame on them if a rapist takes advantage of their vulnerability. One should not have to sacrifice life quality for safety. However, in choosing some course that may not be the safest possible, one can mitigate vulnerability by enhancing the safety of the choice. For example, if a woman chooses to take a walk after dark, she might take a friend or a dog along, choose the least risky path, tell someone when she expects to return, take along a flashlight, dress so that she can escape more easily, and so on. In acquaintance and particularly date rape situations, the victim is commonly seen, in hindsight, as having placed herself in a vulnerable position. Actions like having gone to the man's apartment (Muehlenhard, 1988) or having kissed him may be seen by some as justification for rape. But it is important to recognize the role that trust plays in the situation and to place blame on the one who violates that trust, not the one who is violated. Regardless of the woman's behavioral choices, the blame for any rape must remain firmly on the rapist.

We know very little about characteristics of rapists because most rapists are never caught and consequently are not available for study. In the context of the immediate confrontation, there is little that we gain in self-defense from an understanding of the rapist. We would not want to suggest that a victim of an attempt should make an on-the-spot diagnosis of her attacker before deciding what to do.

On the other hand, a better understanding of rapists in general can help shape everyday avoidance strategies and will certainly help make changes in the world. In choosing precautions with regard to acquaintance rape, it is generally more practical to focus on potentially dangerous male behaviors than to try to avoid potentially dangerous situations. However, one of the difficulties in attempting to find danger signals in the everyday behavior of individual men is that socially approved, even lauded, male behavior may contain many of the elements common to sexual assault—scoring females or telling sexist jokes, for example.

The danger signals discussed here are directly related to the four risk factors of male gender-role socialization discussed earlier (Bateman, 1987). The four factors that would be most important to detect prerape behavior among dates and acquaintances are: feelings of sexual entitlement; needs for power and control; expressions of hostility and anger; and acceptance of interpersonal violence. Each socialization factor is associated with several concrete danger signals. Some of these behaviors are:

1. Sexual entitlement
   Touching women with no regard for their wishes
   Sexualizing relationships that are appropriately not sexual
   Using conversation that is inappropriately intimate
   Telling sexual jokes at inappropriate times or places
   Making inappropriate comments about women's bodies, sexuality, and so on.
2. Power and control
   Interrupting people, especially women
   Being a "bad loser"
   Exhibiting inappropriate competitiveness
   Using intimidating body language
   Game playing
3. Hostility and anger
   Showing quick temper
   Blaming others when things go wrong
   Tending to transform other emotions into anger.

4. Acceptance of interpersonal violence
   Using threats in displays of anger
   Using violence in borderline situations
   Approving observed violence
   Justifying violence.

Malamuth (1986) pointed out the importance of the interaction or over-lap of various factors in predicting sexual aggression. Bateman (1984) also maintained that in taking notice of behavioral danger signals special atten-tion should be given to behaviors that exhibit such an overlap. Overlap between sexual entitlement and any of the other danger factors is a particu-larly potent predictor for acquaintance rape because a belief in sexual enti-tlement can result in the sexualization of power, control, anger, hostility, or violent tendencies. Thus, for example, sexual entitlement coupled with power and control issues may lead to the use of sexually intimidating body language. The sexualization of anger and hostility may be evident in a man who consistently blames women for things that go wrong in his life. The acceptance of interpersonal violence when coupled with sexual entitlement may result in a man's being sexually aroused by rape depictions. Any of these interactions or overlaps are doubly strong danger indicators.

It is important to note that sexual aggression also occurs among same-sex couples. There is little or no research on the topic, but it is likely that the behavioral danger signs for a sexually aggressive lesbian or gay man are very similar to those described for heterosexual males in most studies. Lobel (1986) explored this topic in a collection of anecdotal accounts, but research in this area is desperately needed.

As previously stated, the presence of these warning behaviors does not nec-essarily mean the person in question intends to rape. Nor does their absence guarantee that rape will not occur. However, these behaviors must certainly be considered carefully in any decision to continue a relationship with such a person or in taking precautions within that relationship.

The Stages of Acquaintance Rape

We divide acquaintance rape into three stages: *intrusion, desensitization,* and *isolation* (Bateman, 1982). The first stage, intrusion, is most likely to occur within the realm of everyday life (Tier II). The offender intrudes in some way into the private space of the intended victim. This intrusion may be in the form of sexual or possibly nonsexual touching, suggestive remarks, or conver-sation that assumes more intimacy than is warranted.

If the initial intrusions are made with no overt coercion or in social situations where rape would not be a possibility, the victim may become desensitized over time and no longer regard the offender and his intrusions as alarming. She may consider him "harmless enough," having become desensitized to behavior that would normally be danger signals for her. Intrusion and desensitization could almost be collapsed into one stage because the very prevalence of intrusive behaviors in our society may serve generally to desensitize potential victims.

Isolation is the key to rape, however. The offender must have the time and space to carry out the rape without detection or interruption. If the intended victim has been desensitized, either by the rapist's previous actions or by her experiences in general, she may have difficulty acknowledging that she is in danger of rape until he has the advantage definitively. Once he gets her into an isolated place that is his turf and where he is in control, defending herself will be much more difficult for her.

In addition, she will be very likely to blame herself, thinking that she did something to "lead him on" or she should have known better than to get into that situation with him.

It is important to develop the skills to recognize and resist sexual coercion as it develops. In this way, a woman has a much better chance of escaping or successfully resisting acquaintance rape. For each stage of acquaintance rape, different tasks must be undertaken toward self-protection.

Stage 1: Intrusion

The most important aspects of resistance at this stage are defining one's own limits, recognizing an intrusion on those limits, and defending the limits by effectively communicating that the intrusion is not welcome and must stop. The first step is to discover what kind of intimacy, particularly in touching, is really wanted and from whom. The goal is to be able to identify and stop acquaintance rape at the first stage.

Most if not all women have considerable experience with intrusions into their privacy and personal space and they have developed different ways of dealing with such intrusions. Usually the response is one that assumes that the intrusion is harmless; it usually does seem harmless in the beginning. But it is never really harmless. The harm it does is in desensitizing women so that they do not notice or do not react to intrusions that could be dangerous.

It may be beneficial to change some of the patterns of response to initial intrusions into one's privacy and personal space. The responses that tend to be typical of women and girls may be subtle or indirect (Bateman, 1982): stiffening the body and not returning an unwanted hug; crossing the legs and shifting position when someone's knee makes contact under a table or at the movies; turning the head so that a kiss headed for the lips lands on a cheek; standing or sitting uncomfortably when someone puts an arm around one's shoulders; changing the subject when a topic of conversation makes one feel uncomfortable; or answering questions vaguely that would have been better not asked. These responses are ambiguous, and they do not provide a clear indication of the woman's wishes.

There are many reasons why women respond in these ways. Women are socialized to take care of others' needs and feelings rather than draw attention to themselves or create a scene, and to tolerate minor male sexual assertions. Often they are embarrassed, especially about the possible sexual connotation of the act, and do not want to call attention to what is happening. Some women do not act because they fear hurting someone else's feelings (for example, the host or hostess, or other guests at a party).

Women often are afraid of the possible negative reaction from men if they speak up. Such concerns are legitimate. Research documents assertive behavior as sometimes eliciting a negative reaction from the recipient (Woolfolk & Denver, 1979). In addition, various "stoppers" are often used to silence women when they are trying to express their own needs rather than comply with those of another (Schaef, 1981). Stoppers that might be experienced in the intrusion stage of acquaintance rape include accusations of being frigid, stuck-up, crazy, having sexual hang-ups, or being a lesbian (Bateman, 1982). Coercive males will often try to make women feel guilty for speaking up by pretending to have hurt feelings or displaying anger. However, the positive effects on women's self-esteem will likely far outweigh any possible negative consequences of asserting themselves and communicating displeasure. Being clear in communicating limits is important in both stopping the behavior in question and in allowing one to gather some vital information in the second stage.

Stage 2: Desensitization

In the second stage, desensitization, there are two tasks. One is to resist desensitization by not allowing oneself to get used to sexually coercive behavior. The second task is to be cognizant of the fact that the man is receiving clear communication and is ignoring it (Bateman, 1982). If communication is clear and direct, it will be easy to identify men who have little or no regard for stated limits. This identification is essential to avoid acquaintance rape.

It is important to place the issue of communication in the proper perspective. Clear communication is obviously important, but date rape is not caused by women's failing to communicate clearly. Even when clear communication is present, rapists frequently do not listen to the woman's message or choose to hear "no" as "yes" (Warshaw, 1988). It is misleading and potentially damaging to focus rape awareness efforts on advising women to communicate better, to the exclusion of other solutions. This simply adds to the survivor's guilt and shame if her communication failed to stop an assault.

After identifying potentially dangerous men, it is important to consider how to limit or end interactions with them. If some sort of association cannot be avoided, plans must be made to avoid isolation, the third stage of acquaintance rape (Bateman, 1982).

Stage 3: Isolation

The best way to deal with isolation is to prevent it in the first place. If that is not possible—and frequently it is not—it is important to anticipate those situations in which isolation is likely and to identify strategies for safety. This will provide an opportunity to *plan* to avoid isolation, whether by not accepting rides with the person, not working late with the person, or lining up allies who will help if the person is likely to maneuver for isolation.

Isolation may not be only physical. Sexually aggressive persons often harass a number of people in the same circle. When women do not talk to each other about what is going on, they are isolated in another way. Talking with other women about their experiences can help build allies, which can be very important in the case of an attempted rape or in a formal sexual harassment complaint in a work situation.

TIER III: CONFRONTATION

In the confrontation stage, the choices are most limited (Bateman, 1984). The intended victim has, to a certain extent, already been harmed. Even a close call or a successfully thwarted attempt often causes considerable emotional distress. Women's choices for limiting that harm are essentially confined to verbal or physical resistance, escape, third-party intervention, or submission.

Planning for Self-Defense

If all of a woman's prevention strategies fail and she is actually confronted with a rape situation, advance planning is more likely to enable her to respond quickly and effectively. Although 70% of women in one study fought back against their attackers (Warshaw, 1988), many women are more reluctant to actively defend themselves when the assailant is a date or acquaintance than when he is a stranger (Quinsey & Upfold, 1985). This may be due to the greater emotional complexity in acquaintance rape. Women may fear embarrassment, blame, or other repercussions from mutual friends or relatives. They may be hurt, shocked, and in a state of disbelief at such behavior from someone known and trusted. Women may feel guilt and shame because they were with him willingly and may mistrust their own ability to make good choices for dates. Many women fear that men have greater strength, coordination, control, and credibility. Each of these reactions can keep women from effectively defending themselves from acquaintance rapists.

Many of these obstacles to resistance can be overcome by planning and by considering beforehand a number of questions (Bateman, 1982). Would I physically resist? Under what circumstances? Would I be willing to hurt or injure someone? Would I treat an acquaintance just as I would a stranger trying to rape me? Would I yell for help? Am I worried about others' reactions? How would I handle the reactions of mutual friends or relatives if I resist or report? It is important to know one's own reactions in the situation. Planning enhances the chances of reacting with resolve in an attempted rape, but there are always uncertainties. Whatever choice women make at the moment—to resist or not, and how to resist—and whatever the success of the chosen strategy, the blame for the rape attempt lies solely with the rapist. Each situation needs to be assessed individually, and there are no guarantees that a given strategy will work.

When confronted by a rapist, women have been advised to respond in a variety of ways. Prentky, Burgess, and Carter (1986) advocated the use of nonaggressive strategies. Although escape is the optimum outcome, they believed it should be obtained with caution because resistance may increase some rapists' arousal. They felt that confrontative resistance will be met with increased aggression. Their advice for women was to talk to the rapist, engaging in dialogue related to the present situation. They suggested empathizing with what the rapist is saying by demonstrating some sense of interest, concern, and caring.

These researchers' conclusions are strikingly different from the majority of research findings in this area, which indicated that victim resistance is not related to increased rapist aggression (Bart & O'Brien, 1984, 1985; Levine-MacCombie & Koss, 1986; Quinsey & Upfold, 1985; Warshaw, 1988).

Quinsey and Upfold (1985) examined the effectiveness of various resistance strategies and whether those who physically resisted were injured more than those who did not. They found resistance of any kind was usually associated with an incomplete attack. Bart and O'Brien (1984) found that rape avoiders generally used a greater number of strategies than rape victims, who often used none. Quinsey and Upfold's (1985) temporal analysis of the data showed that any resistance lowers the probability of injury; victims resist more strongly when they are being injured. There appears to be no association between victim resistance and probability of increased subsequent injury. This is true whether the assailant is an acquaintance or stranger. The assumption that if a woman fights back she will pay the penalty is not supported in these studies. In addition, these authors and others note that advising compliance assumes rape itself is not injurious (Bateman, 1986).

Bart and O'Brien's (1984) results also showed that rape avoiders responded actively, whether they knew the assailant or not. Rape victims, however, screamed and yelled less and used fewer cognitive strategies than when they knew the perpetrator.

Acquaintance rape avoidance has been studied to a lesser extent than stranger rape avoidance (Levine-MacCombie & Koss, 1986; Warshaw, 1988). Levine-MacCombie and Koss (1986) indicated that those strategies that are effective in stranger rape situations are also effective in acquaintance rape situations. They found active strategies to be most effective in acquaintance rape avoidance. Verbal reasoning or conning the offender were less effective. Physical resistance, it is surprising to note, was not helpful in avoiding acquaintance rape. However, this may reflect the method of physical resistance used rather than its effectiveness. Physically "struggling" as defined by Levine-MacCombie and Koss (1986) may be less effective than the physical blows and punches typical of self-defense training (Quinsey & Upfold, 1985). Though the latter are less likely to be utilized on dates and acquaintances than on strangers, they are more likely to be successful (Quinsey & Upfold, 1985).

Rape avoiders differed from victims in their appraisal of the assault, emotional response, and use of active avoidance strategies Levine-MacCombie & Koss, 1986; Warshaw, 1988). The avoiders experienced less fear and guilt, perceived the assault as less violent, and more often fled from the perpetrator. Neither group differed in the amount of anger experienced. While quarreling was an ineffective strategy, crying and pleading were somewhat more helpful, although inferior to active avoidance. A preexisting relationship may enhance the assailants' responsiveness to strategies that are usually unsuccessful with strangers (Levine-MacCombie & Koss, 1986).

Although acquaintance rape avoiders and victims do not differ on personality dimensions (Koss, 1985), one distinction is the woman's primary concern when attacked (Bart & O'Brien, 1984, 1985). Rape avoiders' goal is to avoid the rape; rape victims are more concerned with avoiding death or mutilation. Women's extreme fear of rape and rapists may be related to fear of death or mutilation and may result in the use of fewer self-defense strategies. Such fears, as mentioned earlier, are exacerbated by media presentation of the typical rape as one that is both completed and extremely injurious; both characteristics are at odds with the reality of rape. Most rapes are attempted but not completed and the woman succeeds in escaping with little or no injury.

A personal approach to avoiding and resisting acquaintance rape requires each individual to choose methods that will be consistent with her own life-style and values rather than to adopt some standard set of safety measures. Each individual is faced with making choices that will maximize her resources for both avoidance and resistance.

The task, then, in the construction of a truly personal plan of rape prevention, divides into three areas (Bateman, 1990): the gathering of information; the withholding of information about oneself; and the maximization of resources for getting help, escaping, and verbally or physically resisting.

Gathering Information

It is helpful to gather as much information about the man in question as possible. Observation of his behavior and attitudes toward others with whom he is better acquainted is an excellent way of predicting how he will later relate to oneself. A woman should be aware of the behavioral danger signals mentioned earlier, and ask other people about him, especially other women whom he may have dated. In the dating situation, one can gather information about the planned activities or, better yet, take an active role in planning the date to maximize one's own safety and comfort. It is useful to share one's dating plans with a friend or relative who could track one's movements if needed.

Withholding Information

It is beneficial for women to be careful about the information about themselves that they share with acquaintances or dates, particularly in the early stages of a relationship. Personal information such as where one lives, the keys to the safety features of one's home environment (security gates, alarms), or details of one's daily routine are best kept to oneself until the relationship is better established. Arranging to drive one's own car and meeting at an agreed-upon restaurant or some other public place is one way to maintain privacy as well as autonomy.

Maximizing Resources for Help, Escape, and Resistance

Women can maximize their resources for help from others by keeping others informed of any apprehensions they may have about a particular acquaintance. Sometimes double-dating or engaging only in group activities in the early stages of a relationship can help relieve such apprehensions. Enlisting the help of others in avoiding isolation with a new acquaintance may be helpful.

Maximizing resources for escape is best facilitated by having access to one's own car, plenty of cash, and a good idea of the route to and from one's current location. It is also useful to take note of any unusual feature in the environment such as a car with no inside door handle on the passenger side.

Women can maximize resistance by making advance decisions about what sort of actions on the part of another would prompt resistance. This requires knowledge of one's own limits as well as having the resolve to defend them. One can decide specifically how to resist in various situations by gauging the level of resistance to an assessment of the level of risk. Higher perceived level of risk will require more strenuous resistance. By learning a few simple but effective techniques of physical self-defense, one can maximize choices of action in any given situation.

Because the risk of rape is shared by all women, it is useful to consider rape prevention efforts collectively with other women. Women can get together to establish police and judicial review boards to monitor the handling of rape cases. They can pressure universities and colleges to provide adequate lighting and to use appropriate sanctions against known date rapists, whether individual men or members of fraternities or athletic teams. Class action civil suits against rapists as well as against employers who refuse to provide a safe work environment have also been effective.

Women can also send the message individually and collectively that rape is a *men's* issue, not a women's issue. It is men, not women, who are responsible for rape. Men must begin to protest rape as actively as women do by setting a nonaccepting standard for other men; by refusing to engage in rape jokes or victim-blaming and discouraging other men from doing so; and by joining with women in making the social and institutional changes that will eliminate rape.

In presenting rape prevention as a three-tier system of resistance we hope to illuminate several important points. First, any rape prevention effort that addresses only individual-level solutions and fails to give equal consideration to the social and institutional supports for rape is extremely limited, particularly in reducing the incidence of sexual assault in general. Second, interventions aimed primarily at behavioral change among women place an unwarranted responsibility on individual women for their own safety. To live a life free of the fear of sexual assault ought to be a right afforded us by the society in which we live. Most women choose to effect some behavioral changes while working for the social change that will make the behavioral approach unnecessary. But a singular focus on the behavior of the potential victim lends itself to the victim-blaming that has for so long inhibited women's resistance. Finally, an individualistic focus ignores: the role of the rapist; social and institutional supports for violent behavior, including socialization practices, media portrayals of women, and legal and judicial limitations in the definitions and prosecution of rape; and the foundation that supports each of these, the nonconscious ideology of a patriarchal system that values males over females.

If anti-rape educators pursue all three tiers in rape prevention programs, it may be possible to build an alliance between the individual woman and society as a whole. Such an alliance will not only greatly enhance individual safety but will lead to the social changes that will allow women the freedom to shed that "second skin of caution" that bears such an impact in their everyday lives.

REFERENCES

Abbey, A. (1982). Sex differences in attributions for friendly behavior: Do males misperceive females' friendliness? *Journal of Personality and Social Psychology, 42,* 830–838.

Ageton, S. S. (1983). *Sexual assault among adolescents.* Lexington, MA: Lexington Books.

Bart, P. B., & O'Brien, P. H. (1984). Stopping rape: Effective avoidance strategies. *Signs: Journal of Women in Culture and Society, 10,* 83–101.

Bart, P. B. & O'Brien, P. H. (1985). *Stopping rape: Successful survival strategies.* New York: Pergamon.

Bateman, P. (1982). *Acquaintance rape: Awareness and prevention.* Seattle: Alternatives to Fear.

Bateman, P. (1984). *Alternatives to fear volunteer training manual.* Seattle: Alternatives to Fear.

Bateman, P. (1987). *Resisting acquaintance rape.* In R. Hill, J. J. Sutherland, & P. Giggins (Eds.), *Women's self-defense: A complete guide to assault prevention* (pp. 38–40). Los Angeles: Los Angeles Commission on Assaults Against Women.

Bateman, P. (1986). Let's get out from between the rock and the hard place. *Journal of Interpersonal Violence, 1,* 105–111.

Bateman, P. (1990). *Alternatives to fear in the workplace.* Seattle: Alternatives to Fear.

Bem, S. L., & Bem, D. J. (1976). Training the woman to know her place: The power of a non-conscious ideology. In S. Cox (Ed.), *Female psychology: The emerging self* (pp. 180–191). Chicago: Science Research Association.

Borden, L. A., Karr, S. K., & Caldwell-Colbert, A. T. (1988). Effects of a university rape prevention program on attitudes and empathy toward rape. *Journal of College Student Development, 29,* 132–136.

Burt, P. B. (1980). Cultural myths and supports for rape. *Journal of Personality and Social Psychology, 38,* 217–230.

Check, J. V. P., & Malamuth, N. M. (1983). Sex role stereotyping and reactions to depictions of stranger versus acquaintance rape. *Journal of Personality and Social Psychology, 45,* 344–356.

Clark, L. M. G., & Lewis, D. J. (1977). *Rape: The price of coercive sexuality.* Toronto: Women's Press.

Feild, H. S. (1978). Attitudes toward rape: A comparative analysis of police, rapists, crisis counselors, and citizens. *Journal of Personality and Social Psychology, 36,* 156–179.

Furby, L., Fischhoff, B., & Morgan, M. (1989). Judged effectiveness of common rape prevention and self-defense strategies. *Journal of Interpersonal Violence, 4,* 44–64.

Gordon, M. T., & Riger, S. (1989). *The female fear.* New York: Free Press.

Groth, N. A. (1979). *Men who rape.* New York: Plenum.

Jenkins, M. J., & Dambrot, F. H. (1987). The attribution of date rape: Observer's attitudes and sexual experiences and the dating situation. *Journal of Applied Social Psychology, 17,* 875–895.

Kanin, E. (1967). Reference groups and sex conduct norm violations. *Sociological Quarterly, 8,* 495–504.

Kanin, E. (1984). Date rape: Unofficial criminals and victims. *Victimology: An International Journal, 9,* 95–108.

Koss, M. P. (1985). The hidden rape victim: Personality, attitudinal, and situational characteristics. *Psychology of Women Quarterly, 9,* 193–212.

Koss, M. P., Leonard, K. E., Beezley, D. A., & Oros, C. J. (1985). Nonstranger sexual aggression: A discriminant analysis of the psychological characteristics of undetected offenders. *Sex Roles, 12,* 981–992.

Lee, L. (1987). Rape prevention: Experiential training for men. *Journal of Counseling and Development, 66,* 100–101.

Levine-MacCombie, J., & Koss, M. P. (1986). Acquaintance rape: Effective avoidance strategies. *Psychology of Women Quarterly, 10,* 311–320.

Lewin, M. (1985). Unwanted intercourse: The difficulty of saying no. *Psychology of Women Quarterly, 9,* 184–192.

Lobel, K. (1986). *Naming the violence.* Seattle: Seal Press.

Lott, B. (1987). *Women's lives: Themes and variations in gender living.* Monterey, CA: Brooks/Cole.

Mahoney, E. R. (1983). *Human Sexuality.* New York: McGraw-Hill.

Malamuth, N. M. (1981). Rape proclivity among males. *Journal of Social Issues, 37,* 138–157.

Malamuth, N. M. (1983). Factors associated with rape as predictors of laboratory aggression against women. *Journal of Personality and Social Psychology, 45,* 432–442.

Malamuth, N. M. (1986). Predictors of naturalistic sexual aggression. *Journal of Personality and Social Psychology, 50,* 953–962.

Malamuth, N. M. (1989). Attraction to the sexual aggression scale: Part I. *Journal of Sex Research, 26,* 26–49.

Muehlenhard, C. L. (1988). Misinterpreted dating behaviors and the risk of date rape. *Journal of Social and Clinical Psychology, 6,* 20–37.

Muehlenhard, C. L., Friedman, D. F., & Thomas, C. M. (1985). Is date rape justifiable? The effects of dating activity, who initiated, who paid, and men's attitudes toward women. *Psychology of Women Quarterly, 9,* 297–310.

Muehlenhard, C. L., & Linton, M. A. (1987). Date rape and sexual aggression in dating situations: Incidence and risk factors. *Journal of Counseling Psychology, 34,* 186–196.

Prentky, R. A., Burgess, A. W., & Carter, D. L. (1986). Victim responses by rapist type: An empirical & clinical analysis. *Journal of Interpersonal Violence, 1,* 73–98.

Quinsey, V. L., & Upfold, D. (1985). Rape completion and victim injury as a function of female resistance strategy. *Canadian Journal of Behavioral Science, 17,* 40–49.

Rapaport, K., & Burkhart, B. R. (1984). Personality and attitudinal characteristics of sexually coercive college males. *Journal of Abnormal Psychology, 93,* 216–221.

Riger, S., & Gordon, M. (1981). The fear of rape: A study in social control. *Journal of Social Issues, 37,* 71–94.

Riger, S., Gordon, M., & LeBailly, R. (1982). Coping with urban crime: Women's use of precautionary behaviors. *American Journal of Community Psychology, 10,* 369–386.

Roark, M. L. (1987). Preventing violence on college campuses. *Journal of Counseling and Development, 65,* 367–371.

Rozée-Koker, P. (1987). Cross-cultural codes for seven types of rape. *Behavior Science Research, 21,* 101–117.

Rozée-Koker, P. (1988, August). *The effects of fear of rape on working women.* Paper presented at the annual meeting of the American Psychological Association, Atlanta.

Rozée-Koker, P., & Polk, G. A. (1986). The social psychology of group rape. *Sexual Coercion and Assault: Issues and Perspectives, 1,* 57–65.

Rozée-Koker, P., Wynne, C., & Mizrahi, K. (1989, April). *Workplace safety and the fear of rape among professional women.* Paper presented at the annual meeting of the Western Psychological Association, Reno, NE.

Russell, D. E. H. (1984). *Sexual exploitation: Rape, child sexual abuse, and workplace harassment.* Beverly Hills: Sage.

Schaef, A. W. (1981). *Women's reality: An emerging female system in a white male society.* San Francisco: Harper & Row.

Smithyman, S. D. (1978). *The undetected rapist.* Unpublished doctoral dissertation, Claremont Graduate School, Claremont, CA.

Warr, M. (1985). Fear of rape among urban women. *Social Problems, 32,* 238–250.

Warshaw, R. (1988). *I never called it rape: The Ms. report on recognizing, fighting, and surviving date and acquaintance rape.* New York: Harper & Row.

Woolfolk, R. L., & Denver, S. (1979). Perceptions of assertion: An empirical analysis. *Behavior Therapy, 10,* 404–411.

Youn, G. (1987). On using public media for prevention of rape. *Psychological Reports, 61,* 237–238.

CHAPTER 22

Institutional Response: How Can Acquaintance Rape Be Prevented?

ANDREA PARROT, PhD

Acquaintance rape and sexual assault are problems on most college campuses in the United States today. Some colleges are making an effort to educate their students regarding the causes, consequences, and prevention strategies related to acquaintance rape. However, many campuses are not preparing their students because they do not perceive acquaintance rape to be a problem or because they do not want to call attention to it, assuming that if the problem is ignored it will go away. Unfortunately, ignoring the problem will not make it go away. Faculty, students, administration and law enforcement personnel, counseling staff, residence life staff, and judicial boards must be educated to become aware of the problem, and to be able to prevent or deal with the large number of acquaintance sexual assaults occurring on campuses.

Implementation and enforcement of judicial policies may be the key to acquaintance rape prevention. However, educational programs are also necessary so that all students, faculty, and staff know: what acquaintance rape is, and that it will not be tolerated on campus, and what they can expect if acquaintance rape does occur. Judicial policies and procedures that condemn acquaintance rape and carry harsh sanctions are important to send a message to all potential acquaintance rapists that they will be severely punished if they are found guilty of committing an acquaintance rape on campus. (Judicial policies and procedures are the focus of Chapter 23; education, training, and alcohol policies are dealt with in depth in this chapter.)

ADMINISTRATION PHILOSOPHY REGARDING
ACQUAINTANCE RAPE

College administrators need to acknowledge that acquaintance rapes and sexual assaults happen on their campuses. Only then can college policies address the issues regarding condemnation of these behaviors, identifying exactly which behaviors constitute acquaintance rape and sexual assault, and how these cases will be dealt with administratively. The policy and the programs should inform potential assailants that they may be both civilly and criminally liable for psychological and physical injuries resulting from sexual assault or acquaintance rape. College personnel need to be trained in counseling strategies and protocol, to deal with the cases they are likely to encounter. In addition, prevention programs and services for victims and assailants must be developed and information on the services and programs must be made available to students.

Once the administration has developed a policy regarding acquaintance rape, that policy should be disseminated to all students during new-student orientation. But, because not all students read the materials they are given or hear what is presented during orientation, the policy should be explained in posted written statements and in presentations about acquaintance rape. It is not enough to provide students with this information only once during orientation week. They should be reminded of the policy on an ongoing basis throughout their four years in college.

DEVELOPMENT AND DISSEMINATION OF INFORMATIONAL MATERIALS

Policies and information should be delivered in both traditional and nontraditional formats. In addition to printed media (newspapers, pamphlets, flyers, posters, and so on), information may be effectively directed to students through computer-accessible information systems and nonprint media (films, songs, videos, and television, for example). This option is most available if the college has a well developed department of telecommunications.

One possible way to decrease the incidence of acquaintance rape is to publicize data regarding acquaintance rapes that have occurred on campus—and the resulting penalties—in the campus newspaper, radio broadcasts, and television shows. These media may also be used to make public service announcements on rape awareness or prevention. An ad in the student newspaper will reach almost all students with information about what acquaintance rape and sexual assault are, what related campus policies are regarding sexual assault, and where to go if it happens to students or someone they know.

Any media coverage should be proactive and preventive in addition to being reactive. It is better to educate people about acquaintance rape in an effort to prevent any acquaintance rapes from occurring than to present information on the issue only when a rape has been reported. However, if an acquaintance rape triggers a public outcry, then reactive media coverage would also be valuable.

A formal brochure, developed specifically for each campus, should be made available to all students. It should identify rape myths, explain what behaviors constitute acquaintance rape, advise on how to avoid it and what to do if it happens, and describe the types of feelings the victim is likely to have. A list of resources and educational programs relating to acquaintance rape should be provided to counselors and health professionals, so they will be able to make appropriate referrals and recommendations.

Admissions literature should address the problem and should state that the campus administration is committed to preventing and prosecuting acquaintance rape (if this is true) (Adams & Abarbanel, 1988). Under the laws in some states, admissions literature must contain campus crime statistics.

At Cornell University, a letter sent to all parents of incoming students explains that acquaintance rape is a problem on *all* campuses. Parents are encouraged to discuss acquaintance rape with their children (male and female) who will be coming to college, to help them avoid acquaintance rape involvement. A list of recommended readings is included and information is given about what is being done at Cornell to combat acquaintance rape. Many colleges may find this strategy threatening because they are fearful of presenting their college in a negative light. However, because acquaintance rape is realistically a problem on every campus, colleges will have to address the issue sooner or later. It would be better to deal with acquaintance rape prophylactically rather than remedially.

The most efficient way to conduct comprehensive prevention programs is to make sure all campus programs are coordinated. To prevent overlaps or gaps in services, there should be some mechanism to coordinate the prevention efforts, perhaps through a campus sexual assault services coordinator. Because this position probably does not exist on most campuses, it will need to be created. Efforts should also be made to include community representatives (from local women's or men's groups, rape crisis centers, community mental health professionals, and others) in the planning and implementation of programs.

It is unrealistic to expect that one or two people on each campus could carry out all the educational programs necessary on this issue. Colleges need to invite speakers, both men and women, and to train people who can lead discussion groups. It is best to have as many students as possible as members of the speakers' bureau because students are less likely to dismiss information about student life that they receive from other students. Student facilitators are very effective, especially if they are respected by their fellow students. Students are likely to be the best informed speakers about the concerns of other students.

It is essential to develop a speakers' bureau of interested faculty, students, and staff to conduct on-campus programs. The speakers must be trained appropriately so that they will have the knowledge and skills necessary to provide quality programs that meet the needs of various groups. If speakers are provided with course credit or a stipend for their work, they will be more likely to take their task seriously and not allow the speaking to take a low priority in their busy lives.

A campuswide "speak out" is one way to sensitize the campus community to the issues of sexual assault and acquaintance rape. St. Lawrence University, in Canton, New York, has conducted such an event successfully by cancelling classes for one day and strongly encouraging students to attend the day-long event. Another possibility is staging a "mock trial" of an acquaintance rape case, using local attorneys and judges or law students to play the roles. The trial should be at least partially scripted so that the defendant is found guilty, to deliver the important message that acquaintance rape is a serious crime.

When programs are advertised, announcements should be posted in male living quarters, locker rooms, and activity areas, to ensure male attendance. Males should cofacilitate programs on acquaintance rape so that males attending the programs will not feel that this is *only* a women's issue and will recognize that the programs are addressing male *as well as* female concerns.

ALCOHOL-RELATED EFFORTS

One of the greatest contributing factors to acquaintance rape is the use and abuse of alcohol by college students (Polonko, Parcell, & Teachman, 1986). Seventy-five percent of men and 50 percent of women involved in a rape had been drinking at the time of the assault (Warshaw, 1988). One obvious way to decrease the probability of acquaintance rape is to limit the amount of alcohol available to students. If the college sponsors nonalcoholic events, students will discover that they can have fun in an alcohol-free environment. It is important that the events be **interesting** and be scheduled at "party times" that coincide with alcoholic affairs (Parrot, 1987). If an alcohol-free comedy club is scheduled too early in the evening (7:00 P.M., for example), then some people will go to late-night alcoholic parties after the comedy club and the original purpose of the nonalcoholic event will be defeated. Colleges have successfully sponsored a variety of popular alcohol-free events such as night clubs, dances, movies, and concerts.

The consumption of alcohol by students should be discouraged: not only is alcohol illegal for most students, but it creates an environment in which acquaintance rapes are more likely to occur. There is a tendency for college personnel to take a tough stand on public drinking and to be much more lenient toward drinking that takes place in residence hall rooms. Consequently, students choose to drink in their residence halls—and they drink hard liquor, which is often easier to conceal than beer. Allowing drinking in residence hall rooms, but not in public places, forces drinkers into private places where acquaintance rapes are more likely to occur. Campus policies regarding alcohol must be stringent and must be enforced rigorously in all locations. The selective enforcement that currently exists may be creating a more serious problem than existed prior to the introduction of the age-21 requirement for drinkers.

A number of policies and recommendations implemented at various colleges and universities may help to reduce the alcohol problem on college campuses. Brown University, in Providence, Rhode Island, has a Dean of

Substance Abuse who identifies high-risk students and works with them on a one-to-one basis. At some institutions, any time a student is brought up on charges and is found to have consumed alcohol prior to the alleged offense, the offender must attend a mandatory education program about alcohol; for a second offense in which alcohol was involved, the offender must partici- pate in a drug and alcohol treatment program (Bausell & Maloy, 1990).

Some campus authorities are taking action for drug and alcohol offenses occurring beyond campus limits. If an assailant is drunk at the time of an offense, he or she may be subject to future involuntary drug testing. For of- fenders caught using drugs and alcohol while committing an offense on cam- pus, there should be counseling and support groups available.

Alcohol plays a major part in the commission of crimes on college cam- puses. Those at highest risk for crime victimization while in college are most likely to be fraternity or sorority members, juniors or seniors living off campus at the time, and alcohol and drug users (Bausell & Maloy, 1990). Those who commit acquaintance rapes often have low self-esteem and are particularly susceptible to peer pressure, which may be why they joined the group. Stu- dents from high-income households, as compared to those from lower-income households, are more likely to both victimize and be victimized through the ploy of getting another intoxicated to gain sexual favors (Lane & Gwartney- Gibbs, 1985). Since many college students come from high-income families, this is a serious potential danger in the college community. (A more thorough analysis of the relationship between acquaintance rape and alcohol is pre- sented in Chapter 6.)

TRAINING FOR FACULTY AND STAFF

All support staff (residence life, counselors, Office of Equal Opportunity officers, public safety, and so on) who deal with this problem and any front- line person who is likely to be sought out by a victim should be trained. Victims may or may not label what has happened to them as rape, so the staff person must know what behaviors constitute acquaintance rape and what procedures and protocol to follow in the event of an acquaintance rape.

Resident advisors (RAs) need to be trained to identify those who are at high risk of acquaintance rape involvement and those who have been victims. RAs may be the staff members most likely to notice a change in behavior in the residents on their floors. They need information about crisis intervention specifically directed to this issue, and they must learn how to refer victims to the appropriate resources on their campus or in their community.

Medical personnel should know how to collect evidence and provide those services which are necessary to meet the physical and psychological needs of victims (pregnancy prevention measures, sexually transmitted diseases test- ing and treatment, examination for injuries particular to sexual assault, and referral to a trained counselor). (See Chapter 19.) The following actual case was an example of victim blaming by a physician, which discouraged the victim from seeking further help.

> Ellen, a college sophomore, was raped in a residence hall room of a man she had dated twice. On the evening of the rape they had been to an expensive dinner, had gone to a party afterward, and went back to his room to "look at his aquarium." Once in his room, he raped her.

> When Ellen went to the campus doctor several weeks later for a pregnancy test, she told the physician about the rape. The doctor said, "You should have known better than to go back to his room when you were drunk. That was not a rape! What did you expect?"

Public safety officers and judicial board members should also be trained because, although they may know the law, they may still believe rape myths and think that if a woman has had sex with a man before, or if she was drunk, she was "asking for it." Judicial board members should receive training in the following three areas: (a) the laws and policies related to acquaintance rape; (b) the particular psychological needs of victims and defendants; and (c) typical acquaintance rape patterns (these can be depicted through audiovisuals or written scenarios). The training for public safety officers and other staff members should take place annually if there is a high turnover rate in these jobs.

Faculty should be encouraged to discuss acquaintance rape in their classes. If students are required to write papers or to study the issue for a test, they are likely to take it more seriously. Unfortunately, because faculty may not know where in the scholarly literature to find references to acquaintance rape, the task of providing resources may fall to the staff of the local women's center, rape crisis center, or women's studies department. The topic of acquaintance rape fits well into the curriculum of psychology, sociology, law, health, education, social work, human service studies, criminal justice, history, human development, and anthropology.

The training of faculty and staff is important, but because students are most at risk for acquaintance rape involvement the best approach is to directly provide students with information that may prevent acquaintance rapes from occurring. The training of the staff to work with victims and assailants would not be necessary if we could keep our students from becoming victims and assailants.

PROGRAMS FOR STUDENTS

Educational programs should be addressed to men as well as women, because rape will not stop until men stop raping. Telling women how to avoid rape will not end the problem. Unfortunately, the approach taken by most educators is to place the responsibility for avoiding rape primarily with the potential victims (i.e., don't go to a man's apartment, don't stay at a fraternity party after 2:00 A.M., don't get drunk). Not only does this kind of advice place blame on the victim, but it also gives women a false sense of security: "If I don't do these risky things, then I can't be raped." Unfortunately, there is nothing a woman can do to *guarantee* that she won't be victimized. This is the reality of rape.

Because a disproportionate number of acquaintance and gang rapes happen in fraternity houses or are committed by members of fraternities or athletes (Warshaw, 1988; Hughes & Sandler, 1987), and because sorority women are likely to socialize with these men, fraternities, sororities, and sports teams should be involved in the planning and implementation of programs. By getting input from these groups, the programs designed for and by them are more likely to meet their needs and to speak to the issues of importance to them. Sororities and fraternities may want to combine for coeducational programs; these may be particularly effective because they allow a dialogue between the men and women.

If acquaintance rape prevention programs are developed and sponsored by students, as opposed to faculty and staff, they are more likely to attract larger audiences and to have greater impact. Students should be involved in every stage of the project: planning, implementation, evaluation, and funding procurement. Programs that include male student leaders such as fraternity presidents and sports team captains are likely to garner even greater support from the student body.

New-student orientation programs about acquaintance rape are most effective when they are optional but are stimulating enough that most students want to participate. If the programs are mandatory, students who do not want to be there will make inappropriate comments and attempt to ruin the message for the students who are there voluntarily. These orientation programs are likely to have best attendance if they are held during orientation week or the first week of school, before students have heavy work commitments. For maximum attendance, the loaded terms "date rape," "sexual harassment," "acquaintance rape," or "sexual assault" should not appear in the program title, because the students who are at risk for acquaintance rape involvement will probably not think these issues pertain to them. Good title choices would be interesting yet related, such as: "Does No Ever Mean Yes?"; "Who Makes the Decisions About Sex in Your Relationships?"; "How to Get What You Want But Not More Than You Bargained for in a Sexual Relationship"; or "Sex Under Pressure." These titles will draw students other than feminists and are not false advertising.

Acquaintance rape education programs should address sexual assertiveness, communication, and power dynamics in relationships as well as causes, consequences, and prevention strategies related to acquaintance rape. Services available for victims should be identified. It is best to conduct the programs early in students' college careers, before they have a chance to become involved in acquaintance rape situations. One program for students is usually not sufficient to change their attitudes. Information and programs should be offered repeatedly through a student's college career.

Programs Specifically for Men

Because many acquaintance and gang rapes occur in all-male living units such as fraternities (Ehrhart & Sandler, 1985; Warshaw, 1988), programs should be tailored for and presented to all male groups that perpetuate this type of behavior. Catchy titles such as "How to Be a Better Lover" may draw better attendance. The men who think they "know it all" will come to show off, but many men will come to learn. The key elements of this type of program should include discussions of sexism, homophobia, and acquaintance rape prevention; they may even be part of a probationary plan following abuse by the men in that group.

Men need to understand that any sexist, objectifying, or exploitative behavior may desensitize them to acquaintance rape. By committing, laughing at, condoning, or not stopping such a behavior directed at women, men are contributing to a rape culture. The sexual objectification continuum shown in Figure 22.1 visually depicts the relationship among these behaviors.

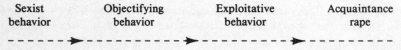

| Sexist behavior | Objectifying behavior | Exploitative behavior | Acquaintance rape |

Figure 22.1. Sexual objectification continuum.

One exciting possibility is to have a famous collegiate or professional athlete present programs to college athletes on what makes a "real man." The emphasis should be on behaviors such as respect for a partner rather than on how to objectify or exploit women. Of course, the presenting athlete would have to be of good moral character and have a good reputation in the area of dealing with women. If professional athletes can sell after-shave lotion and socks, should they not be able to sell the concept of respect for women?

Another group that may become involved in sexual harassment, if not in acquaintance rape, is male foreign students, many of whom do not understand the social norms of this culture. Some foreign students come to the United States thinking that all American women are "loose and easy" sexually and that they always are ready for sex. Forced sex in this circumstance may be a matter of true misunderstanding. An orientation session designed specifically for international students and addressed to issues such as appropriate and inappropriate behavior in sexual situations would be helpful.

Programs Specifically for Women

Women's self-defense classes, including physical techniques and assertiveness training, will not be appropriate for all women on campus. But if a woman has already been the victim of a rape and no longer feels safe, a women's self-defense class may help to empower her. In addition, research has linked training in self-defense and assertiveness with avoidance of rape if a woman is already in a threatening situation (Bart & O'Brien, 1985). Programs that allow women from other cultures to learn about U.S. dating practices and expectations may help to prevent acquaintance rape which results from social misunderstanding.

Programs for Coeducational Groups

Young people who believe in some stereotypic sex role attitudes are at risk for acquaintance rape involvement. For example, women who feel that it is not "feminine" to assert their rights in a physical way may not fight off a man who is forcing them to have sex. If a woman believes that she should not initiate sex on a date and she must say "no" to sex (to protect her reputation) even if she wants it, may be giving mixed signals which her partner has trouble interpreting.

Males may feel that they always have to be ready and willing for sex and that they must "score" sexually to be considered macho. This may result in a man's forcing his partner to have sex so he will have something to report in the locker room to his friends.

Both males and females should learn assertiveness skills. Generally, males in American culture are raised to be aggressive, especially regarding sexual interactions, and females are raised to be passive. Training can teach students of both sexes to interact with their sexual partners in a more respectful and responsible way. Both partners on a date need to determine what their needs are in a sexual situation and to ask for those needs to be met without exploiting their partners or giving up their rights. Assertiveness training may be helpful in providing young people with those skills.

However, unless young people feel that they have the right to ask for what they want sexually, assertiveness skills will not be helpful. Therefore, programs that help to improve self-esteem may enable both men and women to resist peer pressure, which is often a factor in coercive sexual behavior. The case study below illustrates the relationships among sex role stereotyping, alcohol, peer pressure, self-esteem, and acquaintance rape.

John, a minister's son, was pledging a fraternity so he could become a member of one of the "in" groups on campus. He wasn't very popular, and saw this as a way to increase his number of friends and his popularity. He was a virgin at the time and the brothers told him that virgins were not permitted in the fraternity, so John would have to lose his virginity before he could become a brother. He didn't have a steady girlfriend and didn't have any steady prospects with whom he could have sexual intercourse. He told that to the brothers, and they told him that no girl in her "right mind" would turn down an invitation to their fraternity formal. So John should invite a girl, and the brothers would take care of the rest. John invited Ellen, a college sophomore he had gone out with a few times; all they had done sexually was kiss. Ellen was ecstatic. She had come to college interested in meeting a guy whom she might marry. And now she had met a fraternity man who liked her enough to invite her to his fraternity formal. John seemed like a wonderful prospect.

When she got to the fraternity party she had only one drink, but it was spiked with grain alcohol, unbeknownst to her. She wasn't able to handle liquor well and became intoxicated almost immediately. John then took her up to the room of one of the brothers, pushed her up against the wall, pulled up her dress, put on a condom (because he was a "nice" guy and didn't want to get her pregnant or to get a disease), and forced her to have intercourse (against her feeble protests). When he pulled out he discovered that the condom had broken, and Ellen, who also was a virgin, became pregnant as a result.

This event actually occurred, but some of the inconsequential details have been altered to protect the confidentiality of those involved. The case illustrates the way in which a male's poor self-esteem can contribute to acquaintance rape. If John had higher self-esteem, he probably would not have complied with the brothers' rule against virgin members. He might have had the confidence to say, "I don't want to be friends with people who think rape is preferable to virginity." But it was more important for John to be a member of a high status group. Against his better judgment, he succumbed to alcohol and peer pressure and resorted to using force to render Ellen defenseless.

Programs should be designed to empower participants to avoid acquaintance rape by (a) helping them understand the dysfunctional aspects of peer pressure, sex stereotypic behaviors, and drug and alcohol use, and (b) giving them realistic alternative means of interacting with others. Improvisational, interactive theater works well in presenting the message in an interesting and realistic manner.

The Cornell Interactive Theater Program

Cornell University has incorporated interactive theater into its new-student orientation programs on acquaintance rape. The scenes are realistic and specific to the Ithaca and Cornell communities.

Students watch three scenarios presented by actors. The first two scenarios have the same beginning. In the first scene, both the man and the woman on the "date" behave in a sex stereotypic and intoxicated manner, and an acquaintance rape results. The audience then discusses with the actors the dynamics of the situation, to point out the dysfunction of their behaviors. The actors remain in character during the discussion. Audience members are encouraged to make suggestions to the actors to help them avoid involvement in acquaintance rape in the future.

Then the actors present the same scene again, but this time they incorporate the suggestions made by the audience (and modified by the facilitators if necessary). The end result is that the characters like each other much better and the rape is avoided. In the second scene, the woman is more assertive, communicative, and self-assured; the man listens to her, asks her what she wants sexually, and admits his own vulnerability. Both partners act more maturely and responsibly, but there is still room for improvement. Because the actors incorporate ideas that the audience generated, students can see how the suggestions can work, and they will be more likely to carry them out than if the suggestions had been made by the facilitators.

In the third scene, the actors actually *discuss* the advantages and disadvantages of having sex, and the dysfunctions of peer pressure and alcohol use, before they get into a dangerous situation. They consequently decide to *not* have sex. Both partners act responsibly in the third scene.

This approach allows students to feel the emotional trauma associated with acquaintance rape without having to become directly involved. It provides a realistic depiction of an acquaintance rape to which the audience can relate. In addition, students are given opportunities to discuss feelings and thoughts regarding the dysfunctional behavior patterns that lead to acquaintance rape and to participate in developing problem-solving strategies that are applicable to their own lives.

COMPONENTS NECESSARY FOR PROGRAMS TO CREATE SOCIAL CHANGE

To effectively lead groups formed to help educate students about the risks of acquaintance rape and sexual assault, and to teach them about prevention and avoidance strategies, several steps should be followed. First, facilitators must gain student trust and show students that the facilitators are there as allies. This message is conveyed if facilitators are nonjudgmental and if they present the specific local issues and pressures students are facing (Gray, Lesser, & Bounds, 1990). Second, students must be provided with enough information about the world that they become **uncomfortable** with the status quo. Facilitators must create cognitive dissonance, in which students' attitudes and behaviors are incongruous. For example, women may be saying "no" when they mean "yes" sexually, but once they are given new information on how mixed messages may lead to acquaintance rape, they may come to understand that the "no"-meaning-"yes" strategy they employ may be harmful and, only then, may want to eliminate this strategy. Recent research has revealed that almost half of college women admit to giving token resistance on a date, that is, saying "no" when they do not mean it (Muehlenhard & Hollabaugh, 1988).

Students' assumptions are best challenged if students communicate honestly with their peers, instead of being told to make changes by the facilitators. Programs that employ scare tactics or point out only what is wrong with students' current behaviors serve to disempower the students. There *must* be a component to empower them with new behavioral strategies. Therefore, the third component must provide students with alternative ways of interacting with each other and with the world, to help them avoid acquaintance rape situations. All of these elements are necessary for an acquaintance rape program to be effective (Parrot, 1988).

Whenever acquaintance rape programs are being conducted, there are likely to be people in the audience who have been involved in an acquaintance rape. They may never have identified themselves as victims or assailants but may come to think of themselves as victims or assailants by the end of the program. Having a counselor on hand will allow the facilitator to concentrate on the program, while providing the necessary support to anyone who may be in crisis as a result of attending the program. One valuable consequence of acquaintance rape prevention programs is that victims who have heretofore rejected help may decide that they need psychological assistance. If they seek counseling, they stand a greater chance of becoming emotionally recovered, which may protect them, in part, from being victimized in the future.

CONCLUSION

Unfortunately, many campuses attempt to address the problem of acquaintance rape by providing stranger rape prevention strategies (such as tightening security in residence halls, increasing the number of campus police, and installing more emergency telephones on campus). These methods are usually not effective in preventing acquaintance rapes (Miller & Marshall, 1987). The best way to make the educational and prevention programs successful is to make sure they address the needs of the campus community—and to know exactly what those needs are by conducting research at that institution. Many research studies have been conducted nationally, but each college campus is different. The incidence and prevalence of acquaintance rape, the location of rape, and the profile of victims and assailants may differ from institution to institution. Because people will change their attitudes, knowledge, and behavior if they can see the relevance of information presented to them, the best way to maximize change is to present local information to program participants. Lecture formats are not effective in changing attitudes about acquaintance rape; programs should be more dynamic and should include vivid interaction to enhance the desired effect of consciousness raising, attitude change, and empathy toward rape victims (Borden, Karr, & Caldwell-Colbert, 1988).

Education and prevention programs need to become an integral part of the college curricula (Sandberg, Jackson, & Petretic-Jackson, 1987) but should not be limited to reaching students. Research conducted at a given institution may indicate that faculty and staff, as well as students, are at risk for acquaintance rape and consequently are in need of prevention programs targeted at them. Planning programs based on research at another institution may result in presentations that do not address students' needs or educational experiences to which students are unable to relate.

Once programs are developed and implemented, they must be evaluated to determine whether they have had the desired effect of knowledge, attitude, and behavior change and for short-term and long-term pre- and post-change. It might be useful to examine the rates of acquaintance rapes before and after programs are implemented. Ongoing program evaluation will help to improve the programs and will ultimately make the campus a safer place for students, faculty, and staff.

REFERENCES

Adams, A., & Abarbanel, G. (1988). *Sexual assault on campus: What colleges can do.* Santa Monica, CA: Santa Monica Hospital Medical Center.

Bart, P. B., & O'Brien, P. H. (1985). *Stopping rape: Successful survival strategies.* Elmsford: Pergamon.

Bausell, C., & Maloy, C. E. (1990, January). *The links among drugs, alcohol, and campus crime: A research report.* Paper presented at the Fourth National Conference on Campus Violence, Towson, MD.

Borden, L. A., Karr, S. K., & Caldwell-Colbert, A. T. (1988). Effects of a university rape prevention program on attitudes and empathy toward rape. *Journal of College Student Development, 29,* 132–136.

Ehrhart, J. K., & Sandler, B. R. (1985).*Campus gang rape: Party games?* Washington, DC: Association of American Colleges.

Gray, M. D., Lesser, D., & Bounds, C. (1990, January). *The effectiveness of personalizing acquaintance rape prevention programs on perception of vulnerability and risk-taking behavior.* Paper presented at the Fourth National Conference on Campus Violence, Towson, MD.

Hughes, J. O., & Sandler, B. R. (1987). *"Friends" raping friends: Could it happen to you?* Washington, DC: Association of American Colleges.

Lane, K. E., & Gwartney-Gibbs, P. A. (1985). Violence in the context of dating and sex. *Journal of Family Issues, 6.* 45–49.

Miller, B., & Marshall, J. C. (1987). Coercive sex on the university campus. *Journal of College Student Personnel, 28.* 38–46.

Muehlenhard, C. L., & Hollabaugh, L. C. (1988). Do women sometimes say no when they mean yes? The prevalence and correlates of women's token resistance to sex. *Journal of Personality and Social Psychology, 54,* 872–879.

Parrot, A. (1988). *Acquaintance rape and sexual assault prevention training manual* (3rd ed.). Ithaca, NY: Cornell University.

Parrot, A. (1987, April). *University policies and procedures regarding acquaintance rape.* Paper presented at the eastern regional meeting of the Society for the Scientific Study of Sex, Philadelphia, PA.

Polonko, K., Parcell, S., & Teachman, J. (1986, November). *A methodological note on sexual aggression.* Paper presented at the annual meeting of the Society for the Scientific Study of Sex, St. Louis, MO.

Sandberg, G., Jackson, T., & Petretic-Jackson, P. (1987). College students' attitudes regarding sexual coercion and aggression: Developing educational and preventive strategies. *Journal of College Student Personnel, 28.* 302–311.

Warshaw, R. (1988) *I never called it rape: The MS. report on recognizing, fighting, and surviving date and acquaintance rape.* New York: Harper & Row.

CHAPTER 23

Recommendations for College Policies and Procedures to Deal with Acquaintance Rape

ANDREA PARROT, PhD

College and university administrations view and respond to acquaintance rape and sexual assault in a variety of ways. Some administrators may not admit that acquaintance rape exists on their campuses, and some may not believe that acquaintance rape ever occurs. Other administrators may view it as a problem but are not sure how to deal with it, particularly if both parties agree that sexual intercourse occurred but disagree about whether there was consent. Still other administrators are treating acquaintance rape as they would any other serious crime: they do not tolerate it and they are willing to expel a convicted offender from campus. In acquaintance rape cases, a conviction may not result in a prison sentence. The offender may be given probation, community service, or a suspended sentence instead.

Each approach to acquaintance rape is accompanied by implicit messages that reflect the administration's attitude toward acceptable male and female behavior. The way in which administrators deal with acquaintance rape cases that are brought to their attention will determine the extent to which future cases will be reported. A 1986 example illustrates this point.

A junior who was a football player at a large northeastern university was legally charged in criminal court with two counts of first-degree rape for forcing a first-year female student to have sex. The district attorney refused to present the case to the grand jury. The athlete pled guilty to sexual misconduct and the judge sentenced him to three years' probation and 300 hours of community service. In a campus judicial hearing, an administrative tribunal from the university advised no sanctions; the student could continue to attend the university, play football, and retain his scholarship. The university Chancellor overruled the decision of the tribunal, placed the student on probation, and prohibited him from playing the first five games of the season.

Some female students at that institution might have felt that the university would not take them seriously if they came forward to report sexual assault or rape by an acquaintance. If the university had dealt harshly with the athlete, the message would have been different: Women should be believed; sex is not something men have a right to, regardless of the woman's wishes; and men will be held accountable for their actions.

One message that men on that campus probably received was that they could do what they liked to women, even if their behavior was against the law. Perhaps these "relaxed" rules apply only if the offenders are athletes on scholarship. Because the university hearing was closed (only those involved were permitted to attend), there is no way to tell why the hearing board decided that there was not enough evidence of wrongdoing to sanction the alleged assailant. However, when the evidence is questionable, the tendency is to err on the side of the defendant, even though rules of evidence are often less rigid in a campus judicial procedure than in the criminal courts.

Most victims of acquaintance rape and sexual assault do not even attempt to have the assailant arrested; but they would like him to know that what he did was wrong, so that perhaps he will not repeat that type of behavior with others. Even more importantly, victims want and need emotional help so that they can put the assault behind them and get on with their lives. Going to the police often adds to their emotional trauma rather than reducing it, so they choose to talk to someone at a counseling center or to a sympathetic friend.

Even if acquaintance rape cases are reported to the police, these cases rarely go to trial because the police or the district attorney do not believe there is sufficient evidence to prosecute the case. Of those cases which do go to trial, very few result in convictions. It is not unusual for a conviction in such a case to be overturned on appeal (Rowland, 1985). With such poor odds of ever reaching a conviction, it is not surprising that very few victims ever report acquaintance rape to the police.

Campus judicial hearings may be used as an alternative to or in addition to legal criminal proceedings. Usually, the victim determines how many of these proceedings will take place.

To obtain a conviction in the criminal courts, 12 jurors must be convinced of the defendant's guilt "beyond a reasonable doubt." However, in most campus judicial hearings, only a majority of the hearing board members must believe that the alleged assailant is guilty of violating the campus code of conduct. Compared to criminal proceedings, campus judicial board hearings usually apply less rigid standards of proof (such as "a preponderance of evidence," or "clear and convincing evidence"), and the rules of evidence are more flexible.

It should be easier to obtain a conviction in a campus judicial procedure than in a criminal court, but this is not always the case. One of the reasons is that many university administrators are concerned about taking a "hard line" stand in these cases. Even if the law has been broken, if the man who broke the law did not know that what he was doing was wrong, administrators are likely to be lenient with him. Societal messages have provided some men with the notions that men must always be ready and willing to have sex, that a woman never means "no," and that sex is their right if they spent a great deal of money on their dates (Muehlenhard, Friedman, & Thomas, 1985). Some men feel that a woman is "asking" for sex if she gets drunk, goes back to a man's apartment after a party or date, or asks him back to hers. Most states have laws that define rape as a situation in which sexual intercourse is forced on one person by another against the victim's will and without the victim's consent, or if the victim submits out of fear for his or her safety or life. The victim does not have to say "no" more than once, and does not have to explain why he or she wants the offender to stop.

Many people do not believe that an event was rape if the woman is not bruised or hysterical and if the offender was not a stranger (Burt, 1980; Johnson, 1985). But these factors do not have to be present for a rape to have occurred. Why do administrators who know this intellectually find it hard to treat acquaintance rape as a crime? There are several reasons. First, administrators may not have a specific policy on sexual conduct on campus, and they may not even be sure what the law says regarding this issue. Second, they may be worried about being sued by the assailant if the university deals harshly with him while the court finds him "not guilty." Third, they may be worried about a wrong accusation of rape, which could "ruin his life." Finally, in this day of declining numbers of applicants, administrators may be worried that the negative publicity the school will receive because of the rape will hurt its enrollment figures.

Administrators may be experiencing cognitive dissonance regarding acceptable sexual behavior. They may have been in a situation in their own lives where a woman said "no" but meant "yes," and they are generalizing their experience to others. Or, they may have forced women to have sex against their protests but do not think of themselves as rapists and therefore cannot define students' similar experiences as rape.

Administrators must view acquaintance rape as unacceptable and as a crime, if they are to succeed in reducing this behavior on their campuses. Administrators' responses must include evaluating and revising existing campus policies, judicial processes, personnel recommendations, public safety procedures and programs, and services for victims of acquaintance rape.

POLICIES

Existing college policies should be evaluated to determine whether they are sufficient to deal with *any* acquaintance rape situation that may be reported to the college community. The policy in place at the time of the rape is the policy that must be used to deal with the rape. Many colleges are discovering, too late, that their existing policies and procedures are woefully inadequate to address the special needs posed by acquaintance rape situations—solutions include closed hearings, training the judicial board about rape myths, disabusing the judicial board members of their beliefs in the sexual double standard, and so on.

Four actual acquaintance rape cases that illustrate the inadequacy of many existing college policies are described below. Following each case, policy recommendations are provided. Some of the inconsequential details have been changed to protect the confidentiality of the people involved.

Case 1.   Ellen, a first-year student, went to several parties on the first Saturday of the fall semester. She had a lot to drink over the course of the evening. Ellen was then taken by one of the men she had met at one of the parties to his residence hall, where there was a toga party underway. They both dressed in sheets, and drank more alcohol at the residence hall party. Ellen passed out, and when she gained consciousness, she discovered that he was having sex with her.

Policy recommendation: The drinking age in that state at the time was 21; Ellen was 18. Because Ellen could sue the college in civil court for not providing a safe, alcohol-free environment for her, especially in the residence hall, the college should make alcohol policies more stringent, or enforce the current policies if they are adequate. Enforcing alcohol prohibition on campus is crucial to reducing the incidence of acquaintance rape.

Case 2.   Amy, a senior in high school, was visiting her sister Jill, a first-year student at a small liberal arts college, for the weekend. They went to a lacrosse game, and then Jill had a party in her room afterward. One of the lacrosse players, Adam, attended the party after the game, and Amy spent over an hour with him there. Amy and Adam both got drunk and went into an adjoining room for about an hour during the party. When they emerged, he went home, and Amy told Jill that Adam had raped her. Amy and Jill reported the event to the authorities, and Adam was suspended. Adam sued the college on the grounds that the campus policy explicitly stated that the college community would protect its students, but it said nothing about protecting visitors.

Policy recommendation: The campus code of conduct should state that visitors to the campus are covered by the regulations.

Case 3.   During spring semester, Eric, a college senior, was charged with raping a woman while she was drunk at a fraternity party. The case was dismissed by the district attorney for "lack of evidence." Because the rules of evidence for on-campus judicial hearings are more flexible, the case was to be heard by the judicial board on the campus. Eric's attorney kept applying for continuances until the semester was over. By that time, Eric was scheduled to graduate, and he hoped that a guilty charge against him after he graduated would amount to no more than a "slap on the hand." If Eric had been found guilty while he was still a student, he could have been suspended, expelled, given mandatory counseling, put on social probation, and so on. However, once he graduated, the university would be powerless to punish him.

Policy recommendation: Students should not be permitted to register for subsequent semesters if charges are pending against them or until they have satisfied the condition of their penalties. If a case involves a second-semester senior, the defendant should not be given a diploma until the case has been resolved. If he is found guilty, that information should be in his permanent record. Defendants may attempt to postpone the hearing indefinitely or until after graduation. If they are successful, a guilty verdict may be relatively inconsequential.

Case 4.   While visiting from another institution, John got drunk at a fraternity party and raped a woman at the party. His friends, who were fraternity brothers, helped to get the woman drunk and then encouraged the rape by cheering him on. After the party, the woman filed a complaint with the college administration, but since the alleged rapist was not a student at the college, the administration was not able to do anything to him.

Policy recommendation: If a visitor commits a violation that is condoned or encouraged by an organization on campus, the campus code of conduct should allow for sanctions to be permitted against the organization.

These are only a few of the many possible circumstances in which acquaintance rape may occur on a college campus. The four policy recommendations should have been in place before the rapes occurred; campus policies should be prophylactive, not remedial. These recommendations do not address all of the possible problems relating to acquaintance rape. Policies should address institutional concerns, while providing some protection for both male and female students. Given below are several suggestions for policies that should be incorporated into comprehensive acquaintance rape prevention programs on college campuses.

1. Each college should develop a policy, similar to those for alcohol and drug abuse, regarding unacceptable sexual behavior (Hughes & Sandler, 1987). The policy, including clearly outlined penalties related to specific behaviors, should be made known to students early in their college career. Although many institutions express a concern over acquaintance rape, most do not have adequate policies: they are often incomplete or hidden in a section dealing with other behaviors such as sexual harassment (Parrot, 1988, 1989). Sexual assault does not fit well in the sexual harassment section of college policy (Hughes & Sandler, 1988) because sexual harassment usually covers only situations dealing

with employment or professor–student relationships. Most cases of acquaintance rape and sexual assault take place between students and therefore do not fall within this category. The policy should be in a section titled "Acquaintance rape" or "Sexual assault" so that it is easy to find within the table of contents or the index of the policy manual. A student who wants to know what the policy is should be able to locate easily the section that relates to the specific offense.

2. If policies are in place, minimum associated sentences should be indicated. The possible penalties for sexual assault should be listed in the campus code of conduct so students understand the consequences of each type of behavior.

3. Terms such as "sexual abuse," "sexual assault," "acquaintance rape," or "consent" should be clearly defined. If the meaning of these terms is vague, students reading the campus regulations may not clearly understand which behaviors are a violation of the policy. For example, the policy may state: "Forcing a person to have sex without consent is considered sexual assault." The reader may assume that if a woman gets drunk and passes out, sex is not sexual assault because she did not resist or say "no." The law, however, recognizes that a woman who has passed out cannot give consent; sex under those circumstances constitutes rape. To avoid possible misunderstandings, legal terms should be defined.

4. Each college should establish a written protocol for dealing with sexual assault cases (Adams & Abarbanel, 1988). The following elements should be included: (a) the college policy regarding which offenses are identified as sexual assault on campus; (b) information regarding the specific personnel to notify, the notification procedures to follow, and the names of those to whom reports should be made (with victim consent); (c) the specific legal reporting requirements and procedures for the college, county, and state; (d) services available to victims, both on and off campus; (e) approaches for ongoing case management; (f) procedures for guaranteeing confidentiality for both the victim and the defendant as required by the Buckley amendment protecting defendants' rights; (g) (optional) *in loco parentis* policies, which were common 20 years ago, to protect students, especially in relation to alcohol use (Fenstermaker, 1988).

JUDICIAL PROCESSES

In addition to revising policies and the campus code of conduct, judicial procedures should be revised to address the specific issues presented by acquaintance rape and sexual assault cases. Personnel responsibilities and training, a closely related coordinating element, is discussed in the next section.

Judicial Board Recommendations

In sexual assault cases, members of the hearing board may need considerable guidance in interpreting the law. A legal expert should be appointed chair of the judicial board as a nonvoting panel member. The legal expert can help the judicial board members understand the evidence. This is especially important because campus representatives may not understand the intricacies of the law well enough to make informed decisions about whether a rape occurred.

Generally, hearing boards are comprised of three to seven members of the campus community, including students, staff, faculty, and/or administrators. The exact composition of judicial hearing boards will differ from campus to campus—and possibly within a campus, depending on the defendant. Some campuses have a policy that the majority of the members of the hearing board must be the same status (student, faculty, staff, or administration) as the defendant.

Regardless of whether a legal expert is on the board, the board members should be trained in interpretation of the statutes dealing with rape or sexual assault. The definitions of rape and lack of consent should be clearly spelled out in judicial board members' training as well as in the campus code of conduct, so that members of the campus community know which behaviors are acceptable. (Training of the hearing board is discussed in greater depth in Chapter 22.)

Hearing Recommendations

Some victims may choose not to be there, but the victim should have the option to be present during the hearing, in the same way that complainants are permitted to be present in civil cases. Her presence may be important, especially if the defendant did not make a statement before the hearing, so she can refute any false statements he may make during the hearing. If a victim is considered simply a witness for the institution, she may not be given the option to attend the entire hearing. If the campus judicial proceedings are similar to those of a criminal proceeding, witnesses who are not complainants are permitted to be present only when they testify. When an institution brings charges against a defendant, the institution is the complainant and the victim is only a witness; consequently, she will be permitted to be present only during her testimony.

The hearing should be closed (with only the board, the defendant, essential witnesses, and advisors present), or the victim may be unwilling to go through with it. The victim should have the option to have counsel or an advisor present; she may need emotional support and she may not be thinking clearly enough to make good decisions without advice.

The names of any witnesses for either side should be made available to the opposing party 72 hours prior to the hearing, to give both sides enough time to adequately prepare their cases. Rape shield laws (laws that protect the victim by preventing irrelevant past sexual history from being presented during a rape trial) or their equivalent should be incorporated into the rules of evidence for sexual assault cases heard on campus. The victim will probably be reluctant to file charges if she thinks that any aspect of her past sexual history may be brought up during the case. If her past sexual history is irrelevant, its presentation should not be allowed during a hearing, but previous sexual experiences with the assailant are generally considered relevant.

Treatment of the Accused

Even before an official hearing, the accused can and should be moved from a residence hall if he appears to be an imminent threat to another student. There is precedent for such action in other matters concerning residence life on college campuses. Therefore, if the victim is in emotional distress and feels that by remaining in the same residence hall as the accused she is in physical or emotional danger, the accused or the victim should be moved at the victim's request, pending the outcome of the judicial board hearing. If the college fails to comply with the victim's wish to have the assailant moved and the victim is harmed by him, a civil lawsuit against the college could result.

As in Case 3, on page 371, the accused may attempt to delay the hearing indefinitely until he has graduated. If he is successful in doing so, the institution may not have much leverage to ensure that penalties are carried out. For example, if the hearing board recommends expulsion, the sentence will have no impact after a student has graduated. A clause in the campus policy that prevents a student from graduating while a charge is pending against him or her will eliminate that problem.

Once the board has determined a verdict, minimum recommended sentences are important. Historically, when hearing boards have found assailants guilty of rape, the defendants have been given very light sentences, such as community service and counseling. To ensure that the sentences are carried out, a student should not be permitted to register for subsequent semesters until he or she has fulfilled the conditions of the penalty. Some institutions are requiring, as minimum punishment, expulsion for rape and suspension for sexual assault. If the accused assailant transfers to another school to avoid possible or pronounced sentence, the victim's recourse would include a lawsuit in criminal or civil court.

If a rape has occurred, there are many steps the administration can take to deal with the situation effectively and perhaps to serve as a deterrent to future acquaintance rapes. First, the administration must take a tough stand with assailants. If a rape occurs within an organization (such as when a fraternity brother commits an acquaintance rape at a fraternity house) or is condoned by an organization (such as when a pledge, as a condition of pledging, has sex with a woman who is drunk and has passed out), members of that organization should be punished or the organization should be eliminated.

Because fraternities are often implicated in acquaintance or gang rapes (Ehrhart & Sandler, 1985), the administration should carefully examine the fraternity system and structure and revise or eliminate it if necessary. The first proven violation of the policy should be dealt with swiftly and harshly. Regardless of whether the case results in a criminal conviction, if a student is proven to have violated the university code of conduct, the appropriate punishment should ensue.

It may be clear that an acquaintance rape occurred, but because of a technicality, the defendant still may be found "not guilty" in the criminal court. That does not preclude a guilty verdict in a later campus hearing. The case may be heard in both places without causing "double jeopardy" (trying a person twice for the same crime) if in the criminal court the defendant was tried for rape and in the campus hearing he is being tried for having violated some aspect of the campus code of conduct or college policy.

PERSONNEL RECOMMENDATIONS

Each campus should establish a position for a "sexual assault services coordinator" who would train judicial board members, safety officers, counselors, and medical personnel; confer with university counsel; monitor all cases; and provide support for victims and alleged assailants. Unless one person is responsible for all of these functions, they are likely to be carried out in piecemeal fashion.

A rapid response team should be in place, ready to become mobilized in the event of a rape. The team should include representatives from public safety, the counseling office, the medical staff, the office of the dean of students, victim advocacy, and the local rape crisis center. The team would go to the victim so that she would not have to seek out each member of the team and tell her story repeatedly, but the decision for when and how to tell her story would be up to the victim. The University of Northern Illinois, which has a model rapid response team in place, has found it to be very successful.

A sexual assault task force or coalition should be created on campus to oversee the efforts related to acquaintance rape and to provide guidance to the sexual assault services coordinator and the administration. Representation should be drawn from various groups: the office of the dean of students, residence life, campus police, health center (including members from the health education department, psychological services, sexuality counseling department, and the medical services), religious organizations on campus, and the Office of Equal Opportunity. Academic faculty should also be represented. Faculty groups with a professional interest in this subject include: women's studies, political science, nursing, psychology, sociology, human development and family studies, philosophy, criminal justice, law, social work, human service studies, medicine, physical education, and health education. Members of community agencies with a vested interest in acquaintance rape, such as the local rape crisis center and the battered women's task force, should also be included. Finally, it is important to include students on the task force, particularly those who are members of organizations such as womens' and mens' groups, fraternities and sororities, and sports teams.

PUBLIC SAFETY RECOMMENDATIONS

Because some campus rapes are reported to off-campus police, reporting and evidence collection efforts should be coordinated with local policy agencies.

Low report and conviction rates are generally characteristic of simple rapes (those with no violence, a single attacker, and no other crime committed at the time) (Estrich, 1987), and acquaintance rapes are usually simple rapes. Report and criminal conviction rates are much better for aggravated rapes, but their occurrence is less likely, especially on a college campus. Therefore, more assailants may be punished if acquaintance rape cases are heard by the college judicial board or officer, rather than by the criminal courts.

A mechanism should be maintained to collect and disseminate accurate statistics regarding the incidence and the disposition of acquaintance rape cases on campus. It will be impossible to determine whether education and prevention efforts have been successful in a campus community without knowing what has happened in the past and what the needs of the campus community are. The more that is known about acquaintance rape patterns on a campus, the greater the likelihood of developing programs to meet the specific needs of a particular campus community.

Security measures should be implemented to reduce the likelihood of acquaintance rape and sexual assault victimization. Campus crime prevention protocols primarily provide resources to deal with stranger rape; the measures needed to prevent acquaintance rape are different. Specific prevention protocols related to acquaintance rape include informing all students of the fact that sexual assault can and does happen on campus between people who know each other. Female and male students should be educated regarding their rights and the law. Safety officers and medical professionals should be trained to deal with sexual assault victims and assailants. (See Chapter 22 for more information on these educational programs.)

Safety programs can make the campus less dangerous for students. Direct phones to the campus police, placed throughout the campus at locations that are well-publicized, would make it easier for a woman who is being harassed by her date to call for help. An escort service and/or special free after-dark buses routed to stop at the police-phone locations would provide a student with transportation home, in the event that she was feeling uncomfortable and did not want to rely on her date for a ride. Although these programs are probably most useful in stranger rape prevention, they may also help to prevent acquaintance rape. For example, if a woman and a male acquaintance are walking home from the library at night and he begins to sexually assault her, the availability of a direct phone to the campus police may be helpful in preventing her from being raped.

Certified "safe houses," with occupants trained in crisis intervention, emergency measures, and self-defense, would provide women with "safe harbor" if they are being threatened while away from home.

SERVICES FOR VICTIMS

Institutions should provide victim support but should not pressure a victim to pursue a particular course of action. If the victim wants to press charges, the institution should help her with that process, but if she does not want to pursue legal recourse, her wishes should be respected. The services for victims should be comprehensive, including counseling, medical services, and victim advocacy. Counseling for acquaintance rape victims may be provided on a one-to-one basis or in a group setting. Counseling referrals should be made to therapists trained in acquaintance rape issues, and this counseling should be free of charge. A trained victim advocate should be able to help the victim make sense of her options in the criminal justice system and deal with any problems she is having with the college.

Support groups should be available for individuals close to the victim. Medical personnel should be prepared to provide counseling as well as medical care, especially if the victim is uncomfortable seeking help from psychological services personnel.

These resources will not reduce the incidence of acquaintance rape on campus immediately. Interim procedures dealing with offenders may also be necessary before all students have been exposed to information on acquaintance rape presented at new-student orientation. If colleges institute these suggestions, more women victims will probably come forward not only to press charges but to utilize the counseling services available to them. Fewer men will consider it acceptable to take advantage of women sexually. And colleges will be a better place for students to study, learn, and develop into well-rounded adults.

Funds should be allocated to carry out all of the policy, procedural, and educational recommendations aimed toward prevention of acquaintance rape on campus. In addition, research should be funded to determine the acquaintance rape patterns on campus: where it happens; how often; and under what circumstances. Prevention efforts will be most effective if they are customized to the specific patterns and problems on a given campus.

CONCLUSION

Acquaintance rapes and sexual assaults on college campuses are quite common, but because they are infrequently reported to police, many institutions do not think the problem exists on their campus. As a result, most institutions do not have any official policy against such behaviors (Parrot, 1989). Students are given the implicit messages that acquaintance rape and sexual assault are tolerated on campuses and that the legal system will usually not help the victim obtain a conviction in a criminal court.

Schools with a sexual assault policy do not necessarily have higher report rates than those with no policy. Several factors may account for this. Even if a policy exists, it may not be well-publicized and students may be unaware of it. If the policy is known to students but is not enforced when a violation occurs, victims may be less likely to report a case of acquaintance rape or sexual assault. On the other hand, if a policy is in effect and harsh sanctions are carried out (such as expulsion, or fraternities' charters being revoked), students will learn that acquaintance rape and sexual assault behaviors will not be tolerated on campus and eventually there may be a reduction in the rate of acquaintance rape and sexual assault. This situation may be possible in the future, but few colleges have taken the necessary steps to strive for this reduction now.

Acquaintance rape and sexual assault cases on campus will not stop until institutions of higher education take this problem seriously. The first step toward its elimination is the development of a campus policy on acquaintance rape and sexual assault, with related sanctions made clear to students. In addition, through research, colleges and universities must determine the extent of the problem on individual campuses. Education efforts must inform men and women about acceptable forms of sexual interaction; this would include not only educating students but training faculty and staff. The role of alcohol on a campus must be carefully examined, because alcohol is so often a factor in acquaintance rapes (Bausell & Maloy, 1990; Polonko, Parcell, & Teachman, 1986). (The role of education about alcohol in acquaintance rape prevention efforts is discussed in Chapter 22.) Finally, when a case is reported, the victim must receive support and, if the allegations are proven, the assailant should be dealt with to the fullest extent permitted by the campus policy. This will give to others who would commit a similar act the message that such behavior is not acceptable on that college campus.

It is possible to change attitudes toward acquaintance rapes on college campuses. Policy recommendations are a most important first step, but administrators can pursue many other avenues to make college campuses safer. All members of the college community will benefit from decreasing the number of acquaintance rapes on campus.

REFERENCES

Adams, A., & Abarbanel, G. (1988). *Sexual assault on campus: What colleges can do*. Santa Monica, CA: Santa Monica Hospital Medical Center.

Bausell, C., & Maloy, C. E. (1990, January). *The links among drugs, alcohol, and campus crime: A research report.* Paper presented at the Fourth National Conference on Campus Violence, Towson, MD.

Burt, M. (1980), Cultural myths and supports for rape. *Journal of Personality and Social Psychology, 38,* 217–230.

Ehrhart, J. K., & Sandler, B. R. (1985). *Campus gang rape: Party games?* Washington, DC: Association of American Colleges.

Estrich, S. (1987). *Real rape: How the legal system victimizes women who say no.* Cambridge, MA: Harvard University Press.

Fenstermaker, S. (1988). Acquaintance rape on campus: Attribution of responsibility and crime. In M. Pirog-Good & J. Stets (Eds.), *Violence in dating* (pp. 257–271). New York: Praeger.

Hughes, J. O., & Sandler, B. R. (1987). *"Friends" raping friends: Could it happen to you?* Washington, DC: Association of American Colleges.

Hughes, J. O., & Sandler, B. R. (1988). *Peer harassment: Hassles for women on campus.* Washington, DC: Association of American Colleges.

Johnson, K. M. (1985). *If you are raped.* Holmes Beach, FL: Learning Publications.

Muehlenhard, C. L., Friedman, D. E., & Thomas, C. M. (1985). Is date rape justifiable? The effects of dating activity, who initiated, who paid, and man's attitudes toward women. *Psychology of Women Quarterly, 9,* 297–310.

Parrot, A. (1988, May). *University policies and procedures regarding acquaintance rape.* Paper presented at the 21st annual meeting of the American Association of Sex Educators, Counselors, and Therapists, San Francisco.

Parrot, A. (1989, October). *Acquaintance rape patterns and college response in New York State.* Paper presented at the New York State Conference on Acquaintance Rape on College Campuses, Albany, NY.

Polonko, K., Parcell, S., & Teachman, J. (1986, November). *A methodological note on sexual aggression.* Paper presented at the annual meeting of the Society for the Scientific Study of Sex, St. Louis, MO.

Rowland, J. (1985). *The ultimate violation.* New York: Doubleday.

Author Index

Subject Index

(*continued from front*)